UNLIKELY ALLIES

Unlikely Allies

Britain, America and the Victorian Origins of the Special Relationship

Duncan Andrew Campbell

hambledon
continuum

Hambledon Continuum, A Continuum imprint

The Tower Building   80 Maiden Lane, Suite 704
11 York Road   New York, NY 10038
London SE1 7NX
www.continuumbooks.com

British Library Cataloguing-in-Publication Data
A catalogue record for this book is available from the British Library.

ISBN: 978–184725–191–6

Library of Congress Cataloging-in-Publication Data
A catalog record for this book is available from the Library of Congress.

Typeset by YHT Ltd, London
Printed and bound in Great Britain by MPG Books Ltd, Bodmin, Cornwall

Contents

Acknowledgements

Samuel Johnson claimed that 'in order to write, a man will turn over half a library to make one book'. In the experience of this author, he also will turn over half his friendships. This work could never have been written without the help of many judicious and considerate individuals who contributed to the thought and research that this study has entailed. Dr Phillip Myers of Western Kentucky University has generously and continuously shared both the fruits of his research and his thoughts on nineteenth-century Anglo-American diplomacy since even before I began this work. For this and for reading several of my chapters in rough draft, I am profoundly thankful. Mr Jon Latimer provided me with a great deal of assistance in my research and writing on the War of 1812. His advice and critique of that chapter was invaluable and I remain in his debt. In addition, both of these scholars generously allowed me to read and quote from their forthcoming works on Anglo-American diplomatic relations during the Civil War and the War of 1812 respectively, for which I am also very grateful.

My thanks also go to Professor Andrew Lambert of King's College, London, who reviewed my chapters on both the War of 1812 and the later Anglo-American diplomacy offering much insightful criticism and counsel. Professor Peter Mandler of Gonville and Caius College, Cambridge read and critiqued my chapter on the early political relationship between Britain and the United States, among others, providing me with much useful information, advice and encouragement for which I am very grateful. I also owe a debt of gratitude to Professor Miles Taylor of York University, who also read and critiqued the chapter on Anglo-American political relations.

I remain indebted to both Dr Gerard Barrett of St Edmund's College, Cambridge, and my colleague Dr Stephen McVeigh, of the University of Wales Swansea, who kindly read and commented upon the chapters on Anglo-American literary relations. I am further grateful to Dr McVeigh for providing me with information about Buffalo Bill's Wild West Show that I would never have found on my own.

Professor Martin Daunton, Master of Trinity Hall, Cambridge, was especially helpful when it came to the question of Anglo-American economic relations and provided guidance and references that greatly helped my understanding of this topic. For that and his advice on other matters broadly relevant to the subject of this book, I am profoundly thankful.

I am also extremely grateful to Professor Jon Roper, my Head of Department at the University of Wales Swansea, who not only provided me with information about the Anglo-American political relationship of the nineteenth century, but also arranged for me to have the necessary time away from my teaching schedule to finish writing this book. In these and other matters, he has been unfailingly helpful and will always have my thanks.

My colleague at the University of Wales Swansea, Dr Craig Phelan, editor of *Labor History*, has been a consistently good listener and his assistance and advice in the area of comparative British and American labour history has been invaluable. I can only hope that I have made good use of his ideas and suggestions.

On the subject of colleagues, I have been very fortunate to work in one of the best departments of American Studies in the United Kingdom. Working with the faculty and staff at Swansea these nine years have immeasurably broadened my horizons, introducing me to a range of topics about which I previously knew nothing. I would like to thank especially Dr Dave Bewley-Taylor and Dr Alan Bilton.

I was introduced to two of the pivotal individuals in this book, Charles Dilke and W. T. Stead, by Professor Gareth Stedman Jones of King's College, Cambridge and Professor Ann Robson of the University of Toronto, respectively. The former, in particular, suggested looking at Dilke when I was writing my last book and I now understand why. That was advice I should have taken then, and I hope that I have made up for that lost opportunity. I also hope I have done something resembling justice for Stead.

Special thanks must go to my original editors Tony Morris and Martin Sheppard of what was formerly Hambledon and London, who first commissioned this work, originally to be titled *The Victorians and America*. It is but simple truth to say that without them, this book would never have been written. At the time, none of us realized just how large a topic this would prove to be (nor, for that matter, how long it would take me to write). Throughout this process both Tony and Martin not only provided encouragement and counsel, but allowed me to draw upon a deep reservoir of patience. Every author should be blessed with editors like these.

I am also grateful to the new crew at Hambledon Continuum, including my editor Ben Hayes, as well as Eva Osborne and Slav Todorov. My thanks also go to Sarah Norman who acted as copy-editor of this work.

I should also like to acknowledge my thanks to the staff of the British Library, the Library of Congress and the University Library of Cambridge, all of whom provided invaluable help in tracking down various works that I required.

Some of the ideas in this book have been presented at various levels of development to certain individuals, all of whom had ideas that proved valuable, including Dr Murney Gerlach, Professor William Jones of Cardiff University, Dr Steve Sarson, Dr Alan Finlayson, Dr Richard Watermeyer and Dr Chris Walsh. My thanks go to all of them. I am also grateful to my two PhD students, Ms Kate Saunders and Ms Tracy Rex, for their help and assistance.

Thanks, too, go to my parents, Dr Neil and Mrs Sheila Campbell, who always end up reading my rough drafts and whose advice is always for the best. I also remain grateful to Harvey for constantly reminding me that I live in the twenty-first and not the nineteenth century.

It goes without saying that while this book could never have been completed without the help of all of those named above, they are in no way responsible for any errors or omissions; these are entirely my own.

Finally, I should like to express my appreciation, thanks and love to my wife, Bobbie Jo who, being an American born and bred, has her own views on Anglo-American relations. It is to her that this work is dedicated.

List of Illustrations

1. Sir George Cockburn as Admiral of the Fleet and First Sea Lord. The most unwelcome visitor ever to dine at the White House. The city burning in the background is Washington DC. The question was: would this be the face of Anglo-American relations in the nineteenth century? *(National Maritime Museum)*

2. Frances Trollope, called a 'censorious harridan' for her acerbic (and unfair) account of the domestic lives of the Americans, but other visitors proved more sympathetic, including her son, novelist Anthony Trollope. *(National Portrait Gallery)*

3. Immigrants departing for the United States. An estimated 4.25 million Britons migrated to the United States during the course of the nineteenth century, most doing so in the latter half of our period. Called 'invisible immigrants' by some, they nonetheless made their presence felt. *(The* Illustrated London News*)*

4. 'Pass the Mustard'. This *Punch* cartoon humorously underscores the widespread British belief that American society was inherently violent. (Punch Cartoons, Victoria 1841–1901)

5. Lord Palmerston, one of the nineteenth century's greatest statesmen. His continual difficulties with the United States, from the War of 1812 to the American Civil War, personified the ambiguous nature of the two nations' relationship. *(National Portrait Gallery)*

6. Telegraphic message — Queen Victoria exchanged greetings and best wishes with President James Buchanan in the first official transatlantic telegraphic communication. Her Majesty proved to be more pro-American earlier than most of her ministers or, for that matter, most of her people. (Picture History)

7. James Bryce, British statesman. Perhaps the most accomplished of the 'young liberals', his *American Commonwealth* represented an important landmark in British understanding of the United States. *(Bodleian Library, Oxford)*

8. Colonel Jonathan J. Bull or what John Bull may come to: the origins of the Americanization of the world, as the Pax Britannica began to give way to the Pax Americana. *(W.T. Stead,* The Americanisation of the World *(1901))*

9. Mark Twain, called the father of American literature and a transatlantic phenomenon, his career in many ways personified the changing relationship between Britain and the United States. *(The* New York Times *Photo Archives)*

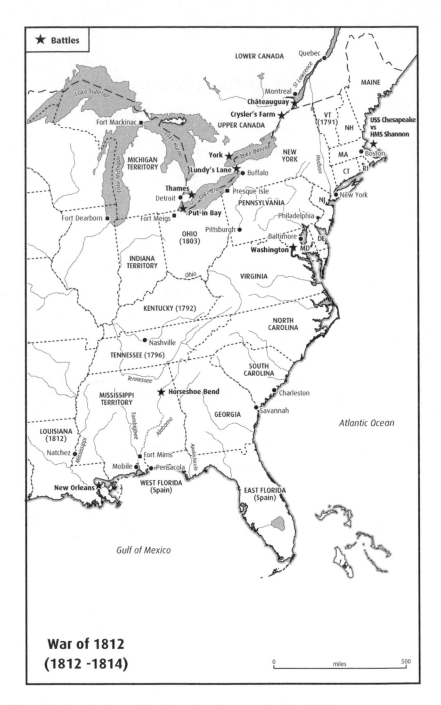

**War of 1812
(1812 -1814)**

Map of the Napoleonic wars' North American theatre or, the War of 1812.

Introduction: Very Distant Cousins

O wad some Power the giftie gie us
To see oursels as ithers see us!
Robert Burns

Almost a century and a half ago, on 16 August 1858, Queen Victoria sent a telegram to James Buchanan, President of the United States. The occasion was the laying of the first successful transatlantic cable the previous month. Victoria hoped it would prove 'an additional link between the nations whose friendship is founded on their common interest and reciprocal esteem'. Buchanan – who had earlier met the Queen while serving as American minister to the Court of St James – replied, including the fervent wish, 'May the Atlantic telegraph, under the blessing of heaven, prove to be a bond of perpetual peace and friendship between the kindred nations, and an instrument destined by Divine Providence to diffuse religion, civilization, liberty and law throughout the world.' Alas, within a month, the connection was broken and this communication breakdown was to worsen. For despite the wishes expressed in the respective heads of states' messages, within three years the United States would be wracked by civil war and Anglo-American relations would be placed under serious strain.[1]

Otto Von Bismarck was reputed to have said the most important fact of the nineteenth century was that Great Britain and the United States of America shared a common language. While many historians would argue it was a more salient fact of the twentieth century, the German Chancellor's observation contained a measure of truth. That the Americans and the British both spoke English was an important fact. Unfortunately it was sometimes as much a hindrance as a help to their relationship. As Royal Naval Captain Basil Hall noted, in his review of Alexis de Tocqueville's *Democracy in America*, 'The Englishman, it is said, has the advantage [of] knowing the language better; and this is true, but only to a certain extent, as it sometimes leads him into serious mistakes ... The Englishman never suspects he is taking up the wrong idea; the Frenchman distrusts himself and inquires.' The Captain, with equal justice, could have said the same about American understanding of Britain.[2]

On the subject of understanding, it must be acknowledged that the title of this work, *Unlikely Allies: The Victorian Origins of the Special Relationship*, is somewhat misleading as it does not confine itself to the period of Queen Victoria's reign, 1837–1901, but instead discusses the era from the War of 1812 to the First World War. Or, to put it simply, from the last military conflict between the two nations during the Napoleonic wars, to the great rapprochement cemented by 'the war to end all wars' where they fought as allies. As this work hopes to demonstrate, there are reasons why it is sensible to examine Anglo-American relations within the context of the long nineteenth century.

When the United States won their independence, many in Europe and America believed that it heralded the end of Britain as a world power. Instead Britain went from strength to strength to the extent that it became the pre-eminent power on the globe, ushering in the period called the 'Pax Britannica'. Equally, when the American War of Independence ended, many doubted the ability of the United States to build a successful nation. Instead the United States grew in power until it eclipsed that of Britain's, turning the twentieth century into the American one. The evolving social, political, cultural, economic and diplomatic relationship between the two nations during this period is the central theme of this book.[3]

Obviously this is hardly virgin territory and this work has a lot of illustrious predecessors, including Sir Winston Churchill's *History of the English-Speaking Peoples* (1956–58) and H. C. Allen's slightly older *Great Britain and the United States: A History of Anglo-American Relations, 1783 to 1952* (1954) to say nothing of the hundreds of more recent scholarly monographs, discussing the vast – and at times bewildering – array of political, social, economic and diplomatic Anglo-American connections. This, of course, is leaving aside the countless subsequent published and unpublished studies on various aspects of nineteenth-century British and American history. Many of these are, of course, cited throughout this work.[4]

Despite all of this research, the two venerable studies cited above still cast a long shadow. For when it comes to the grand narrative of nineteenth-century Anglo-American relations, we are still being told a familiar tale, that of a common and, at times, almost mystical, political and cultural transatlantic community, which although initially split by the American War of Independence, gradually re-united, at least in sympathies, despite various snags, to the point of rapprochement by the end of the nineteenth century. This reunion was effectively completed by the entry of the United States, as a British ally, into the First World War. The process described is virtually an inevitable one, based on the concept that there was more that united the two nations than divided them. As for the various inconvenient snags along the road to rapprochement, they are usually blamed on British conservatives' hatred for America's democratic experiment (running up against radicals' love for the same) and Britain's attempts to contain the United States' territorial growth; conversely, evident American Anglophobia is attributed to either anger at British arrogance and activities or the increasingly large and influential Irish-American electorate within the United States. According to this narrative, the second problem was solved by the increasing growth of American power and the democratization of Britain which, in turn, marginalized the first. Thus, the inevitable rapprochement came about.

This is, of course, a highly simplified summation of the standard account of nineteenth-century Anglo-American relations. Indeed, virtually every scholar on the subject makes a point of installing a veritable battery of qualifiers about and within his work precisely in response to (or anticipation of) such an abbreviated summary outlined above. That being noted however, qualify this account how you will, or add the usual observations that Britain ended slavery before the United States, and one is still presented with an almost triumphal account of Anglo-American liberty leading the world, the United States in the vanguard with Britain, thanks to its politically radical elements, following closely in the American wake. Thus, you have the story of the English-speaking peoples from 1783 to the twentieth century.[5]

Let us start with Churchill's *History of the English-Speaking Peoples,* the title of which was borrowed from R. B. Mowatt's and Preston Slosson's work of the same name published in 1943. The very term 'English-speaking peoples' probably has no older pedigree than the 1870s, being most likely invented by William Gladstone around the time of his article 'Kin Beyond Sea' (1878). This, the first published declaration by a British statesman underlining political, cultural and social links between Britain and the United States, which included the prediction that the latter would one day surpass the former, represented a milestone in Anglo-American relations. Gladstone's article, along with Charles Dilke's earlier *Greater Britain: A Record of Travel in the English-Speaking Countries* (1868), really mark the origins of the idea of the

Anglosphere – a common Anglo-American cultural and political heritage based not only on the English language, but on similar notions of liberty and freedom, representative government, the supremacy of the law, the separation of political powers, and so forth. These notions were given a major fillip by racial (as opposed to cultural) notions of Anglo-Saxon supremacy that became increasingly common as the century wore on. Further, Dilke's and Gladstone's works were very much products of the period surrounding the Treaty of Washington (1871), a treaty that established the framework for settling not only Anglo-American grievances arising from the Civil War, but also several other older ones, including the almost century-long, and, at times, seriously disruptive, disputes relating to the Canadian-American frontier. In other words, both works appeared at a time of improving Anglo-American relations and, indeed, were part of this process of increased reconciliation. In other words, the very idea of 'English-speaking peoples' has a birth-date and political pedigree, being the by-product of later nineteenth-century diplomacy.[6]

This brings us to another aspect of Churchill's and indeed Allen's works: both were published in the period shortly after the victory over Nazi Germany and Imperial Japan and at the same time as the Cold War was gathering momentum. Both were written before the end of the British Empire (or, at least, Harold Macmillan's 1960 'Winds of Change' speech), the Suez crisis and, indeed, the creation of what is now the European Union. In other words, this account of Anglo-American relations is very much conditioned by, and is the product of, a precise, and in some respects exceptional, point in history. In part because of this, it ignores or deprives the nineteenth-century Anglo-American story of a crucial European dimension or component which, far from being marginal to the relationship, often in fact determined the direction it took. In truth it is not too much of an exaggeration to say that it is impossible to understand early nineteenth-century Anglo-American relations without reference to France – meaning that we are really dealing with a *ménage à trois*. Later on, of course, Germany became an important influence for better and for worse. Then there was the British imperial dimension, which was also highly significant in more ways than one.

As regards the alleged snags on the road to rapprochement, there is in fact not a great deal of evidence supporting the notion of a serious radical/conservative split when it came to British views of the United States, which were always more ambivalent and complex than is generally recognized. Regarding America's growing power, meanwhile, given the geographical realities, among other things, the United States was never an especially weak nation in comparison to Britain, a fact of which British statesmen were perfectly aware – even before the War of 1812. This argument also overlooks the fact that Britain reached an entente with two other imperial rivals, France and Russia, at approximately the same time as it did with the United States. Finally, when it comes to the Irish-Americans, they only became a strong political force within the United States after Anglo-American relations had begun to improve. Insofar as they were responsible for Anglo-American animosities, the Irish Americans, at worst, delayed better relations (and even this is debatable); they did not initiate the difficulties that existed. In fact, this tendency to lay the blame at the door of the Irish reminds the author of the verdict delivered by Justice Thrasher in Henry Fielding's *Amelia*.[7]

In many respects, when it comes to nineteenth-century Anglo-American relations, too many have put the cart before the horse. Working on the presumption that the British and Americans shared many similar cultural and political attributes, they treat the rapprochement concluded by the First World War as an inevitable fait accompli and downplay the serious difficulties, differences and disputes that plagued the two countries' ambiguous relationship. Strange as it may seem, Britain at times enjoyed better relationships (and not just at the diplomatic level) with European states such as Portugal, Spain and Prussia. For example, it is often easier to find expressions of Germanophilia in British society for most of the nineteenth century than it is pro-American sentiment.[8]

This is not to deny that Britain's relationship with the United States was, in several crucial respects, different to those of European nations. Yet until nearer the end of the nineteenth century, it was less different than we perhaps like to think. This brings us to another point. Jean Baudrillard has stated that 'America is the original version of modernity', adding 'We [Europe] are the dubbed or subtitled version.' This argument depends heavily upon a specific historical perspective. For most of the nineteenth century, the idea of the modern was associated with Britain, the first nation to industrialize, and urbanize, and the political liberalization of which, while different to that of the United States, attracted world-wide attention until well into the twentieth century. Not only that, the economic, political and cultural exchange between the United States and Britain flowed largely from a British direction for most of the century and, in some respects, beyond. For example, in 1916, the American social critic Randolph Bourne, calling for a more heterogeneous and cosmopolitan American culture, bemoaned his nation's 'melting pot' as little more than a combination of 'English snobberies, English religion, English literary styles, English literary reverences and canons, English ethics, English superiorities'. As late as 1924, meanwhile, Briton Q. J. D. Whelpley confidently asserted, 'British influence upon American life is really far greater than that of American influence on British life.'[9]

Baudrillard's reference to Europe raises another point. Speaking of the nineteenth century at least, the dichotomy between American culture and European culture is an inaccurate one. Leaving aside that the United States was a nation (certainly after 1865) while Europe was a continent consisting of nations, counting Britain in with Europe on either a political or cultural basis is a risky proposition in reference to the nineteenth century. Britain was, after 1815, the world's foremost power or, if one prefers, the superpower of its day, leading the way in technological progress, industrialization, urbanization and many aspects of political development including national consciousness. Then there was its burgeoning world-wide empire which made it an increasingly genuine global and cosmopolitan nation in a manner such as few others. Further, although Britain certainly suffered periods of political unrest, it endured no such upheavals comparable to those which beset Europe in the 1840s or the United States from 1861–65 (although the Empire presented a different story). Its political development in the nineteenth century was thus very dissimilar to most. In light of all of this and the fact that the nineteenth century was in many respects the British one, to lump Britain in with the nations of Europe is about as judicious as equating the American republic with the Latin American ones.

Indeed the existence of the British Empire raises another problem with the 'Old World/New World' dichotomy. Britain founded or developed new worlds of its own, including Australia, New Zealand and Canada, all of which, being settler societies, democratized far more quickly than the motherland, and all took on an increasingly important role in the development of the British national identity, particularly by the end of the century. As regards the United States, however, it was the Canadian colonies which initially caused the most friction. Far from pursuing a containment strategy or engaging in a balance of power policy against the United States, Britain and America were in fact involved in an imperial rivalry, or scramble for North America. Although it is true that the Empire was generally taken for granted until the latter half of the century, the British did pursue a policy of expansionism and defence of their territory and they certainly paid attention to perceived threats from foreign powers. The United States, itself an expansionist power, rubbed up against British North American imperial interests for most of the nineteenth century. Although the two nations usually tried to avoid open conflict after the War of 1812, that struggle and their subsequent disputes did much to foster an atmosphere of suspicion and distrust.

Nor were these disputes only of importance to statesmen or the political elites on either side of the Atlantic. The nineteenth century was, among other things, the age of nationalism. These diplomatic collisions often resulted in popular excitement and animosities on the part of the British and American peoples. For example, for much of the nineteenth century, one only finds British references to the United States if one looks specifically for them, and when one does find them, they most often concern diplomatic difficulties. The War of 1812, the manoeuvrings resulting in Monroe Doctrine, the 1837 Canadian rebellions, the quarrels over the Oregon Territory, the difficulties in Central America, American complicity in the international slave trade, the animosities aroused during the Civil War – or, failing that, activities of prominent Americans in Britain – all combined to make up the overwhelming bulk of British commentary on the United States prior to 1871. Added to all of this was each country's own national identities and mythologies which were augmented by these difficulties and disputes. How John Bull viewed his own nation and the United States differed as much as how Cousin Jonathan saw his own country and Britain.

For most of the nineteenth century, understanding was in short supply on both sides of the Atlantic. After reading dozens of Anglo-American travel accounts as well as published and private correspondence concerning each other's nation, what strikes this historian is the indifferent quality of the observations. Harriet Beecher Stowe had no deeper understanding of Britain than Frances Trollope had of America; the same is true for James Fenimore Cooper and Captain Frederick Marryat. British and American observers more often than not simply saw what confirmed their own national (or personal) prejudices instead of accurately reporting on what actually existed. Despite some outstanding exceptions, it is a measure of just how comprehensive was this failure to understand each other, on the part of both, that a Frenchman,

Alexis de Tocqueville, wrote far more astutely on Britain than did any American and on the United States far more adroitly than did any Briton. In fact, it was not until quite late in the century that Tocqueville actually faced any serious competition on this score (from Henry James and James Bryce, as it happens). In short, until quite late in the nineteenth century, most Britons' or Americans' views of the other's nation need to be taken with a generous heaping of salt.

There were, of course, forces working against these perceptions. The common language certainly helped to misinform, but it also aided conciliation. The increasing trade links, immigration as well as personal and group connections across the Atlantic, all played a role in easing Anglo-American animosities and helped bring about reconciliation – although as we shall see, they sometimes achieved the reverse. What needs to be borne in mind about these, however, is that they usually represented a minority and frequently exceptional point of view. As such, these connections have been too often treated, by those wedded to the idea of predestined Anglo-American accord, as representing the inevitable future; they are too easily assumed to be the norm rather than the exception long before they became such.

In essence, from 1812–71, the relationship between the United States and Britain was one of a hostility that thawed to the point of chilly politeness (and sometimes less than this). At various times, British views of the United States were not essentially unlike their views of France or Russia. Equally, nineteenth-century British cultural dominance and the reaction against this in the United States meant that the impact of America on British cultural and political thought was fairly marginal. It is impossible, for example, to demonstrate that the United States had greater hold on the British imagination than France, Prussia or Russia. It was only after the Treaty of Washington that the British started to pay serious attention to the United States. In other words, only when it ceased to be a potential foe did the British begin to look at the United States from a very different perspective. Thereafter, their relationship underwent a serious change, largely for the better.

As it will probably be clear from the above, this work leans more towards a British perspective of the United States than an American view of Britain. As this work hopes to demonstrate, much of the story of nineteenth-century Anglo-American relations has been told from a largely American perspective. The reasons for this will be raised within the body of the text, but in any case, this work attempts to restore some balance by discussing the imperial and European dimensions often overlooked by studies based primarily from the perspective of the North American continent. This work cannot, of course, discuss in detail all of Britain's relationships with the wider world, any more than it can that of the United States' – that would require a different study. Yet it attempts to place Anglo-American relations within the wider context of international events.

It will also probably be clear that this work is largely uninterested in notions of American exceptionalism (or, for that matter, 'British exceptionalism'). The reason for this is simple: the author finds them unconvincing. Belief in American exceptionalism is largely based on the denial of other nations' uniqueness. This author, for example, could just as easily construct arguments demonstrating French exceptionalism based on France's revolutionary heritage, Chinese exceptionalism based on China's almost 4,000-year-old culture or Swiss exceptionalism based on Switzerland's being the world's oldest democratic republic that knits together four linguistic groups. Or put another way, this author recognizes that the United States has unique traits in the same manner as does Japan or Germany; all nations, from vast Russia to rather smaller Swaziland, are in some way exceptional.[10]

This work, which follows both a chronological and thematic approach, thus explores the complicated and intricate nineteenth-century relationship between Britain and the United States by treating them as nations among nations and, instead of assuming the inevitability of the rapprochement, tries to answer the question of how and why it came about. Because this work covers a span of over a century and is a survey, the reader will not agree with everything he encounters in here – nor should he. At the same time, none of the arguments made above or in the course of this work should be treated as a dismissal of either Churchill's or Allen's pioneering studies. Few of us write works which deserve to be read over half a century after first publication as these two rightly still are. Nonetheless, neither man could take advantage of the vast amount of subsequent scholarship, much of which has not merely questioned but disproved many of their assumptions. This work has the advantage of using these numerous studies and additional primary sources to retell the story of the Anglo-American relationship in the long nineteenth century. Some years ago this author reviewed a study in which the scholar declared that his intention was to replace pat answers with fresh questions and to stimulate debate. If this work achieves the same goals it will have contributed to an understanding of the two nations' shared history.[11]

1

The War Both Sides Won

The night of 24 August 1814 found Rear Admiral George Cockburn in an excellent mood. During the course of the war, the enemy had placed a bounty of $1,000 on his head and $500 on each of his ears, yet Cockburn had not only retained these but, along with members of his company, was now quaffing Madeira from cut-glass decanters, cheerfully dining at a banquet set for others, an uninvited guest in the most important address and headquarters of those who had put a price on his person. Indeed, from the Rear Admiral's perspective, justice could scarcely be more poetic: this same enemy had declared war on Britain when the latter had apparently been losing the life-or-death struggle with Napoleon Bonaparte. Now the British had defeated the Emperor of Europe and were presently settling accounts with those opportunists who had attacked them during that time of peril. Earlier that day, Cockburn's forces had met the enemy by the hamlet of Bladensburg and, despite being outnumbered almost 2–1, had routed them, resulting in the capture of the foe's capital and the Rear Admiral's present dinner libations. Cockburn's troops had already begun burning public buildings in retaliation for arson committed by the enemy against British subjects earlier in the war and would soon turn their attention to the site of the current festivities, but first the toasts. Cockburn and the commander of the British land forces, Major General Robert Ross, drank to the health of the Prince Regent and to the success of His Majesty's land and naval forces. One member of the company, perhaps attempting to be magnanimous in victory, proposed a further toast, to 'peace with America and down with Madison'. The toast made sense: this impromptu banquet's location was in Executive Mansion – only later called the White House – in Washington, the federal capital of the United States of America; the home of the fourth President, James Madison.[1]

Although Cockburn had no way of knowing it, he was actually enjoying the high-water mark of British success in the War of 1812. Indeed, his comrade-at-arms, Ross, who had promised his wife this was his last campaign, would be killed during the unsuccessful British assault on Baltimore a mere three weeks after the feast at the White House. Then there was the Battle of New Orleans, which, although taking place after the signing of the Treaty of Ghent (1815) that officially ended the hostilities, was a decisive American victory resulting in the deaths of 291 British soldiers (and many more wounded) at the cost of 13 American lives. Despite all of this, the treaty signed at Ghent was an admission by both sides that neither had won the conflict which, despite the claims of later scribes, was not, in fact, the second war of American independence any more than it was the 'stab in the back' that Britons of the day, and later, called it. In actual fact, the War of 1812 was an avoidable conflict that was in the interests of neither Britain nor the United States and one in which neither side held the moral high ground. Despite, or perhaps because of this, both sides ultimately benefited – a curious example of the law of unforeseen consequences. This, however, would only become clear later on. Initially, the War of 1812 cast a long shadow over nineteenth-century Anglo-American relations that lasted up to, and really only dissipated after, the American Civil War. To properly understand the Anglo-American relationship in the first half of the nineteenth century, therefore, requires a discussion of this 'forgotten conflict' as one historian has called it.[2]

The causes of the War of 1812 were, simply put, distraction on the part of the British, cupidity on the part of the Americans and over-weening pride on the part of both. Although, at first glance, a second war between the two nations was the logical or inevitable result of unresolved differences dating from the War of Independence, the truth is rather different. Contrary to what might have been expected, Anglo-American relations after that conflict improved to the extent that they were just about as cordial as they could be. One historian has even described the period prior to the War of 1812 as 'the first rapproche-ment', in anticipatory reference to the genuine one that occurred much later in the nineteenth century.

From 1783 to 1801, both governments took sensible steps to settle the outstanding problems left over from the Revolution. The British still occupied land ceded to the United States by the Treaty of Versailles (1783), in response to American failure to pay compensation to the United Empire Loyalists (or 'Tories' as the Americans called them) who had suffered at the hands of the rebels (or 'Patriots' to use the American term). Until the ratification of the Constitution in 1788, the American states were bound together in a loose confederation and had no authority competent to handle the question of compensation. The ratification of the Constitution in 1788, which established the United States as a federal republic as opposed to a league of autonomous states, helped the resolution of these problems. In 1794, the new federal government sent a commission headed by the first Chief Justice of the Supreme Court, John Jay, to settle the situation. Jay's treaty successfully resolved the issue of reparations (ultimately agreed at two and a half million dollars) and British evacuation from the north-west posts in the United States. It also allowed a limited right of American vessels to trade with the British West Indies. The Senate approved the treaty by the necessary majority, demonstrating that, irrespective of the War of Independence, both nations could settle their differences peacefully and, indeed, establish a workable relationship.[3]

Unfortunately for the fate of the first rapprochement, just as the history of individual countries does not take place in an international vacuum, nor do nation states' relationships. Anglo-American relations would be caught up in that phenomenon which followed the War of Independence: the French Revolution and the rise of Napoleon. The War of 1812 was a theatre of the Napoleonic wars, and cannot be properly understood except within this context.

The French Revolution, which began the same year George Washington was inaugurated as the United States' first President in 1789 (the ceremony took place on present-day Wall Street, New York), caused his administration to split into two camps, later to become two parties. The first group, later called the Federalists, led by Alexander Hamilton, first secretary of the treasury, generally favoured Britain and its political stability to France and its revolutionary uncertainty. Hamiltonian or Federalist sentiment was greatest in New England and the Middle States. The second group, later called the Republicans, then the Democratic-Republicans and, finally, the Democratic Party, led by Thomas Jefferson, secretary of state, generally favoured France and its apparent bright new dawn to Britain and its supposedly corrupt stasis. Jeffersonian or Republican sentiment was strongest in the South and the West. While it is true that the Republicans were more inclined towards greater political representation and a wider electoral suffrage than the Federalists, the latter were far less enamoured with slavery and westward expansion (into Indian territory) than the former. Further, despite the Republicans' claim that the Federalists favoured the rich, the former's strongest supporters included the southern plantation gentry – of which Jefferson was a member.[4]

Thus, when Britain and France went to war – as they did in 1793 –

Americans were divided as to the merits of each side. Initially, Fran-cophilia held the upper hand. French assistance had been a crucial factor in the achievement of American independence; Britain was the recent enemy. Further, when the French abolished noble privileges and became a republic, Americans naturally enough celebrated what they saw as the spread of their revolutionary principles. Clearly, the example of the new republic was already having an influence on world affairs. With King Louis XVI executed and the Terror begun, however, pro-French sentiment began to wane, at least on the part of the Federalists. The Republicans, on the other hand, saw things differently. Jefferson, for one, declared in 1795, 'I should have little doubt of dining with Pichegru [a French general] in London next autumn; for I believe I should be tempted to leave my clover for awhile, to go and hail the dawn of liberty & republicanism on that island.' Sentiment was one thing; sound policy, however, was quite another. Washington issued a proclamation of neutrality – a position supported logically on the part of Hamilton and sensibly on the part of Jefferson. When Washington decided against seeking a third term three years later, his Farewell Address advised the infant republic against involvement in the affairs of others or, as he put it, 'foreign entanglements'. This was easier pro-claimed than achieved. The election of 1796 resulted in the Federalist John Adams being elected President with the runner-up Republican Jefferson serving as Vice President. Thus, the United States was gov-erned by a divided administration and these divisions would have a determining influence on Anglo-American relations.[5]

At first, it was Franco-American relations that proved problematic. France, now ruled by a dictatorial executive board called the Directory, announced that the Jay Treaty repudiated the 1778 Franco-American Alliance from the War of Independence. The French were under-standably angry that the United States had not repaid France's assis-tance in the War of Independence by allying with them against the British. Neutrality, so the French held, was a betrayal of the most profound kind. Diplomatic relations were severed and France began seizing American merchant ships. Attempts by Adams to negotiate a peaceful settlement were rebuffed and conflict soon followed. From 1798 to 1800, the United States and France fought an undeclared war as their ships engaged each other at sea. Overall, the Americans had the better of it, not least because the Royal Navy also inflicted defeats on the French and provided protection for US merchant vessels. In short, Britain and the United States formed an alliance – unofficial though it was – against

Revolutionary France. In light of this, the War of 1812 appears almost inexplicable; it certainly calls into question the notion that the conflict was somehow a continuation of the War of Independence.

Circumstances, however, were about to change. While the Adams administration performed deftly in foreign affairs, it proved less adept domestically. Riding on a wave of anti-French sentiment in 1798, the Federalists gained congressional seats at the expense of the rather more Francophile Republicans. Then they overreached themselves, passing laws such as the Sedition Act that equated ordinary dissent with treason, and anti-immigrant and alien legislation aimed largely at Irish and French immigrants. These acts attracted growing opposition – especially in Republican-leaning states. The Kentucky and Virginia state legislatures, for example, passed measures to undermine them. In Pennsylvania, meanwhile, a small rebellion took place that was suppressed with an unnecessarily heavy hand. Although Adams made peace with France, now under the rule of the rather more skilful Napoleon, he was defeated in the 1800 election by Jefferson, largely because of the anger engendered by the Federalists' illiberal activities. The election of the Francophile Jefferson, to say nothing of the rise of Napoleon, marked the beginning of the end of the first rapprochement and the erosion of Anglo-American cordiality.[6]

The first sign of a Franco-American détente was the purchase of the Louisiana territory. France's acquisition of the territory from Spain in 1800 had initially raised concerns in the United States regarding French control of the Mississippi River, and discussion of the forcible seizure of the territory, particularly the important port of New Orleans, was mooted. Jefferson himself observed, 'The day France takes possession of N. Orleans ... we must marry ourselves to the British fleet and nation.' While this might have suited some Federalists, it did not satisfy the primary author of the Declaration of Independence. Napoleon, however, already facing war with Britain, did not need the United States as an enemy. This, combined with a desire to drive a wedge in the Anglo-American relationship, plus his defeat at Saint-Domingue (now Haiti), soured Napoleon's taste for North American entanglements and he proved receptive to an offer by Jefferson to purchase the territory. The bargain was made in 1803. For $15 million (which the Emperor quickly squandered on war) the United States acquired Louisiana, enlarging 'the empire of liberty' as Jefferson pithily put it. Whether or not the Louisiana Purchase would have occurred had not Napoleon been facing war with Britain is a question as interesting as it is impossible to answer, but America virtually doubled its territory, paving the way for a continental empire that would ultimately allow it to (temporarily, looking at events in the long term) disengage politically – though not, initially, economically – from European affairs.[7]

The same year of the Louisiana Purchase witnessed the renewal of war between Britain and France (and each nation's allies). While the British were able to defeat Napoleon at sea, notably at Trafalgar in 1805, Napoleon prevailed on land; his victories at Austerlitz, Jena and Auerstadt in 1806, and Eylau and Friedland in 1807, placed Europe at his mercy. Although sometimes forgotten now, before the War of 1812 events were moving decisively in the Emperor's favour – Austria, Prussia and Russia were forced to seek peace. This left Britain as his remaining serious foe.

In order to address this outstanding problem, Napoleon issued the Berlin (1806) and Milan (1807) Decrees, later called the continental system, to bar British goods from European ports (and neutral ships that stopped at British ports would also be subject to confiscation). In retaliation, the Duke of Portland's Tory administration introduced orders in council (1807) which placed a blockade on France and nations under French occupation. Although London allowed neutrals to trade with said states provided they first obtained a licence from a British port (and paid duty), under the Milan Decree, any neutral ship paying British duty or visiting a British-controlled port was subject to seizure. In other words, neutrals were placed in the position of being seized on the high seas by the Royal Navy, or being detained in European ports by Napoleonic officials.

The neutral nation most adversely affected by this situation was the United States. Although Jefferson tried to retaliate with the Non-Importation Act (1806), which basically barred Americans from trading with either belligerent, the harm it did to his own nation's merchants ensured that it was widely disregarded. Transatlantic trade, it must be noted, did not entirely cease: Napoleon often had to turn a blind eye to violations of his continental system because he needed certain goods and the British, meantime, continued to trade with the United States. US exports to Europe thus held steady and actually increased with Britain. For Jefferson, and his secretary of state, James Madison, however, the idea of Britain regulating American trade was intolerable. From the perspective of the United States, Britain was treating it as a colony, seizing its ships (the British impounded almost a thousand American vessels that challenged the blockade) and thus violating its neutral rights. With the Royal Navy dominating the seas, American vessels ran afoul of British, rather than French, authorities and this increased anti-British sentiment.

Resentment was reciprocated on the other side of the Atlantic. Napoleon's continental system, while ultimately unsuccessful in its aims, nonetheless caused the British economy serious difficulties. British shipping, while able to trade with the colonies, was largely barred from Europe, allowing the American merchant marine to expand rapidly. William Cobbett's radical *Political Register* accused the United States of aiding and abetting France in the destruction of British commerce. He was joined by the lawyer James Stephen, whose pamphlet *War in Disguise, or, the Frauds of Neutral Flags* (1805) went a step further, arguing that the Americans' activities, by undermining Britain's commercial operations, were 'fatal to the last hope of liberty in Europe'. From the British perspective, their campaign against Napoleonic despotism – a war of survival for their own, and Europe's, liberty – was being undermined by the United States, the same nation that had recently helped fill the Emperor's coffers by the Louisiana transaction. Further, it was Napoleon who had extended the conduct of the war into vistas that harmed neutrals – Britain had had no choice but to retaliate.[8]

The British policy of impressment further damaged Anglo-American relations. With the war against Napoleon going badly and serving conditions in the Royal Navy harsh, desertion and, indeed, a shortage of sailors was a serious problem. To meet the need for manpower the navy employed press gangs who forcibly 'impressed' British subjects, usually sailors, into active service. Although the press gangs usually operated in British or neutral ports, the Royal Navy also called upon vessels flying the Red Ensign or even neutral flags at sea. In short, the British were stopping American vessels and impressing their sailors into the Royal Navy. To the modern mind, this was an egregious violation of another nation's sovereignty; at the time, however, there was no international agreement on this matter. But there was a reason the Royal Navy targeted American shipping: no other nation's merchant marine so often provided sanctuary to British deserters as that of the United States.

Part of the problem was there was no agreement on what constituted a British subject and an American citizen. Despite claims otherwise, neither nation allowed its citizens/subjects to expatriate themselves. The British declared that anyone residing in the United States before 1783 or born there subsequently would be recognized as a citizen, while American federal law (after 1802) required that an immigrant should have resided in the country for five years before taking on nationality. This last, however, was a difficult requirement for the 'ashore-today-tomorrow-afloat' life of a sailor. Thus, few British-born sailors could claim genuine American citizenship. Further, fraud was rampant. American notaries from New York to New Orleans issued papers of citizenship to any British sailor or deserter willing to pay appropriate fees. As a result, British naval officers treated such documents with more than a little scepticism. Although the Admiralty did investigate claims of American nationality by impressed sailors, and released men whose bona fides were established, this process took time, during which the individual in question was subject to the dangers of war and the ferocious discipline of the Royal Navy. How many Americans were impressed by the Royal Navy will probably never be known. Although the oft-cited total number of 6,257, derived from Madison's report to Congress, is simply incorrect – his report contained many duplications where individuals were counted three or four times – the number of impressed Americans was at least in the low thousands. The United States had a genuine grievance.

The Royal Navy further added fuel to the fire by its aggressive conduct not just on the high seas, but frequently close to the American shoreline, too. British ships lurked off the North American seaboard, stopping ships as they saw fit and removed alleged British deserters and nationals. One ugly incident took place in 1807, off the coast of Virginia, when the HMS *Leopard* ordered the USS *Chesapeake* to halt and receive boarders searching for deserters. When the *Chesapeake* refused, the *Leopard* opened fire, killing three and wounding eighteen, forcing the American ship to surrender (only one deserter was found). Had it not been for the fact the US was too absorbed with former Vice President Aaron Burr's trial for treason (he had tried to establish a secessionist state in Louisiana) and that London immediately disavowed the act, this single outrage may have sparked a War of 1807 instead of 1812. As it was, the Americans had their revenge four years later, when the frigate USS *President*, mistaking the British sloop *Little Belt* for another ship, HMS *Guerrière*, which had seized an alleged deserter, opened fire on the smaller ship, killing nine sailors. It was as aggressive an act as had been the *Leopard*'s firing on the *Chesapeake*, and marked the rapid deterioration of Anglo-American relations.[9]

There were still other factors in play besides disagreements over blockades, impressment or, indeed, the magnitude of the Napoleonic threat. Another cause of the war came via the American west and was bound up, inextricably, with the question of the boundary with Canada (then British North America, a collection of colonies). American settlers had already begun their long march across the continent and, as they would continuously do, encountered Indian resistance. In the atmosphere of already poor relations, many westerners blamed the Indian attacks on the British, one American newspaper going so far as to state, 'We have had but one opinion as to the cause of the depredations of the Indians, which was, and is, that they are instigated and supported by the British in Canada, any official declaration to the contrary notwithstanding.' Yet there was an air of disingenuousness about these claims. The British were not stirring up the Indians against the settlers – the latter achieved that themselves when they moved into Indian territory. As events moved towards war, Britain certainly did form an alliance with several tribes, but that was a defensive, not offensive, manoeuvre. Further, many westerners made no secret about the fact they coveted Canada itself. If France had been forced off the North American continent thanks to the Louisiana Purchase, could not the same be done to Britain, especially as it was now already distracted by a war against Napoleon? Many westerners, eager for territory, decided that it was now time to complete that which had been left undone at the conclusion of the War of Independence. Little wonder, then, that anti-war US representative John Randolph declared of the westerners' clamour: 'we have but heard one word – like the whip-poor-will, but one monotonous tone – Canada! Canada! Canada!'[10]

The congressional spokesman, if not leader, of the so-called 'war hawks' who included Richard Johnson of Kentucky, Felix Grundy of Tennessee, John C. Calhoun of South Carolina, George Troup of Georgia, and Peter Porter of New York was Henry Clay of Kentucky. When the Republican-dominated Twelfth Congress met in November 1811, Clay took the position of Speaker of the House of Representatives and packed important committees with his supporters and began to press the case for war upon James Madison, now President. Their hand was strengthened by the battle of Tippecanoe, November 1811, when Governor William Henry Harrison defeated the forces of the Indian chieftain, Tecumseh. The fact that Tecumseh's braves had British-manufactured weapons was transformed into a claim that the British had equipped, armed and directed his forces against the Americans. In truth, Tecumseh had formed an alliance among several tribes on his own recognizance in an attempt to defend their territory, but blaming the British proved more useful to the war hawks.

Their tactics paid dividends. On 9 March 1812, Madison's administration levelled a charge of its own against Britain when the President informed Congress that he had evidence of a British plot to detach the New England states from the Union with the help of the Federalists. The proof consisted of communications provided by one Comte Edouarde de Crillon, between John Henry, an Irishman living in New England, and Sir James Craig, governor general of Canada, outlining the scheme. Alas for Madison and the Republicans, the 'Comte' was a French adventurer, not noble, and Henry, while certainly having received travel expenses from Craig after a fact-finding trip to New England, was no British conduit to the Federalists. The papers which cost Madison $50,000 – the entire secret service budget – were a mere collection of reports from newspapers and general gossip and proved nothing. The charge backfired, particularly when the Federalists in Congress demanded to question Henry, only to be told by secretary of state James Monroe that he was out of the country.[11]

Yet the Federalists and New England raise a crucial point: namely, that although the Republicans of the West and South were ready for a war with Britain, the Federalists and New England remained opposed. Indeed, part of the cause of the Henry fiasco was the Republicans' desire to discredit New England and Federalist opposition to conflict by linking it to treasonous dealings with the British. As we have seen, the Federalists were generally less anti-British and, as such, were less inclined to blame Britain for the current difficulties and more disposed to negotiate than fight. Some even believed that France was the true author of America's woes. The Federalists' views were broadly representative of their electoral base, New England. Trade with Britain and Europe remained the lynchpin of the region's economy. The loss of the occasional ship or encounter with British high-handedness on the ocean may have rankled, but commerce would be hurt far more by a conflict with the world's pre-eminent maritime power that Madison and the war hawks appeared determined to provoke. Indeed, on the subject of trade, Jefferson's and Madison's embargo acts had hurt New England, while western expansion and the Louisiana Purchase provided few, if any, benefits to the region. Not only would New England representatives and senators vote against the war in Congress, the region would, to all intents and purposes, be a non-participant in the conflict, which they referred to as 'Mr Madison's war'.[12]

If New England and the Federalists did not want war, nor did the British. The years 1810–12 were, from their perspective, bad ones. The

economic situation was deteriorating. Sweden had joined the continental system and British exports to northern Europe declined by 20
per cent. Exports to South America had declined by 65 per cent and
those to the United States were down by 76 per cent. Money was
draining out of the treasury as gold payments to Spain and Portugal (in
an attempt to keep up the struggle against Napoleon) led to the
depreciation of the pound and inflation. Lancashire was now working a
three-day week and there was serious unrest. In 1810 there were the
Burdett riots. From 1811–13, the Luddite riots, caused in part by the
economic distress, took place in Yorkshire, Lancashire and Scotland. In
the political realm, meantime, in 1811, George III's mental illness
necessitated the establishment of the Regency. Then, on 11 May 1812, the
Prime Minister, Spencer Perceval, was assassinated in the lobby of the
House of Commons by an aggrieved bankrupt, John Bellingham. Thus,
in the middle of a major war, the economy was foundering, the people
were rebelling, the king was mad and the Prime Minister was assassinated. It must have appeared to many that Britain was on the verge of
complete collapse. In some respects, complete economic disaster was
fended off only because Napoleon, his own empire suffering similar
hardship, allowed some backdoor trade through a licensing system.

Things were not much better on the battlefront. Although as a
lieutenant-general, Arthur Wellesley, made Duke of Wellington in 1814,
had defeated the French in Portugal in 1808, two British incursions into
Spain the following year were forced to withdraw. Another failure that
same year was the British expedition to Walcheren Island by Antwerp,
which cost over four thousand casualties. The next two years found
Wellington fighting a defensive campaign from behind his fortified lines
of Torres Vedras, Portugal, fending off French assaults. The war in the
Iberian Peninsula had thus apparently stalemated and the reputation of
the British army, meanwhile, was poor – a fact not missed by the
American war hawks who assumed that Napoleon must ultimately
prevail in the struggle. True, Wellington captured the fortress of Ciudad
Rodrigo, a strategic stronghold near the Spanish–Portuguese border, in
January of 1812; however, that was not an obvious beginning of a
turnabout in British fortunes. In short, while the British failed to
promptly acknowledge American grievances, this was mostly due to the
desperate straits they were in. It was less a case of arrogance towards the
United States that determined British conduct, than the see-sawing
fortunes of a desperate struggle for survival.[13]

This dangerous situation meant that Britain wanted to avoid fighting a two-front war. Learning that the United States was increasing the size of its regular army, the driving force behind this development being Clay and the war hawks in Congress, London decided to act. In an effort to stave off conflict, the Tory administration of Robert Banks Jenkinson, Lord Liverpool, revoked the orders in council on 23 June 1812. Had he been left to his own devices, Madison might have proven receptive, for in early spring he had considered sending a final peace mission to Britain. Unfortunately, in April, two months before Britain revoked the orders in council, Clay, accompanied by a group of representatives from the Republican caucus of congressmen on whom Madison's nomination for re-election depended, paid the President a visit at the Executive Mansion. What, exactly, they stipulated remains a point of dispute, but there is little doubt that it included a demand for war against Britain.

On 1 June 1812 Madison's war message was read to both houses of Congress. Some of the grievances were real: impressments and ship seizures; others questionable: the orders in council; others spurious: 'warfare just renewed by the savages on one of our extensive frontiers'. Despite the best efforts of the Federalists, the House of Representatives passed the declaration 79 to 49 three days later, to be followed by the Senate which, on 17 June 1812, voted 19 to 13 in favour of war. Madison signed the declaration on 18 June 1812. His administration believed that any war would be limited in scope and probably brief. Confident of the outcome, they expected the mere declaration of war to force Britain to give way on impressment or, failing that, Canada would be taken within months.[14]

This confidence was not, on the face of it, unwarranted. With the British apparently losing the war to Napoleon, and greatly outnumbered militarily in North America, their odds of holding Canada looked remote. Certainly the declaration of war came as an unpleasant surprise. The fact that the United States had thrown in its lot with Napoleon at the lowest point in Britain's fortunes was a shock. So this was the Americans' idea of liberty? The United States had launched an attack on Britain, the last remaining opponent of Napoleonic despotism, by stabbing it in the back. Yet it was not really the entire United States that had declared war. For, even from the beginning, the Americans were divided. For example, Massachusetts, Rhode Island and Connecticut, all Federalist-dominated, refused to provide troops or call the state militia into national service. The Chief Justice of the US Supreme Court John Marshall, meanwhile, declared himself to be mortified by his nation's 'base submission' to Napoleon. Nonetheless, the pro-war party represented the majority. In the 1812 presidential contest, Madison was re-elected, defeating the allegedly anti-war Federalist candidate De Witt Clinton.[15]

Despite Madison's re-election, events in Europe, and thus ultimately in North America, were not going in quite the direction the war hawks had surmised. For on the very same day as Madison signed the declaration of war, Napoleon's *Grand Armeé* crossed the River Niemen. Its destination was Moscow – and destruction. Thus, although not immediately apparent, for the British the conflict in Europe had suddenly taken a turn for the better and because of this, Mr Madison's war was going prove a lot tougher than either he or the war hawks had bargained for.

Had the United States launched a coordinated, full-scale invasion of Britain's Canadian territories, it might have won the war outright. Unfortunately for American plans, it did not. A three-pronged assault was attempted: the first aimed eastward, from Fort Detroit at the western end of Lake Erie; another westward, between Lakes Ontario and Erie; and the last at Montreal. The first invasion prong, entering Canada on 12 July, led by William Hull, began badly when the general's papers, contained in a trunk on a schooner, were seized by the British, giving their commander, Major General Isaac Brock, a clear idea of his enemy's plans. Hull soon found himself outflanked when a force of British regulars and Indians, led by Captain Charles Roberts, captured Fort Mackinac, which guarded the straits between Lakes Huron and Michigan. In response, Hull ordered the evacuation of Fort Dearborn (now Chicago), hoping to strengthen his forces by adding the troops there to his total muster. Unfortunately, the Fort's population – which contained women and children – while evacuating, was attacked by Tecumseh's forces and massacred. On 15 August, Brock arrived at Fort Detroit, were Hull was stationed, with a small force and demanded his surrender, noting, 'It is far from my intention to join in a war of extermination, but you must be aware, that the numerous body of Indians who have attached themselves to my troops, will be beyond control the moment the contest commences.' Although this was a bluff as Brock lacked the necessary troops to take the fort, Hull surrendered.

Brock then hurried east to defend against the anticipated second American assault between Lakes Ontario and Erie. This came on 11 October, when General Stephen Van Rensselaer's forces crossed the Niagara River and met Brock's forces at Queenston Heights. During the fighting at the Heights, Brock was killed leading a counter-attack against Rensselaer's forces lodged in a strategic redoubt. An obvious target, he

was fatally shot in the left breast, and although the assault was successful, his oft-quoted last words, 'Push on the York Volunteers', thus
urging the militia on with his dying breath, are apocryphal. The fighting
over the redoubt on the Heights continued throughout the day. The
American forces led by lieutenant colonel Winfield Scott, losing their
best opportunity when their reinforcements, the New York militia,
refused to cross into Canada. The militia claimed their job was to
defend American soil, not invade foreign territory. Finally, after losing
some 300 casualties to 92 British, Scott and his men surrendered. That
was two prongs blunted. The third, which should have been the key
thrust, never really started. This force was led by the dithering Major
General Henry Dearborn who wasted time trying to acquire more
volunteers in anti-war New England, and setting off after Brock's
posthumous victory at Queenston Heights, simply halted at the Canadian border when the state militia refused to cross.[16]

Thomas Jefferson had boasted in August 1812 that 'The acquisition of
Canada this year as far as the neighbourhood of Quebec, will be a mere
matter of marching, and will give us experience for the attack on Halifax
the next, and the final expulsion of England from the American continent.' That was how it should have been, but for American military
mismanagement, Isaac Brock, his small supply of British regulars,
Canadian militia and Indian allies. Further, in the broader scheme of
things, events were likewise beginning to shift in Britain's favour. For,
that October, in the same month as Queenston Heights, Napoleon had
begun his retreat from Moscow, his army to be destroyed by Russia's
three greatest generals: November, December and January.[17]

The Americans did win some victories in the war's first year and
from an unexpected quarter. For, ironically enough, while they did
badly where they should have done well, they did well where they
should have done badly for, if they failed on land, they did much better
at sea. The Royal Navy was overstretched, with too many ships concentrated in European waters – only one ship of the line, seven frigates
and a number of smaller ships operated off the North American coast –
and it was here that the Americans pounced. The USS *Constitution*
defeated the HMS *Guerrière* in August and frigate *Java* in December, the
USS *Wasp* got the better of the HMS *Frolic* in October, and the USS
Hornet sank the HMS *Peacock* in February. The crowning moment for
the US Navy was when the frigate USS *United States* brought in the
frigate HMS *Macedonian* into New London as a war prize on 4
December 1812 (the only Royal naval vessel to suffer such an indignity).

After the defeats on land, these unexpected victories against the world's pre-eminent navy greatly improved American morale and surprised, if not shocked, the British.

Despite some rather extravagant claims both at the time and repeated since, such as that ship for ship, the US Navy proved more than the equal to those of the Royal Navy which eventually prevailed simply by sheer weight of numbers, most of the American naval victories were larger, heavier ships defeating smaller British ones. Also, while the Royal Navy was powerful, it was not invincible: during the Napoleonic wars, individual French ships had also beaten single British ships in combat. Finally, the Americans did not have it all their own way. The *Wasp*, for example, was captured the day after it defeated the *Frolic*; also captured were the frigates *President* and *Essex*; and when the equally matched frigates HMS *Shannon* and USS *Chesapeake* duelled within sight of Boston Harbour, on 1 June 1813, it was the Americans who yielded, in just 11 minutes, despite the order of Captain James Lawrence, 'fight 'til she sinks, boys. Don't give up the ship.' The US Navy undeniably landed some blows, but the Royal Navy returned the compliment.[18]

Further, the American victories simply ensured that the Royal Navy would be reinforced in order to do its job properly and blockade the American coast. Most of the American men-of-war that entered harbour during the winter of 1812–13 never got out again. By the autumn of 1812, Delaware Bay and Chesapeake Bay were under blockade, as were New York and New England by the following spring. By the end of 1813, the American seaboard was effectively shut down. American privateers had better luck initially, capturing over a thousand vessels, but the British moved to a convoy system which sharply reduced their losses. As the war progressed, the Royal Navy's pursuit of the privateers became increasingly aggressive and, by the conflict's end, they had captured over a thousand ships themselves. With the Atlantic seaboard under their control, the British began raiding the American coastline. By the spring of 1813, Rear Admiral Cockburn was launching hit-and-run attacks in Chesapeake Bay, burning canon foundries and munitions stores and either sinking or capturing what ships he encountered.[19]

On land, however, the United States still had the advantage and demonstrated this by raiding York, present-day Toronto, then the capital of Upper Canada in April 1813. Despite its status, York was poorly defended. Strategically it was less important than Kingston, gateway to the St Lawrence River and, besides, desperately short of troops, the British could hardly guard everywhere. Thus when on 27

April American general Zebulon Pike's forces landed three miles west of York, they outnumbered the British, Canadian and Indian forces by at least 2–1. After some fierce resistance, the British regulars were withdrawn to Kingston, leaving the militia to put up token opposition. The situation deteriorated when the latter detonated their supply of powder to prevent it falling into enemy hands. Caught in the blast, however, were numerous American soldiers – including General Pike – and lust for revenge, plus an obvious slackening of discipline, led to homes being looted and buildings – private and public – being burned, including the parliament buildings of Upper Canada. When the Americans departed a week later, they left an enraged populace behind.[20]

Belatedly recognizing that control of the great lakes was necessary for any invasion of Canada to succeed, during the winter of 1812–13, the Americans, thanks to the relative closeness of the manufacturing centre of Pittsburgh, constructed a small squadron. On 10 September, this squadron, led by Oliver Perry, fought an equally ramshackle though smaller British one (both were crewed by militia, backwoodsmen and a minority of professional sailors) compelling it to surrender. Perry's famous declaration 'we have met the enemy and he is ours' was an accurate summation; the later claim that it was one of the few times in the annals of the Royal Navy that an entire squadron surrendered was less so: few of the British crew or commanders were Navy regulars. Nonetheless, the Americans now controlled Lake Erie.[21]

This would have consequences in the war's western theatre. Although General William Harrison, marching from the Ohio River toward Detroit in January, found three of his divisions engaged and defeated by British general Henry Procter before they could unite at Frenchtown on the Raisin River in January 1813, it only delayed, not halted, his advance. Further, Procter's failure to supervise his Indian allies resulting in a massacre of prisoners gave the Americans reason for revenge. After Procter's failure to capture either Forts Meigs or Stephenson, for, despite the aid of the Indian allies commanded by Tecumseh, he lacked the manpower and artillery to take either, Perry's victory on Lake Erie forced him to abandon Detroit. Harrison then engaged both Procter and Tecumseh near Moraviantown, on the Canadian side of the border, and greatly outnumbering them, defeated them at the Battle of the Thames in October. Here, Tecumseh, who had struck terror into the hearts of north-western American settlers, was killed and 600 British soldiers were captured.[22]

Despite these victories, the United States failed to follow up on their success. They directed a pincer movement towards Montreal in Lower Canada. The first column of 7,000 men under General James Wilkinson sailed from Sackets Harbor down the St Lawrence, while General Wade Hampton with 4,500 men marched from Plattsburg on Lake Champlain. The latter encountered a mixed force of British regulars and French Canadian militia led by the Lieutenant Colonel Charles de Salaberry (a French-Canadian British army officer) at Chateaugay in October. Despite outnumbering his foes by a greater than 3–1 margin, after an exchange of fire Hampton retreated. Wilkinson proved even less effective. Harassed by British units under the command of Lieutenant Colonel Joseph W. Morrison, he sent part of his army to deal with this nuisance. Unfortunately for him, the harassers turned out to be seasoned British regulars who routed his men at Crysler's Farm on 11 November, 'Never have so many Americans been beaten by such inferior numbers on foreign soil', bemoaned one later commentator. Wilkinson retreated back to the American side of the frontier.[23]

American fortunes were no better in the Niagara area. In May, US forces, led by Dearborn, wrested Fort George from Brigadier General John Vincent. Vincent won the re-match, however, when he defeated the American advance on Hamilton at Stony Creek in June and in December and recaptured Fort George, driving the Americans back across their frontier. The Americans, in retreat, burned much of the Canadian village of Newark to the ground – sending the 400 inhabitants out into a blinding snowstorm. Retribution followed swiftly. Within a week, the British, under the command of Lieutenant-General George Drummond, seized Fort Niagara, and then captured Buffalo, New York, defeating an American force at the town of Black Rock and put both places to the torch in retaliation.[24]

If the war in North America was stalemated on land, however, the situation in Europe was altogether different. In October of 1813, after a series of battles, Napoleon's forces facing the combined armies of Sweden, Austria, Russia and Prussia were smashed at Leipzig. As the allies converged on Paris from the East, in the South the Duke of Wellington drove the French from Spain. In June, Wellington crushed Joseph Bonaparte's army at Vitoria and the following year crossed the Pyrenees to defeat Marshall Soult at Orthez (February) and Toulouse (April). Paris fell to the allies on 31 March 1814, forcing Napoleon's abdication. Although the British were tied diplomatically to Europe, they were freed up militarily and this meant they could now pay rather closer attention to the North American theatre.

Indeed, the mood against the United States had hardened. Although Francis Jeffrey, the editor of the *Edinburgh Review*, while on a visit to Washington in April 1814, had replied to Madison's question what the British thought about the war that, 'Half the people of England do not know there is a war with America, and those who did had forgotten it', he was being diplomatic. By this time, the reports of the burning of York and Newark were well circulated, and the news that innocent civilians had been forced into a Canadian blizzard while the American burned their homes to the ground caused outrage. That the British ships bearing news of Parliament's repeal of the orders in council had been seized as war prizes and that America had sided with Napoleon at the lowest point in Britain's fortunes had taken on the role of serious grievances. Troops started to be shipped across the Atlantic; Britain was now preparing to go on the offensive.[25]

Until the British reinforcements arrived, however, the Americans still had the advantage on land and used it. In May they attacked Port Dover, Upper Canada, and put it to the torch, in retaliation for the British assault on Buffalo. In response, Drummond captured Fort Oswego, New York. In July, the United States made what was to be their final invasion of Upper Canada. Initially things went well: the under-manned Fort Erie was forced to capitulate and a force of British regulars was compelled to retreat at Chippawa after a fierce engagement. At that point, the tide turned. The American forces ran into Drummond and his troops at Lundy's Lane, Niagara Falls. The battle that followed was the bloodiest of the war, each side taking close to a thousand casualties. Although neither side was dislodged from its position, by nightfall the Americans had had enough and retreated under the cover of night. Despite claims of a draw both at the time and afterward, an army in retreat has conceded defeat. In truth, Drummond had halted the invasion and ended once and for all any chance that Canada would be annexed by the United States.[26]

In August, the British began their offensive. With an army of almost 10,000 men in Montreal, most of them veterans of the Peninsula campaign, under the command of General Sir George Prevost, the danger to the United States was acute. Prevost's leadership, however, proved no better than that of his enemy's. Unnecessarily insisting on controlling Lake Champlain, when an American squadron, led by Thomas Macdonough, defeated a British one (a mere eight ships in total were engaged), in the misnamed 'Battle of Plattsburg' (which the British had already taken by land in September), Prevost ordered a general retreat – to the fury of his field commanders. Prevost was summoned home to face a court martial that he did not live to endure. He had served as governor-general of Canada since 1811 and, as chief of his Majesty's forces in Canada and the Atlantic colonies, had held the territories together administratively and successfully defended them. As a defender, Prevost met the challenge, but in 1814 Britain needed generals to take the offensive and a more aggressive one might well have captured Albany, if not New York City. Either way, the war on the Canadian-American frontier was effectively over.[27]

Elsewhere the war continued, as British raiding parties were now attacking towns and villages up and down the Atlantic seaboard. One even sailed up the Connecticut River and destroyed twenty-seven American ships. Emboldened by this success, Vice Admiral Sir Alexander Cochrane recommended an assault on Washington in July 1814. Permission granted, a British fleet sailed into Chesapeake Bay and then up the Patuxent River. On 19 August an invasion force of just over 4,000 men under the command of Major General Robert Ross, accompanied by Cockburn, disembarked at the tiny port of Benedict, some forty-five miles from the capital. Cockburn, in an act worthy of Horatio Nelson, ignored an order from Cochrane, who had developed cold feet, to abort the attack; the British force marched towards Washington.

In the capital, the British landings caused consternation. Even though Madison had announced at a cabinet meeting on 1 July that he expected an attack on Washington, little was done to prepare for it. Indeed, the British force that moved through Maryland encountered virtually no resistance, until they met the hastily gathered American army consisting of some 7,000 men, commanded by General William Winder, outside Bladensburg, five miles from the capital. Overseen by President Madison – the only time a US President was ever present on the battlefield as a commander in chief – the Americans awaited the British assault from a reasonably strong defensive position. The engagement that began at noon lasted some three hours but, in the end, each of three American lines broke and ran, Madison leading the retreat that soon became a rout. That the British took more casualties at Bladensburg was to be expected – they had attacked a larger force in a good defensive position and one that fell back as soon as the advancing columns closed in. The American retreat was so rapid the British could not even follow in pursuit for, as Cockburn put it, 'the victors were too weary and the vanquished too swift'. Ross and Cockburn had won a decisive victory.[28]

Once in Washington, the British had their revenge for the burning of

York and Newark, even if they restricted their arson to public buildings and structures from which brave or foolhardy individuals had fired upon them. They set fire to the Capitol, the White House and the Treasury Building. The tale that Cockburn's troops sat in the place of the congressmen and passed a unanimous motion in favour of 'burning this hive of Yankee democracy' is a myth, as is the story that the White House was originally pink and only later painted white to cover the British arson. What is true is that had it not been for a sudden torrential downpour, many of these buildings would have burned to their foundations. One act of arson especially pleasing to Cockburn was the burning of the premises of the *National Intelligencer*, a newspaper responsible for printing scurrilous stories about him (making him one of the few individuals to get satisfaction at the expense of the American press). At the same time, Cockburn put a guard on the late George Washington's home to protect it from local looters. Otherwise, British soldiers collected 'souvenirs' from every building they torched. When Cockburn's forces departed – unmolested – on 26 August, they took with them 206 guns, 500 barrels of powder and some 100,000 musket cartridges.[29]

Those who claim that the capture of Washington was of prestige value only, and was more than outweighed by Andrew Jackson's victory at New Orleans, are committing considerable violence to history. As the nineteenth-century Swiss military strategist – and therefore impartial judge – Antoine Henri Jomini later put it, 'The world was astonished to see a handful of seven or eight thousand [*sic*] Englishmen making their appearance in the midst of a state embracing ten millions of people, taking possession of its capital, and destroying all the public buildings – results unparalleled in history.'[30]

Although war-weariness was growing across the United States, the burning of Washington, in many respects, marked the tipping point. Indeed, when Madison's wife Dolley attempted entry into a tavern filled with refugees from the capital, she was turned away; they blamed her husband for their distress. In New England, meanwhile, opposition to the war now moved in a secessionist direction. When James Monroe, now secretary of war, insisted Canada could still be taken, many called him mad. Much of Maine was now under British occupation, the New England economy was in ruins, and the British were apparently able to strike with impunity. Even the capital was not safe. The Massachusetts legislature issued a call for a regional convention to examine the question of secession from the Union. Several other states concurred and delegates from Massachusetts, Rhode Island and Connecticut met in convention in Hartford in December, joined by unofficial delegates from New Hampshire and Vermont. As the proceedings were held in secret, it is unknown if secession was actually avowed, but several amendments to the Constitution were publicly proposed including an end to slaves being included in state censuses for the purposes of seats in the House of Representatives (a move to weaken the South); a two-thirds majority in both Houses of Congress would be required to declare war; and that new states could only be admitted into the Union with a two-thirds majority in both Houses of Congress (aimed at weakening westward expansion and western power), among others. True, the American victory at New Orleans completely discredited the Hartford Convention, but Madison, facing the dissolution of the Union and having been driven out of Washington, now had to seriously consider making peace.

As it happened, the United States had made peace overtures almost as soon as the war began, offering an armistice on the basis of Britain's withdrawing the orders in council and ending impressment. The Foreign Secretary, Robert Stewart, Viscount Castlereagh, however, was initially disdainful – as far as he was concerned, Britain had already made a major concession by repealing the orders in council and had had war declared upon it for its efforts. Another attempt at peace was made in 1813 by Tsar Alexander I who offered to mediate between the belligerents, an offer the Americans accepted, but the British declined, not the least because of Monroe's foolish suggestion that the British should consider surrendering either a portion or all of Upper Canada. Finally, after Leipzig, with the British in something resembling, if not a position of strength, at least equal terms, Castlereagh offered to negotiate directly with the Americans. Negotiations began at Ghent in August 1814, but Madison's insistence that the British renounce impressment as a precondition for peace was simply a non-starter. Although he had allowed the American negotiators to give way on the issue of impressment, they could only do so in the final extremity. The burning of Washington proved to be just that and impressment was dropped as a precondition. In a reciprocal measure, and in response to their repulse at Baltimore, the British government abandoned its demands for an Indian buffer state in American territory. The treaty, signed on 24 December 1814, to all intents and purposes, established the *status antebellum*.[31]

In many respects, it was the wisest course for both nations. After their successful raid on Washington, Cochrane and Cockburn decided

another such attempt should be made on Baltimore. Baltimore, however, proved much better defended. Besides being guarded by several
forts, including McHenry, the city authorities had constructed a defence
of massive earthworks in response to the capture of Washington. To
circumvent the forts, the British, in September, landed several miles
away and marched towards Baltimore. At a narrow point on the North
point peninsula, however, they encountered entrenched American
troops who, when driven from one set of defences, simply fell back to
even stronger ones. In order to outflank these defences, Fort McHenry
would have to be taken. Throughout the night, Royal Navy vessels fired
on the fort to little effect. One witness to all of this was Francis Scott
Key, who, as a prisoner on the British ship, could only tell of Fort
McHenry's continued resistance by the American flag flying from the
battlements. The sight inspired him to pen 'Star Spangled Banner' –
later the American national anthem (sung to the tune of the old English
drinking song 'To Anacreon in Heaven'). Unable to outflank the
Americans, and lacking either the troops or artillery to break their
earthwork defences, the British withdrew, taking a large number of
escaped slaves with them to freedom, something that did not endear
them to the citizens of Maryland. Although repulsed at Baltimore, the
British could at least console themselves with the fact that casualties had
been light – they would have no such consolation at New Orleans.[32]

New Orleans was one of the great defensive victories of the war,
courtesy of general, later President, Andrew Jackson. 'Old Hickory' as
he was known, a former major general of the Tennessee militia and a
staunch supporter of seizing Indian and British territory, raised
volunteer regiments to help do just that. Jackson was instead sent south
to capture territory in present-day Florida and Alabama, including
Mobile. This last was supposedly included in the Louisiana Purchase,
but remained under Spanish occupation. That Spain was Britain's ally
in the war against Napoleon was the justification – but Spain had
committed no offence against the United States. The Americans simply
took from French-occupied Spain what they could not from Britain.
Jackson spent much of the war fighting – and in some cases massacring
– Creek Indians, finally forcing them to concede half their lands – three-
fifths of the present state of Alabama and a fifth of Georgia. The
argument that they would have helped the British was, and is, a dishonest excuse. It was also a foretaste of what Jackson would do to the
Indians as President.

Jackson faced a large British assault force under the command of

Major General Edward Pakenham. The plan was to occupy as much of New Orleans and gulf territory as possible to be used as bargaining pawns for peace (the negotiations at Ghent were underway, but nothing was as yet agreed to, much less signed). Jackson initially misread British intentions, believing they would land at Mobile, and had to scramble to New Orleans, when their advance forces landed. Jackson, with superior numbers, launched an assault on this advance guard at the Villere plantation, only to be driven back. Deciding that defence was the key, he accordingly constructed a solid rampart behind Rodriguez's canal, a ditch four feet deep and twenty feet wide. Had Pakenham moved with alacrity, he may well have been able to brush Jackson's forces aside. As it was, he wasted time gathering reinforcements, and allowed Jackson to finish building his defences. Pakenham at this point had two realistic options: he could either clear the American defences with artillery, or flank them. Instead, Pakenham, 'not the brightest genius' as his brother-in-law the Duke of Wellington put it, chose the worst option of all: a frontal assault over open ground by infantry against troops ensconced in heavily built defences. Pakenham lacked even the necessary 3-1 advantage in manpower required for such an offensive, his forces amounting to only 5,300 men to Jackson's 3,500. Pakenham's attack resulted in a one-sided massacre. Thirteen Americans were killed to 291 British with at least 1,262 wounded, Pakenham being one of the fallen. Although the British captured Mobile after the debacle of New Orleans, the War of 1812 had concluded on a high point for the United States.[33]

Occurring after the signing of the Treaty of Ghent, New Orleans was, militarily speaking, a pointless battle. Despite claims that Britain would have held on to New Orleans and whatever part of the Louisiana territory it could get – a charge that, originating as it did with Monroe, is immediately suspect – there is no evidence to support this. In the first instance, the British had already passed up such an opportunity in 1805 when Jefferson's Vice President, Aaron Burr, approached the British with a bid to detach Louisiana from the United States (the offer was refused – undeterred, Burr went ahead and tried to turn the territory into an independent republic, only to be betrayed and tried for treason for his pains). In the second, if the British had been so inclined to break the peace treaty, they would have held on to Mobile or even the swathes of easier-to-defend Maine under their possession.

From the British perspective, America was a secondary problem; the real threat, once again, came from Europe. In March of 1815, Napoleon escaped from Elba, and although his career would end bloodily at

Waterloo on 18 June 1815, the diversion of troops to North America limited the number of British forces available for the European campaign. One of the reasons why the army Wellington commanded at Waterloo was both inexperienced and less than one third British was because of the demands of the American war. Indeed, Wellington was nearly not at Waterloo himself – he had been asked to replace Prevost after the latter's bungling at Plattsburg (and there were demands in the British press that Wellington take charge and do to the Americans what he had done to the French). Wellington, regarding the war in North America as a pointless sideshow and dissatisfied with the European situation, declined – fortunately as it turned out. Although there was never any formal alliance between Napoleon and the United States, to all intents and purposes it was the Emperor's useful ally – and, from his perspective, the arrangement was very nearly finer still.

This aspect was lost on many in the United States at the time, and by some historians since. Understandable, perhaps, considering that Madison was succeeded by Monroe, whose famous eponymous doctrine (1823) effectively caused America to enter its first period of isolationism, and away from European events. Popular memory, following suit, confined itself to events on the North American continent, the larger international picture forgotten. Further, the end of the Napoleonic wars marked the beginning of Britain's status as the pre-eminent world power – and it was that mighty force that the United States, according to popular American memory, had engaged with, not the weakened nation on the ropes in a life-or-death struggle. Jackson's defensive victory at New Orleans, which placed the general firmly on the road to the presidency, gave both he and his supporters obvious grounds to mythologize it. Once this became the decisive engagement, the entire conflict was conflated into a stunning American triumph. This version of events was set in stone by the American historian George Bancroft, whose account in his multivolume *History of the United States* (1834–73) was largely confirmed by Henry Adams in his *History of the United States during the Administrations of Jefferson and Madison* (1889–91). In some respects, all subsequent histories of the conflict remain influenced by this interpretation.

That the war's last major engagement ended with an American victory, despite occurring after the Treaty of Ghent was signed and ratified, played an important role in the development of the American national identity. Certainly, Jackson's victory was the death knell for the New England-dominated anti-war Federalist Party, particularly as the now

Democratic-Republicans, later the Democrats, portrayed the war as a resounding triumph and damned their opponents with impunity. Although both New England and the ghosts of the Hamilton and the Federalist Party (in the form of Lincoln and the Republicans) would later have their revenge on the Democrats, and the South especially, during the American Civil War, Jefferson's southern and western Democratic-Republicans were now the dominant party. The United States would make the transformation from a liberal republic into a democratic one. In this respect, the War of 1812 or rather, the mythological account, would prove to be crucial to the United States.

The British view was somewhat different. In many respects, the Treaty of Ghent was unpopular. There were demands for revenge – demands in no way confined to any social or political class – for this perceived opportunist attempt to seize British territory. Further, the repulse at New Orleans only increased the strength of such sentiment. Napoleon's escape from Elba, however, vindicated the British government's actions. Europe was always the first priority in the nineteenth-century British mind, and the threat of Napoleon and the French would always render the problem of Madison and the Americans to a secondary concern.

Nonetheless, the animosity against the United States caused by the war took longer to abate than historians have generally recognized. It is difficult to overestimate the importance the Napoleonic wars held in the nineteenth-century British imagination. Although comparisons made between the Emperor of Europe and Adolf Hitler are often wide of the mark, the struggle against Napoleon played a similar role in the nineteenth-century British imagination that the Second World War and the 'finest hour' does in the present. For the Americans to ally with France to win their independence was one thing; to side with Napoleon was quite another. In British eyes, the new republic behaved in the same fashion as the despotisms of Europe. Clearly, American belief in liberty did not extend beyond its own borders. Further, Britons were frequently reminded of this conflict by American nationalists' attempts to turn the stalemate into a resounding victory. It did not take long for the British to retaliate in kind. Captain Edward Brenton's *The Naval History of Great Britain* (1825) pointed to the ultimate British victories on the high seas, the capture of Washington and reminded the Americans of their failure to take Canada. Another, more popular analyst was the lawyer, William James, who, having been detained in Philadelphia in 1812, scoffed at American claims of victory in his *A Naval History of Great*

Britain, which went through several editions: 1822, 1826, 1837 and 1859. Indeed, so thorough was his analysis that the Admiralty used it for formulating plans for a future war against the United States right up until 1865. This British version of events has been almost forgotten, but it was important in its day. One individual whose views of the United States were certainly shaped by this 'forgotten conflict' was Henry Temple, Viscount Palmerston, who acted as secretary of war and later served as Foreign Secretary as well as Prime Minister. This point would prove important in future Anglo-American relations. In the end, however, the War of 1812 could never be more than a sideshow to the Napoleonic wars and British public memory eventually atrophied.[34]

If the American national identity was greatly enhanced by the War of 1812, the national identity conceived by the war was Canada's. That the Canadian militia proved crucial to the defence of the colonies, despite the fact British officers and regulars were more militarily significant, established a clear sense of separateness from the United States. This is why those who insist that such arguments are anachronistic because Britain's North American colonies did not confederate until 1867 have missed the point. All national identities, to some degree, are defined by what a people are not. Thus, as the American national identity was originally based on not being British (later extended to not being European), so the Canadian identity was founded on not being American. Indeed, without the real or perceived external threat of the United States, it is difficult to see how French- and English-speaking Canadians would ever have unified politically (and it is interesting that the linguistic-political division reappeared after all serious threat from the United States receded). The process was helped by the British who, struck by the loyalty of their colonists, reversed their policy of neglect, and moved in the direction of strengthening their colonies' political development. Prior to the War of 1812, the United States might well have been able to purchase Canada in much the same way it did Louisiana or later, Alaska. That option was now gone and, as a result, a new nation was conceived, if not born.[35]

At the conclusion of the negotiations at Ghent, the most cerebral member of the American delegation, John Quincy Adams (later President), remarked 'I hope this will be the last treaty of peace between Great Britain and the United States'. It was – the numerous war scares during the rest of the century notwithstanding. This was why both sides won. They had fought each other to a standstill and whatever each had gained, they had, at least, not taken it from the other. Each had given as good as they had got, and if Britain had been distracted, America had been divided. While the war left a legacy of animosity and distrust which would shadow Anglo-American relations, particularly as both nations expanded their reach across the North American continent, it nonetheless left both convinced that there had to be better ways of settling future disputes. British and American expansionism would certainly result in future quarrels and threats but they would avoid open conflict with each other. The United States might expand into Spanish or Mexican territory but, whatever future hotheads might declare, Britain's North American territory was off-limits. All the later bombast surrounding Jackson's victory at New Orleans could not quite drown out the sounds of Rear Admiral Cockburn's impromptu – and incendiary – dinner party.[36]

As for the Rear Admiral, his war ended on a slightly unsatisfactory note. He was preparing for another major assault on the United States – this time against Savannah, Georgia – when, much to his chagrin, news of the peace arrived. His new assignment was to convey Napoleon, aboard the HMS *Northumberland*, to the latter's final exile on St Helena, a rock in the mid-Atlantic from which there could be no escape. On the day Cockburn arrived at the White House, he had facetiously inquired after James Madison, only to be told that the President was not in. Cockburn never did get to meet the President of the United States, but perhaps making the acquaintance of the Emperor of Europe proved to be an adequate substitute; he, after all, was the real architect of Mr Madison's war.

2

Who Reads an American Book?

Sam Slick, itinerant Yankee peddler, currently trading in Nova Scotia, was delighted by his latest transaction, the likely successful sale of a timepiece to Deacon Flint and his wife. Slick's sales technique was carefully planned and cleverly executed. Earlier, he had complimented the deacon by (deliberately) miscalculating the extent and worth of his land, 'why there aint such a location in all New England', and had replied to the other's self-deprecating remarks regarding his age, 'why you are worth half a dozen of the young men we see, nowadays'. This was American '*soft sawder*', or softening up, for, as Slick observed, 'An Englishman would pass that man as a sheep passes a hog in pasture, without looking at him.' No Englishman, of course, could make a sale like an American.

Having thus gained admission into the deacon's home, Slick then, with feigned reluctance, showed his last remaining clock to the Flints, informing the deacon when the latter declared that he had no occasion for it, 'I guess you're in the wrong furrow this time, Deacon, it aint for sale ... and if it was, I reckon neighbor Steel's wife would have it, for she gives me no peace about it.' Then, 'in apparent surprise', he noted the time and, declaring that he could not make his destination that evening, asked the Flints to hold onto the clock overnight. Slick would pick it up before his departure 'to the States', the following day. This was the work of a consummate salesman, for, as Slick pointed out afterwards,

> Mrs. Flint will never let Mrs. Steel have the refusal – nor will the Deacon learn until I call for the clock, that having once indulged in the use of a superfluity, how difficult it is to give it up. We can do without any article of luxury we never had, but when once obtained, it is not '*in human nature*' to surrender it voluntarily.

Slick's talent for '*soft sawder*' and his knowledge of '*human nature*' paid dividends. For, as he pointed out, 'Now that clock is sold for 40 dollars – it cost me just 6 dollars and 50 cents.' Thus could an American 'sell his wares, at whatever price he pleases, where a blue-nose [Nova Scotian] would fail to make a sale at all'.

In many respects we have here a quintessential stereotype: the American as salesman and a slippery one at that (the name 'Slick' rather gives the game away). A shameless huckster (he boasts of his techniques) palming off his shoddy products on the gullible (the clock is described by the narrator as 'a gawdy, highly varnished, trumpery-looking affair'). This is the crafty, amoral, if not downright immoral, American – one who alternately insinuates himself into people's confidence and talks tall, all for the express purpose of deceiving them into purchasing his cheap junk. But what was one to expect from a representative of so mercurial a culture where, as Slick himself says, 'We reckon hours and minutes to be dollars and cents'? This notion of the American as salesman, its literary apotheosis being Willie Loman in Arthur Miller's *Death of a Salesman* (1949), is now something of a cliché, but Sam Slick is the original. He never existed, of course, being the creation of Thomas C. Haliburton (1796–1865), born in Windsor, Nova Scotia, lawyer, provincial assembly member, provincial Supreme Court judge and Member of Parliament in the House of Commons at Westminster; the creator of a character that almost anticipated Miller's eponymous protagonist by over a century.

Haliburton was to publish twenty-one 'Sam Slick' stories in the newspaper the *Nova Scotian*, later to appear as a single collection, *The Clockmaker: or, The Sayings and Doings of Sam Slick of Slickville* in 1837. It was a measure of the travelling Yankee trader's popularity that Haliburton was able to make something of a literary career out of his exploits. Later titles followed, including, among others, *The Attaché; or Sam Slick in England* (1843–44) and *Nature and Human Nature* (1853). Indeed, Haliburton's books were bestsellers on both sides of the Atlantic, being as popular in America as they were in Britain. They were less popular in the author's native Nova Scotia, however, doubtless in part because the inhabitants recognized that they, not the Americans, were the real butt of the joke (Haliburton's stories deliberately contrast the industriousness of the Americans to the sloth and avarice of the Nova Scotians). As Haliburton has Slick declare in a letter to the editor in the first collection, 'It wipes up the blue-noses considerable hard, and don't let off the Yankees so very easy neither ... and although it aint altogether jist gospel what's in it, there's some pretty home truths in it, that's a fact.'[1]

Having noted that, for all Slick's dialect comedy (which anticipates that of Mark Twain and probably influenced Dickens), Haliburton's works express the author's ambivalence about Americans and their imperial confidence. Politically, Haliburton was a Tory, albeit of a liberal bent, supporting both Catholic emancipation and removing education from the control of the Church of England (as he grew older, as is so often the case, his conservatism hardened – he later opposed self-government for the Canadian colonies). Yet Haliburton's portrayal of Americans owes little, if anything, to this. His concerns about America's imperial confidence were a logical concern for an inhabitant of Britain's North American colonies whose formative years were spent during the War of 1812. Yet the image of the Americans that the Victorian reader carried away with Sam Slick was that of a people very different to both the British and their North American colonists, a tall-talking, not-to-be-entirely-trusted, crafty and acquisitive folk whose dialect was English of a very different variety. Americans might appear friendly, charming or amusing, but if not watched closely one might find oneself out of pocket – or worse.

Haliburton's portrait of the Americans at least contained some measure of affection. Earlier British writers were not even prepared to grant that. Poet Laureate Robert Southey, writing in 1812, remarked of the Americans, 'They have in the course of twenty years acquired a distinct national character of low and lying knavery; and so well do they deserve it that no man ever had any dealings with them without having proofs of its truth.' Comments such as these, written in wartime, were to be expected – even by radicals, for Southey, at this time, had yet to renounce his Jacobin sentiments (like Haliburton he, too, would become far more conservative with age). Yet, as one scholar has observed, in the peace that followed the War of 1812, bitterness appeared to intensify, rather than subside, as insults and rebuttals regularly appeared in both nations' journals and newspapers. One taunt among the many hurled most frequently at the Americans was that old slander: they lacked culture.[2]

One man who first levelled this charge was that witty Whig and literary critic Sydney Smith who, after reviewing a book on the United States, in the *Edinburgh Review*, January 1820 (a journal he co-founded), loudly expressed his opinion of the nation. After declaring that, 'Thus far we are the friends and admirers of Jonathan', Smith stated that the chief merit of the United States was its British heritage. Pointing out that the great patriots of the American Revolution were all born and brought up as subjects of the King, Smith then listed several distinguished Britons active since the War of Independence and, turning to the 'self-adulating race', that was 'too fond of glory', on the other side of the Atlantic, he contemptuously asked what the world owed to American scientists, doctors and manufacturers, and who 'sleeps in American blankets'? That covered science, medicine and industry, not to mention bedclothes, but there remained the arts, and Smith sarcastically inquired, 'In the four quarters of the globe, who reads an American book? or goes to an American play? or who looks at an American picture or statue?' In short, what was the point of the United States?[3]

If the British were not reading American publications, the Americans were certainly reading British ones – and Smith's contemptuous dismissal of their nation and culture provoked a roar of outrage that echoed long after his death. Herman Melville, for example, in an 1850 essay on Hawthorne, belatedly fired back by demanding to know who read an British book that was modern. The *Review*'s editor, Francis Jeffrey, whose second wife was American, and who courted and won American readers, tried to persuade Smith to soften his pronouncements, to no effect. Declaring himself 'as much a Philoyankeist as you are', Smith then criticized the Americans for being 'so extremely sensitive and touchy' and remarked, 'We really thought at one time they would have fitted out an armament against the *Edinburgh* and *Quarterly Reviews*, and burnt down Mr. Murray's and Mr. Constable's shops as we did the American Capitol.' Despite his talent to annoy, Smith was not, in fact, anti-American. His articles in the *Edinburgh Review* and elsewhere did, in fact, praise examples of American egalitarianism and use them to illustrate British iniquities (and anyone familiar with Smith's works knows he was an unsparing critic of his own society, too). Further, some of his later articles were written in response to the state of Pennsylvania repudiating its interest payments on bonds in which he had foolishly invested (although his dismissing the United States as a nation of pickpockets in the liberal *Morning Chronicle* was probably unnecessary, even if the Americans had referred to him as the 'Rev. Shylock Smith'). Yet, in the end, Smith's dismissal of American culture and, worse, his taunt that there was no possibility of an emerging American literature 'for centuries to come', caused the most irritation, particularly as it reflected a point of view prevalent in Britain. Most offensive of all, however, was the unspoken upshot: that because the Americans were incapable of portraying themselves, someone would have to do it for them; in this case, the British. Understandably, however, Sam Slick's folk were not about to accept this state of affairs with equanimity.[4]

Shortly after Smith's taunts were published, at least one representative of American letters achieved a degree of modest success in Britain. It was success well deserved for while Anglo-American animosities were at their height, he tried to soothe tempers and to bring about reconciliation between the two estranged peoples. In the opening of his British edition of *The Sketch Book*, Washington Irving informed his readers that his work would probably only be interesting to Americans. He shared it only reluctantly, being mindful of the 'austerity with which the writings of his countrymen have hitherto been treated by British critics'. It is not difficult to imagine which British critic he had in mind. Yet Irving's attempts at peacemaking were sincere and he, like many on either side of the Atlantic, came to the issue of Anglo-American relations from the turmoil of the War of 1812. Irving's British-born father was a supporter of the War of Independence and the son inherited the father's patriotism, for, as he declared during the second Anglo- American conflict, 'The disgrace of defeat will not be confined to the contrivers of the war, or to the party in power, or the conductors of the battle; but will extend to the whole nation, and come home to every individual.' He served as a colonel in the New York militia but because he did so largely as state governor's aide and secretary, saw no military action. The conclusion of hostilities did not end his patriotic perspective, but tempered it, for he now wanted reconciliation with Britain – genuine reconciliation.[5]

The beginnings of Irving's urge for reconciliation lay, at least in part, in Walter Scott's praise of his satirical Knickerbocker's *History of New York* (1809). To be praised by one of the greatest novelists of the day did much for Irving's reputation. Further, Scott performed an even more important service for Irving, when he persuaded John Murray to publish *The Sketch Book* (and Irving was to be later embarrassed when an Anglophobic friend of his published a parody of Scott that was attributed to him). His works enjoyed modest success in Britain and, travelling there, he made the acquaintance of numerous leading literary figures, including Thomas Moore, Thomas Campbell and, of course, Scott. Indeed, Irving even gained admittance into Britain's most prestigious literary circle, Holland House. The seeds of an Anglo-American literary culture seemed about to be sown.

Unfortunately, anti-Americanism in Britain, like Anglophobia in America, to say nothing of provincialism in both, was still very much a presence. When in 1820, the actor Charles Matthews organized a committee to place a memorial to Shakespeare at Stratford-upon-Avon, he nominated Irving as a member on the strength of the American's tribute to the Bard in the *Sketch Book*. The notion of an American on the committee was deemed unacceptable to the weekly *John Bull*, which strongly opposed Irving's membership. After the usual familiar disclaimers that inevitably accompany such attacks, 'Mr. Washington Irving is a very pleasant and gentlemanly man', the journal got to the heart of its case:

> ... but Mr. Washington Irving is an American ... Now, really, what an American Sketcher can have to do in a London committee, formed to commemorate Shakespeare, we cannot see. If it is meant as a compliment to the Americans, which we suspect it to be, it is paid at too great a sacrifice. We repeat, we have no personal feelings against Mr. Irving; far from it – we are prepossessed in his favour; but as a *general* question, we certainly must say, that it does appear that a *national* monument could have been raised to Shakespeare without selecting as a Committee-man, a member of a republic which has denationalised itself.

One might consider this to be the opening shots in the quarrel over the propriety rights of the English-speaking world's cultural and political heritage. As it was, numerous American publications responded to the British journal, insisting that as Americans were English subjects in Shakespeare's day they were claiming him as an American, along with John Hampden, Sir Philip Sidney, John Locke, Sir Isaac Newton, John Milton and Alexander Pope. A full-pitched transatlantic battle of the press began – not for the first, or, indeed, the last time – which foreshadowed later disputes about American involvement in what we might call British heritage – echoes of which are still heard periodically to this day. Although the London literary circuit bravely stood its ground and refused to expel Irving from the committee, the controversy nonetheless revealed the levels of undisguised hostility that Irving was determined to dilute.[6]

Irving's descriptions of Britain in the *Sketch Book* for Americans sounded a note that would be repeated, with variations, throughout the nineteenth century. 'My native country was full of youthful promise; Europe was rich in the accumulated treasures of age. Her very ruins told the history of times gone by, and every mouldering stone was a chronicle. I longed to wander over scenes of renowned achievement ... and lose myself among the shadowy grandeurs of the past.' According to one British reviewer, his essays on the Bard read very much like a tourist's guide to Shakespeare's country. The idea of Britain as an established, ancient nation set in its ways would bedevil the American understanding throughout the nineteenth century. For, despite Irving's declarations, the Britain which he visited was anything but settled. In the first instance, the Industrial Revolution was now fully underway, in the second, so too in several crucial respects was a political one as well. The economic depression following the end of the Napoleonic wars had led to a rise in radical activity. There was the Spa Fields Riot of 1816, after the radical Henry Hunt had addressed a gathering of around 10,000 people demanding universal male suffrage, the secret ballot and annual parliaments had turned into a virtual insurrection when part of the crowd marched on London with weapons stolen from a gun shop. The following year bore witness to the dispersal, by cavalry, of the so-called 'blanketeers' (unemployed Manchester weavers, so named because they carried a blanket and a petition to the sovereign) as well as the more serious, although equally futile, 'Pentrich Rising' in Derbyshire, where several hundred men were mobilized by Jeremiah Brandreth, expressly to overthrow the government. The year 1819, in turn, witnessed the notorious 'Peterloo' massacre where a meeting of 60,000–100,000 people addressed by Hunt was broken up by yeomanry on horseback, resulting in eleven deaths and hundreds of injuries, many serious. In response to this, Parliament passed the Six Acts. These prohibited large meetings and seditious libel, allowed homes to be searched without a warrant and, to curtail the radical press, increased the tax on newspapers. The last measure was aimed particularly at William Cobbett's incendiary *Political Register*, a journal the radical often found himself editing while in prison. Despite, or because of this, in 1820 the Cato Street conspiracy was exposed, in which Arthur Thistlewood, a former army officer, and several fellow conspirators planned the assassination of the Prime Minister, Lord Liverpool, and his cabinet. As the Scottish Whig Henry Cockburn put it, 'I have never known a period at which the people's hatred of government was so general and so fierce.' Britain was no bucolic theme park but a dynamic and developing society, both economically and politically, the eventual future of which could not easily be foreseen. Certainly its inhabitants had concerns far more pressing than past glories. Paradoxically, the image that Irving created was already dated.[7]

Although none of Irving's publications were as popular or well-received as his *Sketch Book* (which contains the stories for which he is best known: 'Rip Van Winkle' and 'The Legend of Sleepy Hollow'), he took his place as Britain's first American man of letters. In 1830 he was awarded a medal from the Royal Society of Literature and an honorary LL.D. from Oxford. Unfortunately the future and his fellow countrymen were to prove to be somewhat less kind. After serving in the American Legation in Madrid (1826–29), he became the secretary of the American Legation in London. This position did much to erode his Anglophilia and ideas of transatlantic brotherhood. Diplomatically, Anglo-American relations were strained and it was, perhaps, a case of theory meeting practice. Returning home to a triumphal reception in 1832, Irving continued his career as an American man of letters. Despite being hailed as the first American author to have achieved international fame (certainly, he had managed to effectively rebut Sydney Smith), Irving was continually dogged by accusations from American nationalists that he was too Anglicized, for, in the words of *The North American Review*: 'His literature is not national', and he wrote 'in England, on English subjects, and for an English public'. These accusations continued even after he published *A Tour on the Prairies* (1835). There was an unpleasant incident with the poet William Cullen Bryant, who, through an intermediary, accused Irving of censoring Anglophobic lines in some poems published in a British edition. Irving had, indeed, done so, but the collection would never have been published in Britain had it not been for these minor changes. Bryant's grievance and his method of settling it reflected poorly on him.[8]

In some respects, Britain was kinder to Irving than his native land. In the 1840s, he was to begin a correspondence with an up-and-coming young British author whose admiration for the older American was abundant: 'There is no living writer, and there are very few among the dead, whose approbation I should feel so proud to earn.' The young Briton was Charles Dickens. Although their relationship would later cool because of Dickens's portrayal of the United States and its inhabitants in *American Notes for General Circulation* (1842) and *The Life and Adventures of Martin Chuzzlewit* (1843–44), Irving promoted Dickens just as Scott had endorsed and promoted Irving. Despite the Sydney Smiths, William Bryants, *John Bull*s and *North American Review*s, something resembling an Anglo-American literary community was forming – despite the formidable odds.[9]

It is easy to exaggerate the strength of the Anglo-American relationship and there has been a tendency to identify any thaw in relations as a harbinger of an inevitably cooperative future. Relations between the two nations were still very difficult and the writings (and opinions) of Dickens regarding the United States serve to illustrate this. Dickens left for the United States on 4 January 1842, a month shy of his thirtieth birthday, accompanied by his wife. The trip should have been a triumphant success for, as has been observed, he was almost an example of what American society allegedly represented, a young man of modest origins who had succeeded through his own efforts and who was instinctively a radical. Surely such a man was well-suited to the New World? While this is true, it simply establishes that neither radicalism nor humble origins automatically instilled pro-American sentiment in a Briton – indeed, such individuals could easily be the reverse. Broader issues were always in play, as was to be the case with Dickens. When he arrived back in his native land in June 1842, he almost immediately began work on his *American Notes*, but did not do so in a complimentary frame of mind for, as Mary Shelley reported, 'Dickens has just come home in a state of violent dislike of the Americans – and he means to devour them in his next work – he says they are frightfully dishonest.' Dickens had gone to the United States with a favourable view of the country, and was already renowned there for his novels – indeed, during the serialization of *The Old Curiosity Shop* (1841), the first thing an American pilot had asked upon boarding a British ship to guide it into New York harbour was, 'What of Little Nell?' So what went wrong? The answer, in part, lies with Little Nell, or rather, the medium in which she appeared.[10]

Dickens arrived in Boston to a triumphal reception. Indeed, the reception he was accorded in America went far beyond anything he had ever received at home. Besides Washington Irving, he met Henry Wadsworth Longfellow, Edgar Allan Poe, Oliver Wendell Holmes Sr, and the President of the United States, John Tyler (who apparently had little to say). Writing to his friend, John Forster, Dickens remarked, 'How can I give you the faintest notion of my reception here ... of the crowds that pour in and out the whole day; of the people that line the streets when I go out; of the cheering when I went to the theatre; of the copies of verses, letters of congratulation, welcomes of all kinds, balls, dinners, assemblies without end?' This was true for much of his trip, which included visits to New York, New Haven, Washington, Philadelphia, Baltimore, Richmond, Pittsburgh, Cincinnati and Columbus. It was in America that, for the first time in his life, Dickens understood the extent of his fame or, what he would call on another occasion, his 'Power'. Alas, pride goes before a fall. Dickens began making speeches demanding the establishment of some copyright agreement between Britain and the United States, a reasonable enough demand one might have thought, considering his books sold as many copies in America as in Britain and yet he received not a penny in royalties. How swiftly the applause died down. Newspapers that had hailed him now damned him as a hypocritical mercenary cockney who had simply come to the United States to make more money. Dickens, who suffered from the handicap of needing to be loved, took the abuse to heart, declaring that 'the scorn and indignation I have felt under this unmanly and ungenerous treatment has been to me an amount of agony such as I never experienced since my birth'. In another letter to a friend, William Macready, Dickens lamented, 'This is not the Republic I came to see. This is not the Republic of my imagination.' He was not to be the last Briton to express this sentiment.[11]

American Notes was not, however, a mere exercise in score-settling. In fact, he avoided discussion of the copyright issue therein and allowed himself to be persuaded by Forster to leave out an introductory chapter that contained some very uncomplimentary observations, including this tart opening:

> If this book should fall into the hands of any sensitive American who cannot bear to be told that the working of the institutions of his country is far from perfect; that in spite of the advantage she has over all other nations in the elastic freshness and vigour of her youth, she is far from being a model for the earth to copy; and that even in those pictures of the national manners with which he quarrels most, there is still ... much that is just and true at this hour; let him lay it down, now, for I shall not please him.

American Notes largely confines itself to general observations of architecture and institutions, particularly factories, prisons, workhouses and asylums. Dickens expressed genuine delight at improvements in public institutions and the general condition of public welfare, and cited areas in which he believed American society had the advantage over Britain's. His work, however, was by no means all complimentary. His disgust at American table manners and intrusive personal questions was palpable. His particular disdain at the habit of chewing tobacco and expectorating was comically expressed by his suggestion that the spittoon be made America's national symbol. He complained that 'The people are all alike, too. There is no diversity of character. They travel about on the same errands, say and do the same things in exactly the same manner.' Sharp business practices in the United States attracted his condemnation and he also attacked slavery at length, having seen the institution close up in Richmond (and South Carolina considered banning the book for this). The only thing he despised more than slavery was the press and here Dickens did settle scores by blaming it for keeping Americans ignorant of the wider world. Attacking the press is always risky, for unless one is in the position of Rear Admiral Cockburn one can be assured it will always have the last word. The press generally damned *American Notes* as being anti-American and exaggerated the criticisms while ignoring the praise.[12]

Nonetheless, the work of Dickens that caused more offence was *Martin Chuzzlewit* (1843–44), often referred to as his 'American novel' and written almost immediately after *American Notes*. The part that caused offence was when the serialized novel's eponymous hero crosses the Atlantic to seek his fortune (on board *The Screw*), for Dickens' description of the United States is very uncomplimentary. One of the earliest conversations with an American, Colonel Diver, editor of the *New York Rowdy Journal*, upon arrival, sets the tone:

> 'To the Palladium of rational Liberty at home, sir, and the dread of Foreign oppression abroad', returned the gentleman, as he pointed with his cane to an uncommonly dirty newsboy with one eye. 'To the Envy of the world, sir, and the leaders of Human Civilization. Let me ask you sir', he added, bringing the ferule of his stick heavily upon the deck with the air of a man who must not be equivocated with, 'how do you like my Country?'

This sort of arrogant boasting, followed by a question with a set answer, is commonplace throughout the novel. New York, surprisingly enough, turns out to be a place of snobbery and ludicrous pretension. Further, the part of the novel where Chuzzlewit purchases land purportedly in the southern township of Eden from a fraudulent corporation which turns out to be nothing more than a poisonous swamp and nearly loses his life when he falls ill with fever, takes the concept of Sam Slick's America to unpleasant depths. That numerous of the American characters, General Cyrus Choke (who believes Queen Victoria resides in the Tower of London), for example, sport bogus military titles (and decorations) was treated as an affront; so too was the frequent portrayal of Americans as tobacco-chewing buffoons on the make. Dickens's portrayal of the United States stung because of the affection for which Americans felt toward his works and, of course, because he was an international figure whose views were perceived to matter. In some respects, however, the criticism of Dickens – then and since – has not been entirely fair. There is a reason for the term, 'Dickensian', because the author was as sharp a critic of his native land as he was of the United States.[13]

Dickens's relationship with the United States probably reached its nadir from 1861–65 when he sided with the South in the American Civil War, his journal *All the Year Round* defending the Confederacy with some determination. This was not the first time a celebrity made foolish statements about foreign affairs, nor was it to be the last. Despite his *American Notes*, *Martin Chuzzlewit* and his support for the Confederacy, Dickens continued to receive invitations to visit the United States. He visited again, less than three years before his death, from November 1867 to April 1868, going on a reading tour that earned him an extraordinary £19,000. This trip was, on the whole, more successful than his earlier one and, at a dinner in his honour in New York on 18 April 1868, Dickens noted how both he and America had changed considerably since his last visit. He commented on the excellent treatment he had received this time around and promised to include these words in an appendix to every copy of his two books in which he referred to the United States. There had been significant changes in the Anglo-American relationship since his first visit, most of which were for the better, but even more so than Irving, Dickens was a transatlantic phenomenon, and by the 1860s, a true representative of an Atlantic literary tradition.

James Fenimore Cooper was another contributor to this literary exchange, which helped misinform as much as inform Britons and Americans about each other. Unlike Irving, as far as Cooper was concerned, the British would have to accept both he and his nationality as they were. Indeed, Cooper was scornful of Irving's apparent Anglophilia, denouncing him as 'A man who takes the money of the U. States with one hand and that of the [anti-American] Editor of the *Quarterly Review* with the other.' He also denounced Irving for the picture of American society the latter laid before British readers, particularly condemning 'Rip Van Winkle' and 'The Legend of Sleepy Hollow' for their failure to reflect 'the diversities of passion, sentiment and behaviour' of the United States. This was ironic on two counts. First, Cooper's earliest novel was *Precaution* (1820), a novel of British manners inspired by Jane Austen's *Persuasion* (1818). That the creator of *The Last of the Mohicans* (1826) began his career with a novel of domestic manners in the mode of Austen suggests that Cooper – at least initially – suffered from what is now referred to as cultural cringe far more so than Irving. Indeed, it was Cooper's sloughing this off (and escaping Austen's tutelage), and deliberately striking an American path and writing on specifically American themes, starting with *The Spy* (1821), set in the War of Independence, that brings us to our second irony: his novels, especially his *Leather-Stocking Tales* (1823–41), with their hero Natty Bumppo (Hawkeye), almost single-handedly created the image of the American frontier in the British popular imagination. Seventy years before Frederick Jackson Turner's 'The Significance of the Frontier in American History' (often referred to as the 'Frontier Thesis'), which argued that the frontier was the key to American history and character, making it distinctive from Europe's, was propounded in 1893, Cooper introduced the British (and his fellow countrymen) to an image of America that resonates to this day. In many respects, for all Cooper's condemnation of Irving, he simply presented the British with an even more fantastic image of his native land. It was not for nothing that he was soon labelled 'the American Scott' (a nickname he disliked, because he did not much care for Sir Walter on either a personal or literary level).[14]

That Cooper deliberately followed a distinctly independent American route stemmed from his demand that the United States achieve what he called 'mental independence' from Britain and Europe. As he put it on one occasion: 'Her [America's] mental independence is my object, and if I can go down to the grave with the reflection that I have done a little towards it, I shall have the consolation of knowing that I have not been useless in my generation.' To an extent he succeeded, although it took the historian Turner to give Cooper's wish intellectual gloss. Cooper, like Irving before him and Henry James later, had complained of the poverty of materials, particularly the shortage of national history, available to an American writer as compared to a British one. By turning towards nature, most especially the inspiring and unique wonders of the American wilderness and, also to a degree anticipating Turner, deploring the rapid disappearance of that wilderness, Cooper had found the solution to his dilemma. There was, of course, a debt owed to Scott (which was yet another reason Cooper disliked him) and that was both authors' emphasis on the futility of the untamed wilderness ideal. Scott's highlanders are pushed aside by the forces of modernity as surely as Cooper's backwoodsmen. Ultimately, both authors' visions are tragic ones. Yet Cooper's debt to Scott should not be allowed to overshadow his essential achievement, the beginning of a uniquely American literary vision.[15]

Just as Dickens would do less than a decade later, Cooper published a travel account. In this case, it was an American's view of Britain rather than a Briton's view of the United States. That was the difference; the similarity was that both caused offence. Part of the problem was that

Cooper's *England with Sketches of Society in the Metropolis* (1837) was already out of date when published. The political structure he described was that prior to the Great Reform Act of 1832. His claims of a politically ossified society ripe for revolution like that of America's had thus already been disproved (and whom the British were supposed to secede from was unclear). Nor, as a nationalist, was Cooper one to avoid giving offence: his claims that 'Power in America, has nothing to apprehend from English example, while power in England, has much to apprehend from the example of America', was a standard American claim that misled then and afterwards. Imbued with the American interpretation of past relations between the two nations, he blamed British dislike of the United States on the fact that, 'In the collisions between the two people, in the main, America has won and England has lost. The winner is usually complacent, the loser soured.' He then expressed his surprise regarding the War of 1812 that,

> There is a very general notion prevalent in England that we seized the moment to declare war against them, when they were pressed upon hardest, by the rest of Europe. A portion of their antipathy is owing to this idea, though the idea itself is altogether owing to their prejudices against America, for there is not a particle of truth in it. I do not remember to have conversed on the subject with any Englishman, who did not betray this feeling.

There was, in fact, rather more truth to this 'general notion' than Cooper was willing to recognize. Generally, Cooper observed essential differences between the two cultures, which he believed were so completely the 'converse of each other' that it was surprising so many resemblances survived. Cooper complained of what he believed to be the palpable deference of the subordinate classes to their superiors, claiming that the opposite was true in America. At the same time, Cooper noted that an unfortunate result of American egalitarianism was the 'moral cowardice' where men bowed down 'before what is called public opinion', and concluded that there was 'more honesty of public sentiment in England than in America'. In light of all of this, it was no surprise that he came in for criticism. The most common charge was that Cooper had focused on the trivial at the expense of the fundamentals and that his analysis was based on too meagre an experience. Yet British journals such as the *Literary Gazette*, the *Spectator*, the *Athenaeum* and the *Examiner* were mostly positive in their reviews, although his work was savaged by the *Quarterly Review, Blackwood's* and *Fraser's*.[16]

If Cooper offended the British, he irritated his own countrymen even more with his next publication, *The American Democrat: or Hints on the Social and Civic Relations in the United States of America* (1838). This work had been preceded by *A Letter to His Countrymen* (1834), a bitter attack on American cultural provincialism (the eternal complaint of American intellectuals). Despite the accusations of his critics, Cooper was not opposed to democratization, but rather the tendency for democracies to mistake public opinion for principle, for, as he put it,

> In a country where opinion has sway, to seize upon it, is to seize upon power. As it is the rule of humanity that the upright and well intentioned are comparatively passive, while the designing, dishonest and selfish are the most untiring in their efforts, the danger of publick opinion's getting a false direction, is four-fold, since few men think for themselves.

To prevent this, Cooper demonstrated how, with its constitutional checks and balances, the American republic could bring about enlightened leadership, control of demagogues, protection of property rights and encouragement of the arts and the amenities. This was accompanied by constant warnings of the tyranny of the majority. The work provoked an angry response, expressing as it did a low opinion of the people and filled with such acerbic comments as, "'They say", is the monarch of this country, in a social sense. No one asks "*who* says it", so long as it is believed that "*they* say it".' Cooper was to be vilified as having been in Britain so long that he had put on airs – an ironic charge to apply against him.[17]

Cooper's popularity in his own day was immense, but he is now, perhaps unfairly, remembered almost more as a literary curio than as a great author and it was his fellow Americans who proved to be his most astute critics. In some ways his reputation never recovered from Mark Twain's savage and funny, 'Fenimore Cooper's Literary Offenses' (1895), a sample from which gives the gist:

> Another stage-property that he pulled out of his box pretty frequently was the broken twig. He prized his broken twig above all the rest of his effects, and worked it the hardest. It is a restful chapter in any book of his when somebody doesn't step on a dry twig and alarm all the reds and whites for two hundred yards around. Every time a Cooper person is in peril, and absolute silence is worth four dollars a minute, he is sure to step on a dry

twig. There may be a hundred other handier things to step on, but that wouldn't satisfy Cooper. Cooper requires him to turn out and find a dry twig; and if he can't do it, go and borrow one. In fact, the Leatherstocking Series ought to have been called the Broken Twig Series.

Yet Cooper's influence in the nineteenth century should not be underestimated, least of all his vision of the American frontier which, for many in Britain, remained the romanticized view both at the time and for many years after.[18]

Another American keen to defend his country's reputation was John Neal, an author of Gothic romances who, having made himself unpopular in his native land, retreated to Britain in 1823, where his novels had received favourable reviews. Once there, by posing as an Englishman, 'Carter Holmes', who had returned from America, he managed to persuade *Blackwood's Edinburgh Magazine* to publish five articles on some 135 American writers in 1824. Although the quality of literary criticism was uneven (an inordinate amount of attention and praise was lavished on one John Neal while Cooper was dismissed as a cut-rate Scott), the 'American Writers' series was the first ever published effort to detail and critique American literature. William Blackwood, despite learning of his deception, continued to employ him, making Neal the first American to break into the British periodical press. Neal also enjoyed modest social success, becoming, at least for a time, a friend of Jeremy Bentham, before returning to the United States in 1827.[19]

Although it has been claimed that Neal's work would never have been published in *Blackwood's* had it not been for his pretending to be British, there is little evidence to support this. The journal, after all, was open-minded enough in the first place to publish a series on American writers – a mere three years after Sydney Smith's taunts. Further, *Blackwood's* was to remain a conduit for Anglo-American literary development. Not that it received any thanks for doing so on either side of the Atlantic. Both nations' opinions of each other remained very low. Each believed the other meant ill, and American writers still raged about the apparent cultural cringe still suffered by the United States. Take, for example, the views of Edgar Allan Poe expressed in 1845:

We *know* the British bear us little but ill-will; we know that in the few instances in which our writers have been treated with common decency in England, these writers have either openly paid homage to English institutions, or have had lurking at the bottom of their hearts a secret principle at war with Democracy: – we *know* all of this, and yet day after day, submit our necks to the degrading yoke of the crudest opinion that emanates from the fatherland. Now if we *must* have nationality, let it be a nationality that will throw off this yoke.

Poe then went on to damn *Blackwood's'* ability to make or break an American author's reputation. Poe's American targets in this case were Irving and Cooper but, as we have seen, both shafts fell wide of the mark. Yet Poe's rant reveals common nineteenth-century American accusations (and prejudices) against Britain: that the British hated them and that the British only appreciated Americans who toadied to them and who shared Britain's hatred of American democracy. This last accusation, that all British dislike or criticism of the United States was based on anti-democratic sentiments, was made repeatedly throughout the nineteenth century by Americans and has subsequently been parroted by some historians who muddy the waters further by claiming anti-Americanism was an exclusively Tory vice. *Blackwood's* is a case in point – the British periodical most interested and most prone to promote American fiction was Tory in politics (the *Edinburgh Review*, by contrast, which published Sydney Smith's sneers, was Whig).[20]

Poe himself spent part of his childhood in England (aspects of which are immortalized in his *Doppelgänger* story 'William Wilson') and for all his complaints about *Blackwood's* he mined its collection of macabre stories ruthlessly for plots. He also made the acquaintance of Dickens and persuaded him to try to secure British publication of his stories. Although Dickens failed in this, Poe's works were nonetheless widely reviewed in *Blackwood's*, thus reaching a wider British audience. One member of that British audience, who came to Poe's stories after the latter's death, was Sir Arthur Conan Doyle. Doyle was especially taken with Poe's brilliant French detective, C. Auguste Dupin, and his powers of deduction. So much so that he created his own, Sherlock Holmes who made his debut in 1887. Thus, although he did not live to see it, for all his complaints about the British reception of American fiction, Poe's own work was to be emulated by British authors.[21]

We are, however, getting a little ahead of ourselves, for Anglo-American relations, both literary and otherwise, were in the 1880s vastly different to those of the 1840s and 50s, as the career of Nathaniel Hawthorne, another American writer who assiduously read *Blackwood's*, illustrates. Although Hawthorne was unsuccessful in his attempts to persuade *Blackwood's* to publish his work, his novel *The*

Scarlet Letter (1850) won a wide audience in Britain, impressing such literary luminaries as William Thackeray and, especially, Anthony Trollope. By the time he published *The House of Seven Gables* (1851) and *The Blithendale Romance* (1852) the *Athenaeum* felt confident enough to declare 'Mr. Hawthorne's third tale, in our judgment, puts the seal on his reputation of its author as the highest, deepest, and finest imaginative writer whom America has yet produced.' To a certain extent, British critics were even more enamoured of Hawthorne's output than his fellow countrymen. This enthusiasm was at least partly responsible for his decision to accept a consulship in Britain beginning in July 1853.[22]

Hawthorne's impression of Britain, according to his journals, was that of returning to an ancestral homeland, going so far as to declare on one occasion, 'My ancestor left England in 1635. I return in 1853. I sometimes feel as if I myself had been absent these two hundred and eighteen years . . .' Hawthorne's tours of Britain were, in essence, literary pilgrimages, visiting places associated with Shakespeare, Scott, Robert Burns and William Wordsworth. In short, what was positive in his views of Britain was, like Irving's, that of a past. Of the future he was silent and of the present he was less enamoured (and less informed).[23]

It must be noted that Hawthorne's view of Britain was always a divided one – the War of 1812 took place during his childhood – and, as has been observed, his American patriotism was inextricably bound up with a traditional and deep enmity towards Britain. This side of him came out when his backwards-looking view of Britain ran into present-day realities. Hawthorne became involved in the efforts of an American woman, Delia Bacon, to whose frankly half-baked work, *The Philosophy of the Plays of Shakespere Unfolded* (1857) he wrote a foreword. The British press was merciless towards Hawthorne, wondering, rightly, how he could have put his name to such nonsense. Hawthorne complained, too, of English abrasiveness and hostility towards America, blaming it, as usual, on anti-democratic sentiment, a view that owed more to his notion of a British past than to the present.[24]

Hawthorne's discussion of Britain in *Our Old Home*, published in 1863 while Anglo-American relations were at a low ebb during the Civil War, reveal a certain lack of self-awareness that an ordinarily intelligent observer should have held. For example, the administration he nominally represented as an American consul was that of the anti-British Franklin Pierce. Further, as we shall see, there were a number of diplomatic squalls during this period that reflected at least as badly on the

United States as on Great Britain. In terms of British domestic politics, Hawthorne somehow managed to miss noticing the movement to extend the franchise in Britain, despite the fact it was gathering pace during his time there. Nor was Hawthorne quite the cosmopolitan observer he sometimes professed to be: his staunchest British admirer, Anthony Trollope, once noted that the former 'withered me with scorn which was anything but mystic or melancholy because I expressed a patriotic preference for English peas'. As it happened, Hawthorne's apparent indifference to the American Civil War was badly received in his native land, as were whatever compliments he dared make about the British during an atmosphere of poisoned Anglo-American relations (not that British reviewers, operating under the same circumstances, were much kinder). In essence, Hawthorne's view of Britain was a curious hybrid of romance and resentment – and one not atypical of his countrymen's views of the 'Old Home'.[25]

Intellectual collaboration and influence continued, albeit hesitantly, during the nineteenth century and this can be seen in the curious relationship between Thomas Carlyle and Ralph Waldo Emerson. Although on the face of it, it is difficult to think of two individuals less temperamentally akin than Carlyle and Emerson, the latter was an admirer of the former from at least the 1820s. Fond of quoting some of Carlyle's ideas in his own sermons when serving as a minister, Emerson sought out the Scottish sage on a visit to Britain in 1833 and obtained an introduction. On a Sunday afternoon, the two men walked for miles discussing government and society, literature and religion. Despite some differences over the last, and the exact merits of Socrates, Emerson informed a friend that Carlyle is 'the most simple, frank and amiable person'. Carlyle meanwhile observed that Emerson was 'like an angel, with his beautiful transparent soul'. Upon Emerson's return to the United States, the two men corresponded, Emerson offering (generally well-taken) critiques of Carlyle's Sartor Resartus (1833–44) and the latter peppering the former with questions about American life and society. Before long, each was informing the other of personal matters and concerns.

The literary alliance was strengthened when Emerson supervised the American publication of Sartor, The French Revolution (1837), and Past and Present (1843); Carlyle returned the favour by arranging British publication of Nature (1836) and two volumes of essays. In addition, they both favourably reviewed each other's works to increase appreciation (and sales) on their respective sides of the Atlantic. This alliance bore fruit: Emerson became known as the American philosopher in Britain, while Carlyle's reputation in the United States was greatly augmented. His work on Oliver Cromwell (1845), in particular, received a wide audience. One of its most avid readers was none other than John Brown, the militant abolitionist who would help spark the secessionist crisis of 1860 by his raid on the federal arsenal at Harper's Ferry, Virginia, 1859, in a doomed attempt to initiate, and arm, a slave uprising. On the other hand, Carlyle's works appealed equally to the pro-slavery Virginian George Fitzhugh, whose work *Cannibals All* (1857) robustly defended the institution.[26]

In 1847, Emerson made another trip to Britain, this time to undertake a lecture tour (a practice for which he was already famous in America) and stayed with Carlyle before travelling (he also met Dickens, John Stuart Mill and William Coleridge). The tour was largely a success, certainly amongst Britain's literary and social aristocracy, although some of the more religious found his theological musings, if we may call them that, suspect. His statement that, 'Man, wheresoever thou seest him, in brothels, gaols, or on gibbets, is on his way upward to all that is good and true', caused controversy. Carlyle was largely unenthused, dismissing Emerson's talks as 'rather *moonshiny*', a comment the American resented. The two intellectuals also had a dispute on the merits of their respective countries, Carlyle arguing for the superiority of British culture and Emerson, referring to the geography of his nation, responding, 'that we play the game with immense advantage; that there and not here is the seat and culture of the British race ... and that England, an old and exhausted island, must one day be contented, like other parents, to be strong only in her children'.[27]

In the end, however, it was not really nationalism or nationality that ultimately divided them. Indeed, Emerson's *English Traits* (1856) was deemed by some British critics to be too complimentary. On the surface, Emerson and Carlyle had similar intellectual concerns. Both became estranged from their religious faith and sought a substitute; both expressed concern about impersonal economic forces and the replacement of communal values by isolated individualism; and both were influenced by German romanticism. Indeed, although Emerson had stated that he wished to 'extract the tape-worm of Europe from America's body' and 'to cast out the passion for Europe by the passion for America', and although Oliver Wendell Holmes referred to *Nature* as 'our intellectual declaration of independence', German thinking, via Carlyle's interpretations, had a marked influence on Emerson's ideas.

New England Transcendentalism, the nineteenth-century American philosophy, bore, in some real respects, Carlyle's intellectual finger-prints. Yet there remained important differences and one of the most profound lay in the fact that while Emerson retained a faith in man, Carlyle largely lost that as well. Whereas Emerson remained liberal in outlook, Carlyle became increasingly attracted to authoritarianism. Emerson, while not a pacifist, did not place much faith in the virtues of force in the manner that Carlyle did. Then there was slavery; while Emerson broke with most of his fellow countrymen and became an abolitionist, Carlyle departed from the majority of his by defending the institution, most notably in his 'Occasional Discourse on the Negro Question' (only later changed to the 'Nigger Question') in 1850. Oddly, the existence of American slavery did little to incline Carlyle favourably towards the United States, which he dismissed as the land of 'Eighteen million of the greatest *bores* ever seen in this world before.' Emerson was displeased by comments such as these, as well as by Carlyle's dismissal of Walt Whitman's poetry. The Civil War, meantime, nearly ruptured their friendship: Emerson the abolitionist (and patriot) seeing the Union's cause as 'the battle for Humanity', Carlyle brutally dismissing the conflict as a contest between people 'cutting each other's throats, because one half prefer hiring their servants for life, and the other by the hour'. Nor did his views change with the North's victory. Despite all of this, the two men met up again when Emerson made a third trip to Britain in 1872 and, by all accounts, maintained the old friendship – a strange personification of the awkward nineteenth-century Anglo-American relationship.[28]

Another Transcendentalist influenced by Carlyle was Henry David Thoreau. One of his biographers has gone so far as to claim that during his college days at Harvard, Carlyle was Thoreau's favourite modern writer. Certainly the influence of *Sartor* can be seen in Thoreau's masterpiece *Walden, or Life in the Woods* (1854), including the obser-vation about how men would behave if divested of their clothes, and he also wrote an appreciative essay, 'Thomas Carlyle and His Works'. Thoreau, like a number of American intellectuals, took an interest in British history (he was particularly fascinated by Sir Walter Raleigh) and at the same time saw Americans turning away from their wilder natural heritage towards a refinement closer to that of the English gentry (a point he regretted). *Walden*, itself, concludes with consideration on Britain and the United States, referring to the Empire as 'very large and respectable', and America as 'a first-rate power'. Both nations, however, had life spans, much as people do and, addressing John Bull and Cousin Jonathan equally, Thoreau warned, 'I do not say that John or Jonathan will realize this; but such is the character of that morrow which mere lapse of time can never make to dawn ... There is more day to dawn. The sun is nothing but a morning star.' A quiet rebuke, then, to both nations' patriotic self-image.

Although *Walden* was initially ignored, from the first it had its admirers – including in Britain. One of these was the poet Arthur Hugh Clough who, on a visit to America, met with Emerson and Thoreau. He, in turn, wrote a letter of introduction for a friend of his, a young man named Thomas Cholmondeley. Cholmondeley and Thoreau, being idealists who shared an interest in the subject of man and nature, became friends; the former reporting his views on the 'brighter Britain' he saw developing in New Zealand. More importantly, when back in Britain, Cholmondeley sent Thoreau a virtual library of 21 rare books (44 volumes) on ancient Hindu literature. Thoreau, already an admirer of the *Bhagavad Gita*, devoured these Hindu classics, which would have an influence on his thought, including notions of non-violent protest and civil disobedience. The Transcendentalist reciprocated as best he could, sending Cholomondeley hard-to-find American works, particularly on flora and fauna, and an edition of Walt Whitman's *Leaves of Grass*. This last the Briton found even more impenetrable than ancient Hindu philosophy.[29]

Cholmondeley, who attempted to compliment Whitman's work as 'very brave and American', was hardly alone in his bafflement. Yet Whitman was another individual influenced by Carlyle, one scholar stating that the latter may have been the catalyst for the latter's transforming into a poet, the first edition of *Leaves of Grass* (1855) being almost a reply to *Sartor*. Certainly many of the same themes – clothing, animalism, observations on the nature of squalor and injustice seen from a distance and a host of other topics – are seen in both works. Carlyle's idea of the poet as hero and his praise for Robert Burns as the poet of humble origins who wrote in dialect anticipates Whitman's poet of democracy. If in the end, Whitman, like Emerson, was angered by Carlyle's view of the American Civil War, responding to the Scot's essay 'Shooting Niagara and After?' (1867) with his article 'Democracy' and later, *Democratic Vistas* (1871), he never did quite shake off Carlyle's influence. In the meantime, while *Leaves of Grass* did receive an initially frosty reception in Britain, as it did in America, Whitman's work's reputation began to improve after W. M. Rossetti and Algernon

Swinburne began promoting it in the late 1860s (and the poet, ever alert to an opportunity, started sending them revised editions to assist them in their endeavour). As Whitman's work began to gain recognition in Britain, this had a ripple effect in the United States, preparing the way for him to assume the title of America's national poet.[30]

Another American author whose transatlantic career played an important role in his literary reputation, albeit posthumously, was Herman Melville. Melville had spent his early years as a sailor, and had sailed to Liverpool in 1839 at the age of 19. His impression was not entirely favourable, for he found the poverty of the city's slums worse than anything he had encountered in the United States, a point he made clearly in his semi-autobiographical novel, *Redburn: His First Voyage* (1849). Indeed, the sight of Liverpool's slums never left Melville for, as one scholar has observed, some of the author's satiric attacks on western civilization can be explained in part by the profound impact they left upon him. Visiting Britain again, a decade after his first visit and this time not a sailor but a published author, Melville discovered the British did not much care for an American's observations of their social problems. *Blackwood's* review, one of the longest *Redburn* received, dismissed his observations on Liverpool's poverty as 'more than improbable' and 'utterly absurd'. As for Redburn's adventures in London, they were 'utter rubbish'. Fortunately, no one ever pays any attention to reviewers: Melville's British publisher Bentley presented him with a cheque for £100 – the royalties accrued from the novel. This was a large part of the reason Melville was in Britain: to secure British publication for his next and future novels. The copyright problem still existed. British and American novels were pirated on either side of the Atlantic, depriving authors of revenue. Only a separate copyright in each nation (and that required a local publisher) could guarantee an income.[31]

To say that the periodic appearances of British characters and locations in Melville's fiction were simply a method to ensure publication there would be wrong. His novel about a neglected hero of the American Revolution living in penury in Britain, *Israel Potter: His Fifty Years of Exile* (1854–55), was based on an autobiographical account, *The Life and Remarkable Adventures of Israel R. Potter* (1824), which Melville had acquired on his British visit. Indeed, Anglo-American themes were a staple of Melville. Each of his Anglo-American scenes, 'The Two Temples', 'Poor Man's Pudding and Rich Man's Crumbs' and 'The Paradise of Bachelors and the Tartarus of Maids' (1854) are set half in

America and half in Britain. While these Anglo-American landscapes of Heaven and Hell, discussing, among other issues, religious hypocrisy, charity, solidarity and, above all, poverty, certainly make distinctions between the two nations, their central targets – those who see suffering and injustice around them and fail to respond – are clearly shown to exist on both sides of the Atlantic. In other words, Melville is another marker in the change from simple one-upmanship to the recognition of common problems and, just possibly, common solutions.

Melville is, of course, best known as the author of *Moby Dick or The Whale* (1851), which he arranged to have published as simultaneously on both sides of the Atlantic as was possible. His British publisher, Richard Bentley, was sent a set of proof sheets from the American edition. Melville appended a note defending his use of American terms, insisting that most were neither American corruptions nor inventions but the preservations of early English lost in Britain. This was a defence of the pedigree of the American language, vigorously upheld by many nine-teenth-century Americans. Alas, his views were little heeded. *Moby Dick*, first published as *The Whale* in Britain, was heavily bowdlerized. It was not just Americanisms that suffered, but Melville's use of religious imagery – all biblical allusions or reference not strictly referential were cut out, due at least in part to Britain's blasphemy laws. Less excuse could be made for the deletion of chapter 25 because of its less than respectful tone regarding coronations. Despite these changes (it is hard to claim because of), *Moby Dick* was as much a commercial failure in Britain as in America although a few perceptive critics recognized its literary worth.

Melville's literary career marked a new direction in Anglo-American literature. Instead of mere denunciation or aggressive assertion of national worth, some sense of common present and future was anticipated. Indeed, one of Melville's greatest works, *Billy Budd, Fore-topman* (written 1891; published 1924) takes place on a British man-of-war. As a result, it was appropriate that it was the British who initiated the Melville revival. Melville had been almost forgotten by the time of his death, his literary reputation's rebirth being generally credited to both the centenary of his birth and Raymond Weaver's *Herman Mel-ville: Mariner and Mystic* (1921). Yet, as one scholar has pointed out, by that time D. H. Lawrence had already published two essays on *Moby Dick* and other Britons publishing on Melville before this time included poet John Masefield, and novelist and journalist Henry M. Tomlinson. Tomlinson, in fact, secured the publication of *Moby Dick* in the World's

Classic Series of the Oxford University Press in 1920. Finally, between 1922–24 Constable of London published *The Works of Herman Melville*, in which *Billy Budd* first appeared.[32]

At the same time Melville was publishing his works containing British characters and scenes, so too was a British novelist, no doubt partially inspired by Dickens, writing novels set in the United States containing American characters. This was William Makepeace Thackeray, most famous for *Vanity Fair* (1847–48), in his novel *The Virginians* (1857–59). The sequel to *Henry Esmond* (1852), *The Virginians* takes place in the period from the struggle against the French in Canada to the War of Independence. The novel's American-born protagonists, the Warrington brothers, George the bookish, Harry the boisterous, carry on a separate existence for much of the novel when the elder is believed killed by the French in Canada. Released from the oversight of his more sensible sibling, Harry returns to Britain to get himself into a series of scrapes only to be rescued by his brother, who, far from being dead, has only just escaped from the French. During the War of Independence, the siblings fight on opposite sides: George for the Crown; Harry for Washington (an old personal enemy of his brother's). The novel ends with George settling in Britain, Harry in Virginia, the Warringtons living separate lives, united still in love for one another. Although there is always a risk, especially with Thackeray, of extrapolating too much from a novel, it seems safe to say that the Warrington siblings, at least in part, personify Britain and America. If so, Thackeray had a clearer idea of the two countries' relative relationship – more akin to that of siblings than to the parent–child. Furthermore, the American characters in the novel are not a collection of grotesques or inclined to sharp practice or, at any rate, no more so than the British ones.[33]

If Thackeray's fiction marked a point of greater maturity in the Anglo-American literary relationship, he was to receive little acclaim. *The Virginians*, unusually for Thackeray's works, lost his publisher money. Whether this was due to the fact there was a dearth of interest in reconciliation on either side of the Atlantic, or because of the slackness of the plot, *The Virginians* still remains something of a milestone. Thackeray was, after Dickens, the most important author of his day. With the leading lights of British literature now setting their novels in America, the relationship between the two nations was certainly undergoing change. Like Dickens, Thackeray toured the United States twice, but unlike Dickens, in quick succession: 1852–53 and 1855–56. Thackeray's lecture tours, the first being *English Humorists of the*

Eighteenth Century, the second being *The Four Georges*, were both unqualified successes. This was perhaps unsurprising, as Thackeray's fame in Britain, as with Dickens, was matched in the United States.[34]

If Thackeray and Dickens represented the first British transatlantic literary sensations, complete with grand tours of adoring fans, the greatest phenomenon of them all in the 1850s was a woman from Connecticut, Harriet Beecher Stowe. In terms of transatlantic popular cultural sensations, her abolitionist novel *Uncle Tom's Cabin* (1851–52) was almost impossible to match, with 2,000,000 copies sold world-wide by 1857. The novel spawned card games, toys, songs and even plays (or spin-off merchandise as it is now called), all of which were made possible by the rapidly developing consumer societies on both sides of the Atlantic. As popular as the novel was in America, however, it was still more so in Britain. In its first year of publication it sold 150,000 copies in the United States, but it sold over a million in Britain. Not that Stowe saw much in the way of royalties, thanks to the continuing transatlantic disrespect of copyright. Sententious, sentimental and self-righteous, the novel's success was aided by the fact that its denunciation of slavery made it a safe bet (at least outside the southern states, where the work's reception inevitably differed). It should also be remembered that at least part of the reason for the novel's popularity in Britain was that it laid into America's great crime – slavery. Although *Uncle Tom's Cabin* is by no means an anti-American novel, it was certainly read as such by some Britons.[35]

If Stowe was less skilled than Melville in accruing the maximum financial gains from her novel, she was perfectly competent when it came to using her literary celebrity to promote her cause, abolitionism. She sought to enlist influential Britons in the American anti-slavery cause, including Prince Albert, the Duke of Argyll, the Earls of Carlisle and Shaftesbury, Thomas Macaulay, Dickens, Charles Kingsley and many others. A presentation copy of the novel accompanied each letter. If, like many Americans of her day, Stowe's knowledge of British policy was somewhat shaky (she believed Britain was going to close Canada off to fugitive slaves – a policy no administration had ever contemplated), she did stir up some support. A group of leading British ladies sent a document, 'An Affectionate and Christian Address from the Women of Great Britain to the Women of America', calling for the abolition of slavery and a Christian education for the freed slaves (and, to avoid any accusations of anti-Americanism, acknowledged Britain's responsibility for introducing slavery into the American colonies). More than half a million British women signed the document and, as an added bonus, Stowe was invited by a British anti-slave society to visit Britain at their expense.

Although Stowe was received in Britain with enthusiasm, there were also rumblings of discontent. For one thing, Anglo-American relations during the 1850s had been difficult. Deep suspicion of the United States, especially as regards to its foreign policy, remained. These animosities, as one scholar has pointed out, often meant that anti-slavery sentiment transformed into anti-American opinion. This was something both Stowe and her husband complained of in letters home. This phenomenon would become especially apparent a mere decade later during the American Civil War – a conflict fought ostensibly to end slavery. Yet if Stowe on occasion expressed dissatisfaction, so too did several of her British admirers. Lord Carlisle was more than a little outraged by her comparison of the British aristocracy to southern slave-owners: 'Whenever you speak of England and her institutions', he observed in a letter, 'it is in a tone which fails to do them justice.' The parallel drawn between the British aristocracy and capitalists and the south's slave-holders was 'wholly inapplicable'. Indeed, 'Our capitalists are very much the same sort of persons as your own in the Northern States.' This was an acute observation. Southern slave-owners, after all, defended their peculiar institution precisely by claiming they took better care of their human chattel than northern industrialists treated their workers. Despite his lordship's astute objections, Stowe's erroneous parallels would retain some currency, particularly in the United States, where it would later be believed that the British aristocracy sided with the South out of a sense of kinship (untrue on both counts, as it happened). Other members of the British aristocracy, meantime, ignored the comparison and praised *Uncle Tom's Cabin* to the skies. Lord Denman, for example, entered into a furious dispute with Dickens over the latter's not-entirely-unfair criticism of the novel; a work which retains its great popularity in the present day.[36]

Despite these rumblings, Stowe's visit to Britain was largely a success. Her memoirs of the trip, *Sunny Memories of Foreign Lands* (1854), was broadly appreciated and she was to visit Britain again, three years later and again in 1859, when she was honoured by no less a personage than Queen Victoria herself. She could probably claim, in the 1850s, to be Britain's favourite American – she was by far and away the one most read. Unfortunately, Stowe's triumph was, in a manner not dissimilar to the first rapprochement at the end of the eighteenth century, almost a false dawn in the Anglo-American relationship. The very issue at the heart of her novel – slavery – was to be one of the main points of contention between the northern and southern states of America; points of contention that would lead to bloody civil war and a rapid, and at times apparently dangerous, decline in Anglo-American relations. Many of those who honoured Stowe would damn both sides in the conflict equally or, in some rare cases, actually support the South. Yet that was in the future. For now at least, Sydney Smith's taunt, 'who reads an American book?', had been definitively rebutted. The United States, in part thanks to its authors, loomed larger in the British consciousness than ever before. Culturally, at any rate, the country of salesmen had found some common ground with the nation of shopkeepers. Sam Slick's descendants had found a new market for their wares – now if only they could settle copyright.

3

Trade, Immigration and the Transfer of Capital and Technology

President Andrew Jackson was not one to overly concern himself with constitutional limits while in office. Whether or not he actually dismissed a Supreme Court ruling against his Indian removal policies with the words, '[Chief Justice] John Marshall has made his decision, now let him enforce it', Jackson nonetheless generally behaved as an elected dictator. It was therefore a little unusual that, in 1835, he found it necessary to request that Congress grant him permission (in the form of legislation) to accept a special bequest to the United States from a foreign national. Even stranger still was the bequest itself, namely a gift of over $500,000 (roughly the equivalent of over $9 million today) to 'the United States of America, to found at Washington, under the name of the Smithsonian Institution, an Establishment for the increase and diffusion of knowledge', from one James Smithson (1765–1829), a scientist of some repute (in mineralogy especially), a member of the Royal Society of London and the illegitimate son of the Duke of Northumberland. Jackson may well have disliked Britons almost as much as Blacks and Indians, but as neither irony nor looking a gift horse in the mouth played much part in his psychological composition, the seventh President decided to accept the bequest, hence his request of Congress.[1]

If Jackson's Anglophobia was temporarily placed in abeyance, the same was not true of all members of Congress. One of the staunchest opponents of Smithson's bequest was Senator John C. Calhoun of South Carolina, a former war hawk of 1812 and best remembered today as the leading proponent of the states' rights doctrine, privileging the authority of the state legislatures over that of the federal government. Indeed, Calhoun depended upon states' rights to argue that Congress had no authority to accept the gift on behalf of the United States and further declared that it would be 'beneath dignity' for the nation 'to accept presents from anyone'. His fellow senator from South Carolina, William Campbell Preston, meantime, questioned Smithson's motives and expressed concerns about what sort of precedent acceptance of the

bequest might set. After all, reasoned the senator, 'every whippersnap-
per [and] vagabond ... might think it proper to have his name distinguished in the same way'. As the question of accepting bequests from
people who might have earned their money through dubious means has
vexed a number of institutions in recent years, senators Preston and
Calhoun's concerns should not, perhaps, be lightly dismissed. Those in
favour, led by former President John Quincy Adams, prevailed, however, a fact probably as much owed to the value of the bequest as the
strength of their arguments. On 1 July 1836, therefore, Congress
authorized the acceptance of the Smithson bequest and Jackson
instructed the diplomat Richard Rush to secure it.

Rush, one of the negotiators of the Rush-Bagot Treaty (1817) was to
spend a while in Britain pursuing the United States' claim. For, if there
was disquiet in Congress about accepting the money, there was concern
in Britain about allowing such a large sum to be handed over to the
United States. For many in Britain, the United States was an unfriendly,
virtually hostile, power. In fact, to say that relations between the two
nations in the 1830s were in a state akin to a cold war would only be a
slight exaggeration. Both Anglophobia and anti-Americanism were
genuine and widespread sentiments. There was thus not a little satisfaction in Britain when the mother of Smithson's nephew and desig-
nated heir filed a counterclaim in the Court of Chancery. Britain,
however, was a nation under the rule of law, which meant that the legal
system was independent of government and the government, whatever
its misgivings, could not interfere in the judiciary process. Although the
Court of Chancery was notoriously slow in its proceedings (as
immortalized by Dickens's 1852–53 novel, *Bleak House*, in the litigation
of Jarndyce vs. Jarndyce), Rush won the United States' claim in a
remarkably short time, securing a successful verdict on behalf of his
nation in less than two years. On 9 May 1838, the Court awarded
Smithson's properties to the United States and in the summer of 1838
Smithson's estate, including his library and mineral collections, crossed
the Atlantic; the monetary value of Smithson's estate being more than
one hundred thousand gold sovereigns.

In many respects, the battle over Smithson's estate, far from being
finished had, in fact, only just begun. A furious debate took place in
Congress as to how Smithson's bequest would be fulfilled. Suggestions
included, among others, a national library (the Library of Congress then
was not quite the institution it is today) and a national university. After
heated debate and the disappearance of the money (into dubious state

funds, which the Treasury ultimately had to replace), a compromise was reached to establish an institute. Thus, on 10 August 1846, President James Polk signed into law a bill establishing the Smithsonian Institution which, of course, exists to this day, as an educational, research and associated museum complex (19 in all) with over 142 million items in its collections.

So what motivated Smithson to leave his considerable estate to the United States, a nation that, as we have seen, was not exactly on good terms with his own? The answer to this question remains elusive. Smithson did not, in either his public or private writings, establish a reason for his bequest. Popular claims, therefore, that he viewed the United States as a model for humankind are purely speculative; as are the claims he sought revenge on the British aristocracy for his status as an illegitimate child. The origins of these claims can be traced back no further than to the pronouncements of John Quincy Adams who needed reasons for the United States to accept the money and whom, in his private correspondence, wondered about Smithson's sanity. Further, it should not be forgotten that the United States was not, if one may describe it thus, Smithson's original heir. That honour went to his nephew, Henry James Hungerford. It was only if Hungerford died without children – legitimate or illegitimate – that the estate would pass to the United States. Certainly, although he travelled extensively in Europe, Smithson never visited America in his entire life.[2]

Thus, the reason for Smithson's bequest remains one of the intriguing mysteries in the Anglo-American story. Yet the bequest itself and the events surrounding its eventual acceptance, obtainment and fulfilment are representative, at least in part, of another aspect of the two nations' developing relationship, for it represents the transfer of capital, investment and knowledge, and ultimately, ideas, across the Atlantic. This chapter concentrates on trade relations, the movement of people, capital, capital goods and intellectual property, within the framework of the growing transatlantic economy.

When discussing Anglo-American trade in the first half of the nineteenth century, it is important to keep in mind the notion, suggested by one scholar, that, rather than thinking of two separate economies, Britain and the United States, it is more useful to think of a single, Atlantic economy. The War of Independence had not fundamentally altered the pre-colonial economic relationship as radically as it did the political one. The transatlantic web of trading relations had certainly been stretched by the War of Independence and Napoleonic

wars, but not torn apart. Furthermore, in the aftermath of these conflicts, political affairs from an Anglo-American perspective moved in
favour of economic cooperation, as both nations agreed that the
Americas were off-limits to further European colonial expansionism
and, not to put too fine a point on it, American foreign policy in the
shape of the Monroe Doctrine was simply hyperbole without the
enforcement of the Royal Navy. Thus the American republic, at least in
its formative years, was, along with the South American republics, a
member of Britain's informal trading empire.[3]

At this period, Britain was the workshop of the world, the progenitor
of the Industrial Revolution and the first nation where a majority of its
population became urban dwellers (city-states excluded). This prior
urban and industrial transformation that took place greatly strengthened Britain's internal trading competences and advanced its trade
capacity to the point where it became the pre-eminent trading nation in
the world. This virtuous circle of industrialization, trade and development was supported by the world's largest merchant marine fleet,
transporting manufactured goods to all corners of the globe, selling at
prices no other nation could match and in return bringing back the raw
materials necessary to sustain and advance further the nation's industrial development. This grand trading empire and merchant marine was,
of course, supported and protected by the Royal Navy – the primary
agency with the global reach capable of maintaining freedom of passage
on the high seas.[4]

One of the sources of these raw materials was the United States
which, in the early nineteenth century, had a rural-based population
engaged in an agrarian economy, well endowed with land and other
natural resources, but lacking capital and the skills necessary to develop
the resources. Initially, the United States provided Britain with foodstuffs such as corn, beef and pork and significant amounts of raw
cotton, while purchasing manufactured goods in return, absorbing
nearly a quarter of all British manufacturing exports. The development
of American territory required emigrant labour, technical skills, durable
and consumer goods, long-term investment capital, much of which
would be supplied by a rapidly industrializing Britain. In this sense, the
extension of the American frontier meant also the expansion of the
Anglo-American trading sphere.[5]

The process of trade and development was assisted by the progressive
removal of trade barriers by the British authorities and the continuation
of America's low tariffs prior to the War of 1812. This helped to

encourage commerce between the two nations. The path to free-trade in Britain, however, did not follow a smooth course. For example, laws protecting British agriculture were passed in 1791 and 1804, and these, the Corn Laws, culminated in the Act of 1815. The 1815 Corn Law stipulated that foreign grain – particularly wheat, barley and oats – could be imported and warehoused free of charge, but could only be sold on the British market when the domestic prices reached certain levels. The reason for the Corn Laws was twofold: (1) they protected the British agricultural sector (which had strong representation in Parliament) from cheaper European and later American grain; and (2) they theoretically ensured British self-sufficiency in foodstuffs – a not unreasonable concern following years of war with Europe. Despite being revised in 1822 and 1828, chiefly in the areas of the sliding scale of prices at which foreign grain could be sold and changes in the amount of duty charged, the Corn Laws continued to serve as protectionist legislation in the early part of the 1800s. The Corn Laws attracted opposition very early on from free-trade advocates such as David Ricardo and Jeremy Bentham. They argued that allowing Europeans to export their grain to Britain would provide them with the money to purchase British manufactures. Growth of British industry would increase opportunities for workers who, in turn, because of cheaper bread would see their cost of living decline, allowing them more purchasing power. This was the intellectual firepower for free trade; the vociferous campaigning came from the Anti-Corn Law League, founded in Manchester in 1838, two of whose spokesmen were Richard Cobden and John Bright. Although the influence of the League was exaggerated both at the time and afterwards, it formed a powerful lobby to repeal the Corn Laws, organizing bazaars, publications, advertising and holding public meetings.

As is so often the case, one lobby begets another and in 1844 the Anti-League was established by agricultural interests, including tenant farmers, to counter the efforts of the free-traders. Relying mostly on the argument that Britain needed to be self-sufficient in grain production, the Anti-League used many of the same tactics as their opponents. Despite this, by 1845 the Whigs were in favour of scrapping the Corn Laws, leaving the Conservatives as the voice of protection, despite Prime Minster Robert Peel's reduction of duties in 1842. Peel, facing an economic crisis and concerned about the conjunction of high food prices and mass unemployment, concluded that the abolition of the Corn Laws was the price of political stability. In 1845, using the Irish potato famine as political cover, he proposed total repeal of the Corn Laws,

successfully doing so in 1849 and in the process splitting the Conservative Party into a free-trading minority and protectionist majority.
Increasingly, Britain moved to free-trade policies, granting the United
States full trading privileges in the West Indies in 1830 and repealing the
remnants of the Navigation Acts in 1849. Thus, at least in Britain,
politically speaking protectionism was identified with conservatism; free
trade with liberalism.[6]

In many respects, the opposite happened in the United States. In the
immediate deflationary years following the War of 1812, and to protect
the domestic industries that grew up during the conflict, American
nationalists pushed for tariff increases citing among other things
arguments in favour of 'infant industries' (a policy of temporary
assistance to enable newly formed domestic industry to compete successfully with foreign enterprises until such time as the 'infant industry'
becomes viable). The result of these efforts was a bill introduced in 1816
by William Lowndes and John C. Calhoun of South Carolina that
applied import duties, ranging from 7.5 per cent to 30 per cent, on
imported cotton goods, woollens, iron and other commodities. From
that point until 1833, demands for additional tariff protection continued
to grow.

During this period, the free-trade arguments were increasingly
attacked as not being appropriate for the American economic envir-
onment. One of the spokesmen advocating more tariffs in support of
domestic industry was Henry Clay, the leading war hawk of 1812. Clay
has been credited with coining the term, 'the American system' which,
among other things, harboured the embryonic policies of economic
isolationism. The 'American system' soon became a populist credo,
which promoted the idea of improving the national infrastructure by
means of government investment, strengthening intra-domestic trade.
This argument was promoted on the basis that by improving the
infrastructure, the exchange of domestically produced commodities
would be made more efficient, benefiting both the farmer and the
industrialist, and, in the process, reduce the country's dependence on
foreign trade.

On this point, however, divisions appeared within the United States.
While the states of New York, New Jersey, Pennsylvania and Ohio were
early converts to protectionism, the rest of the nation preferred free
trade. New England, for a time, was split between protectionist manufacturers and free-trading shipping interests, but by the 1830s the
former had won the argument. This soon left parts of the West and

especially the South as the anti-protectionist regions. The shift can be seen in the political careers of New Englander Daniel Webster and South Carolina's Calhoun. In 1816 Webster opposed tariffs while Calhoun supported them; by 1830, both men had reversed their positions.[7]

As the tariff debate in the United States increased in volume, so too did the divisions among the regions of the country. American manufacturing was generally located in the north-eastern states, and increasingly, these areas demanded tariffs in order to protect their industries from cheaper British manufactures. The southern states, which exported raw cotton to Britain and imported manufactured goods in return, saw no reason to support any tariffs which would force them to purchase more expensive (and, frequently, less well-made) northern-produced manufactures. Despite this, tariffs were introduced in 1818, 1824 and finally in 1828 when, under Jackson's presidency, the United States passed the highest duties on foreign imports, at least until the Civil War. This last tariff increase, however, called the 'tariff of abominations' by its opponents, resulted in a backlash, particularly when amendments were made to it in 1832. The state of South Carolina led the resistance by passing the 1832 Ordinance of Nullification. This, the brainchild of Calhoun, stated that federal tariffs were unconstitutional and forbade the collection of duties within the state. A contest of wills began between the federal government and President Jackson on one side, South Carolina and Jackson's former Vice President, Calhoun, on the other, which included threats of secession and military coercion. Finally, thanks to intercession by the other states, a compromise tariff was introduced by Clay, which significantly lowered duties and peace was restored.[8]

This, the Nullification Crisis, which in many respects began the estrangement of the South from the rest of the nation and set the United States on the path to civil war, was intimately connected to the tensions within the American economy. Meantime, the South, because of its economic circumstances, wished to preserve the existing system, while the rest of the country, particularly the north-eastern states, wanted to bring it to an end and thereby supposedly advance their economic development. Although the tendency of tariff rates was downwards from 1832 until the Civil War, the Union's victory meant it was the north-eastern states' vision of national development that prevailed (tariffs of increasing steepness being passed in 1861, 1862, 1864 and 1875). In this sense, the American Civil War completed the War of Independence, enabling the United States to cease being a colonial economy. At the same time, the South went from being an economic colonial appendage of Britain to being one of the United States.

As the century wore on, American tariffs began to be increased, up to the level of the Dingley tariff of 1897 that imposed duty of 57 per cent. Even though this was the high-water mark, tariffs would be a hallmark of American economic policy well into the twentieth century, culminating in the Smoot-Hawley tariff of 1930 that would greatly lengthen the world economic downturn of the 1930s. Therefore, although the early part of the century saw a significant agreement between Britain and the United States on the issue of free trade, as the century wore on, this became less and less the case. Indeed, as Britain converted to free-trade ideology and practice, the United States became increasingly more protectionist. Not for the first time, Anglo-American views diverged, rather than converged. Eventually, of course, the American tariffs and increasing competition from Europe would lead to Britain following similar policies by imposing Imperial tariffs in the twentieth century. These, in effect, turned the Empire into a protectionist bloc. Thus, the first great era of international free trade came to an end, the consequences of which would reverberate throughout the twentieth century.[9]

Notwithstanding the infighting on protectionism during the early part of the nineteenth century, both Britain and America were largely *laissez-faire* societies (although the examples of the Factory Acts in Britain and the state-funding of education in the United States should remind us that both nations always had some degree of government involvement in their economies). As such, there was relatively little government interference in the movement of capital goods and services. The economic driving force behind American continental expansion was based on an oceanic partnership in which New York was partnered with Liverpool, Boston with London, and New England with Old England, and together they supplied the inputs and demand for western expansion. By the first half of the nineteenth century, the United States was Britain's primary export market and the United States was largely dependent on British manufactures to support its domestic economy. Between 1820 and 1860, nearly half of American exports went to Britain and roughly 40 per cent of America's imports came from Britain. Of foreign tonnage entering American ports in 1860, four-fifths was British. Despite the difficult diplomatic relationship of the first part of the nineteenth century, it would appear that British and Americans traders were not prepared to let politics interfere with business. Small wonder then that a later American minister to Britain, Edwards Pierrepont, declared, 'The two nations *surely sympathize in trade and finance if in nothing else.*'[10]

The two American crops of especial importance to Britain were wheat and cotton, which successively determined the growth of markets and the flow of capital and credit, demonstrated most notably by the notorious railway booms and collapses of the 1850s. Initially, it was the cotton trade that was especially important, as the demand for raw cotton in Lancashire helped the development of the South's economy – an economy based on slavery. When it came to the cotton trade, Liverpool's importance dwarfed that of all other British ports, completely overshadowing its only two serious rivals (London and Glasgow) by the 1830s. As one scholar has pointed out, Liverpool's dominance in the cotton trade stemmed from the fact that by the early years of the nineteenth century the city had become the principal centre of American trade. London might serve as the headquarters for the bankers of American trade, but Liverpool handled the consignments, the volume of which increased steadily throughout the first half of the nineteenth century. Thus, not only was Liverpool the centre of American trade in Britain, but this trade was probably the single most important business conducted by the city's merchants. This made sense: cotton made up almost 60 per cent of American exports to Britain by 1850. The cotton, in turn, was turned into textiles, which accounted for 60 per cent of British exports and 30 per cent of these went to the United States. After this, wheat, thanks to the repeal of the Corn Laws, overtook cotton as America's most important export crop and the great cycle of business activity that accompanied it was also, like cotton, financed by British capital.[11]

Liverpool, however, handled more than just cotton. Its geographic location, with canals and later railways, meant it had access to the cutlery of Sheffield, the woollens of Yorkshire and the North, the pottery of Staffordshire and the hardware of Birmingham, as well as the textiles of Lancashire. Liverpool's merchants swiftly developed connections with their counterparts in New York and Philadelphia. This existing network of merchants and brokers was complemented by British manufacturers who sold directly to American wholesalers. By the 1820s, representatives of Staffordshire potteries, Sheffield cutlers and Birmingham hardware manufacturers were established in New York. Indeed, the New York–Liverpool axis was to prove crucial in establishing New York as the most important port in the United States.

British involvement in the lucrative Atlantic economy was diverse: the Royal Insurance Company of Liverpool established a New York branch under Henry Eyre, while others, like Alexander T. Stewart, established a series of dry good stores in New York.

British merchants in New York soon established clubs and, as the British do in most places, formed a small expatriate community complete with societies and newspapers. Some, of course, became naturalized Americans, but most seemed to have regarded Britain as 'home', and several, having made their fortunes, returned home to retire. As one contemporary observer noted, 'few Englishmen residing in America renounce their allegiance to their own Government. They are patriotic John Bulls. They take British papers, frequent British beer-houses, drink British ale, and are proud and happy to call themselves "British residents".' These, however, were not immigrants, but mostly representatives of British companies and other commercial interests operating in a foreign land and, as such, behaved in a manner as would be expected from subjects of a world-wide trading empire. Initially, transatlantic trade was run almost exclusively by British merchant houses, but by the 1830s Americans began to appear in larger numbers, even if the British companies continued to dominate.[12]

Another area of British involvement in the American economy was in financing state and national bonds. So, for example, of the $11 million worth of bonds issued for the Louisiana Purchase, some $9 million worth was purchased by Britons. By 1837, there was some $125 million foreign capital invested in the United States, most of it British. This, of course, was the year of 'the Panic' of 1837, which revealed the downside to investing in the United States when shortly thereafter public debt was repudiated and individual private fortunes were lost. The political response to the economic crisis of 1837 underlined another point of difference between Britain and America. Whereas the British government in the 1830s and 40s, concentrating on creating an effective legal framework for a stable currency, made Bank of England notes legal tender in 1833 and, via the Bank Charter in 1844, ensured the Bank's notes once issued were supported by gold bullion, in America the opposite occurred. There, President Jackson terminated the licence of the Second Bank of the United States by refusing to renew its charter despite the objections of Congress. The Bank, which was modelled on the Bank of England and was the second attempt to establish a central bank, had helped to stabilize the American economy by periodically demanding that state banks honour their issued notes with specie.

Jackson, ever the populist, dismissed the bank as the instrument of aristocracy, privilege and monopoly, and made pointed references to conspiracies supposedly organized by British investors. Politically, Jackson's tactics worked and, winning re-election in 1832, allowed the Second Bank's charter to expire in 1836. The president's actions are said to have set back the development of America's monetary policy for at least a generation, for it was not until the 1863 National Banking Act that a system of national banks was instituted and even these did not prevent bank panics in 1873, 1893 and 1907. In fact, it was not until two years after the establishment of the Federal Reserve Act in 1913 that the United States established a monetary institution equivalent to a central bank. Until then, this absence made the management of fiscal policy more problematic.[13]

The immediate effect of the demise of the Second Bank was that, freed from the Bank's oversight, state banks issued notes rather freely and, in some cases, with abandonment. At this point, British banks and other investors demanded these notes be redeemed by specie. The result was a chain of American bank closures from New Orleans to New York and, ultimately, an economic depression which lasted from 1837 until 1843. It was during this period that several states defaulted on their bonds, including Mississippi (the future President of the Confederate States of America, Jefferson Davis, was one of the spokesmen for the state's repudiation, something a number of Britons remembered during the American Civil War) and, perhaps more ominously, Pennsylvania (where Sydney Smith lost his money). Unsurprisingly, British investment was reduced during this period, only to be seriously revived in the 1850s. By that point, however, the Americans took increasing hold of their part of the continent and their economy became less colonial and increasingly a centre of manufacturing itself.[14]

While these trade and financial dealings between Britain and the United States were undeniably important, in some cases too much emphasis has been placed upon them as a reason for improving Anglo-American relations in the first half of the nineteenth century. In the first place, the diplomatic thaw took place only very slowly and became noticeable before British investment to the United States began to recover following the 1837 crisis. In the second, during this period Britain enjoyed improved trading relations with other nations without there being a corresponding amelioration in the diplomatic sphere. For example, in 1860, Britain and France signed the Cobden-Chevalier Commercial Treaty which liberalized trade between the two nations (the French reducing tariffs on British manufactured goods and coal while the British reciprocated with respect to wine and cognac, among other products). Despite the undoubted economic benefits of the treaty, it did very little to allay either Francophobia in Britain or Anglophobia in France – nor did it much influence the arms race taking place between the two nations as represented by the construction of ocean-going ironclad warships. Nations that trade with each other may well have better reasons to avoid conflict, but trade in itself is neither a guarantee of peace, nor of friendship. Further, as regards to Anglo-American relations and the financial crisis of 1837, creditors rarely have much respect, let alone love, for debtors who default on their loans, to say nothing of those who repudiate them altogether.[15]

That being said, the Americans did not cease to take lessons from British industrialization. Indeed, after the American Civil War, the so-called 'British model' of industrial relations impressed numerous social observers in the United States who hoped to emulate aspects of it in their homeland. As this phenomenon occurred very much in the latter part of the nineteenth century, it is dealt with in a later chapter. Yet the idea of Americans learning from British industry was an old one even by the end of the nineteenth century. Although in 1825 Britain raised the ban on the export of artisans and machinery, and emigration policy shifted from discouragement to indifference, many artisans long before this, lured by the offer of financial incentives, high wages or partnerships, or sometimes just lump sums of cash, disguised themselves as labourers and crossed the Atlantic, carrying plans of their machines and, more importantly, their skills, to America, irrespective of the laws. Two lessons may be taken from this: (1) that the 'brain drain' to America has an ancient pedigree, but (2) more importantly, no nation – or at least, no liberal state – can prevent ideas or skills from travelling and spreading elsewhere.

One of these British émigrés was Samuel Slater who migrated from Derbyshire in 1789. He was an apprentice of one of Richard Arkwright's partners, inventor of the spinning jenny for cotton. Slater, after copying the design of Arkwright's latest models, disguised himself in a beard and sailed to America. Upon arrival, he took over the management of an American merchant's cotton mill in Rhode Island and replicated the entire set of Arkwright's machines. Thus, the most advanced mill in America was opened in 1790 – a date which is traditionally held by historians as marking the beginning of the Industrial Revolution in the United States – based on an audacious act of industrial espionage. It must be noted, however, that the Americans learned from the British in other, more reputable ways, too. By the early nineteenth century, American states began to take their cue from the Acts of Trade passed by the British Parliament and enacted various measures to stimulate economic development within their boundaries. Corporate charters, introducing limited liability, began to appear, reducing the risks to investors and encouraging entrepreneurs.[16]

The notion of British emigrants carrying industrial methods and technologies from Britain to America has been described by one historian as the 'Transatlantic Industrial Revolution', for Slater was one of hundreds of thousands of British migrants who crossed the Atlantic during the nineteenth century. The motives of those who crossed the Atlantic were as various as the types of individuals. Some certainly went across for reasons of political freedom or religious principle, but these (the chief exception being the Irish) were a distinct minority. For one thing, British migration to the United States was consistently lower during periods of political upheaval in Britain than during periods of political peace. Indeed, emigration to the United States was lower during periods of economic downturn than in times of prosperity.[17]

Of the estimated four and a quarter million Britons who crossed the Atlantic to the United States between 1820 and 1930, there were three prominent waves of migration: the first from the mid-1840s to the mid-1850s, the second from the late-1860s to mid-1870s, and the third in the 1880s. The first took place as the difficult economic and political climate of the 'Hungry Forties' gave way to what one historian has described as the 'age of equipoise', the improved economic and political circum-stances of the 1850s. The second took place during the middle of the 'Great Victorian Boom', which stretched virtually unbroken from 1850 to 1873, a period of increased economic opportunities and political progress that included the 1867 Reform Act. Even the last, and by far the largest, took place during a similar period of political and economic stability.[18]

Why people chose to move in good times, rather than bad, is perhaps best explained by the argument that the increase in emigration was owed to the positive side of economic growth. Personal prosperity whetted the appetite for even further economic advancement. Further, to emigrate to America required a reasonable amount of capital. For although the price of a ticket across the Atlantic declined during the nineteenth century, it was still, in relative terms, expensive. Even at mid-century, £5–6 was the absolute minimum cost of a ticket to cross the Atlantic. For a family of four the cost was approximately £20. As an annual income of £25 was the average wage for a factory operative (and agricultural labourers often received only two-thirds of that), migration to America was not usually an option for the poorest members of British society.[19]

In other words, most of the British who went to America had, for the most part, already enjoyed at least modest economic success at home and were probably sufficiently ambitious to advance further. Politics seems to have played, at most, a very minor part in determining British motivation for migration. Indeed, industrial workers emigrated to the United States in such low proportions that Britain's expanding economy seems to have provided sufficient opportunity for most such potential migrants. The expanding economy meant that industrial emigration was not of a distressed nature and rarely served as a safety valve. In this respect, at least, British emigrants to America differed to those from Europe such as the Germans who went across during the revolutions of the 1840s or the Irish who went across because of the famine. The exception to this might have been the nonconformists, who were somewhat more likely to migrate than Anglicans. On the other hand, this larger migration of nonconformists may well have been as much owed to the fact that some of them, such as the Methodists, maintained stronger institutional links and networks on both sides of the Atlantic than did the Church of England. These nonconformist networks must surely have increased emigration opportunities. This aspect of British migration, however, became less significant after the laws barring nonconformists from political office and the universities were repealed in 1828.[20]

The cost of passage brings us to our next point: at least part of the reason for the increase in British migration to America can be found in the fact that ship technology improved throughout the nineteenth century. By sail, the journey from Liverpool to New York was usually five weeks, although bad weather could increase that time to 14 weeks. The new transatlantic steamers that appeared in the 1850s reduced the length of the trip to 12 days although the sailing ships dominated the trade until well into the latter half of the century (and it is obviously no coincidence that the greatest period of migration occurred towards the end of the century when the steamships assumed dominance). These changes in technology, plus the fact that increased competition greatly reduced the costs of transatlantic travel (fares fell to £3.10s), meant more people were willing to make the journey. Further, one must not forget the psychological advantage these changes represented, namely, that the trip to America was no longer potentially irreversible – it was easier to return.

None of this should allow us to forget that the trip across the Atlantic could still be a harrowing ordeal. For example, of the roughly 90,000 emigrants who crossed to Quebec from Britain in 1847, more than 15,000 died of disease either at sea or in Canadian hospitals – a casualty rate of just over 16 per cent. Typhus or cholera epidemics could reduce a ship's passengers (and crew) with terrifying swiftness. Shipwreck was another potential obstacle – Thomas Liddle's ship departed Liverpool in 1851, but was shipwrecked off Newfoundland, depriving him of every- thing save the clothes he was wearing. William Bosomworth's vessel sprung a leak and had to hastily return to Liverpool. These were all sailing ships, but the example of Jane Chadwick, apprentice dressmaker, who crossed the Atlantic by steamship on a visit to America and was so ill on the outward voyage across that she refused to return to England with her family, thus becoming an unintended immigrant, helps demonstrate how uncomfortable the trip could be even with the improvements in transportation.[21]

Insofar as opinion regarding British migration to the United States went, both public and political views were ambiguous. Although there was no suggestion that people should not be allowed to go freely where they wished (and the departure by some groups, such as the Irish, was less regretted than others) the question of whether or not migration was good for the emigrants was debated. Newspapers hostile to emigration published letters by immigrants relating a catalogue of sorrows, weal and woe, while those in favour reproduced letters proclaiming the opposite. This makes the use of such letters somewhat problematic, but as many journals supported neither one school nor the other, and published both favourable and unfavourable accounts, these commu- nications do provide some idea of the information available to those who, lacking any connections in America, were considering making the trip. Certainly, some scholars have insisted published letters had a greater influence on potential emigrants and perceptions of the United States than did manuscript letters because they reached a far wider public. For example, by 1846, it was estimated that two-thirds to three- quarters of the British population was literate and this, plus the large increase in periodicals, provided a forum for these letters. As expected, the numbers of letters published shadowed the number of emigrants going out, meaning the period following the American Civil War up to the 1880s was the golden age of the immigrant letter writer.[22]

The immigrant letters were sometimes written specifically for publication. In some cases – human vanity has not changed much – people simply wanted to see their name in print. Other individuals found a published letter spared them having to write multiple ones to different family members and friends. Thus, in August 1844, a letter to the Welsh-language journal *Y Bedyddiwr* (the Baptist), by one Robert Williams of New York, directly asked the editor to print his communication because it would save him the trouble of writing to all those to whom he had promised a missive, noting that all his friends and acquaintances read the publication. More common was for immigrants to request recipients to arrange for the publication of the letters or occasionally the recipients acted on their own initiative. In either case, journal editors tended to edit out information they deemed too personal or libellous. The advantage of such letters to a potential emigrant was that, being mainly addressed to a local community of which the immigrant was a former inhabitant, it was easier to determine their trustworthiness. Certainly the sheer variety of topics covered by the letters makes them difficult to classify. Some pointed to the material advantages they enjoyed or lacked, and what sorts of people resided in the area to which they had emigrated including religious denomination and ethnicity, while others gave detailed descriptions of political developments. For many Britons, even those disinclined to emigrate, given the relative dearth of American coverage in the British press, these letters served as a source of information – albeit of varying quality – about the United States.[23]

This information was important, because while many British immigrants prospered many did not. Indeed, during periods of economic crisis in the United States, many regretted the move so much that they returned home in large numbers. Indeed, some scholars have claimed that of those who went out as many as one third returned. For example, in 1857 during another economic crisis that left over 200,000 people unemployed, thousands of recent immigrants crowded the eastern ports, hoping to return home. As *The New York Times* reported in October of that year, 'Every ship for Liverpool now has all the passengers she can carry, and multitudes are applying to work their passage if they have no money to pay for it.' It must never be forgotten that immigration carried grave risks as well as great rewards. Further, returning immigrants came back with a decidedly different view of the United States than those that went out and stayed.[24]

That said, until the last decades of the nineteenth century, the United States remained the favourite destination for British migrants. At that point, Australia, Canada and New Zealand became increasingly popular and finally, as a collective, overtook the United States as the first choice of destination for British migrants. Without a doubt, the United States offered a lot of opportunities. As Michael Chevalier pithily observed in 1839, 'In Europe work is often wanting for the hands, here that is, (in the United States) hands are wanting for the work.' Although in comparison to Britain, America was overwhelmingly rural, with some four-fifths of its labour force engaged in agriculture in 1840, this ignores regional differences. By 1850, fully one third of New England's and two-fifths of the Mid-Atlantic States' workers were engaged in manufactures. In New England's textile mills alone, British mechanists, engineers, dyers, managers and operatives could find employment at relatively high wages. Even in the coal mines of Pennsylvania and Illinois, as well as the lead, copper and iron mines of Wisconsin, Michigan and Illinois, British miners could earn in excess of twice what they could expect at home. Those who made it as far as the California gold mines sometimes did even better still. As we have noted, British immigrants in the United States tended to come from the classes of the skilled, rather than unskilled, labourers. The shortage of skilled labourers in various American industries represented an opportunity unmatched anywhere else.[25]

As Britain was the only urban and industrialized nation even in the middle of the nineteenth century, so its labour force was the most diversified. That Americans and Britons shared a common language undeniably facilitated migrants' entry into the American labour force, but it was their skill and experience that made them especially attractive. So, for example, workers in Sheffield's crucible steel and specialized tool-making industries were in especially high demand. American businessmen in the 1840s visited Britain to learn Sheffield methods and returned with workers they had recruited. Thus, not only did American employers welcome skilled Britons – they actively recruited them. This occurred despite the fact that British industrial migrants to America had a reputation for independence and indeed militancy even by the mid-nineteenth century. Indeed, the tendency for British workers to organize and fight for improved conditions was also noted – particularly as the century progressed – a case, perhaps, of Britons demonstrating the principles of liberty to the Americans. Certainly in later years, American employers began to prefer the allegedly more passive and docile workers from southern and western Europe.[26]

Skilled British migrant workers of the mid-nineteenth century fell into two camps: pre-industrial craftsmen inexperienced in technological change and industrial workers who had experienced change and possible technological displacement. Thus, handloom weavers, threatened by power looms, immigrated in sizable numbers in the first half of the century. One family of such migrants from Scotland brought with them a young son, Andrew Carnegie, who would, by the end of the century, become the richest man in the world. Carnegie was the ultimate immigrant success story, but many others prospered, too. Yorkshire weaver William Broadhead, arriving in 1843, used his technological know-how to eventually establish nine weaving factories in New York State. More common than textile workers were engineers and ironworkers. In fact, by mid-century, engineers were overrepresented, if anything. Ironworkers, meantime, were drawn largely by the railroad booms of the 1840s and 50s (and suffered when the booms inevitably collapsed). Most common, however, were pre-industrial craftsmen, including those connected with the building trades and miners. Many in the first group were from agrarian locales and, finding themselves displaced by the increasing depopulation of rural areas in Britain, tried their luck abroad. A large number of these individuals had agricultural experience as well, and, as a result, many switched to farming upon arrival in America.

Indeed, individuals involved in agricultural pursuits – whether part-time or full-time as labourers or farmers – represented a significant proportion of British migrants to America. As well over half of British emigrants to the United States would either farm, or attempt to farm, land was an obvious lure. During the 1840s and 50s it was possible to buy outright land in America for the cost of renting it for a year or two in Britain. The attraction of American land was increased during this period by the government's reducing the price of it still further. British migrants were thus as keen on western expansion as native-born American settlers. Further, with the abolition of the Corn Laws, British agriculture was denied protection from foreign, mostly American, competition. The resulting competition certainly made British agriculture more efficient, but that resulted in a serious loss of employment opportunities in rural areas. As a result, there were very much 'push' factors as there were 'pull' when it came to rural migrants.[27]

Like their compatriots in manufacturing, British farmers were usually skilled in their profession and often, but not always, superior to the local variety. As one migrant Briton observed, 'The Yankee farmers are the most careless in their operations of any agriculturalists I ever saw.' These new arrivals were thus able to introduce advanced and innovative methods already practised at home. Indeed, migrant British farmers' improved practices were renowned enough that advanced methods in farming were often referred to as 'English methods' of agriculture. This should not be too surprising – it was, after all, an agricultural revolution in Britain that had preceded the industrial one. Improvements included better drainage techniques, more effective breeding of livestock, more efficient blends of livestock farming and mixed crops, maintenance of land fertility by rotating crops with nitrogen-rich plants and collecting manure for fertilizer. Farm labourers, who were especially hit by the end of protectionism, had a tougher time of it. Pooled family savings were often the only source of money to pay for the trip across the Atlantic. Once in America, the labourers would then work hard, live frugally and remit their savings to their families – for whose arrival they might well make preparations. It was an obviously risky process if the one sent across proved wastrel or simply unlucky. Still, the number of British farm labourers who eventually saved enough to purchase land for themselves meant the risks were often worth it – British farm workers in America could typically earn twice as much as they could at home and three times as much was not unusual.[28]

The view that British immigrants were of higher quality than other groups of migrants was expressed by numerous American observers by the late nineteenth century. Although this was in part due to improved relations between the two countries, as well as notions of 'the Anglo-Saxon race', which had become commonplace by the century's end, it was also based on a measure of truth. By the mid-nineteenth century, Britons involved in the clerical, commercial and professional sectors arrived in numbers not much less than those of general labourers – a feat not replicated to the same extent by any other migrant group. For certain of these groups, clerks especially, movement across the Atlantic was a bold gamble: the United States was not short of literate individuals who could perform clerking duties, nor was the profession oversubscribed to in Britain until the end of the century. Other professions, however, such as doctors, were in demand. By the mid-nineteenth century, the British medical profession had instituted meaningful qualifications in comparison to those that prevailed in the United States – many American doctors being little more than semiliterate quacks. This persisted for a longer time than is generally realized. For example, when President James Garfield was shot by an assassin, in 1881, part of the reason he did not recover lay in the fact that while Joseph Lister's ideas on antisepsis had become standard in Britain, they had not yet been widely accepted in the United States. Garfield died in part because American doctors were operating on him with unsterilized instruments. That said, one should not exaggerate nineteenth-century medical prowess – British or otherwise; there was a reason doctors were commonly referred to as 'saw bones'. Teachers were another class who migrated to the United State in numbers – despite the profession's relatively low pay in America.

Despite the long-standing myth that the British upper classes hated the United States and its democracy, a surprisingly large number joined the flow across the Atlantic, exclusive of those who went across on business. In fact, the numbers of British 'gentlemen' arriving were high enough that numerous contemporary observers remarked upon them, as one might imagine, for refined, upper-middle to upper-class individuals must have seemed wholly out of place on the American frontier. These individuals often purchased acres of land which they ran in the fashion of absentee landlords, going back and forth across the Atlantic. Many others, however, established small communities in the United States, Robert Owens's failed community in New Harmony, Indiana (1825) being the most famous example, and even larger numbers came across after the conclusion of the Civil War. Le Mars, in north-western Iowa (which now calls itself the ice-cream capital of the world), was established by adventurous Cambridge graduates. Another location was Victoria, Kansas, established by George Grant, former silk merchant who introduced Aberdeen Angus cattle into the United States and who hired an architect from London to lay out the new town. Most of these colonies, for want of a better term, either died out or, more often, were subsumed into the greater American whole, as most immigrant communities were destined to be.[29]

In many respects, because of the common language, the British were indeed what one scholar has described as 'invisible immigrants'. They were not so invisible, however, that they did not take part in transatlantic movements, such as temperance (prohibition of alcohol) or abolitionism (as regards slavery) – two areas in which British migrants made themselves conspicuous. Although one does not want to exaggerate the numbers of British involvement in either – most migrants did not practise temperance (most Britons then, as now, enjoyed drink) nor belonged to abolitionist organizations – the strength of their presence was noted by contemporary American observers. In the case of the temperance movement, nonconformists made up by far the majority of participants, although members of the Church of Scotland and others were also well represented. Where one places the temperance movement on the scale of progress is obviously a matter for the individual concerned. In this case, however, British migrant influence was clearly a mixed blessing when one considers the end victory of the temperance movement: the Eighteenth Amendment to the Constitution (ratified in 1913) or, prohibition, as it is usually known.[30]

More positive, then, was the British migrants' contribution to American abolitionism (although the temperance and abolitionist movements were so closely entwined that it is almost inadvisable to treat them separately). Part of the reason mid-century British immigrants tended (there were always exceptions) to be more hostile to slavery was because the institution had been abolished by Britain and its colonies in 1833, while the Royal Navy attempted to stamp out the international slave trade. This sentiment was felt rather more fiercely at home. So much so that some Britons cited slavery as the reason they refused to join family members in America. Thus, John Woodhouse of Sykehouse, Yorkshire, writing to his brother in Illinois in January 1853, declared, 'For my own part I never think of coming to America. I deem it a cursed land. The curse of slavery is on it. You may call it a free country but the Blacks are not free, but are bought and sold as Cattle.' Indeed, British views of American slavery did much to determine their views of the country, never more so than during the American Civil War. In many respects, then, it was unsurprising that numerous British migrants became involved in American abolitionism, not the least because of its transatlantic nature, the significance of which will be discussed in the next chapter.[31]

With all of this, it was not surprising that Britons remained one of the very few migrant groups to vote Republican, rather than for the Democrats, then, as now, the preferred party of America's immigrants. This, however, may have owed as much to the growing influence of anti-British Irish Americans' influence within Democratic ranks as the Republican Party's policies. Indeed, nothing brought Welsh, Scottish and English immigrants together as Britons more effectively than Irish-American animosities. The rise of the sectional Republican Party was, of course, another marker on the road to civil war in America, and migrant Britons found themselves embroiled in the conflict.

According to one scholar, more than 54,000 British-born individuals served in the Union army, a disproportionately high number when factoring in the percentage of immigrants eligible to serve. Having noted that, very few Britons, in comparison to Europeans, joined the northern armies once the war got underway, secretary of state William H. Seward complaining that British volunteers were very rare in comparison to the 'generous enthusiasm of those States which send us soldiers by the hundreds of thousands to uphold the American Union'. Further, British consuls had their hands full throughout the war with Britons (and Irish) claiming to have been illegally conscripted into the Union's armies, not having become American citizens – one issue, among many, that would bedevil Anglo-American relations during this period. Indeed, the government of the United States insisted on special oaths of loyalty from British immigrants, that they 'renounce forever all allegiance and fidelity' to Queen Victoria. Both British migrants and visitors during this period complained of hostility towards them on the basis of their nationality. For some migrants, of course, this merely acted as a spur for them to prove themselves loyal Americans, sometimes to a ridiculous extent. So, for example, the editor of the Anglophobic *New York Herald*, a widely popular, pro-slavery and pro-Democratic newspaper that caused serious damage to the reputation of the Union in Britain during the American Civil War, was one James Gordon Bennett – an immigrant Scot. Certainly Bennett is one example of the British immigrant going, as the phrase has it, native.[32]

An example of a more salubrious immigrant from Scotland was Alexander Graham Bell, who arrived in America during the 1870s, as many British immigrants did, via Canada (and is thus claimed by all three countries). Bell was a philanthropist and holder of eighteen patents, inventor of the hydrofoil, respirator and metal detector, and most famously for one invention that caused H. L. Mencken to remark, 'No man can hear his telephone ring without wishing heartily that Alexander Graham Bell had been run over by an ice wagon at the age of four.' Winter 1903 found Bell, in his fifties and already famous, in Genoa, Italy. He was there to rescue a body, buried for three-quarters of a century, from an old British cemetery which, unfortunately located next to a marble quarry, was about to be demolished by blasting. Having little time, up against the formidable obstacle of Italian government bureaucracy, at both the local and national level, not to mention the objections of some French individuals claiming distant relation to the deceased, Bell declared himself an official representative of President Theodore Roosevelt (untrue) and by virtue of a cannily distributed thousand lira won permission to exhume the body. On 7 January 1904, the old bones were loaded on board a passenger steamer for transportation to New York. Although the US government had initially paid little attention to Bell's activities, by the time the corpse was half-way across the Atlantic, the mood had changed. A US Navy vessel met the steamer in New York Harbour, took charge of the body and, after placing an American flag over the casket, carried it to the Navy Yard in Washington. There it was met by an Honour Guard of US Marines who, along with a troop of cavalry, escorted the body to the Smithsonian Institution, there to finally be interred, by the Institute's main entrance, on 6 March 1905.[33]

The body was, of course, that of James Smithson, who had died in Genoa in 1829. Bell was a member of the Smithsonian Board of Regents, and the only one who found the idea of Smithson's body being dumped into the Mediterranean to be unacceptable – hence his bodysnatching trip. Thus did one British migrant and North American inventor recover the body of a British scientist responsible for an important institution in American intellectual life. Bell, although hardly a typical British immigrant to the United States, was at least a recognizable representative of their contribution to America. Smithson, on the other hand, was so entirely different but, then, to some degree they all were – investors, visitors and immigrants alike. In Smithson's case, although he never in his life visited the nation to which he generously bequeathed his estate, it was appropriate that in the end he was finally buried there.[34]

4

Taking Liberties and Beacons of Freedom

Peter Porcupine, British resident of Philadelphia, pondered his position.

> I thought my situation somewhat perilous. Such truths as I had published,
> no man had dared to utter, in the United States, since the rebellion. I knew
> that these truths had mortally offended the leading men amongst the
> democrats, who could, at any time, muster a mob quite sufficient to destroy
> my house and to murder me. I had not a friend, to whom I could look with
> any reasonable hope of receiving efficient support; and, as to the *law*, I had
> seen too much of republican justice, to expect anything but persecution
> from that quarter. In short, there were in Philadelphia, about ten thousand
> persons, all of whom would have rejoiced to see me murdered; and there
> might, probably, be two thousand, who would have been very sorry for it;
> but not above fifty who would have stirred an inch to save me.

Peter Porcupine was the *nom de plume* of William Cobbett, and the
current source of his distress was a letter sent to his landlord, John
Olden, signed by 'A Hint'. The anonymous correspondent was outraged
by Cobbett's writings, which 'repeatedly traduced the people of this
country, [and] vilified the most eminent and patriotic characters among
us'. Warning that 'the time of retribution' was approaching, the writer
urged Olden to expel his property's 'rascal' occupant, for '[i]n this way
only you may avoid danger to your house and perhaps save the rotten
carcase of your tenant for the present'.[1]

Mr Hint, for such we shall call him, was one of many – both then and
later – offended by Cobbett's commentary. This account is taken from
Cobbett's 'The Scare-crow', a pamphlet published in 1796, and contains
his rebuttal, particularly regarding his abuse of the United States and its
people. Cobbett had been encouraging the Federalists against the
Democratic Republicans, urging the United States to support Britain in
its war against France. His landlord's angry correspondent was thus of
the opposing party – as were the majority of Philadelphia's inhabitants.
In short, Cobbett was contending with the rough and tumble politics of
the early American republic.

Yet as the quote above reveals, for all the declarations regarding the bright new dawn of liberty represented by the birth of the American republic, there were serious and profound differences between what was proclaimed, and what was practised, by the United States. The land of liberty could prove intolerant of contrary opinions; 'republican justice', while not an oxymoron, was hardly perfect – mob rule and violence were not uncommon. Further, there was the issue of slavery, which, although not an important issue at the time this account was written, would increasingly become one. Finally and too often forgotten, there was American Anglophobia, which waxed and waned throughout the nineteenth century. All of these issues, to one degree or another, greatly determined how the British liberal state viewed the American republic and its version of democracy. Few Britons were uncritical observers and most, irrespective of political persuasion, recognized that declarations were one thing and reality quite another. Cobbett, like most other radicals both then, and later, quickly understood this. Thus, his career both in the United States and in Britain (his adult life was almost equally divided between the two) is a good starting point for discussing the complexities of the Anglo-American political discourse during the first part of the nineteenth century, because many of the radical's concerns would continue to preoccupy his successors in later years.

Cobbett's introduction to the United States came via his service in the British army (he became a sergeant-major) while stationed in New Brunswick, 1784–91. There, hearing the stories of the exiled United Empire Loyalists, he questioned the values of the new republic to the south that had persecuted them in the name of freedom. His experiences in the French Revolution, following his departure from the army, especially during the Terror, however, gave him reason to give the United States another chance. Living there from 1792–1800, he acquired a reputation as one of the most scandalous pamphleteers in the United States, attacking the politically powerful and eventually coming to the attention of President John Adams, who contemplated deporting him. Cobbett thus left the United States before he was thrown out. Back in Britain, he soon assumed the same role he had taken in the United States – that of political scourge – and the British establishment found itself as roundly abused as had the American. His radical *Political Register*, established in 1802, soon sold nearly as many copies as *The Times*. As in the United States, he was frequently sued; unlike in America, however, he spent time in prison for seditious libel and had to edit his journal in gaol. In 1817, after the British government suspended the writ of *habeas corpus* Cobbett thought it advisable to return to

America. His career, however, was already on the wane. He was unable to rekindle his reputation in the United States and, upon return to Britain in 1819, found he had equally lost much of his power there. Having noted that, he ended his days as an MP (for Oldham) in the first Parliament after the 1832 Reform Act – an event to which he, as much as anyone, had contributed.

When in the United States, Cobbett justified Britain in its war against France; when in Britain, he defended (up to a point) the Americans in the War of 1812. Thus, when in the United States, he was a John Bull; when in Britain he was a fervently pro-American Briton. So, while Cobbett generally admired the United States and its people, he was also a British patriot. This is a crucial point, one that always needs to be remembered when it comes to any discussion of Anglo-American relations – including especially political thought – in the nineteenth century. For, to properly understand British views of the United States, one first needs to comprehend British conceptions of themselves, their society and its political structure. How Britons, radicals included, viewed the United States, its society and political order, was very different to how America saw it. Of particular importance were the competing nationalisms or national myths of both nations – something that is all too often forgotten when it comes to discussion of what was arguably the most nationalist century in history.[2]

The story of the development of democracy – including the usual battery of qualifiers defining what is meant by the term – is a topic beyond the parameters of this study. To even hope to do the subject anything approaching justice would require a separate book. What the above example is meant to illustrate is that there was, during the nineteenth century, a transatlantic dialogue (or, if one prefers, a debate) on the nature of both representative and liberal government – to which we refer in shorthand as 'democracy'. Until the 1960s, historians were generally content to repeat the story – which, by no coincidence, was largely conceived in America during the celebrations surrounding the 1876 centennial of the nation's founding – that British radicals and liberals greatly admired the United States for its democratic order while conservatives and reactionaries generally despised the latter for the same reason. One might call this the 'beacon of freedom' interpretation after a popular work published in the 1950s. Despite its still being rather lazily repeated, subsequent and rather more rigorous scholarship has established that this model is far too simplistic, and that throughout the nineteenth century British views of the United States, its society and

political order, were always far more complicated, complex and, ultimately, sophisticated than this.[3]

For example, the precise meaning of the term 'democracy' remained
in flux in Britain throughout the nineteenth century. While the term
'republic' evoked numerous models, from Switzerland to the United
States, through to the historical examples of the Dutch Republic or the
city-state of Venice, it at least usually implied rule of law and the
defence of personal liberty. This was why that acerbic visitor to
America, Frederick Marryat, could claim that 'It is singular to remark,
notwithstanding her monarchical form of government, how much more
republican England is in her institutions than America.' By contrast, the
term democracy almost always evoked the French Revolution and the
Terror that is mob rule and the suppression of individual rights. This
primarily illiberal and negative definition endured in Britain even after
the appearance of Alexis de Tocqueville's *Democracy in America* and the
American Civil War. This was unsurprising as nineteenth-century
Britons always paid far more attention to political developments in
Europe than they did to America. Indeed, as late as 1880, Edward Dicey
complained that the term democracy in Britain was synonymous with
the French Revolution, not the American – a fact he bemoaned. The
People's Charter, meantime, never used the word 'democracy' or
'democratic' even though its call for universal (male) suffrage was, in
our eyes, democratic. Even John Bright and Richard Cobden, who loved
the United States not wisely but well, even after most other radicals had
given up on it, both eschewed the term democracy. Bright specifically
denied being a democrat, declaring, 'I never accepted that title, and
believe those who know me and speak honestly of me never applied it to
me. What I am in favour of is such freedom as will give security to
people, but I am not in favour of that freedom which will destroy it.'
Cobden, meantime, while stating in 1835 that Britain must match the
'improved [political] management of the Americans', nonetheless
added, 'let us not be misconstrued. We do not advocate Republican
institutions for this country ... Democracy forms no element in the
material of English character.' Here Cobden was going even further
than most conservatives, who acknowledged that Britain was at least
partially democratic. For example, as early as 1835, the conservative
Quarterly Review cited no less of an authority than Sir William Black-
stone's declaration in his *Commentaries on the Laws of England* (1765–
69) that the British Constitution was a combination of three elements:
monarchy, aristocracy and democracy. In nineteenth-century Britain

the political discourse centred on the idea of liberty under law and the promotion of liberal institutions. This certainly involved the extension of the electoral franchise, but it included a lot more besides and democracy was a term that even most political radicals avoided.[4]

As for the United States, while the term democracy enjoyed a more positive reputation, even here there were reservations. The Framers of the Constitution took a dim view of the term democracy (although some later changed their views) which they also associated with mob rule and put in place the checks and balances precisely to curtail it. Further, while the word democracy was undeniably used in the public discourse by the 1830s, and the Democratic Party (which only jettisoned the word 'Republican' in 1844) existed, American politicians remained circumspect when it came to the term. Andrew Jackson avoided the word in his public addresses and Abraham Lincoln, meanwhile, preferred the expression 'popular government'. In fact, the first President to refer to the United States as a democracy in a public address was Woodrow Wilson during the First World War. In any event, using the term democracy in relation to nineteenth-century societies means overlooking restrictions on race and sex. Considering that women make up over half the population in all societies that do not practise female infanticide, not to mention the civil rights movement and anti-colonial struggles in the second half of the last century, the truth is that democracy is not a nineteenth- but a twentieth-century phenomenon.[5]

During the nineteenth century, the United States regarded itself as the land of liberty. The Declaration of Independence and its second paragraph's 'We hold these truths to be self-evident, that all men are created equal, that they are endowed by their Creator with certain unalienable Rights, that among these are Life, Liberty and the Pursuit of Happiness', in addition to a Constitution whose opening words are 'We the People', certainly represented a further development in the history of political liberalization – as did both the English Civil War (1642–51) and Glorious Revolution (1688–89) which preceded them. Even if the United States began as a republic with property qualifications for the franchise, by the end of the 1840s, and the era popularly referred to as 'Jacksonian America', these were either largely being done away with or were greatly reduced. This process, it should be noted, was not always peaceful or even properly completed. For example, Rhode Island was the site of Dorr's rebellion, where the urban poor, finding themselves denied the vote enjoyed by wealthy landowners, organized a 'People's Convention' to agitate for the franchise in 1841–42 – actions remarkably similar to the Chartist activism in Britain. Faced with the continuing unrest, even in the face of martial law, Rhode Island's politicians instituted a new constitution offering some reform but which still restricted the franchise to property owners and tax-payers. It also maintained overrepresentation of the rural at the expense of the urban areas – a process not entirely dissimilar to Britain's 'rotten boroughs'. That said, a process of democratization in the United States was clearly underway – even if at this point it was limited to white males. Throughout the century, Americans would associate their national identity with liberty. Certainly, many agreed with them both then and since – as the waves of immigrants and refugees to the United States clearly attest.[6]

The Americans, however, were not the only people who equated their national identity with liberty. As numerous scholars have demonstrated, the notion of Britain as the land of liberty was a crucial part of the British national identity – both before and long after the War of Independence. Indeed, it was during this period that Thomas Babbington Macaulay was identifying such a past for the British in his *History of England* (1848–62) in the manner akin to American George Bancroft's efforts for his fellow countrymen in his *History of the United States* (1834–1873). Further, there is plenty of evidence demonstrating that numerous Europeans agreed with this British self-assessment – even after the War of Independence. For example, the father of Arthur Schopenhauer (1788–1860) had wanted his son to be born in Britain because that would ensure a claim to British nationality and all the rights and privileges that came with it (alas for British philosophy, Schopenhauer's mother frustrated the plan). A young Russian sub-lieutenant posted to Sebastopol in the Crimean War by the name of Leo Tolstoy, recorded the lectures on British liberty he received from British prisoners-of-war. Friedrich Engels, certainly no uncritical admirer of Britain, declared in his preface to Karl Marx's *Das Kapital* that it was 'undeniably the freest, or least unfree, country in the world'. Polish-born Joseph Conrad declared that 'liberty can only be found under the British flag all over the world'. Sigmund Freud expressed similar sentiments in 1875 although he, ultimately, would move to America – after having been detained by the Gestapo in the 1930s. Yet this example brings us to the Second World War when, even as late as this, Simone Weil, the Parisian writer, Marxist and anarchist, wondered why Britain alone had maintained 'a centuries-old tradition of liberty guaranteed by the authorities'.[7]

Furthermore, if the United States offered a refuge for European radicals and immigrants, so too did Britain, for the latter had a long history of doing so, starting with the Huguenots in the seventeenth century. One refugee, the German radical, Gottfried Kinkel, declared in 1866 that Britain was the only country 'which has never expelled a refugee', adding 'It gives elbow room to every man, a field for his labour and energy, and full liberty to build up his house by his labours, without demanding in return a denial of his principles or the sacrifice of his character.' Many Europeans took refuge in Britain after the failed revolutions of 1848, including Italians, Hungarians, French and Germans. Among the more famous asylum seekers in Britain during the nineteenth century were Giuseppe Mazzini, Italian patriot; Victor Hugo, who resided in Guernsey; and Karl Marx; Marx's analysis of capitalism being based in large part on what he witnessed while living as an asylum-seeker in Britain.[8]

Britain also provided a haven for large numbers of Jews throughout the nineteenth century (some 65,000 lived there by 1880), seeking sanctuary from pogroms and other anti-Semitic activities on the continent. Although anti-Semitism undeniably existed in Britain as well – there are the examples of Fagin in Dickens's *Oliver Twist* (1837–38) and Augustus Melmotte in Anthony Trollope's *The Way We Live Now* (1875) plus stereotypical cartoons in the British press – it was apparently less virulent in Britain than elsewhere. Certainly British society was tolerant to the extent that Benjamin Disraeli could become Prime Minister in 1868. Disraeli, of course, was not an immigrant – but his father was one. Nor was Disraeli's political success an isolated example. By 1869 there were six Jewish MPs in the House of Commons and many more individuals had been ennobled or knighted.[9]

Even European governments commented on Britain's reputation for being a place of asylum. The Italian ambassador's protest that Britain, in effect, acquiesced in the large migration from his newly unified nation in 1874 (some three-quarters of a million people left Italy as a result of the political upheavals), attracted a response from *Chamber's Journal* that 'England is very chary of making restrictions on the freedom of entry of foreigners on our shores. Deposed emperors and kings, princes in trouble, defeated presidents and past presidents, persecuted ecclesiastics, patriots out of work – all find an asylum in little England.' Indeed, it was not merely radicals who took advantage of British sanctuary: Louis Philippe, one time King of France, Prince Metternich of Austria, and the French Empress Eugénie Bonaparte, not to say

Napoleon III himself, were all, at one time or another, asylum seekers in Britain.[10]

It was, in fact, this European view of Britain as the home of liberty that Alexis de Tocqueville in part sought to challenge with his *Democracy in America* (the two volumes of which appeared in 1835 and 1840, respectively) by specifically demonstrating to Europeans, particularly to his fellow countrymen, that instead of looking across the English Channel for lessons in political reform, they might instead more profitably gaze upon the republic across the Atlantic. This is not to claim that *Democracy in America* was an exercise in taunting *les rosbifs* – that would be absurd – it is merely to point out that the notion of competing liberalisms was apparent to those who were neither British nor American.

As it happened, Tocqueville visited Britain in 1833, the year after his trip to the United States, partly for romantic reasons (to pursue his courtship of Mary Mottley whom he married) but also because he was already at work on his *magnum opus* and, as the editor of his correspondence observes, he probably believed that he could not completely understand American political and social institutions without some familiarity with British ones. Making the acquaintance of numerous British liberals and radicals, including John Stuart Mill, John Arthur Roebuck and George Grote, among others, Tocqueville was given a good introduction to the British political system. Indeed, Tocqueville visited shortly after another milestone in the democratization of Britain, the 1832 Reform Act, something that helped convince him of the proof of his theory, expressed in his masterpiece, that democracy represented the future. This also meant that his account held different lessons for the British – or rather, they took from it different lessons – than did either American or European readers; an important point that has generally not been recognized.[11]

This would account for the near-universal acclamation with which *Democracy in America* was received in Britain: the conservative *Quarterly Review* praising it as much as liberal journals. Considering the work predicted that democratization represented the future, this appears virtually impossible, but there were reasons for this. Tocqueville's proposition was a far less incendiary version than that of the French Revolution. Nor was he entirely semantically clear in his use of the term '*démocratie*'; which was interpreted to mean either a bourgeois, capitalist society or an egalitarian society at large. Further, as too many readers of Tocqueville forget, the Frenchman had numerous criticisms regarding the United States, including references to the 'tyranny of the majority' and the threat to individual independence of thought. Sir Robert Peel, for one, quoted from the work in Parliament, and at his inaugural address as Lord Rector of the University of Glasgow cited it as evidence of the superiority of the British political system. As Tocqueville's English translator (and friend) Henry Reeve noted in 1861,

> It was hailed with equal satisfaction by the ardent friends of democracy and by those who dread the exclusive predominance of democratic power. The former were gratified by M. de Tocqueville's admission of the preponderance of this great element in modern societies, and by his prediction of its future dominion over the world; the latter were no less struck by the acuteness with which he pointed out its tendency to favour absolute government, and to degrade the noblest faculties of man.

Indeed, so often did conservatives cite *Democracy in America* with approval that John Stuart Mill complained they 'fancied it was a Tory book'.[12]

Despite Mill's comment, conservative thought regarding the work showed a remarkable degree of variety. Take the response of *Blackwood's* review of the second volume. Here, Tocqueville's nationality was faulted, his work being judged to be the product of typical French theorizing. American democracy, insisted the reviewer, was piecemeal and practical, earthy and concrete in the British fashion, rather than abstract like the French: 'The words democracy and equality have a noticeable diversity of signification in the apprehension of the Frenchman and the American.' Indeed, the reviewer argued that Tocqueville might have been (allegedly) less pessimistic about the future had he realized 'that the *Real* in the two freest countries on the face of the globe, is much more than an overmatch for the *Ideal* in France, and is able to counter-balance and counteract its effects very sufficiently'. By this reading, American democracy was merely another form of British liberty – rather than a genuinely new departure in human history.[13]

Further, while Mill might have complained about British conservatives' appropriation or misrepresentation of Tocqueville's work, ultimately a similar charge could be laid against him. In many respects, he was second only to Henry Reeve in determining British understanding of *Democracy in America* by his analyses of the two volumes in the *London Review* in 1835 and the *Edinburgh Review* in 1840. As one scholar has pointed out, Mill somewhat amended Tocqueville's analysis, and in doing so made the work more palatable to the middle class. Mill insisted that Britain was already transforming into a democratic society, proposing that the process of democracy in America was equivalent to British commercialization (meaning industrialization, urbanization and bourgeois values). In fact, he went so far in his review of Tocqueville's second volume as to claim that,

> To most purposes, in the constitution of modern society, the government of a numerous middle class is democracy. Nay, it not merely *is* democracy, but the only democracy of which there is any yet example; what is called universal suffrage in America arising from the fact, that America is *all* middle class; the whole people being in a condition, both as to the education and the pecuniary means, corresponding to the middle class here.

Mill argued that the supremacy of the middle class had been achieved by the 1832 Reform Act and that even the aristocracy was turning bourgeois. In effect, Mill downplayed the revolutionary element of Tocqueville's analysis in favour of the evolutionary one by claiming that the differences between the British and American political systems were essentially superficial and that, in effect, they were arriving at the same destination by alternative routes.[14]

There was another aspect to Mill's interpretation that ought to be noted. Both Mill and Tocqueville believed to some degree that democratic societies were essentially philistine, their inevitable homogeneity of thought resulting in intellectual stagnation, particularly in the fields of philosophy, morality and culture. In order to offset this, Mill offered a solution: in order to push public opinion in the correct direction, 'there should exist somewhere a great social support for opinions and sentiments different from those of the mass'. It just so happened that such a support could be found in Britain's leisured and learned class and that its existence was the great natural advantage Britain had over the United States: as Mill added: 'and we believe that the interests of the time are greatly dependent upon preserving them'. Mill pursued this idea in his *Considerations on Representative Government* (1861) and again in an amendment to the 1867 Reform Act. Although he failed in the last measure, his notion of the demos being guided by political elites enjoyed a certain degree of success. In some respects, this concept of how democracy should function remains a distinction between the British (and for that matter, European) and American versions – an elitist, rather than genuinely popular, democracy.[15]

In any case, Tocqueville's ideas were subtly altered even before Mill's analysis by the work's first translator, Henry Reeve, who had his own agenda. Although Reeve was a cosmopolitan who championed liberty in Europe, he was no democrat and proved unsympathetic to radical aspirations in Britain. Much as Reeve personally liked Tocqueville and admired his work, he nonetheless believed that while *Democracy in America* revealed much about the United States and held lessons for France, the institution in Britain would have to be modified to suit the nation's peculiar national heritage. As Reeve once declared, Tocqueville was writing for the people of France just as Machiavelli wrote *The Prince* for Caesar Borgia. Reeve's position was recognized by Tocqueville himself who admonished him in 1839: 'I think that, influenced by your opinions, you have, in your translation, unwittingly coloured too highly all I say against democracy.' Reeve replied by arguing that the British people were monarchical, not republican and that, lacking America's vast territory, Britain had less room for political experimentation. He thus remained sceptical regarding the relevance of the work to British conditions – an argument Tocqueville accepted, up to a point.[16]

In some respects, both Reeve and Tocqueville were proven correct, but Reeve's, Mill's and numerous conservatives' analyses of *Democracy in America* all point to an unavoidable conclusion – that when it came to the American political system, the British approach was always *à la carte*. This was to be expected. With a tradition of representative government that could be credibly traced back to the seventeenth century, combined with a history of evolving and expanding liberties, to say nothing of a marked world lead in modernization in the form of industrialization and urbanization, or indeed that Britain was an international, rather than regional, power, the example Britons would draw upon from a largely agrarian republic (and one that maintained slavery as an institution) was always going to be extremely limited. It would be an unusual Briton indeed who viewed the United States in the same manner as a French liberal, coming from a different political, philosophical and historical tradition, in the manner of Tocqueville.[17]

In any case, British political thought regarding the United States was never static or monolithic – even within the radical, conservative and liberal camps. Indeed, by the time both volumes of Tocqueville's work appeared, British radical thinking regarding the United States had undergone something of a shift. Although British radicalism had always been divided on the subject of the United States – there was always an anti-American William Hazlitt for every pro-American William Cobbett – it was in the decades immediately after the Napoleonic wars, in the 1820s and 30s, that the high-water mark of radical interest in the

United States occurred. Led by the Utilitarians, including founder Jeremy Bentham, James Mill (father of John Stuart), George Grote, Harriet Martineau and John Arthur Roebuck, radicals made positive references to the United States and its lack of aristocracy (albeit tempered by criticism of both slavery and tariffs). Even so, Utilitarian admiration for the United States illustrates how radicals could use aspects of the American political system to argue a point, while ignoring others inconvenient to their thinking. So, for example, Bentham's contempt for Lockean (and thus, Jeffersonian) notions of inalienable natural rights and the contract theory of government led to his dismissal of the Declaration of Independence as 'a hodge podge of confusion and absurdity', consisting of 'jargon'. Yet this document, even more so than the Constitution, was the fundamental basis of the American political creed, illustrating a clear difference between Benthamite radicalism and the United States' founding ideals.[18]

More significantly, by the 1840s and 50s, British radicals' admiration for the United States began to decline. There were a number of reasons for this. In the first instance, the increasing amount of available information about the United States, thanks to improved methods of transport and communication, made it increasingly difficult to selectively cite those aspects about the United States that upheld one's arguments in the manner of the Utilitarians. There was now contradictory evidence on hand for the critics, and the problems of American society could no longer be ignored. In the second, insofar as many middle-class radicals were concerned, the liberalization of the British state, including the repeal of restrictions against Dissenters and Catholics by 1829, a process that culminated in the 1832 Reform Act, essentially gave them what they wanted. Having thus secured the vote for themselves, they found the example of the United States to be increasingly less useful.[19]

At the same time, working-class radicals, frequently abandoned by their former allies, increasingly rejected middle-class doctrines of laissez-faire and began exploring the necessity of what we now call 'economic justice', an issue regarding which the United States held no obvious lessons. By the 1850s, opposition to laissez-faire ideals was established among the ranks of organized labour. Demands for economic justice, and curbs upon the powers of the market, were now commonplace. Chartists such as James 'Bronterre' O'Brien, Ernest Jones and John Francis Bray had all made reference to 'wage slavery' and the need for economic justice by the 1840s. By 1851, looking towards the

United States, Jones declared, 'Wealth [in America] is beginning to centralize. It is in its nature – all other evils follow in its wake. It should be the duty of government to counteract that centralisation by laws of a distributive tendency.' In other words, Jones was discussing government redistribution of wealth – or, if one prefers, proto-socialism. Something Jones, and most every other working-class radical, knew was not practised in the United States.[20]

These changing radical views of the United States were already apparent during the period of Chartism (1837–54). One can, of course, locate positive references to the United States in Chartist writings and speeches – provided one expressly looks for them. What is more notable about Chartist references to America is their comparative rarity. Further, such references as there are to the United States in Chartist literature are not necessarily positive, especially on the part of those who actually visited the place. Thus, John Alexander, correspondent to O'Brien, writing in *The Reformer* declared that 'I expected to find America a few degrees better than England, but it is not – it is worse; it is, in fact, a hopeless condition as regards either moral, political or intellectual progression.' Another radical who went out to the United States and returned disillusioned was Thomas Brothers, who published *The United States of North America as They Really Are: Not as They Are Generally Described* (1840). Finally, G. J. Harney, editor of the *Northern Star*, remained sourly sceptical of the United States, to the extent that commentary on America within the journal's pages was as often hostile as friendly. These were hardly unique assessments; as one scholar, sympathetic to the 'beacon of freedom' school of thought acknowledges, while workers left for America in their thousands, they also returned in very large numbers (as we have elsewhere noted, by possibly as much as a third of those who went out). When these men returned, they frequently did so angry and embittered against the United States.[21]

The example of American universal white male suffrage certainly carried appeal for numerous Chartists, but was tempered by the increasing awareness of the society's problems, particularly those pointed out by disillusioned visitors. Indeed, by 1846, even the conservative journal *Blackwood's* noted increased Chartist dissatisfaction with the example of the United States. Not all radicals abandoned the example of the United States, but fewer and fewer shared Cobden's and Bright's admiration for it. Nor is this to claim that working-class radicals became anti-American, merely that as the nineteenth century progressed, their enthusiasm tempered and their views became decid-edly more critical and noticeably less inherently pro-American.[22]

In the case of British conservatives, they rarely referred to the United States, the American example having little influence on their thought. When, on rare occasions, conservatives did refer to the United States, their response was determined less by political notions and rather more by America's conduct towards Britain. For conservatives, there was no essential difference between the United States or any one of Britain's other imperial rivals – as the War of 1812 and continued diplomatic squalls, in their eyes, conclusively demonstrated. Disparaging comments by conservatives about American democracy certainly exist, but they are greatly outnumbered by criticisms of the nation's foreign policy. Fur-ther, nineteenth-century conservatism was sophisticated enough to tackle the United States on a variety of issues, such as the various American states' repudiation of their debt, which offended many commentators. As Voltaire had observed as early as 1733, the British gave 'the name of infidel to none but bankrupts'. Sectionalism, as demonstrated by the Nullification Crisis, political corruption, violence, American-Canadian boundary disputes, and Manifest Destiny resulting in a war of aggression against Mexico, all provoked far more con-servative commentary on the United States than any theoretical 'beacon of freedom' arguments such as they might occasionally hear from British radicals or, far more likely, from American chauvinists.[23]

What conservatives were aware of was the importance of the United States to British commerce, and they tailored their views accordingly. As early as 1820, Robert Banks Jenkinson, 2nd Earl of Liverpool, the Prime Minister, informed the House of Lords that, 'of all the powers on the face of the earth, America is the one whose increasing population and immense territory furnish the best prospect of a ready market for British produce and manufactures. Every man, therefore, who wishes pros-perity to England, must wish prosperity to America.' This theme was to be a staple of *Quarterly Review*'s contributor John Wilson Croker, who pointed out that 'New York is but a suburb of Liverpool, or, if you will, Liverpool of New York ... We are not merely brothers and cousins – the ties of consanguinity, we know, are not always the bond of friendship – but we are *partners* – *joint tenants*, as it were in the commerce of the world.' Not that all conservatives viewed America in terms of trade – one of the reasons *Blackwood's* retained the American John Neal as a contributor was expressly to increase its coverage and thus understanding of the United States. John Barrow, meanwhile, contributor to the *Quarterly Review* during the 1820s and 30s, was generally pro-American – except when it came to the nation's foreign policy. Conservative thinking about the United States, then, was shaped by numerous factors, both positive and negative, and this was reflected in its commentary which was, in short, highly ambiguous.[24]

If British conservatism's and radicalism's views of the United States varied, those of the liberals or Whigs are even more difficult to qualify. Whigs tended to sympathize with the broad characteristics of American liberalism and emphasized the economic links and similarity of the political traditions between the two countries. American public education, cheap government and aspects of its political system all came in for praise. (The issue of separation of church and state in America received much less attention than is commonly alleged, chiefly because established churches existed in individual states until 1833 or, in other words, up until restrictions against Catholics and dissenters had been lifted in Britain.) Liberal esteem for the United States, however, was always liable to be disillusioned, not because of radical notions of economic justice, but because of many of the same complaints conservatives cited, such as American foreign policy, the repudiation of states' debts, and Manifest Destiny. British liberals complained of American 'swagger', criticized their culture (or, as they saw it, the lack thereof) and could never reconcile themselves either to slavery or to tariffs. As free trade was virtually the Gospel of British liberalism, which they saw as being as much a moral, as commercial, issue, American adherence to protectionism was always going to be taken as an affront. Thus, while not necessarily hostile, most British liberals regarded the United States with a fair degree of scepticism or suspicion.

This scepticism was liable to be applied to the American system of government. Not all, certainly, but many British liberals were suspicious of written constitutions such as the American version, which they regarded as inflexible and a bar to progress. Indeed, one of the problems with slavery in the United States was its constitutional protection. One example is Nassau Senior, who said of America, 'with the exception of our own, we know of no country whose institutions we prefer', but nonetheless complained,

> It [the constitution] has on the whole been successful, but it is an unpleasant symptom that its success has not been progressive ... In the British Islands, where apparent changes have been the least, the real changes, and the real improvements, have perhaps been the greatest. But in

the constitution of the United States, few changes have been made; and most of those have been either unimportant or mischievous.

Other liberal complaints regarding the United States included the spoils system, presidential patronage, corruption, violence and Anglophobia, the last of which they regarded as wholly unreasonable and a barrier to closer cooperation between the two nations. Again, this is not to suggest unremitting hostility towards America on the part of British Whigs, merely that their views of the United States were always malleable. Essentially, for liberals, the United States was the quintessential curate's egg: excellent in parts, execrable in others.[25]

That British political views of the United States varied so widely, changed and generally remained in flux, reflected the relationship between the two nations. Another reason is that the information Britons received about the United States became more sophisticated as the century wore on. This was true of British travel accounts of the United States, the range of which improved from the 1830s onwards as the trip across the Atlantic became easier. An increase in published accounts meant that individuals' claims were now subject to scrutiny by others, resulting in a greater degree of accuracy and honesty, if not understanding. Indeed, according to one scholar, some 230 travel accounts of the United States were published in Britain between 1836 and 1860. Thus, British understanding of the United States, for better or for worse, increased as the century wore on; this rather more 'warts and all' portrait, to use Oliver Cromwell's phrase, to say nothing of the rocky diplomatic relationship between the two countries, could not help but affect British views of America far beyond any idealized notions regarding its political structure. So, although scholars have attempted to compartmentalize British travel writing of the United States into various political camps, much of it resists this categorization. Indeed, only a minority of accounts expressly concerned themselves with the American political system, authors being more likely to make observations on the society and its inhabitants as a whole.[26]

This was certainly true of that infamous nineteenth-century British travel account, Frances Trollope's *Domestic Manners of the Americans* (1832) which, far from being a reasoned political critique – and she was not a Tory but if anything an early feminist – simply attacked the society as a whole. The great offence Trollope's work caused is now almost proverbial (and she followed up on her success with a series of insulting novels about the United States, too). In many respects, her book achieved the success that eluded her on a sojourn America in 1827–31 where she had tried to establish a business in Cincinnati. Her trenchant and frankly contemptuous observations, which included sneers about American prudery (she claimed Shakespeare was described as obscene), backwoods piety (she described hysterical scenes at a Methodist camp-meeting in Ohio) and boastfulness (she noted bragging about the War of 1812) would be repeated by a score of other British writers. As would her denunciations of American materialism, about which she was especially scathing:

> I heard an Englishman, who had long been resident in America, declare that in following, in meeting, or in overtaking, in the street, on the road, or in the field, at the theatre, the coffee-house, or at home, he had never overheard Americans conversing without the word DOLLAR being pronounced between them. Such unity of purpose, such sympathy of feeling, can, I believe, be found nowhere else, except, perhaps, in an ants' nest. The result is exactly what might be anticipated. This sordid object, for ever before their eyes, must inevitably produce a sordid tone of mind, and, worse still, it produces a seared and blunted conscience on all questions of probity.

Of course, if we are going to mention stereotypes, this account is a classic example of two expatriate Britons being condescending about the natives. There was not, in fact, a lot about the United States of which Trollope approved but not all her criticism was spurious. For example, she condemned slavery and the high levels of violence in America – something that concerned a lot of other writers as well.[27]

The notion of political divisions within British travel writing is especially problematic when it comes to the two most widely read British accounts after Trollope's (and Charles Dickens's) in the years prior to 1860, Captain Frederick Marryat's *A Diary in America* (1839) and Harriet Martineau's *Society in America* (1837). Although they have been described respectively as the conservative and the liberal view of the United States (and, more crudely, as negative and positive accounts), this fails to do either author justice and obscures a lot. Certainly nineteenth-century Americans did not make such a distinction between the two – they hated Martineau's work almost as much as they did Marryat's. Further, just how much of a Tory was Marryat is debatable. His one foray into politics was to stand for election as Liberal MP in 1833 (he lost). Further, Marryat was no intellectual, being instead a man of action and a popular author of nautical novels based on his experiences in the Royal Navy during the Napoleonic wars. Marryat's views of the United States were thus less theoretical and rather more practical – he had fought in the War of 1812, in which he had won innumerable certificates for personal gallantry. Then there were the circumstances surrounding his trip, which would have coloured the views of any individual and gave Marryat apparent reasons for declaring that America was not a republic, but a 'mobocracy'.

Marryat arrived during the depression of 1837 and thus visited the United States at a time of crisis. Further, although he initially received a warm reception from a nation still angry at Martineau's and Trollope's accounts (his novels were popular in America, too), events conspired against his trip. In 1837, there were rebellions in Upper and Lower Canada (and that they were celebrated by the Americans resurrected concerns in Britain about the former's annexationist impulses). Marryat, ever the loyal subject, volunteered his services to the Crown and saw action in the thickest part of the fighting at two engagements (St Eustache and St Benoit) between the rebels and colonial forces. That did not endear him to the Americans. What endeared him even less was Marryat's speech at a public dinner in Toronto on St George's Day where he toasted the Canadian militia who burned the *Caroline*. This was a rebel boat that was set alight in American waters, an event, as we shall see, that sparked not one, but two, diplomatic crises. When Marryat returned to the United States, he had the dubious pleasure of seeing not just his books fuelling bonfires, but his being burned in effigy at least twice. His riposte, that he would celebrate British victories on British soil, hardly helped matters. Indeed, on two occasions, he had to confront angry mobs who wanted to make their dissatisfaction with the Captain even clearer.

In light of such an eventful trip, one that included becoming publicly embroiled in a sexual scandal with one Mrs Collyer (the lady was willing, her husband was not, and ambushed them together in a hotel room – only Marryat's threat of a duel ended the matter), it was hardly surprising that the Captain took a dim view of the United States. Not that his account was altogether negative. Besides his expressed appreciation of American women, he also took America's side against Frances Trollope, reporting (rather ungallantly) the views of Cincinnati's citizens that, because she was a married woman travelling without a chaperone, the decent elements of society had avoided her. Further, the Captain declared outright that 'with all its imperfections, democracy is the form of government *best suited to the present condition of America*, insofar as it is the one under which the country has made, and will continue to make, the most advances'. He also expressed a number of honest concerns derived from his circumstances. Considering, as he saw it, the likely possibility of another Anglo-American war, Marryat declared 'the Americans have been ready to bully or quarrel with any-body and about anything', and warned:

> The idea of their own prowess will be one cause of danger to their insti-
> tutions, for war must ever be fatal to democracy. In this country [Britain],
> during peace we have become more and more democratic; but whenever we
> are again forced into war, the reins are again tightened from necessity, and
> thus war must ever interfere with free institutions.

While one applauds this view that neither nation's free institutions would be helped by conflict, there was always the other side of Marryat. Despite his repeated public declarations that he had come neither to ridicule the United States, nor to spy on it, he proved otherwise on both points: besides the acerbic opinions in his account, one of his souvenirs for the Admiralty was a map of the New York Navy Yard. More important, however, is the fact that the Captain's contemporaries never treated his work as a serious political analysis of the United States and this is especially true of British conservatives. The Tory press, for example, entirely ignored his book. Thus, there is no evidence to sup-port the contention that the opinions of this rake – or, if one prefers, rough diamond – represented serious conservative thought regarding the United States.[28]

Harriet Martineau's views of the United States were more cerebral and penetrating than the Captain's and she worked from a more solid base, for she lived there from 1834–37. Martineau, who became closely involved with American abolitionism, was largely positive about the United States and its society. Yet, even so, her account contained numerous serious criticisms. She considered the 1836 presidential campaign of Martin Van Buren to be duplicitous and corrupt, noting, for example, that some individuals cast as many as nine votes. This was a staple complaint of British visitors in the age of Tammany Hall. This, the Democratic Party organization in New York, effectively became the controlling interest of the city's elections from the 1830s until the end of the century. Violence, intimidation and political corruption were hall-marks of the Tammany Hall's activities – and, as such, made a mockery of the ideals of representative government. It was, of course, hardly fair to tar the entire American political system with the brush of Tammany Hall, but because New York was an almost guaranteed starting point for any British visitor to the United States, that city's peculiar political proclivities were invariably noted. Besides political corruption, Martineau, as expected, denounced slavery in no uncertain terms as well as moves towards protectionism and she complained of the high level of violence within American society. Further, for all her thoughtful consideration of the American political system, she claimed that the United States had failed to live up to the principles upon which it was founded. She also expressed serious misgivings about introducing its political notions into Britain. Despite or perhaps because of this, her book was well received in Britain even if not in the United States. It must also be noted that Martineau's reservations were echoed by other sympathetic travel writers such as Alexander MacKay whose work *The Western World* (1850), while generally positive, also noted both political corruption and violence in American society and likewise questioned whether the society's institutions could or should be introduced into Britain.[29]

Without a doubt, Britons saw a very foreign society on the other side of the Atlantic. American egalitarianism in the personal realm struck most visitors, especially the ease with which the President could be visited. Travellers were astonished at how easy it was to meet the chief executive with no more of an introduction than their personal calling cards (in fact, visiting the President soon became almost *de rigeur* for British tourists). The White House receptions where some 3,000 people would crowd in to meet the President also astonished many visitors. J. S. Buckingham, who dedicated his work to Queen Victoria's consort, Prince Albert and declared his hopes of promoting Anglo-American accord, marvelled that, 'the only qualification for admission ... is that of being a citizen of the United States'. Charles MacKay witnessed President James Buchanan shaking hands with ambassadors and 'the veriest "Rowdies" from New York, or "Plug-Uglies" from Baltimore, who either have, or fancy they have, business with him'.[30]

That said, when it came to American egalitarianism, most Britons added an important qualifier. As one scholar notes, Americans, they insisted, although assertively egalitarian in their public dealings with each other, were usually the opposite in their personal relations in private life. All talk of equality and egalitarian society became a farce when applied to the last, according to some British visitors. This was especially noted of established cities, such as Philadelphia and Boston. In the case of the latter, even a sympathetic visitor like Martineau noted the daughters of merchants would not speak to those of grocers at a local girls' school. She regarded this aristocracy of wealth as 'vulgar in the extreme'. James Logan, meanwhile, bluntly stated that 'The "liberty and equality" so much boasted of in America have no existence there. Their independence and their free institutions, which they hold up as a pattern to Europe, are incapable of bearing the close inspection of a Briton, who, on examining the different parts of the social compact, finds them rotten at the core.' Indeed such claims, according to this last visitor, were mere shibboleths.[31]

British criticisms regarding a lack of law and order in American society were common, unchecked violence being allegedly frequent, particularly in the South and West. In a section entitled 'Allegiance to Law', Martineau described a catalogue of robbing, mobbing, lynching and murder. The practice of lynching – whites or blacks – was commented upon by numerous other travellers. Examples of mob activity were frequently noted. William Thomson reported a Cincinnati bank, unable to redeem its notes, being destroyed by a mob that first overcame a guard of soldiers who fired upon it. It was perhaps little wonder that a sympathetic visitor such as Buckingham went so far as to declare that the loss of life did not attract as much attention in America as did the death of a dog in Britain. Even the ostensibly more civilized North-East was apparently not exempt from violence. C. R. Weld, for example, described a murder trial in New York, the crime having taken place at the fashionable St Nicholas Hotel. The murderer received a four-year sentence, the judge ruling that killing was excusable 'if not done in a cruel and unusual manner'. Reports such as these called into question the nature of the American judicial system. W. E. Baxter claimed wealth, influence and bribery procured acquittals more easily than in Britain; punishment, he averred, seldom overtook the rich. James Logan, among others, concurred with this assessment.[32]

Most travellers commented on the high levels of Anglophobia within the United States (which not all of them did a lot to help) and they were not simply magnifying a minor occurrence. For example, it is said that Alexander Cartwright of New York invented baseball in 1845 as a patriotic alternative to cricket – many Americans refusing to play a British game (and thus the world now has two methods of organized loafing instead of one). That alert observer, Tocqueville, meantime declared in 1830 that he could conceive of no hatred more poisonous than that which Americans felt for Britain. More serious was the amount of anti-British sentiment expressed in American political life. Captain Basil Hall complained of 'this eternal vituperation of England

and everything belonging to us', and remarked of Congressional debates,

> there was hardly one speech uttered in the House in the course of this debate, or in others which I heard, wherein the orator did not contrive, adroitly or clumsily, to drag in some abuse of England. It might almost have been thought, from the uniformity of this sneering habit, that there was some express form of the House by which members were bound, at least once in every speech, and as much oftener as they pleased, to take a passing fling at the poor Old Country.

Certainly, this phenomenon had a far greater impact on Hall's views of the United States than the fact he was a Tory as is commonly alleged. Not that Hall was actually that ill-disposed towards the American system of government. For example, reviewing *Democracy in America*, he acquiesced in Tocqueville's praise of the inbuilt checks of the American system, and also declared that it depicted 'not only the true situation of that extraordinary people, but the true causes of their social political situation'. Indeed, Hall went so far as to congratulate Tocqueville on correcting many of his own misapprehensions regarding the United States.[33]

Slavery was noted by almost every travel writer, as was anti-black sentiment in the free states. Most travellers to the United States opposed the institution, although there were exceptions – particularly among those who had family or business connections in the South. Yet the racism of the free states attracted attention as well (even Marryat, not especially sympathetic to the plight of African Americans, noticed it). Charles MacKay (who in 1859, dismissed the possibility of civil war) remarked that those who talked loudest of liberty and equality were the most likely to express contempt for blacks. On the other hand, Britons' naïve willingness to discuss the institution, particularly in the South, could land them in trouble, particularly as the sectional crisis intensified. As early as the 1830s, Buckingham declared that the word 'abolitionist' was as bad as the term 'murderer' in the South. By the 50s, British visitors to the South complained of being under surveillance in a region suspicious of strangers who might be abolitionists. Certainly, most commentary about the region was negative. Poverty, decay and retrogression were all noted. Richmond, in comparison to other American cities, was said to be in a state of decay. Much the same was said of the slave-owners' plantation homes, which bore no resemblance to the mansions of popular myth. The Earl of Carlisle effectively

summed up British views of the South when he dismissed it as the
'Ireland of America'. Violence and the supposed moral backwardness of
the South were laid at slavery's door. Southern atrocities provoked
comment as well. Martineau, for example, told of two blacks being
burned alive over a slow flame for the attempted rape of a white woman
in Mobile. Part of the reason the Confederate States failed to win any
level of meaningful sympathy among either the British people or political elites during the American Civil War was surely owed to these
negative reports.[34]

Slavery, of course, was the obvious riposte to claims that America was
a free society. Having abolished the institution in the Empire by 1833
(the apprenticeship substitution for children, the last vestige of slavery,
was ended in 1838), and directing an international effort to wipe out the
trade by use of treaties and the Royal Navy, Britain took the world lead
in abolitionism. What this meant, ultimately, was that if the United
States was a good haven for British radicals such as Chartists George
Holyoake and John Campbell, keen to avoid the authorities at home,
Britain and its colonies proved to be very good places of refuge for
American slaves.

One of these American refugees was Frederick Douglass, escaped
slave and abolitionist, who first visited Britain in 1845 on an 18-month
lecture and fund-raising tour. Douglass, who was still 'at large', as the
expression has it (meaning he would be returned to his owners under
the Fugitive Slave Law if on American soil), was a 'refuge from
Republican slavery in monarchical England', as he described it in his
1855 autobiography. It was in Britain that Douglass purchased his
freedom, thanks to a collection organized by Ellen Richardson of
Newcastle. It was also thanks to his stay in Britain – as two scholars have
noted – that Douglass returned home with a more independent and
radical agenda. Thus, part of the reason Douglass arrived in Britain an
escaped slave and left as an altogether more confident spokesman not
merely for abolitionism, but for racial equality, was a direct consequence of his experiences there.[35]

For, if the corollary of American democracy was a relatively class-free
society in the United States, the consequence of British abolitionism was
a greater degree of racial tolerance in Britain. As Douglass remarked,
'Why, sir, the Americans do not know that I am a man. They talk of me
as a box of goods; they speak of me in connection with sheep, horses
and cattle. But here, how different! Why, sir, the very dogs of old
England know that I am a man!' Douglass was not alone in this

assessment. As Herman Melville noted of Liverpool, 'the negro steps with a prouder pace, and lifts his head like a man ... Three or four times I encountered our black steward, dressed very handsomely, and walking arm-in-arm with a good-looking English woman. In New York, such a couple would have been mobbed in three minutes, and the steward would have been lucky to escape with whole limbs.' White and black Americans equally would note the lower levels of anti-black prejudice in Britain, both in the first, and well into the second, half of the nineteenth century.[36]

This brings us to the subject of transatlantic reform movements which, although of less importance to the history of each nation than is sometimes alleged, were nonetheless a presence during the nineteenth century. The impetus behind these movements was evangelicals among the Presbyterians, Congregationalists, Methodists, Baptists and Episcopalians, to say nothing of Quakers and Unitarians, on both sides of the Atlantic who maintained both theological dialogue and activities, whether it was Hannah More's Religious Tract Society (1799) influencing the American Tract Society (1823) or the British and Foreign Bible Society (1804) encouraging the American Bible Society (1816). Theological concerns aside, drink, war and slavery were the three chief demons that united these transatlantic Christian soldiers in holy crusade.

In the case of temperance, the American Society for the Promotion of Temperance (1826) inspired the British and Foreign Temperance Society (1831) and the two joined forces in 1846 to hold the World Temperance Convention, described by one historian as an Anglo-American jamboree. The War of 1812, meantime, and subsequent Anglo-American diplomatic friction, inspired many of the same individuals to form transatlantic Peace Societies. Although British and American peace societies (led, as one might expect, by Quakers) formed independently of each other, by 1828 they were so intertwined that, as one scholar notes, it is impossible to treat them as anything but a single movement. Insisting on arbitration as a method of settling disputes, both societies published journals, the British *Herald of Peace* and the American *Advocate of Peace*, and in 1843, even before the temperance societies, held a World Peace Convention in London, which was another transatlantic affair. While the cynics among us might point to the subsequent history of the world as a measurement of their success, idealists might fairly riposte that there never was another Anglo-American war after 1815 and that the ending of war in general is still a work in progress.[37]

Although it has been claimed that membership of these groups consisted largely of radicals, it is more accurate to designate them as liberals. Further, the majority of British radicals, concentrating on obtaining the vote and economic justice, had no connection to any of them. More importantly, many radicals were contemptuous of these groups, accusing them of focusing on foreign problems as a way of drawing attention away from, and thus evading, altogether more pressing domestic issues. Further, one needs to be careful not to simply treat British and American movements as identical bodies. For example, American abolitionism in the 1830s and after, in the form given it by William Lloyd Garrison, was very much the preserve of radicals. In Britain, however, the situation was very different. The British anti-slavery movement contained liberals, conservatives, radicals and members of the Establishment alike. The President of the British Foreign and Anti-Slavery Society, for example, was none other than Prince Albert. This marked out a crucial political difference between the United States and Britain. Slavery from the 1830s onwards increasingly became an important issue of American politics, one that contributed to (or, indeed, caused) the growing sectionalism within the United States. In Britain, by contrast, the anti-slavery societies began to dwindle and die out, the victims of their own success. Further, there were a host of issues dominating British politics, none of them essentially sectional in nature and none of which involved slavery. This fundamental political divergence determined both the nature of the activities and type of individuals involved within each nation's abolitionist movements. American abolitionists certainly learned from their British counterparts, particularly when it came to organizing skills, involving speeches, publications and petitions, while the remnants of the latter would form a vocal lobby against the Confederacy during the American Civil War. Nonetheless, it was in both cases an example of limited cooperation rather than symbiotic or even parallel development.[38]

In conclusion, as the nineteenth century continued, so too did Anglo-American relations at both the social and political level. People on both sides of the Atlantic commended or condemned what they saw in the other nation according to both taste and inclination. At the same time, one must take good care not to exaggerate either the breadth or the depth of ties between the two nations. For all our talk of a trans-atlantic dialogue, both Anglophobia and anti-Americanism enjoyed widespread existence. Further, many in the United States and Britain were largely indifferent to the other's existence, paying attention only when a diplomatic incident erupted. Moreover, in such cases, the overwhelming tendency of both was to rally around the flag. The nineteenth century was the age of patriotism, to say nothing of nationalism, a fact that determined Anglo-American relations as much as their relationship with other nations. The national identity of the English-speaking nations on either side of the Atlantic might well be founded upon a belief in liberty, but in both cases this was easily trumped by nationalism.

Nor were political progressives any exception. One need only cite as an example the radical John Arthur Roebuck and the liberal John Stuart Mill. Come the American Civil War, their paths would sharply diverge: Mill would defend the North and oppose interference while Roebuck would support the South and demand intervention. Despite this, both believed the same regarding their own nation. Roebuck declared in the 1850s that Britain was on a great mission to propagate its liberal institutions across the globe, that 'liberty and truth have their sacred sphere only in England', that its people were to be an example to others, so that they might say, 'Why can't we be Englishmen?' and rise up against the despotism under which they lived. Mill's 1859 article, 'A Few Words on Non-intervention', meanwhile, justified both the Empire (it was written shortly after the Indian Mutiny) and Britain's intervention in the affairs of other nations. Mill described Britain (and what would later be called the 'Pax Britannica') as 'a novelty in the world', for, in the past,

> Power, from of old, is wont to encroach upon the weak, and to quarrel for ascendancy with those who are as strong as itself. Not so this nation. It will hold its own, it will not submit to encroachment, but if others do not meddle with it, it will not meddle with them. Any attempt it makes to exert influence over them, even by persuasion, is rather in the service of others, than of itself: to mediate in the quarrels which break out between foreign States, to arrest obstinate civil wars, to reconcile belligerents, to intercede for mild treatment of the vanquished, or finally, to procure the abandonment of some national crime and scandal to humanity, such as the slave trade. Not only does this nation desire no benefit to itself at the expense of others, it desires none in which all the others do not as freely participate.

After this declaration, Mill acknowledged that other nations, unable to understand behaviour so foreign to their own conduct, would impute base motives to Britain, which could hardly expect any thanks for its, as he saw it, selfless conduct. All of this, of course, should sound very familiar to the reader, especially when one considers the history of both British and American foreign policy as a whole. Yet ultimately, it raises an important point: what would happen when British liberty ran up against the American version as it had in 1812? This conundrum is the subject of our next chapter.[39]

5

Squabbles and Squalls: The Scramble for North America and the Diplomatic Relationship from 1815 to 1860

Henry Temple, Viscount Palmerston, the British Foreign Secretary, was not one to hide his exasperation. In 1841, following yet another quarrel with the United States over the boundary between that nation and Britain's North American colonies (now Canada), Palmerston expressed his views of the Americans and their government to Lord John Russell, succinctly:

> [I]t never answers to give way, because they always keep pushing on their encroachments as far as they are permitted to do so; and what we dignify by the names of moderation and conciliation, they naturally enough call fear; on the other hand as their system of encroachment is founded very much upon bully, they will give way when in the wrong, if they are firmly and perseveringly pressed.

The United States, then, menaced the security of the North American colonies and thus the territorial integrity of Britain itself. Palmerston spent much of his political career wrangling with the United States, a process that began in the War of 1812 and continued until the end of the American Civil War. These numerous diplomatic disputes, to the exclusion of everything else, conditioned his views on the United States. To Palmerston, Anglo-American difficulties were owed to the fact that the latter were unscrupulous expansionists and utterly unprincipled.

That was one point of view. Another perspective on the overall situation was that of Andrew Jackson. In 1844, a few years after Palmerston's letter to Russell, the former President, frustrated at the delays surrounding the admission of Texas as a state, and noting the Lone Star Republic's flirtations with Britain, wrote to his old political advisor Frank Blair, 'Texas is the key to our future safety', noting that, 'We cannot bear that Great Britain has a Canedy [Canada] on our west as she has on the north.' Thus, Britain was trying to create 'an iron hoop about the United States', in order to control or, indeed, attack the latter from multiple points on land as well as sea. The acquisition of Texas was thus a matter of national security. Jackson's view of the British was determined by the fact he fought them in both the War of Independence and the War of 1812. To Jackson, Anglo-American difficulties stemmed from the fact that the former were opportunistic imperialists, and completely untrustworthy.[1]

Although both Palmerston and Jackson faced political opposition in their day and have divided historians since, both were largely popular with their respective peoples at large, and never more so than when it came to their foreign policy. So, while it must be granted that the 1840s was a difficult time for the Anglo-American relationship, that Jackson was an Anglophobe while Palmerston was anti-American, and also that not everyone in either man's country entirely agreed with them regarding the other nation's merits, these two statesmen's views nonetheless represent the perspective the numerical majority in each country held of the other from 1815 to 1871: that of suspicion and distrust. The sentiment waxed and waned, to be sure, for some periods were better than others, but wariness, misgiving and mistrust were never far beneath the surface even during relatively placid periods. Thanks to roughly a century of largely positive British and American relations, there has been a tendency to discount or play down this nineteenth-century hostility (either that or it has been incorrectly dismissed as being the preserve of a particular political, social or ethnic group on either side of the Atlantic). Yet this sentiment was nonetheless real and it was widespread. Furthermore, both sides had, on the face of it, good reasons for their suspicions.

Nineteenth-century Britain and the United States were imperial powers. Their methods and approaches differed, of course, but expansionists they undeniably were – as any Indian (Asian or American), Maori or Mexican could have attested. During the century, both nations extended their territory (and power) at others' expense without overly concerning themselves about the morality or ethics of such activities (even though there were always opponents to these actions in both nations). That both nations defended their conduct by declarations such as 'an Empire for Liberty' in Thomas Jefferson's words, or in expository essays such as John Stuart Mill's 'A Few Words on Non-intervention', should not blind us to either the realities of the situation or the atrocities that took place. One does not need to accept that either nation behaved worse than other powers or peoples – in fact this author shares the conceit that they often behaved rather better – but it must be acknowledged that self-interest, to the point of predatory behaviour, was a practice of both. So, while there were always both politicians and private individuals who sought Anglo-American accord, the diplomatic relationship between the two countries was shaped primarily by their respective national self-interests. In short, there was nothing inherently benign about either nation's foreign policy, including when it came to dealings with the other.[2]

Britain was the global maritime empire; the United States was a continental one. Britain was an international power; the United States a regional one. Throughout the nineteenth century, Britain remained the United States' chief focus of foreign policy. Of course relations with Britain could be briefly eclipsed by those with Mexico and occasionally by other powers, but it remained the dominant focus. For the British, there could be no such chief focus on any one nation state. Besides their world-wide trading interests, the maintenance of the British Empire involved careful surveillance of what we shall term the three frontiers: the west, the east and the centre. The western frontier, arguably the least important of the three, consisted of Britain's North American and West Indian colonies, and the foreign power most relevant there was the United States. The eastern frontier, the second most important, was represented most significantly by India, and the foreign power most relevant there was Russia. The centre, undeniably the most important of the three frontiers, was Europe, and the power most relevant there was France (and this excludes the British and French international imperial rivalry). Thus, what we now call maintaining the balance of power in Europe combined with colonial interests meant that when it came to British dealings with the United States, American issues could only occasionally take centre stage for, from the British perspective, there were almost always other, more important, concerns in play. In fact, without acknowledging the existence of these concerns, it is impossible to correctly understand the nineteenth-century Anglo-American relationship at all.[3]

The chief bone of contention between Britain and the United States during most of the nineteenth century concerned the demarcation of the Canadian-American frontier. As it is fair to say that nothing brings out the worst in nations more than disputes over territory, it was this issue, above all others, that affected the two countries' perceptions of the other. Far from there being a balance of power issues between them, both the United States and Britain were, in fact, involved in a scramble for the North American continent. Although some historians have claimed that Canada was, in effect, a hostage for the benevolent conduct of the British toward the United States, this assertion would have astonished the inhabitants of both nations during the nineteenth century. For most Americans, Canada was the likely point of origin of any British land assault on the United States (as Jackson's quote demonstrates). To the British, Canada was territory menaced by a covetous neighbour (as Palmerston's statement reveals). As was true of their respective imperial approaches, the United States held the advantage of proximity by land, while Britain held the advantage by control of the seas. These two respective advantages, and it really came down to these, determined how the two nations would settle their differences and, indeed, treat each other, from 1815–71.[4]

That the Canadian-American boundary represented a proper frontier to the two governments can be seen in the negotiations during the 1815 Treaty of Ghent. There, boundary commissions divided the Passamaquoddy Islands (between Maine and New Brunswick) between the two nations and set the line from the St Lawrence River to the western shore of Lake Huron. This was followed by the 1817 Rush-Bagot Treaty (negotiated by British minister to Washington Sir Charles Bagot and then acting secretary of state, Richard Rush) that limited the number of each nation's warships on the Great Lakes – an early example of a strategic arms control treaty. Although an American initiative, it benefited the British rather more as they would find it difficult to match a ship-building race on the Great Lakes (and it was a measure of how little Britain's Canadian colonists trusted the United States that they opposed even this relatively advantageous treaty). In the following year, the Convention of 1818 was signed in London that addressed – although did not entirely solve – outstanding problems regarding fishing off the coasts of Maine, Newfoundland, Nova Scotia and New Brunswick; established the northern boundary of the Louisiana Purchase at the 49th Parallel, from the Lake of the Woods to the Rocky Mountains, leaving the area west of that – the Oregon Territory – as 'free and open'. This was in addition to the extension of a commercial agreement and having Tsar Alexander I act as arbiter as to whether or not the British should pay compensation to American slave-owners for freeing their human chattel on various raids during the War of 1812. The Tsar found in favour of the United States.[5]

Despite this, Anglo-American relations were tested by events resulting from the ripples of the Napoleonic wars – namely, the decline of Spain as an international power. From 1815 onwards, all over what we now term Latin America, the 300-year era of Spanish imperial rule was ending. Popular revolts against Spanish rule took place across the two continents as Argentina, Chile, Peru, Columbia and Mexico declared their independence – and there were rumblings in Cuba as well. The Americans, seeing these independence movements as a vindication of their own principles and precedent, swiftly recognized these new nations. The assessment by Britain, which had important trading relations with Latin America – up to around ten per cent of its export trade by 1825 – was somewhat more mixed. In the first instance, Spain had been Britain's ally in the Napoleonic wars and the latter did not want to ruin relations. In the second, from the British perspective, American proclamations of liberty were often a precursor to territorial acquisition, attempted or otherwise, as in 1812. Were they simply going to take advantage of the upheavals to seize yet more territory? American actions suggested they might. The United States had already exploited Spanish weakness during the War of 1812 and followed up on this by invading Spain's territory, Pensacola, Florida, in 1818.

The architect of this opportunistic act – and like Sir Charles Napier in India 1843, he acted on his own authority – was Andrew Jackson, who, for good measure, judicially murdered (their trial was a kangaroo court) two Britons, Robert Ambrister and Alexander Arbuthnot, who, he claimed, had been arming the Indians. This atrocity caused a storm of outrage in Britain and was viewed by many as an act of war (the Foreign Secretary, Robert Stewart, Viscount Castlereagh, for one believed the British people favoured revenge for Jackson's actions). The British government, however, was less certain. After all, had an American citizen been caught aiding and abetting a native uprising in British territory by a British general, he would have probably met the same fate. So, on these grounds London accepted Jackson's actions as a precedent – one that, as we shall see, would prove fatal for the American adventurer William Walker when he fell into British hands later in the century. Spain, contending with open rebellion in her colonies and faced with the almost inevitable American annexation of Florida, sold the remnants to the United States under the Adams-Onis Treaty of 1819. Confronted by this, and concerned that Cuba would be the United States' next port of call, the British, in 1822, dispatched a squadron to patrol Cuban waters as a warning. The effect was to convince the Americans that the British intended to seize the island for themselves. Thus, for a time, the possibility of a serious collision over the Latin American situation loomed. Suspicion and distrust, fuelled additionally by outrage, were a combustible mixture. That no confrontation in the end took place was largely owed to two facts: (1) neither nation needed another war so soon after the collision of 1812–15, and (2) Britain's tangled relations with Europe would provide an unexpected opportunity to apparently satisfy both British and American national objectives not just in Latin America but, as it turned out, elsewhere, too.[6]

Britain's chief area of concern remained Europe and what to do with not merely a continent, but a world turned upside down by the French Revolution and Napoleon. This was the issue resolved by the Congress of Vienna, 1814–15 which, despite the justifiable criticism voiced of it both at the time and afterwards, proved to be an altogether more durable achievement than the settlement following the First World War. After years of war, Britain's primary objective at Vienna was to secure a lasting peace and it was to this end that a restored France, rather than a humiliated one, was an overriding goal. As Castlereagh declared, 'The establishment of a just equilibrium in Europe [is] the first objective of my attention.' He even insisted on returning to France the colonies seized by the Royal Navy (although, as ever, British idealism was laced with opportunism – Mauritius was kept as an exception, to serve as a base securing the western approaches to the Indian Ocean). Napoleon, observing from St Helena, scoffed, 'What great advantage, what just compensations, has he [Castlereagh] acquired for his country? The peace he has made is the sort of peace he would have made if he had been beaten.' This was an astute question, yet it also revealed the gulf that underpinned the Napoleonic and the British ideologies.[7]

The defeat of Napoleon and the peace established in the aftermath was a palpable repudiation of one of the standard assumptions about the role and function of government in human history. Namely, that a charismatic leader, a central bureaucracy and a large standing army was the most effective way to run a political community. Such a community held the advantage of both discipline and organization and was thus strong enough to both defend itself and dominate its neighbours – the last being the ultimate goal of any state. From ancient Rome through Philip II of Spain through to Louis XIV, this was how historically great powers had been organized. Napoleon (and the French revolutionaries before him) had revised this model by stripping it of its traditional religious and class accoutrements and instead dressed it up in ostensibly progressive clothing such as citizenship, national identity, and even the rights of man – yet the end goal was essentially the same. Indeed, this time the result would have been even more impressive than in the past;

the huge and increasingly interconnected world of Europe and its overseas colonies in every continent meant that the stakes involved had not merely been European, but global.[8]

This was what the British, along with their allies, had finally halted at Waterloo. What was promoted instead was a new idea of political community and, indeed, how said communities should interact. Instead of an absolute leader and centralized bureaucracy, the British preferred parliamentary authority and limited government. Instead of a society based on a division between those who serve the state and those who obey it, the British promoted a society based on property ownership (whether mobile in the form of commerce and trade or static as in land). This last, of course, determined the notion of how nations should interact. As the 'nation of shopkeepers' (as Napoleon's sneer had it) saw it, instead of attempting to dominate one another, nations should instead trade with one another – and respect one another's sovereignty. Ultimately, Britain would eventually push this notion to its logical conclusion and promote international free trade. This was the new liberal international economic order, as one scholar calls it, that Britain would attempt to introduce, promote and uphold from Vienna until 1914.[9]

This was not, of course, achieved all at once nor was it always applied consistently or without internal political debate. Further, it was a series of events on both sides of the Atlantic which finally pushed Britain onto the path by which she would establish this order. Latin America was not the only part of the world to be convulsed by revolution and nationalist uprisings for in Europe, the genie of popular liberalism, freed once again by the American and French Revolutions, harnessed (in different ways) by the Founding Fathers and Napoleon, was not about to be put back into the proverbial bottle. Where the British and Americans managed the forces of popular liberalism to a greater or lesser extent through their constitutional structures, the Powers of Europe believed in a very different approach: these forces were not to be managed, but destroyed.

These differences between, on one hand, Britain and the United States and on the other, Europe, became apparent with the foundation of the Holy Alliance in 1815. The Alliance, membership of which both Britain and the United States rejected, was the brainchild of Tsar Alexander I committing its signatories to recognize the supremacy of Christ and to acknowledge Christianity as the basis of political policy. The British and the Americans were swiftly vindicated when the Alliance became the driving force of reaction against Europe's liberal revolutions. Events took a turn for the worse at the Congress of Troppau (1820), where the British were presented with the declaration that the Alliance intended to intervene in any state where internal change had come about without permission of the monarch. As far as the British were concerned, this meant a return to the principle of divine right of kings; anathema even to political reactionaries. This was not the Europe that Britain had spent blood and treasure to bring about. By 1823, having achieved success in Europe, most particularly in Spain despite British protests, the Alliance now turned its attention to the upstarts in Latin America. The British, although quietly contemptuous of the new republics, decided that their continued independence represented a better option than that presented by the Holy Alliance. Looking about, it appeared that only one other nation, in a position to help, agreed with them. Perhaps it was time to talk to the Americans.[10]

It was thus, in August 1823, that the Foreign Secretary, George Canning (who replaced Castlereagh upon the latter's suicide the previous year), took the American minister to the Court of St James, Richard Rush, by surprise by positing a simple question: would the United States go 'hand in hand' with Britain in order to solve the crisis? Rush would have to consult with Washington, of course, but asked in response if Britain would first join the United States in recognizing the independence of the new republics. Canning noted that the British government was not yet ready for that step (although it was moving in that direction). Before the end of the month the British question became a straightforward proposal: both nations would declare that they conceived Spain's recovery of the former colonies to be hopeless and that under appropriate circumstances their independence would be formally recognized. Furthermore, that not only would they not allow any other power to despoil the former colonies of their territory, they would both refrain from doing so themselves. While waiting for a response from Washington, Canning informed the Alliance that Britain would not tolerate European military suppression of the new republics, nor would it consider any discussion of Latin America's future unless the United States was also invited into any such talks. Essentially, the British were both promising to use the Royal Navy to halt any military action by the Alliance and, at the same time, to put pressure on the Americans to, as they saw it, take a share of the diplomatic burden. As it turned out, the Alliance could not hope to defeat the Royal Navy and thus the independence of the new republics was guaranteed. The United States, however, proved less cooperative.[11]

To be sure, the British offer came as something of a relief, if not a pleasant surprise. The United States had been observing the Alliance's activities with more than a little concern. In truth, there was little the Americans could have done had the Alliance intervened militarily in Latin America. Upon receipt of the British proposal President James Monroe consulted with the two elder statesmen, former presidents Thomas Jefferson and James Madison, both of whom urged him to accept it. Monroe's cabinet, however, was less satisfied. In the first instance, Canning had blundered – by already threatening to use the Royal Navy to stop the Alliance he had relieved the United States of any need to accept the British offer. A shrewder, if more Machiavellian, manoeuvre would have been to suggest that the British could do nothing to stop the Alliance unless it had American help – thus placing the United States in the position of either cooperating with Britain or facing any potential European military expedition alone. The only reason secretary of state John Quincy Adams could boldly declare, 'It would be more candid, as well as more dignified, to avow our principles explicitly to Russia and France, than to come in as a cockboat in the wake of the British man-of-war', was because he knew the Royal Navy was actually leaving said wake. In the second instance, American politicians were unhappy with any guarantee not to acquire territory from the former Spanish colonies. Any such agreement would limit their opportunities for expansion while the British, meantime, although having given up any such practice in the Americas, would nonetheless be free to extend their territory elsewhere in the world. In that respect, at least, the British were offering a one-sided bargain. Monroe's cabinet decided to, in effect, go it alone – rhetorically, at any rate.[12]

In his annual message to Congress, 2 December 1823, the President made three points which later came to be called the Monroe Doctrine. The essence of the declaration was essentially (1) 'the American continents' were 'not to be considered as subjects for future colonization for any European powers'; (2) the 'political system of the allied powers' was essentially different to that of the United States and therefore 'any attempt on their part to extend their system to any portion of this hemisphere is dangerous to our [America's] peace and safety'; and (3) that while the United States would respect the existing colonies in the Americas, any attempt to oppress or control the newly independent ones would be treated as 'the manifestation of an unfriendly disposition'. Despite its later importance, the immediate impact of Monroe's message was slight. The United States certainly won some easy plaudits in Latin America but neither the former, the latter nor, indeed, Europeans, were in the least bit mistaken as to which nation had really guaranteed the new republics' independence. Nor was that nation, Britain, especially amused by Monroe's declaration.

Although scholars have demonstrated that Monroe's message was not intended to permanently rule out any potential Anglo-American cooperation regarding Latin America, it nonetheless had that immediate effect. For many in Britain, Monroe's declaration simply provided yet more proof that while Americans might pontificate about liberty, it was the British who were expected to do the hard work. Further, Monroe's proclamation that the Americas were off-limits to future European – and that also meant British – colonization after the United States had rejected Britain's proposal that both nations make a mutual agreement not to acquire territory at the expense of the new republics, created the impression that the Americans were attempting to claim both continents for themselves. The British had not protected Latin America from the Alliance merely to hand it over to the Americans. Finally, although Monroe had stated that the United States had not interfered nor would interfere with existing colonies in the Americas, the War of 1812 gave the lie to the first part of that statement while the issue of the unresolved Canadian-American boundary demanded clarification of the second. It was little wonder that Canning, accused of being tricked by the United States, was forced to defend his proposal. After frankly declaring that Britain would not accept American suzerainty over Latin America or interference in its colonial policy towards the same, Canning concluded with his oft-quoted boast, 'I called the New World into existence to redress the balance of the old.' A tart reminder as to who had really guaranteed Latin America's independence.[13]

Nonetheless, for all the suspicion, hostility and accompanying rhetoric, in this instance Britain and the United States had colluded rather than collided. That they had done so was thanks to events in Europe, namely the existence and activities of the Holy Alliance. Yet the whole affair of the Holy Alliance and the South American republics caused the British and Americans to move in another parallel direction as well – the consequences of which remain with us. Britain's attempts to forge its new world order following Napoleon's defeat would require that it remain fundamentally outside of Europe. As Castlereagh had declared as early as 1813, 'The power of Great Britain to do good depends not merely on her resources but her impartiality and the reconciling power of her influence.' In other words, just as the Monroe

Doctrine marked a milestone in the American drift away from Europe (for, as we have seen, the United States was intimately involved in European affairs right up to, during and for a period after, the Napoleonic wars), Britain likewise made a similar diplomatic and political break of its own. In neither case was the separation immediate or ever complete: for example, regarding Britain, the term 'Splendid Isolation' was only coined by the Canadian Prime Minister Sir Wilfred Laurier in 1896, while Monroe's message was only identified as a declaration of separation from Europe (and upgraded to a doctrine) a generation after it was promulgated. As it turned out, Britain, unlike the United States, not having 3,000 miles of ocean between itself and Europe, would find such a separation easier wished-for than enacted. Further, as both the British and the Americans would discover in the early twentieth century, events in Europe affected them, for better or for worse, whether they liked it or not. There was also a distinct difference between the American and British approaches. The United States was essentially seeking a form of isolationism combined with hemispheric hegemony (the Monroe Doctrine was thus not an anti-imperialist decree); Britain was essentially establishing itself, on its own recognizance, as the referee of a new international system. But as far as the British were concerned, both Europe's Holy Alliance and America's Monroe Doctrine had demonstrated that they were going to have to stand alone.[14]

With the retreat of the United States from affairs beyond the Americas, this hemisphere became the chief point of Anglo-American friction for the rest of the nineteenth century. In the Americas, the main issues at stake were, in descending order, the Canadian-American frontier, complicated by the rebellions in Upper and Lower Canada in 1837, each nation's activities in Central America, the international slave trade and the establishment and existence of the Republic of Texas 1836–47. In some cases, notably the Canadian-American frontier and Central America, the disputes were settled by treaty; others, notably Texas and the international slave trade, were solved, much as they were caused, by domestic actions within the United States. Despite being finally resolved, however, all these disputes contributed to animosities and suspicions on each side.[15]

The Canadian-American boundary problem arose almost immediately after the dispute over Latin America. In 1827, the bone of contention was the demarcation line of the American-Canadian north-east frontier (which consisted of the boundary line from Lake Huron to the north-west corner of the Lake of the Woods and the line from the source of the

St Croix River in Maine to the St Lawrence River). Unable to reach agreement, both parties agreed to arbitration by the King of Holland, who, in 1831, awarded most of the disputed territory to the United States. That should have been that, except that Maine's political establishment, angry at not having gained all the territory it wanted, successfully sabotaged the treaty by preventing its ratification in the Senate. This action infuriated the British who, already angry with the Dutch Monarch's apparent partiality towards the United States, started to wonder if the game of negotiating with the United States was worth the candle. As there remained several other points of contention, including the boundary line across Lake Huron and the north end of Lake Champlain, this rejection of a mutually agreed arbiter's decision by the United States boded ill. Further, these failures would help to make the 1830s the most volatile decade for Anglo-American relations until the 1860s.[16]

The secession of Texas from Mexico in 1836 and the rebellions in Upper and Lower Canada in 1837–38, although unconnected, occurred virtually simultaneously, and besides the impact they had on Britain and the United States, profoundly affected how they engaged with each other. Texas was originally part of the Republic of Mexico. In the preceding decade, American settlers had flooded into the territory (initially with Mexican permission) and soon outnumbered the indigenous inhabitants. Before long, these émigrés – *all* American settlers – decided that self-rule was better than Mexican rule and so when Mexico's President, General Antonio López de Santa Anna (Santa Anna), introduced a new constitution increasing the powers of the central government, they declared their independence, establishing the Republic of Texas. This independence was decisively settled when a Texan army led by Sam Houston defeated Santa Anna's forces (and captured the General himself) at the Battle of San Jacinto, in April 1836. The victorious Texans demanded that the United States either recognize, or preferably annex, the new republic. Here, however, American sectionalism presented a problem. The admission of Texas would mean another southern, free-trading, slave state. Although there has been a tendency to overstate the North–South divide over the admission of Texas into the Union – only six states out of twenty-seven objected to the annexation and two of these six, Delaware and Maryland, were slave states – American political divisions thus killed the prospect of immediate annexation and meant that diplomatic recognition was the most Texas could immediately expect. Something it received on the last day of Jackson's presidency.[17]

It was to concentrate American minds that Houston, now President of Texas, recognizing the situation between Britain and the United States, played them off against each other to get statehood for his republic. Surprised (and a little offended) at being rebuffed by the United States, Houston sent out feelers to Britain. Would the British formally recognize the Republic of Texas? At the same time, Houston let his former fellow citizens in the United States know that, as his new republic needed allies to preserve its independence from Mexico, he might have no choice but to consider an alliance with Britain. London, however, was not in fact keen on being drawn into such a game. Despite vigorous mythologizing, no serious 'balance-of-power' policy was contemplated by the British – even though an alliance with an independent Texas was an obvious temptation for a nation currently concerned about American intervention in the rebellions in Upper and Lower Canada (see below). Although Britain, along with France, recognized Texas, the Foreign Secretary, George Hamilton-Gordon, Earl of Aberdeen, specifically declared for the benefit of the Americans that Britain's 'objects are purely commercial, and she has no thought or intention of seeking to act, directly or indirectly, in a political sense, on the United States through Texas'. Upon Texan request, the British did negotiate a truce between Texas and Mexico (the latter still refused to recognize the Lone Star republic's independence) and even went so far as to propose that both Mexico and the United States agree to a formal recognition of both Texas and Mexico's boundaries. This suggestion, however, foundered upon the twin rocks of Mexican refusal to recognize Texan independence and American intention to annex the republic (as well as parts of Mexico, too, as it turned out).[18]

In the end, the Anglo-American manoeuvrings secured Texan statehood. British involvement in Texan affairs wonderfully concentrated American minds. Southerners, always interested in annexation, feared that the British would persuade the Republic to abolish slavery (a rumour even emerged that Britain was prepared to loan Texas money to compensate the slave owners for their losses). This fear became more pronounced when Aberdeen, although denying any plans to provide Texas with money for compensated abolition, nonetheless informed secretary of state John C. Calhoun that, 'Great Britain desires, and is constantly exerting herself to procure, the general abolition of slavery throughout the world. But the means which she has adopted and will continue to adopt, for this humane and virtuous purpose, are open and undisguised' (Calhoun's response was to lecture the British government on the advantages of slavery). The rest of the nation, meanwhile, feared that the United States was being surrounded by, in effect, British satellites. This fear became even more pronounced when the Anglo-American dispute over the Oregon Territory (see below) increased in intensity in 1844. Faced with possible war with Britain on its northern frontier, the existence of Texas as a British ally was far more dangerous to the security of the United States than its admission to the Union as a southern state. Objections to annexation thus began to fade – rapidly. With American internal political divisions overcome, President John Tyler secured the assent of both houses of Congress to admit Texas into the union in February 1845. Houston's manoeuvres had paid off handsomely. Of course, by annexing territory still claimed by Mexico, the United States had placed itself on a collision course with that nation. At this point, however, we must turn northwards.[19]

If political divisions within the United States would lead to rebellion, Britain's Canadian colonists achieved the dubious feat of reaching this state of affairs before the Americans. For, from 1837–38, in the colonies of predominantly English-speaking Upper Canada and largely French-speaking Lower Canada, open revolt against the colonial authorities took place. The causes of both rebellions remain controversial, although the example of the United States – with some exceptions noted below – was slight. In Lower Canada, economic, social and religious tensions were to blame, exacerbated by disputes between English- and French-speaking colonists, which have given the revolt the reputation of an ethnic dispute that is largely undeserved. The revolt in Upper Canada, motivated by abuse of patronage, especially regarding land grants, was a more limited affair and would probably never have actually resulted in a collision of arms had it not been for the example of Lower Canada. In any case, neither revolt enjoyed the level of popular support necessary for success. Each was suppressed without even the need for reinforcements from Britain.

Despite their quick suppression, the revolts resulted in a series of serious diplomatic rows that, in many respects, foreshadowed those which arose during the American Civil War when the United States faced a rebellion of its own. Although President Martin Van Buren issued a proclamation of neutrality on 5 January 1838, American public sympathies were clearly on the side of the rebels. Seeing the unfolding of such events as the inevitable consequence of the example of the United States, the Americans believed the revolts were copies of their own war of independence. This perspective was apparently confirmed when, after being driven from Canada, the leaders of the two rebellions, William Lyon Mackenzie and Robert Nelson, respectively issued declarations of independence for Upper Canada on 13 December 1837 and for Lower Canada on 22 February 1838. These, however, were probably the final nails in each rebellion's respective coffins. The colonial authorities, playing on Canadian annexationist fears, were able to portray the rebels and their leaders as Yankee pawns. Anti-Americanism would prove to be the trump card in British North American and later, Canadian, politics for many years to come.[20]

Yet this was not all simple political opportunism, for there undeniably existed some annexationist sentiment in the United States – the acquisition of Britain's Canadian colonies for the northern states would offset the gain of Texas for the South. Further, there was an undeniable American element in the rebellions (albeit one unsupported by the government). For example, in Upper Canada especially, although the majority of the rebels were native-born Canadians, a number were, in fact, American citizens – settlers who had wandered across the border and who bore the Crown no allegiance whatsoever. For example, Mackenzie's second in command was Rensselaer Van Rensselaer, son of the American general, who undeniably saw himself as a northern Sam Houston. Thus, for many British, and indeed, Canadian colonists, the similarities between what was occurring in both Texas and the Canadas were more than mere coincidence. Further, the number of American volunteers increased when the rebellions' leaders, defeated in Upper and Lower Canada, set up camp on the American side of the border and launched a series of raids throughout 1838 – actions that were in obvious defiance of the United States' proclaimed neutrality – which caused great anger in both Britain and its Canadian colonies.

The rebels and their sympathizers, however, were not the only ones who crossed the border. The situation became increasingly dangerous when, on 29 December 1837, Canadian militia crossed the Niagara River into United States territory and set on fire a rebel steamship, the *Caroline*, killing an American citizen in the process. The incident sparked outrage in the United States and, as if this were not enough, the trouble along the frontier began to spread. From 1838–39 the so-called Aroostook War took place when Canadian lumberjacks crossed into the disputed territory along the Maine–New Brunswick frontier and, at the Aroostook River, engaged in a series of brawls with American rivals (and roughed up a protesting Maine state senator for good measure). Fortunately, because none of these engagements resulted in any fatalities, this event was, on the face of it, farcical (although both the Maine and New Brunswick militias were called out). Rather less so, however, was the burning of the British steamer the *Sir Robert Peel* in United States' waters by Americans in May 1838, ostensibly in retaliation for the *Caroline*. These events, especially the *Caroline* incident, resulted in increasing numbers of Americans, assisted by a belligerent press, clamouring for war. This sentiment was reciprocated among both Britons and their Canadian colonists, furious that the lives of two failed rebellions were being artificially prolonged through apparent American connivance. Add a disputed border to this combustible atmosphere and conditions for war began to materialize.[21]

Resolution to the crisis came in the unlikely form of the British Foreign Secretary Palmerston, and the American President Martin Van Buren. The two men personally knew and, more importantly, respected each other thanks to the American's brief stint as US minister to Britain in 1831. As a result, despite the passions of their peoples, the two men ensured their respective administrations communicated in a sensible and civil fashion. Van Buren sent troops to the border (commanded by Winfield Scott, of War of 1812 fame) to prevent further excursions by the rebels and arrested Mackenzie and some of his lieutenants. With Mackenzie – who was not so much the Thomas Jefferson of 1776 as the Aaron Burr of 1806 – in an American gaol for 18 months and the border secured, the trouble died down fairly quickly. Scott, with the assistance of New Brunswick Governor Sir John Harvey, was even able to arrange a truce in the Aroostook imbroglio. Van Buren did protest the Canadian militia's actions in the *Caroline* affair but did so mildly, and Palmerston accepted the British government's responsibility (although he failed to apologize). The Foreign Secretary did, however, formally thank the United States for its friendly attitude during the rebellion. Yet he could congratulate himself too, because it was the cooperation by the political elites on both sides that brought the crisis to an end (not that Van Buren necessarily benefited politically – it has been claimed he lost his bid for re-election because of being too pro-British, but the 1837 Panic seems a more likely reason).

Unfortunately, such Anglo-American cooperation, instead of being a harbinger of future harmony, proved to be merely an interlude and Palmerston, in particular, would never enjoy so cordial a relationship with any American President ever again. For, figuratively speaking, the fires from the *Caroline* flared up again. In 1840, one Alexander McLeod, formerly of the Upper Canada militia, on a visit to New York, boasted while drunk about having participated in the raid that killed the American citizen, and was promptly arrested by the authorities. London demanded McLeod's release on the grounds that if the former militiaman was guilty, he had been acting under orders of his government and it was from there that redress must be sought. As it happened, the US government agreed. Unfortunately, New York State, led by its governor William Henry Seward, insisted that the affair was a state matter and McLeod was tried for murder. As public opinion in Britain was decidedly in favour of war if McLeod was executed, the situation became genuinely dangerous. In the end, the incident was resolved by sheer luck: McLeod, like so many gents in their cups, had exaggerated his martial prowess. He had, in fact, nothing to do with the affair, provided an alibi and was acquitted.[22]

Recognizing that the delineation of the north-eastern portion of the Canadian-American boundary was a problem that desperately needed to be solved, the Conservative administration of Sir Robert Peel (formed in August 1841) dispatched Alexander Baring, Baron Ashburton, to negotiate with the United States. It is a measure of how foreign the United States was regarded as being that Ashburton was chosen in large part because his bank, Barings, did business there (indeed, from 1843–67 the bank was the sole financial agent of the US government in London) and because his wife was American – it was assumed that he understood the nation and its people. It proved an astute choice: Ashburton's wife was a friend of his counterpart, secretary of state Daniel Webster and further, while Ashburton was a partner in his family's bank, Webster was a partner in an American bank. This meant the two men approached negotiations from a business, rather than political, perspective. This approach paid dividends: the boundary was determined by the Webster-Ashburton Treaty in August 1842.

Yet, as usual, the path of Anglo-American relations could never follow a straight course. Each side had maps that ostensibly proved the other had conceded too much. Ever on the lookout for an advantage, they concealed their respective maps from each other. Webster used his to persuade Maine (which had sabotaged the last attempt to settle the boundary) and Massachusetts to accept the treaty. Palmerston, who was fully aware of the British map's existence, scored some easy points at the Tories' expense by claiming Ashburton had ceded too much, despite the fact the treaty was less generous to the United States than the King of Holland's decision in 1831. If the affair of the Webster-Ashburton Treaty contained some faintly comic activities, they and the treaty were an improvement over the disputes surrounding the Canadian Rebellions, the *Caroline* affair, the McLeod case, the boundary quarrels and continued manoeuvrings in Texas. Within a few years, however, British and Americans required all the skill and luck they possessed to navigate the treacherous shoals of the Oregon boundary dispute.[23]

The entire Oregon Territory had been declared 'free and open' by the 1818 convention, and extended by negotiations from 1825–27, but by the 1840s American and British settlers had flooded into the area, and the United States wanted it to be formally divided between the two nations. This was not necessarily a problem, but domestic American politics muddied the waters. Besides the absorption of Texas, the Democratic Party was gazing covetously at Mexican territory; in particular, California. The problem was the opposition Whig Party opposed a war against Mexico, and northern Whigs, in particular, were against southern expansion. It was to overcome these objections that the Democrats' 1844 presidential election party platform called for the annexation of Texas and asserted that the United States had a 'clear and unquestionable' claim to the entire Oregon Territory, adding for good measure that none of it 'ought to be ceded to England'. Anglophobia paid in American politics; so too did expansionism at the expense of one's neighbours. This was not lost on James Polk, the Democratic candidate, who won the election and, at his inauguration in 1845, repeated the claim that none of the Oregon Territory would be ceded to Britain. At this point, as far as London was concerned, Yankee bluster had become Yankee threat.

The British, however, had a number of other concerns. They had recently suffered a reverse in Afghanistan, where Major-General William Elphinstone's forces, sent to fend off Russian advances, had been massacred by an Afghan army, necessitating a punitive raid on Kabul, in 1842–43; there was an ongoing war with the Sikhs from 1845–46 as well as the Maoris, from 1843–48. In fact the only thing that had gone smoothly for the British was Sir Charles Napier's conquest of Sind in 1843. That was merely abroad. At home, there was the Irish potato famine, from 1845 onwards, which strongly argued in favour of keeping the supplies of American corn coming, to say nothing of Chartist activism that flared up before, during and after the Oregon crisis. Seen from one perspective, Polk had picked as opportune a time for a quarrel as any. Although the president's first proposal to the British government was conciliatory – he proposed dividing the territory along the 49th parallel – his proposition did not include the navigation rights to the

Columbia River that his predecessor, President John Tyler, had offered. Faced with this, the British minister to Washington, Richard Pakenham, refused the offer. Polk, incensed, withdrew his proposal and reasserted his claim to the entire territory.[24]

Events became increasingly unpleasant as American politicians and the press joined the dispute. By November 1845, demands for all of Oregon became the staple of American editorials and, on 27 December 1845, the editor of the *New York Morning News*, John O'Sullivan, declared that the United States was owed the entire territory 'by the right of our manifest destiny to overspread and to possess the whole of the continent'. American expansionism had just been given a formal title. Not only that, but it appeared as if not only Oregon, but Canada and Mexico were now also on the menu (O'Sullivan did not actually mean this, but others using the phrase Manifest Destiny did). That same month, in his annual address to Congress, Polk recommended giving Britain notice of the American determination to end the joint occu-pation agreement. He was cheered on by senators calling for war with Britain unless it ceded all of Oregon up to 54°40'N (the southern limit of Russia's North American settlements, now Alaska). These demands were soon followed by the slogan 'Fifty-four Forty or Fight', a phrase repeated by newspapers and many westerners – Whigs as well as Democrats.

By this point, however, British patience had worn thin. Not wanting war with the United States, but wholly unprepared to concede territory rightfully belonging to it, and having been twice rebuffed by Polk upon requests for arbitration, Peel's administration decided to clarify matters. On 29 January 1846, Foreign Secretary Aberdeen summoned the American minister, Louis McLane, to an interview in which he informed him that if the United States' final offer on Oregon was indeed 'Fifty-Four Forty or Fight', the British would choose the latter. News of the British choice came as a sobering shock to Washington but to a degree it was probably unnecessary. Although Polk had written in his diary, 'The only way to treat John Bull is to look him in the eye', he knew when to blink. His position was largely a bluff and now that it had been called, it was time to negotiate. The president's real interests lay in the direction of Mexico and he had no intention of fighting Britain at the same time. Further, for all the grandstanding in the Senate, when the declaration informing the British that the United States wished to ter-minate the joint occupancy agreement was actually passed, it was nonetheless accompanied by a majority resolution calling on both governments to settle the matter peacefully. The British were only too happy to oblige. Pakenham and the American secretary of state negotiated the Oregon Treaty using the 49th parallel as the boundary, Vancouver Island being ceded to the British, but navigation rights on the Columbia River being rather less than what Britain had originally desired. By the time the treaty was ratified in Washington and at Westminster, the United States and Mexico were already at war.[25]

The Mexican-American war, which lasted from 1846–48, was a stunning success for the United States. The territorial gains were enormous – what is now California, New Mexico, Nevada, Utah and half of Texas, were among the spoils as well as parts of Arizona, Wyoming, Colorado, Kansas and Oklahoma. This conquest of one-third of Mexican land which came at the cost of a few thousand men and $18.2 million (a compulsory sale) increased the territory of the United States by two-fifths. Polk had a serious claim to being a great American President, yet this was not the reputation posterity bequeathed upon him. The reason was that the war, although widely popular in the United States (especially after the territorial gains), reopened the sectional differences between the North and the South and probably committed the nation to eventual civil war. Although sectional differences were numerous (in 1844, Ohio congressman Joshua Giddings accused the South of seeking to increase the number of southern states through territorial conquest in order to increase support for free trade rather than slavery), northern abolitionists attacked the war as nothing more than a campaign to extend slavery. When in 1846 the Wilmot proviso was introduced in the House of Representatives barring slavery from the newly acquired territory (a provision defeated in the Senate) the sectional differences were laid bare. This raises the question: did Britain's stance on the Oregon Territory unwittingly help drive the United States to civil war? Certainly, there was resentment in parts of the northern states at Polk's determination to fight for vast swathes of Mexican territory while negotiating for decidedly less from Britain. Polk, after all, had campaigned on the promise that he would get all of Oregon – not just part of it. Many of those, both in the political and public realm, who cried 'Fifty-four Forty or Fight', meant exactly what they said. Such resentment would never have existed nor would the abolitionist claims that the war was solely for the purposes of extending slavery gained much traction had Britain ceded all of the Oregon Territory.[26]

The Oregon Treaty, however, appeared to settle the American-

Canadian boundary dispute. This apparent removal of territorial disputes from the Anglo-American relationship should have marked an improvement in the relationship but, almost immediately following the treaty, they found new things to quarrel about. In 1852, a serious dispute arose over the question of fishing rights in American-Canadian waters. Both sides accused the other of fishing illegally and each sent warships to patrol the disputed waters. Fortunately, at the diplomatic level at least, both nations were learning to handle each other. After the obligatory display of sabre-rattling, secretary of state William Marcy sent London a draft treaty in September 1853 that compromised on many of the outstanding problems. Britain, with an eye on escalating tensions between Russia and Turkey that would ultimately lead to the Crimean War (see below), proved receptive. The governor general of Canada, Lord Elgin, negotiated in Washington with the secretary of state. The resulting Marcy-Elgin Reciprocity Treaty, signed in June 1854, settled the fishing dispute and also greatly liberalized trade between Canada and the United States by reducing or eliminating duties on various goods, as well as opening important waterways to each other's inhabitants. Although the treaty only lasted a decade – in 1864 Congress, angered by Britain's neutrality in the American Civil War, gave notice that it would not renew it – in the immediate term it successfully cooled passions.[27]

If things improved in the northern part of the continent, however, they became steadily worse in the south, especially in the region of Central America, where an Anglo-American commercial rivalry began to develop. Although neither nation was the sort to fight a war over trade (at least not with each other, but the Chinese during the Opium wars, 1839–42, and the Japanese, faced with Commodore Matthew Perry's fleet in 1854, could tell a different story), both were considering the possibility of a Central American canal (activities were already underway on the other side of the world to build the Suez – an issue over which Britain nearly came into conflict with France). To this end, each nation signed various diplomatic treaties with Central American republics, most especially New Grenada (now Columbia) in the case of the United States, Costa Rica, in the case of Britain. The problem was these republics had various territorial disputes of their own, particularly in the area of a potential canal zone. The distinct possibility of a collision loomed.

Recognizing the problem, the Russell administration, which replaced Peel's in June 1846 and saw the return of Palmerston as foreign

secretary, dispatched Sir Henry Lytton Bulwer to Washington to settle
the dispute. President Zachary Taylor's administration proved receptive
and secretary of state John Clayton signed the Clayton-Bulwer Treaty in
April 1850. The treaty stipulated that neither nation would colonize or
assume dominion over any part of Central America and that any canal
built would be open to all nations on equal terms. Although this should
have settled matters, events conspired to virtually undo all the good will
this treaty, and the others, represented.[28]

Both nations disputed each other's interpretation of the treaty, most
importantly over the fact that Washington believed that it obligated
Britain not to have any dominion in Central America with the exception of its long-established colony, British Honduras (now Belize),
meaning that recent acquisitions such as the Bay Islands and the
Mosquito Coast (now part of Nicaragua) were to be vacated. London
countered that the treaty was prospective only – that no new territory
was to be acquired. Events were further complicated by American filibustering expeditions. These private military expeditions organized by
American citizens were directed at Cuba, Mexico, Nicaragua and other
places and angered the British no end. Although the filibusters were not
agents of the American government, the example of Texas lingered and
many of the filibustering incidents enjoyed popular support in the
United States. Further, at least some of the expeditions were at least in
part inspired by American government activities. For example, in 1854,
the administration of Franklin Pierce offered to purchase Cuba from
Spain (an offer Madrid refused). The British regarded this as a violation
of the Clayton-Bulwer treaty and, alarmed by this and the filibustering
activities, sent a fleet to patrol Cuba's coast – an act that caused great
offence in the United States.[29]

In 1854, it was the US Navy that caused offence when a warship, the
Cyane, bombarded Greytown (now San Juan del Norte, Nicaragua),
then a British protectorate – despite protests from a British officer
present – in revenge for an insult to an American official there. This
incident caused serious outrage in Britain. Palmerston even considered
bombarding American coastal cities in retaliation. Fortunately, because
the captain had acted far beyond his orders, it was relatively easy for the
United States to disavow his actions and apologize. Yet Anglo-American
difficulties in Greytown were not to be so simply resolved. A mere two
years later, the filibuster (freebooter, said the British) William Walker
set himself up as the dictator of Nicaragua, re-introduced slavery and
promptly annexed Greytown. The difficulties caused by this action

which followed in the wake of the *Cyane* affair were compounded by the fact that the US government had formally recognized Walker's Nicaraguan regime. The British were incensed. There was something of a war scare, but the United States, recognizing the dangers posed by Walker's activities, sent a fleet to expel him from Nicaragua. The next time Walker attempted another expedition, this time to Honduras in 1860, the reinforced Royal Navy intercepted him and turned him over to the Honduran authorities, who put him before a firing squad.[30]

All of these events in Central America created tension enough, but they did not occur in a vacuum – in the background loomed the Crimean War, which began in 1853, when Turkey and Russia initiated hostilities (Britain and France only became involved in March 1854). Not a few in Britain believed that the United States was taking advantage of the eastern conflict to run amok in Central America (and the Democrat Pierce administration and Whig annexationists such as William Seward certainly did detect an opportunity). Further, although the United States was officially neutral during the Crimean War, the American public demonstrated a marked predisposition towards Russia. Confidently predicting that French and British forces would meet the same fate as Napoleon's *Grand Armeé*, a vocal portion of the American press made no secret of where its sympathies lay. Considering that, as recently as 1851, the United States had enthusiastically welcomed the Hungarian rebel Louis Kossuth and damned his opponents Austria and Russia, this *volte-face* to pro-Russian position was remarkable. It also did serious damage to the reputation of the United States in Britain – especially among liberals and radicals. Although the Crimean War is now remembered as something of a debacle, some recent historians have argued that it halted Russian expansionism for a generation and therefore succeeded in its objectives (it is also highly unlikely that Russia would have ended up selling Alaska to the United States in 1867 had it emerged victorious). Perhaps more importantly, at the time the conflict was widely seen as a strike against Russian despotism. British liberals and radicals, in particular, hoped it would result in the liberation of Poland. To an extent, American sentiment was more anti-British than pro-Russian – and events in Central America had a hand in this – but to many Britons this distinction meant little.

Relations were further worsened by American outrage resulting from British attempts to recruit its citizens for the struggle in defiance of the nation's neutrality laws (a controversy that would be repeated, vice versa, when the United States attempted to recruit Irish subjects for the

Union armies in the Civil War). Added to all of this was the British discovery that American citizens served as doctors and experts on the Russian side and that the United States built a steamship for the Tsar's government (which reached Russia too late to participate in the war). This American opposition to the success of the allied cause was not forgotten. As far as most in Britain were concerned, the United States had, as in 1812, backed the wrong side in the struggle for liberty. As one scholar has noted, by the time the war was over the United States was the sole remaining nation that openly acknowledged its friendship for Russia. Those historians who wonder about the lack of British sympathy for the North in the American Civil War in the 1860s, especially among liberals and radicals, should pay more heed to the events of the previous decade. Certainly, by the time the war ended in 1856, anti-Americanism in Britain had gained a new lease of life.[31]

The decade continued to be punctuated by disputes, especially over the issue of slavery. In 1841, for example, 135 American slaves, who were being transported from Hampton Roads to New Orleans on the American brig *Creole*, seized control of the ship by killing several crew members, and sailed to Nassau in the Bahamas. Although the British authorities executed the murderers, they refused to return the rest of the mutineers to American custody, Aberdeen declaring that slaves in British jurisdiction by whatever means and from whatever quarters 'were *ipso facto* free'. Although the British paid compensation, or 'hush money', this incident caused resentment in the United States.[32]

Yet the tension created during the *Creole* affair was mild compared to that of the 1858 Anglo-American boarding dispute. This concerned the Royal Navy stopping American ships on the high seas to search for slaves being transported from Africa. The abolition of the international slave trade was an outstanding British policy and although they were able to negotiate treaties for mutual right of search with virtually every major power, the strongest opponent of this policy was the United States, which actually led an international diplomatic campaign against it. The United States contended that it would police its own merchant marine and, under the terms of the Webster-Ashburton Treaty, maintained a squadron off the African coast to do just that. By 1842, however, all serious attempts on the part of the United States had stopped and by that time it was by far the largest importer of slaves in the world, despite the illegality of the trade (although involvement in the trade carried the death penalty in America, no one was successfully prosecuted much less executed until 1862). While most of these slaves were destined for Cuba and Brazil, rather than the United States, the problem for the British was that they had largely stopped all the holes in the net, except those made under cover of the American flag. The United States also rejected a British compromise: no right of search, only a right of visit, in order to verify that a ship flying an American flag had the right to do so. As a result, the British took matters into their own hands and began stopping American ships.

When in May 1858, the HMS *Styx* halted and searched the American schooner *Mobile* in the West Indies, public outrage in the United States, stoked by the press, reached fever pitch. The secretary of state, Lewis Cass, demanded that the British government cease and desist from all such activities. The Senate followed suit, passing a bill to enable the President to take military action to stop the British if necessary. This prompted a counter-wave of anger in Britain and more than a few voices demanded that the anti-slavery campaign had to be maintained even if it meant war with the Americans. In the end, however, Lord Derby's Conservative administration, never as passionate about the slave trade as the Liberals, backed down – a move that disgusted the Liberal opposition.[33]

The following year Anglo-American relations were unsettled by the 'Pig War', an event caused by a dispute over the Oregon Treaty, namely, whether the San Juan Islands were on the American or British side of the channel separating Vancouver Island from the mainland. The British-owned Hudson's Bay Company used the islands for sheep pasturing, but American settlers began to arrive. In June 1859, an American farmer shot a Hudson Bay employee's pig he found rooting in his garden. When the British authorities threatened to arrest the farmer, the American settlers, in the best frontier tradition, called for govern-ment protection. Officials in Oregon obliged and dispatched troops to San Juan Island. Believing the Americans were attempting another land grab, British colonial officials called for help themselves, and soon three Royal Navy warships were patrolling the waters. This, in turn, sparked a reinforcement effort by the Americans which meant more soldiers and artillery. Although the troops on each side had orders not to fire unless fired upon, hotheads in both ranks taunted their opponents in hopes of goading them into attacking and thus begin the show. Nor were their superiors necessarily over-endowed with any great intellectual ability. Noticing the British had over 2,000 marines and 70 guns to the Americans' fewer than 500 men and 14 cannons, the governor of Vancouver Island, James Douglas, ordered the British commander, Rear

Admiral Robert Baynes, to attack before more enemy reinforcements could arrive. Baynes, possibly the only man at the scene of the dispute with any sense, refused, declaring that he would not cause a war 'over a squabble about a pig'.

Fortunately, intelligence can be infectious. Washington sent General Winfield Scott to negotiate with Douglas. Both sides agreed to retain joint occupancy of the island until such time as a more permanent settlement could be reached. Each side left a token force behind and, after that, the only conflicts that took place were a result of drunkenness, the British and American soldiers otherwise enjoying each other's company. Despite all the fuss and furore, the only fatality was the pig and, as it was technically the aggressor, one could hardly complain of any injustice.[34]

The Pig War is remembered, if at all, as one of history's comic performances. Yet the fact remains it could have easily turned out differently and, in that respect, serves as a useful metaphor for nineteenth-century Anglo-American relations from 1815 to 1871. The two nations were not always at loggerheads – they cooperated, along with France, in opening China to foreign trade, for example. Indeed, in the second British war with China, 1856–60, something akin to outright collaboration occurred. In 1860, Royal Navy vessels assaulting the Taku Forts guarding Tientsin, the pathway to Peking (now Beijing), found themselves joined by the American commodore Josiah Tatnall and some of his men, who boarded the British flagship to help with the fighting. Further, during the Indian Mutiny, 1857–58, American public opinion, unlike in the Crimean War, leaned in a distinctly pro-British direction. This last, however, probably owed a lot to the fact that Americans faced their own Indian uprisings, to say nothing of the fear of slave revolts in the southern states, rather than a serious breakthrough in relations.[35]

For, despite the claims that relations between the two nations steadily improved, this is true only up to a point. Yes, the two sides managed to settle the demarcation of their frontier, but it is more accurate to say that in doing so they reduced the potential for conflict rather than developed any serious friendship. Further, despite this successful demarcation, their relationship was marred by a disturbing number of serious incidents that, had they been incorrectly handled, could have resulted in war – and these events were hardly less frequent in the 1850s than they had been in the 1830s. Each one of these occurrences meant that for every two steps towards rapprochement taken by the Americans and British, they took one back. To most Britons and Americans the two peoples were, in every sense of the word, foreigners. Both saw the other as opportunists who had to be stood up to. In the final analysis, neither nation actually wanted to push things to the point of war, but at the same time, while they accepted the need for negotiation and compromise, both absolutely believed – with some justice – that appeasement or any sign of weakness would prove fatal. Contrary to mythology, this sentiment was not the preserve of any particular elite, class, ethnic or political group – this was broadly the view the British and the American people held of each other.

When Commodore Tatnall and his men boarded the Royal Navy vessels to help the British assault on the Taku Forts, the American commander was supposed to have declared, by way of explanation for his actions, that 'Blood is thicker than water'. Perhaps, but blood might not be enough and, indeed, it was about to flow like water. For the year 1860 introduced a third party into the Anglo-American relationship when a wealthy lawyer with connections to the railway industry, Abraham Lincoln, was elected President, on a plurality of the vote. This resulted in South Carolina's secession from the Union, ultimately to be followed by ten other states. America was to divide into two republics: the United States and the Confederate States; the Anglo-American relationship was about to become very interesting indeed.

6

John Bull, Cousin Jonathan and Johnny Reb: Great Britain and the American Civil War, 1861–65

In 1863, during the height of the American Civil War, an anonymous note was sent to the Legation of the United States in London. The message was as simple as it was crude:

> Dam the Federals. Dam the Confederates. Dam you both.
>
> Kill your damned selves for the next ten years if you like; so much the better for the world and for England. Thus thinks every Englishman with any brains.
>
> N.B. P.S. We'll cut your throats soon enough afterwards for you, if you ain't tired of blood, you devils.

This sentiment was reciprocated, if in a slightly more elegant fashion; by the *New York Times*, which promised that 'America will hate England ... until the last American now living goes to his grave'. Considering that, from 1861–65, there was enough killing and hatred within the boundaries of the United States without the need for yet more abroad, and also that Britain had no direct stake in the conflict's outcome, this incredible degree of animosity between the nations appears to be something akin to psychosis. Certainly, the anger Britons and Americans directed at each other during this period was exceeded only by that expressed during the sideshow of the struggle against Napoleon, the War of 1812. Primarily the Civil War was a local event rather than a global one; a rebellion in one nation, not a war among several. This time, however, it was the Americans who believed they were fighting a war for liberty and national survival, while the British were the spectators affected by a conflict in which they wanted no part. There was another important difference as well: despite all this animosity, unlike in 1812, Britain and the United States did not actually go to war.[1]

Although most in Britain refused to support either side and the government never recognized the Confederacy's independence, nor intervened on its behalf, at the war's end both the North and the South damned the British for allegedly sympathizing with the other. In later years, however, a myth arose that crudely divided British national sentiment into two camps: a pro-northern one consisting of the working class, radicals and liberals and a pro-southern one containing the aristocracy, reactionaries and conservatives. The first, admiring American democracy and loathing slavery, supported the Union while the second, despising American republicanism and tolerating slavery, championed the Confederacy. The origins of this myth, which later solidified into a traditional account of Anglo-American relations during the conflict, lie in the opinions of two groups. The first contained several prominent Americans who, demonstrating little understanding of either British society or politics, instead viewed relations between the countries through a decidedly nationalist lens. The second consisted of the very small number of pro-northern British radicals who, attempting to damage their political opponents after the war, dishonestly associated them with the defeated and discredited Confederacy. Despite having been comprehensively debunked, variants of this traditional account are still being repeated, largely by those who focus on the very small number of Britons who actually took sides in the conflict, to the exclusion of society as a whole, and whose classification of each group's outlook and politics is best charitably described as cavalier. In truth, when it comes to Anglo-American relations during the Civil War, as with the War of 1812, mythology still distorts historical understanding.[2]

The creation and perpetuation of the myth will be discussed later in the chapter; what need to be established now are the realities of Anglo-American relations during the war. First and foremost, from the British point of view, it was a foreign conflict. Insofar as these extraneous hostilities were regarded, it was from the perspective of their impact upon British interests. Here, there were two main issues: the first was apprehension regarding the cotton industry, because its main source of supply, the southern states, was cut off; the second concerned Canada, because the western portion of the empire now bordered that most unstable of entities – a nation embroiled in civil war. At both the political and public levels, neutrality was held to be the least worst available option. Not having enjoyed especially friendly relations with the United States before the war, the British were understandably suspicious of both sides in the conflict. This perspective on its own angered a North demanding sympathy for its cause and a South demanding intervention on its behalf, but hostility was further provided by the conflict's two protagonists who, fighting to preserve the nation and struggling to create a new one respectively, both followed policies that ultimately succeeded only in alienating the British altogether. Hence the message shoved through the American Legation's door cited above. When it came to the Civil War, the British demonstrated a broad consensus: they wished a plague on both houses. Yet despite the public antagonism on both sides of the Atlantic, including the threats of hostilities, British and American politicians managed, in 1871, to put together a treaty that not only settled outstanding differences, but also put the two nations on the path to rapprochement. In many respects, the apocryphal Chinese notion that crisis is a combination of both danger and opportunity has never been given a finer demonstration.

In 1860, the long-standing sectional quarrel over slavery, states' rights, tariffs, majority rule versus minority rights, whether the United States was a nation or a union, to say nothing of the competing Hamiltonian and Jeffersonian interpretations of the Constitution, reached breaking point. The new Republican Party's presidential candidate, Abraham Lincoln, won the election on a plurality. Seeing the presidency fall into the hands of a party representing entirely northern sectional interests, the states of the lower south decided that independence was the preferred option and, following the example of their forebears in 1776, seceded. In 1839, former President John Quincy Adams had declared that, 'If the day should ever come ... when the affections of the people of these states should be alienated from each other ... far better will it be for the people of the disunited states, to part in friendship from each other than to be held together by constraint.' Lincoln, however, like Andrew Jackson before him, held a very different view: secession was illegal. As he would later declare, 'Both parties deprecated war; but one of them would *make* war rather than let the nation survive; and the other would *accept* war rather than let it perish. And the war came.'[3]

Indeed it did. Within three months of Lincoln's election, the states of the lower South formed a provisional government, headed by President Jefferson Davis. The states of the upper south held their counsel, but when Lincoln's administration clashed with the rebellious states over possession of the federal fort Sumter, guarding Charleston harbour, in April 1861, prompting the President to call for 75,000 men to suppress a revolution 'too powerful to be suppressed by the ordinary course of judicial proceedings', they too seceded from the union and joined their brethren in the lower south. For good measure, Lincoln also declared that the South was now under blockade. The United States was now officially at war – with itself.

The British had witnessed wars of secession before. Besides the obvious example of the American War of Independence, there had been the secession of Spain's Latin American colonies and from 1848 onwards, the Italians and the Hungarians both fought wars of independence against Austria. Indeed, the British had already seen a broadly democratic confederation fight a civil war, namely Switzerland in 1847. In fact, from the period 1845 to 1870, the British witnessed numerous wars of independence, secession and unification – some successful, some less so – and avoided involvement in all. It was primarily the common language that the British shared with both the protagonists that made the American Civil War different, as they were treated to an unadulterated version of each side's views. This, in many respects, was to prove as much a disadvantage as advantage.[4]

Initially, British sympathies leaned northwards. The belief that the South had no better justification for secession than defeat in a fair election, combined with contempt for its 'peculiar institution', that is, slavery, ensured that the Confederacy was almost universally condemned. A commentator in the conservative *Fraser's Magazine*, among others, noted the obvious problems an independent South would pose: 'the British Government cannot wish these states to establish their independence, when it would involve much danger of getting into a war with them ourselves on the question of the slave trade with Africa, which, however prudent may be their present language the moving spirits among them are bent on re-opening'. The institution of slavery and the spectre of the slave trade put the South beyond the pale of the overwhelming majority of Britons whatever their political alignment – and this was scarcely less evident in the later than in the earlier period of the conflict. Certainly in July 1861, one of the South's first diplomatic envoys to Britain, William L. Yancey, reported to his superiors that the British opposed the Confederacy because of slavery.[5]

The South also outraged the British by its 'King Cotton' strategy – a policy of withholding its cotton crop from Britain. Having a virtual monopoly (80 per cent) on the export of raw cotton underpinning Britain's textile industries (which accounted for almost five-ninths of its exports, and upon which some 20 per cent of the population depended either directly or indirectly for its livelihood), Britain appeared to be in thrall to the South. In theory, Britain thus had a choice: either guarantee Confederate independence or face a cotton famine, economic ruin and political upheaval. Or, as one southerner bragged to a visiting Briton, 'Why sir, we have only to shut your supply of cotton for a few weeks and we can create a revolution in Great Britain.' Fortunately, despite causing some initial alarm, the South's strategy failed. The pre-war bumper crop of cotton meant there was already a surplus supply in Britain; the growth of cotton in India and elsewhere was encouraged; and finally, as the war progressed, the Confederacy had to ship cotton through the blockade in order to raise money for munitions. A shortfall was certainly felt, most keenly in Lancashire, but even here, a massive relief effort that raised almost two million pounds from private subscribers helped to mitigate the worst effects. Nonetheless, this crude attempt at blackmail enraged both political and public opinion and this hostility lingered long after the South gave up the policy. In March 1862, Confederate commissioner James Mason noted of his meeting with the Foreign Secretary Lord John Russell, 'So much as related to the cotton supply and its importance to this country, I thought it best to omit, as I had reason to believe ... that it might be considered obtrusive, having been urged until England had become a little sensitive.'[6]

Despite all of this, the Union managed to alienate the British public. The first problem was Lincoln's failure to make emancipation a war aim. At his inaugural, on 4 March 1861, he specifically declared that 'I have no purpose, directly or indirectly, to interfere with the institution of slavery in states where it exists ... I believe I have no lawful right to do so and have no intention to do so.' The reasons for this approach even after hostilities broke out were twofold: firstly, most northerners did not like blacks and even fewer still had sympathy for abolition, and secondly, the North had to stop the haemorrhaging of seceding states – and this meant securing the slave-owning border states, including, crucially, Maryland. Lincoln was thus in no position, even if he had actually been inclined, to act against slavery at this juncture. Although some Britons recognized the second point, for many it simply confirmed their view that Americans, whether northerners or southerners, supported slavery. This outlook was upheld by several pieces of supporting evidence, including the pronounced anti-black sentiment in the United States – or 'fanatical hatred', as one anti-Confederate journal put it – which was far greater than anything found in Britain. Further, incidents such as Lincoln's repudiating the Union general John Frémont's August proclamation freeing the slaves of rebels in Missouri, among others, strongly suggested that an emancipation programme was not going to materialize. It was perhaps unsurprising, then, that Lord

Palmerston, now Prime Minister, upon being informed by the American John Motley that the Union was anti-slavery, asked if so, why did the North 'not prove their abhorrence ... by joining us in our operations against the slave trade by giving us the facilities for putting it down when carried under the United States flag[?]' On this point, Palmerston eventually got his wish: in April 1862, the Union signed a treaty with Britain for the mutual right of search off the coasts of Africa and Cuba in April 1862.[7]

If the Union's failure to emancipate was a sin of omission, its protectionist policy was one of commission. To British liberals, free trade was as much a moral, as commercial, issue. Or as one of its great apostles, Richard Cobden, put it, 'I see in the Free Trade principle that which shall act on the moral world as a principle of gravitation in the universe – drawing men together, thrusting aside the antagonism of race, and creed, and language, and uniting us in the bonds of eternal peace.' The Union demonstrated what it thought of that theory when it introduced the Morrill Tariff in February 1861. Setting duties at 40 per cent and aimed principally at manufactured goods and thus, British imports, the tariff caused outrage. That great supporter of free trade, *The Economist*, actually flirted with the Confederacy in its rage at the tariff, declaring that there was no interest in a southern victory, 'unless as far as the Protective Tariff of the foolish Federalists has made it so'. Leslie Stephen declared that while 'Free-Trade may not be the great bone of contention between North and South ... it is, perhaps, that point in dispute between them which most immediately affects us.' Harriet Martineau, meantime, raged that while the sin of the South was slavery, the sin of the North was protection.[8]

While neither a failure to pursue abolitionist or free-trade policies was as offensive as either King Cotton or southern slavery, the Union's diplomacy proved to be another thing altogether. It is instructive to compare British behaviour prior to the War of 1812 with the Union's diplomacy in 1861, because it seemed as if everything the two nations had learned in their dealings with each other during the intervening years had been completely forgotten. One problem was Lincoln's appointment as secretary of state, William Seward. An American chauvinist, he had angered the British by his conduct as New York governor during the McLeod case in 1840; his opposition to President James Polk's compromise on the Oregon issue; his regularly stoking of Irish immigrant animosity against Britain; his encouragement, as a congressman, that President Franklin Pierce take advantage of Britain's difficulties in the Crimea to advance American interests in Central America; his constant prophesying of the annexation of Canada; and his expressed belief, in 1859, to the Duke of Newcastle, that civil conflict in the United States could be avoided by causing a quarrel with Britain and engaging in a war against it. Almost immediately, then, Lincoln's administration fell under suspicion.

Relations worsened when, in response to the outbreak of hostilities, the Queen's proclamation of neutrality was issued on 13 May 1861. Forgetting that their own government had issued a similar proclamation during the Canadian rebellions in 1837, and unaware that, by declaring a blockade, Lincoln had, under international law, admitted the existence of a state of war, the northern public and political class were outraged by Britain's action. As far as they were concerned, recognition of the South as a belligerent placed it on the same plane as the Union and, convinced the proclamation was but a prelude to formal British recognition of southern independence, public opinion in the North turned sharply anti-British. Anglophobia, always a factor in nineteenth-century American politics, now enjoyed a free rein.

Although Seward had made anti-British statements even before the proclamation of neutrality, its promulgation apparently persuaded him to increase both the frequency and tone of such comments, going so far as to threaten Palmerston's ministry with war. He was joined by a number of other politicians, including the minister to St Petersburg, Cassius Clay, who accused Britain of betraying its anti-slavery past and threatened future conflict unless it supported the Union. Another source of irritation was the new minister to the Court of St James, Charles Francis Adams, son and grandson of presidents John Quincy Adams and John Adams respectively. A political crony of Seward's (as Lincoln said, upon receiving Adams's thanks for his post, 'Very kind of you to say so, Mr Adams, but you are not my choice. You are Seward's man') and coming from a predictably nationalist family which suffered from the delusion that the British establishment was forever plotting the destruction of their nation, Adams exacerbated tensions. Finding his demands that Britain rescind the proclamation of neutrality and guarantee never to recognize the South to be rebuffed, he spent much of his time as minister misrepresenting Palmerston ministry's intentions to Washington.[9]

Relations were further soured by the Anglo-American failure to secure agreement regarding the 1856 Declaration of Paris (eventually signed up to by over 40 nations) which abolished privateering while clarifying the rules of both naval blockades and contraband. Traditionally, the United States, both opposing blockades and supporting privateering, had refused to sign up to the Declaration. Facing changed circumstances, including a declared Confederate intent to use privateers, the Union changed its tune, only be told by Britain that since hostilities had commenced, the treaty could not be applied retroactively to the current situation in America. Despite a promise not to allow Confederate privateers to bring their prizes into British ports, discussions between Britain and the Union broke down in acrimony and mutual recrimination.

The American press, most ably represented by the *New York Herald*, but joined by others such as the *New York Times*, also contributed to this deteriorating situation by calling upon the Lincoln administration to make war on Britain and seize Canada. Soon it appeared as if Anglo-American relations had taken a step backwards to the days of the Oregon crisis, if not before then. Although much of the North's animosity was owed to fears of British intervention on the side of the Confederacy, by threatening war and an invasion of Canada, the Union essentially reopened issues the British believed were settled and thus re-awakened concerns about American annexationist impulses. This, in turn, provoked memories of previous Anglo-American difficulties, including the 'stab-in-the-back' of 1812, support for the 1837 rebellions, the disputes over the Oregon Territory and Central America, Russian sympathies during the Crimean war, the boarding dispute of 1858 and so on. Add to this the Union's Morrill Tariff and its failure to address slavery, and British opinion towards the North began to turn. The press started to retaliate in kind against its counterparts in America – anti-American sentiment began to grow.

By mid-1861, most Britons regarded the North as aggressive, irrational and rabidly Anglophobic. Or, as one journal observed in June, 'The Americans are, for the moment, transported beyond the influence of common sense ... With all of England sympathizing, more or less heartily, with the North, they persist on regarding her as an enemy, and seem positively anxious to change an ally, who happens to be quiescent, into an open and dangerous foe.' Or, as Palmerston, reading the disturbing reports of the British minister to Washington, Richard Bickerton Pemell, Lord Lyons, noted in September, 'I almost doubt Lincoln and Seward being foolish enough to draw the sword against us, but they have shewn themselves so wild, that any impertinence may be expected from them', and he made arrangements to strengthen Canada's defences and reinforce the Royal Navy's North American fleet. By sending troops to Canada, however, Palmerston simply further stoked American fears of intervention, despite the fact the contingents sent were not actually numerous enough to successfully assault the Union.[10]

It was in this febrile atmosphere in November that a Union warship, the USS *San Jacinto*, halted the mail carrier, HMS *Trent*, in international waters, and forcibly seized the Confederacy's two putative representatives to Britain and France respectively, James Mason and John Slidell, who were travelling as passengers. This assault on British sovereignty touched off a storm of outrage, one that grew considerably when the news arrived that the American captain, Charles Wilkes, was being lionized in the Union for his actions. At a public gathering, for example, Massachusetts governor John Andrew declared that 'Commodore Wilkes has fired his shot across the bows of the ship that bore the British lion at its head'. Palmerston, who had been assured by Adams that the *Trent* would not be molested (Wilkes had acted on his own, hence the minister was not duplicitous, but that took time to establish) took a different view. Convening an emergency cabinet meeting the day after the news of the seizure reached Britain, Palmerston declared 'I don't know whether you are going to stand this, but I'll be damned if I do!' With emotions running high on both sides of the Atlantic, and with neither side apparently inclined to yield, the situation looked grim.

Yet despite their anger, most Britons preferred to make absolutely certain that the North was indeed attempting to provoke hostilities. As one editorial put it, 'The idea of war with America should be to every Englishman unnatural and revolting.' A number of MPs publicly spoke out against conflict, including Edward Horsman, who opposed a war with the Union because that would mean an alliance with the Confederacy and thus British support for slavery, an institution he denounced as 'a disgrace and curse to mankind'. This widespread concern regarding the inevitability of an alliance with the South in a war against the North was echoed in the press: 'We have as little occasion to feel any emotions of interest in, or respect for the Northern States; but we pray earnestly that God may avert from us the great calamity of finding ourselves striking hands with Southern slavery.' The cabinet agreed. Although Palmerston gloomily observed to Russell, 'I am afraid that we shall not get what we ask for without fighting for it', his ministry refused to meet with any of the Confederate envoys demanding an audience. Even the military plan drawn up by the ministry to strike at the North in the event of war excluded an alliance with the South.

1. Sir George Cockburn as Admiral of the Fleet and First Sea Lord. The most unwelcome visitor ever to dine at the White House. The city burning in the background is Washington. The question was: would this be the face of Anglo-American relations in the nineteenth century? *(National Maritime Museum)*

2. Frances Trollope, called a 'censorious harridan' for her acerbic (and unfair) account of the domestic lives of the Americans, but other visitors proved more sympathetic, including her son, novelist Anthony Trollope. *(National Portrait Gallery)*

3. Immigrants departing for the United States. An estimated 4.25 million Britons migrated to the United States during the course of the nineteenth century, most doing so in the latter half of our period. Called 'invisible immigrants' by some, they nonetheless made their presence felt. (*The* Illustrated London News)

LIFE IN AN AMERICAN HOTEL?

Leech 1856

4. 'Pass the Mustard'. This *Punch* cartoon humorously underscores the widespread British belief that American society was inherently violent. (Punch Cartoons, Victoria 1841–1901)

5. Lord Palmerston, one of the nineteenth century's greatest statesmen. His continual difficulties with the United States, from the War of 1812 to the American Civil War, personified the ambiguous nature of the two nations' relationship. (*National Portrait Gallery*)

6. Telegraphic message – Queen Victoria exchanged greetings and best wishes with President James Buchanan in the first official transatlantic telegraphic communication. Her Majesty proved to be more pro-American earlier than most of her ministers or, for that matter, most of her people. (Picture History)

7. James Bryce, British statesman. Perhaps the most accomplished of the 'young liberals', his *American Commonwealth* represented an important landmark in British understanding of the United States. *(Bodleian Library, Oxford)*

8. Colonel Jonathan J. Bull or what John Bull may come to: the origins of the Americanization of the world, as the Pax Britannica began to give way to the Pax Americana. (*W.T. Stead*, The Americanisation of the World *(1901)*)

9. Mark Twain, called the father of American literature and a transatlantic phenomenon, his career in many ways personified the changing relationship between Britain and the United States. *(The* New York Times *Photo Archives)*

That noted, Lincoln's administration apparently still had to be convinced to respect the rights of neutrals. What amounted to an ultimatum was sent to Washington (accompanied by a reinforcement of the North American fleet and troops being recalled for duty in Canada), altered slightly by Prince Albert who inserted a clause declaring there was no doubt that Wilkes had acted without authority, thus providing the Union with a face-saving means of retreat. After a very tense Christmas, Lincoln's cabinet, probably having the 1859 boarding dispute at the back of their minds, bowed to both justice and pragmatism and released the envoys. Their release, however, was preceded by a provocative declaration by Seward who claimed that while the seizure was illegal, the Union was only returning the envoys because they were unimportant, and further appeared to suggest that Palmerston's government was afraid of war. Predictably, this communication further fanned the flames of anti-Union sentiment and convinced the British they had acted correctly. The Americans had violated their neutral rights and had retreated only because they had stood up to them. Or, as Palmerston bluntly replied to a tirade from the pro-northern MP John Bright, who virtually accused him of picking a quarrel with the North over the *Trent*, 'My hon. Friend says that . . . it was criminal in us to take measures ostensibly in defence, but in reality calculated to provoke a war with the United States. But Sir, had we no ground for thinking that it was very doubtful whether our demand would be complied with?'[11]

The results of the *Trent* affair – called the *Trent* outrage by the British – were both positive and negative. The incident served to release much of the tension that had been building up since the proclamation of neutrality, demonstrating to most in Britain and the Union that, despite all appearances to the contrary, neither nation wanted a war. Further, both Palmerston's and Lincoln's administrations made a rather more concentrated effort at communication in order to prevent any future misunderstandings from creating conditions similar to that of the *Trent* or, for that matter, the War of 1812. Conversely, the incident greatly increased Anglophobic sentiment in the North, with many believing Britain had sought to embarrass the United States while it was in difficulties (very few accepted that their nation had violated neutral rights). Meantime, for many in Britain, the entire affair – the incident itself, the Union's behaviour during it, and Seward's comments – was the final straw. They did not develop any particular affinity for the South – slavery was too insuperable a barrier – but they never forgave the North either. Even Lincoln's emancipation proclamation (see below) did little to mollify them.

It was also in part thanks to the *Trent* affair, which helped create a sense that events were spiralling out of control, that, in 1862, the British cabinet considered offering to mediate, in concert with France, in the conflict. As Britain had offered mediation in a prior American conflict – the one with Mexico – there was a precedent. Russell and the Chancellor of the Exchequer, William Gladstone, were the driving force behind the effort and, because they were arguably the two most powerful cabinet members after the Prime Minister, their activities posed a possibility of British intervention in the war – provided that Palmerston could be won over. Fortunately, the Prime Minister demurred, declaring that 'Those who in quarrels interpose, will often get a bloody nose.' While it is true that in September, before the battle of Antietam, Palmerston conceded that if Washington fell to the Confederates, an offer of mediation could then be considered, this was a considerable qualifier. If Robert E. Lee had marched into Washington as Rear Admiral Cockburn had done almost half a century earlier, the South would have almost certainly won its independence irrespective of any British actions. When, in October, the news of the North's defensive victory in Maryland arrived, Palmerston stated that before mediation was suggested, it should first be established that the two parties would even talk to each other – a necessary first step in any peace negotiations.

At this stage, Gladstone complicated events by his speech at Newcastle on 7 October 1862, where he declared that 'Jeff Davis' had 'made a nation'. As the cabinet was discussing mediation, Gladstone – unintentionally – had caused something of a leak. Unfortunately for him, the public outcry was unfavourable, even from those hostile to the Union. In fact, it was not until George Cornewall Lewis, the secretary for war, rebutted the chancellor of the exchequer at Hereford a week later that the outcry subsided; the majority of the British public opposed involvement in the conflict. The combination of this public opposition and the determined resistance to Russell's proposals mounted by Lewis from within the cabinet simply confirmed Palmerston's position. The Prime Minister sided with Lewis and, with that, Russell's proposal was dead.

The Foreign Secretary made a last bid for mediation to the cabinet on 11 November 1862 when he recommended a French proposal which included an armistice and a suspension of the blockade. His failure to secure Palmerston's support, however, encouraged the rest of the cabinet, excluding Gladstone, to rubbish the proposal. Russell had failed to persuade Palmerston when he proved unable to convincingly answer a series of questions posed by the prime minister prior to the meeting: would the North 'consent to an armistice to be accompanied by a suspension of blockades, and which would give the Confederates a means of getting all the supplies they may want'? That was the first problem. 'Then comes the difficulty about slavery and the giving up of runaway slaves, about which we would hardly frame a proposal which the Southerns would accept, the Northerns to agree to, and the people of England would approve of.' That was the second, but then there was the third: 'The French government are more free from the Shackles of Principle and of Right & Wrong as on all others than we are.'

As was so often the case when it came to Anglo-American relations, France was an important factor. There was little trust between Palmerston's ministry and that of the French Emperor Louis Napoleon, a point the two nations' fractious alliance in the Crimean War had tended to confirm, rather than refute. Indeed, in 1859, the volunteer movement had been founded, establishing a sort of home guard to defend Britain against French invasion. Further, the two nations were engaged in a naval arms race, constructing ironclad warships. Then there were the Emperor's activities in Mexico, where he would establish a puppet state in defiance of the Monroe Doctrine, making his interest in the Civil War markedly different to Britain's. In short, Palmerston did not trust the 'spider of the Tuileries' or his proposal.[12]

This effectively ended the debate surrounding mediation. In the following year, Poland rebelled against Russia and in the next the Prussian-Danish War erupted. In terms of foreign affairs, America simply became less important, especially as effects of the cotton shortage eased. Indeed, as regards the British economy overall, the Civil War's impact proved to be far less detrimental than initially feared. For example, from 1862–63, Gladstone as Chancellor of the Exchequer created a budget surplus of £3.75 million – then a significant sum. Nor was the ministry under any political pressure to intervene: when consulted by Palmerston and Russell, regarding America, the leader of the Conservatives, Lord Derby, along with Benjamin Disraeli, let it be known that they favoured a course of 'bona fide neutrality'. In Parliament, meantime, few members of either the House of Commons or the House of Lords regarded the conflict as any of Britain's business. Only one in six referred to it in their public addresses and, of these, a clear majority supported neutrality – irrespective of their political affiliation. The chief exception to this, at least early on, was Lancashire, where, thanks to the cotton shortage, there existed support for intervention. Thus, MPs as varied as the liberal William Massey, the radical J. T. Hibbert, and the conservative Robert Peel, the members for Salford, Oldham and Bury respectively, all called for intervention. Yet these cries were rarely repeated elsewhere. Nearly all MPs, however, even those predisposed in favour of the North, declaimed against Union hostility. Thus, Alexander Kinglake declared that the northerners were 'indulging in language which, had it been used by a state in Europe would undoubtedly have brought about before now an interruption of diplomatic relations between the two Powers'. This sense of nothing good coming from America explains why Palmerston's policy of neutrality enjoyed overwhelmingly widespread support in both houses of Parliament to say nothing of the country at large.[13]

This opposition to intervention also explains why all attempts to gain recognition of the Confederacy in Parliament ended in abject failure. For example, the first attempt, by the Liberal MP, William Gregory, in June 1861, according to one report, 'elicited only four cheers in the House of Commons and was silenced before it was withdrawn'. The second attempt, by the radical MP William Schaw Lindsay, meanwhile, faced cabinet opposition because of his attempt to convey a message from the French government regarding joint recognition of the Confederacy. Russell's rebuff was terse: 'I think the best way for the two governments to communicate with each other is through their respective embassies', and a similar communication was sent to the Emperor for good measure. When Lindsay introduced his motion in July 1862, he secured only four backers, one of them an inebriated Lord Adolphus Vane-Tempest who, in the words of one witness, 'came near to falling over the back of the bench in front of him on several occasions'. The show was brought to an abrupt end by Palmerston's refusal to accept any motions pertaining to mediation.

The third effort, a motion introduced in June 1863 by the radical MP John Arthur Roebuck, also involved Louis Napoleon, and proved a bigger fiasco than Lindsay's attempt the previous year. Breaching parliamentary protocol by announcing to the House that he conveyed a message from the Emperor, repeating French accusations of double-dealing by Palmerston's cabinet, and announcing the imminent arrival of a formal request from Napoleon III in favour of joint intervention in the war, Roebuck discredited himself from the outset. He outraged Palmerston's ministry and its supporters, secured the support of only two other members, and was forced to acquiesce to the Home

Secretary's demand that debate be adjourned until the French request arrived. When, thanks to his own activities, no such communication materialized, Roebuck was forced to withdraw his motion, his credibility in shreds. With studied understatement, one newspaper described events thus: 'He [Roebuck] does so concentrate his sarcasm and bitterness – delivers his opinions with such assertion of their being unanswerable ... that he never fails to interest, if he does not actually convince.' In fact the only result of Roebuck's failure was Confederate realization that British intervention was not going to materialize and so ordered its representative, Mason, to withdraw from Britain.[14]

If the efforts of southern partisans in Parliament proved farcical, the same could not be said of southern ship-building activities in Britain. James Bulloch, the Confederate agent residing in Liverpool directing these efforts, recognized that because the full burden of proof fell upon the Crown when it came to violations of the 1819 Foreign Enlistment Act, he had located a loophole big enough to sail ships through. Working in the leading ship-building nation in the world and by cloaking his activities under a mound of misleading documentation, Bulloch ensued that the ships left British ports as ostensibly innocent vessels of neutral nations, only to be armed on the high seas and converted into raiders. Despite the myth that the British government colluded in allowing these ships to be unleashed on northern shipping, historians have exonerated Palmerston's ministry of collaboration. Indeed, in the case of the most notorious of these raiders, the *Alabama*, the most recent scholarship blames the Union's officials for the ship's escape because they failed to provide the necessary evidence they possessed to the ministry in a timely fashion. Understandably outraged by these developments, Washington demanded that London halt Bulloch's activities. Despite disagreement over who was responsible for the *Alabama*'s escape, the British were broadly in agreement, being perfectly cognizant that these activities represented a dangerous precedent to the world's largest merchant marine. A clampdown on Bulloch's activities followed – despite some outstanding failures such as the release of the CSS *Alexandra* by the courts in June 1863 because the Crown failed to prove that it was indeed a Confederate vessel.

In 1863, an undaunted Bulloch audaciously attempted to have two ironclad rams built for the Confederacy. Attempting to fool British and Union officials both, he cunningly covered his involvement by making it appear that the vessels' putative purchasers were French. Unfortunately for him, neither the Union's officials nor the British government were deceived and, in September, the ships were detained. Despite Adams becoming overexcited and wildly threatening Russell, 'It would be superfluous in me to point out to your lordship that this is war' (a remark that nearly persuaded Palmerston to release the vessels, telling Russell, 'We ought to say to him in civil terms, "you be damned"'), the situation was resolved. Bypassing the American minister by informing Washington directly of the ships' seizure, and faced with Bulloch's ingenious paper maze that prevented legal confiscation of the rams, the Prime Minister came up with the obvious solution – compulsory purchase of the ships for the Royal Navy.[15]

Although finally thwarted, Bulloch's raiders nonetheless drove virtually the entire American merchant marine from the seas. Further, those ships not sunk were themselves converted into privateers, augmenting their numbers. Had the Union followed the British example in the War of 1812 and protected their shipping by means of convoy, the Confederate raiders' effectiveness would have been greatly reduced. Every ship the North had, however, was apparently needed for the blockade. Although the *Alabama* was finally sunk off Cherbourg in June 1864, other raiders continued the fight. Indeed, the last Confederate unit to lower their flag was the CSS *Shenandoah,* which did so in Liverpool on November 1865, some six months after the South's defeat. The activities of these ships would prove to be a major grievance of the Union during and after the war, and they accused Britain of deliberately releasing them upon northern shipping.

Privateering was not the South's only nautical concern; blockade running was even more important. The Confederacy, having little industry of its own, needed to have supplies run through the Union's blockade, in order to prosecute the war. Plenty of individuals, inspired by a combined lust for adventure and avarice, were willing to run the blockade, which remained fairly porous until late 1864. Evading the northern navy after setting out from Bermuda and the Bahamas, these blockade runners were a crucial source of supply for the South, providing not just munitions, but goods of all kinds, including tents, shoes, clothing and even food. Nonetheless, even here the South was disadvantaged. The contribution the blockade runners made to the Confederate cause in terms of material was utterly dwarfed by the amounts purchased from Britain by the North (which, among other things, remained dependent upon British munitions until late 1864).

If Britain's neutrality angered both combatants, the two feuding American republics equally failed to impress the British. In the case of the Union, both northern politicians and the press continued to cause offence. Seward, for example, published his diplomatic correspondence in 1862, the anti-British contents of which caused widespread anger. He was matched by Clay who made several speeches in 1862–63 calling for a Russian-American alliance against Britain. Adams meanwhile informed the leading pro-Union lobby group in 1864 that the North resented British neutrality with a bitterness that would lead to war. The American press, meanwhile, continued to denounce Britain on a regular basis. It was unsurprising, then, that the anti-southern *Spectator* declared in late 1862, 'We have not the slightest sympathy with American ways or American foreign policy. They are collectively to us the most disagreeable of people, and we have as contemptuous a pity for the half-bred vapouring of their public dispatches as any European diplomatist or as Mr. Roebuck himself.' Judah P. Benjamin, the Confederate secretary of state, observing the North's abuse of Britain in 1864, drew a more ominous conclusion: 'The administration papers in the United States, by their party cry of "one war at a time," leave England with little room for doubt as to the settled ulterior motive of that Government to attack England as soon as disengaged from the struggle with us.' British public hostility to the Union during this period simply reflected what was demonstrated towards Britain.[16]

Nor were many, liberals and radicals in particular, overly impressed with the suppression of civil liberties that took place in the North, including the suspension of the writ of *habeas corpus*, the repression of the press, imprisonment of dissenters and the introduction of conscription, all of which appeared to be a throwback to the days of the Napoleonic wars. The behaviour of the Union general Benjamin Butler in occupied New Orleans, particularly his threat to treat any defiant women of the town as common prostitutes and his hanging a man simply for tearing down the US flag, caused disgust. The arrest, trial and imprisonment by a military court of Ohio Democratic gubernatorial candidate, Clement Vallandigham, for denouncing the war in 1863 likewise reflected badly on the North. By 1863 onwards, meantime, Britain's Canadian colonies had become a refuge for northern draft dodgers, as well as other opponents of the conflict, a process that would be repeated a century later during the Vietnam War. In many respects, by the time of Sherman's march to the sea in 1864 – whose armies burned, robbed and raped (although rarely murdered) their way through the South, virtually abandoning nineteenth-century rules of war, particularly as pertained to the treatment of enemy civilians –

many in Britain no longer recognized a civilized society on the other side of the Atlantic. When one adds to this the sheer number of lives consumed by the conflict (the number of casualties at Gettysburg rivalled those of Waterloo), one can understand why many in Britain saw this war as a retreat from civilization.[17]

It was this, in large part, which weakened the impact that the Emancipation Proclamation, issued 22 September 1862, had on British sympathies, even if it was nonetheless better received than is usually recognized. Rather than there being any widespread belief that Lincoln intended or even would cause a slave uprising, most in Britain welcomed his proclamation, even if suspicious of the President's motives: 'He does not think that his notice that the slaves are free will set four millions of revengeful Africans firing, plundering or slaying; but he probably does hope that he will embarrass the Confederate Generals', represents typical commentary. Although the American historian Richard Hofstader claimed the Proclamation 'had all the moral grandeur of a bill of lading', it enabled Lincoln to at least partially reclaim some of the moral terrain he had earlier ceded by not pursuing a policy of abolition – particularly once the Proclamation took effect in January 1863 – even if it could not quite undo all the damage caused by the North's apparent belligerence towards Britain.[18]

The claim that Lincoln's emancipation efforts fell upon stony ground because British racial views had changed from an ethnocentric position to one of Anglo-Saxon congenital racial superiority, rendering their opposition to slavery shallow and encouraging widespread sympathy for the South, is nonsense. It was only after the Civil War that the ethnocentric idea that other races could be inculcated into the social values of British society as easily as whites was seriously challenged by the notion that other races were congenitally inferior. Historians claiming that notions of Anglo-Saxon racial superiority existed before then are reduced to citing the examples of Thomas Carlyle and his 'Occasional Discourse on the Nigger Question' (1853), or the opinions of Dr Robert Knox, two of the earliest adherents of these ideas. Both these men, however, saw themselves as outsiders advancing an unpopular cause even as late as 1865. Indeed, when one of their followers, James Hunt, argued blacks were inferior to whites at a public meeting in 1863, he was booed and jeered. Opposition to the idea of congenital racial inferiority was far more common in Britain than arguments in support of it throughout the conflict. As regards to the term 'Anglo-Saxon', few pushed the notion that the British and Americans were of common racial stock harder than that staunch pro-northerner, Goldwin Smith (indeed, he was one of the earliest converts to the doctrine of congenital racial superiority). Even then, Britons referring to Americans as Anglo-Saxons were not necessarily admirers. Palmerston was always suspicious of Americans, yet he referred to them as 'Anglo-Saxons' on several occasions. Further, at this point in time, the term 'Anglo-Saxon' was most commonly a cultural expression – not a racial one. Indeed, even the term 'race' did not often carry the connotations then that it did later. Britons still frequently referred to the 'British race' – a reference to nationality and culture.

No serious shift in British racial views can be credibly dated before 1859 and Charles Darwin's *On the Origin of Species*, the arguments of which were seized upon and perverted by the believers of congenital racial superiority. This process was not, however, immediate and the controversy surrounding Darwin's work, to say nothing of the hostility it initially engendered, slowed this intellectual corruption. Historians of nineteenth-century British thought on race have long established that the widespread change from the ethnocentric to the racist view occurred only in the aftermath of the 1865 Jamaican insurrection. This event happened after the conclusion of the Civil War. As it happens, that insurrection and Governor Edward Eyre's brutal suppression of it may be usefully compared to the actions of the Lincoln administration towards the Sioux in 1862 where General John Pope, sent to crush the rebellion, declared, 'It is my purpose to utterly exterminate the Sioux ... They are to be treated as maniacs or wild beasts, and by no means as people with whom treaties or compromise can be made.' Once the Sioux were defeated, over 300 of them were sentenced to death. After Lincoln mercifully reduced that number to 38, they were then all hanged together in the biggest mass execution in American history. It should be added that Pope, whose soldiers killed women and children, never faced a large public campaign to have him tried for murder in the manner of Governor Eyre. In the end, however, what was done to the Jamaicans and the Sioux represented the other side of British and American liberty.[19]

In any case, that British opposition to slavery prevented the South from winning any significant number of supporters is undeniable. As Confederate commissioner Mason despairingly noted to his secretary of state, 'In my conversations with English gentlemen, I have found it was in vain to combat their *sentiment*. The so-called anti-slavery feeling seems to have become to them a sentiment akin to patriotism.' Even the

Saturday Review, which detested the Union, nonetheless noted, 'The military vigour and fortitude of the South has been fully appreciated; but, as long as the Confederate cause is identified with slavery, it will never obtain perfect sympathy in Europe.' Then there were the observations of Confederate agent Matthew Fontaine Maury, who in early 1863 declared that Britain's upper classes were mostly abolitionists and, after complaining about a dearth of supporters, remarked, 'many of our friends have mistaken British admiration of southern "pluck" and newspaper spite at Yankee insolence as Southern sympathy. No such thing. There is no love for the South here. In its American policy the British government supports the people.'[20]

It was this realization, combined with the recognition that British intervention was not to be forthcoming, which exhausted the Confederacy's patience. Writing to Slidell in Paris, Benjamin angrily noted that 'the important fact has been saliently developed that France is ready and eager for our recognition and that England is opposed to it'. After Roebuck's failed motion, Benjamin ordered Mason to vacate his post in August 1863. Southern actions against the British then began in earnest. By October, all their consular officials in the Confederacy were expelled, in part because they were preventing an increasingly desperate South from conscripting British subjects. Southern journals, meantime, began to rival the northern press in Anglophobic sentiment. The British press, as it had with its northern counterparts, began to return the compliment. The Confederacy's record of perfidy was repeated in whole: its adherence to slavery, its plans to reopen the slave trade and its attempt to blackmail Britain through the King Cotton strategy. As one journal irritably declared, 'The South, now realising that nothing can be gained from forbearance, is taking up the anti-English cry, and Mr. Davis is as "bitter", if not as vulgar as *The New York Herald* ... Therefore we are well pleased at the close of the year to add to our record that the South is as angry with us as was the North.'[21]

By 1863, however, American events had already been eclipsed by European ones. The start of the Polish rebellion of that year and the Prussian-Danish War in the one following diverted attention away from events in America. Newspapers paid considerably less attention to the Civil War, as did the British public and politicians. To put it bluntly, from the British perspective there were simply more important things to worry about. As it turned out, the years 1861–62 proved to be the high-water mark of British interest in the conflict. By 1863, it was obvious that both sides were hostile to Britain and its refusal to choose between them, and the British, in turn, dismissed them both. This would remain the state of affairs until the collapse of the Confederacy in 1865.

While it is true that a small minority of Britons championed either the South or the North, usually on the grounds of national self-determination in the case of the first (equating the Confederate cause with Poland's or Italy's) and for anti-slavery reasons in the case of the second (which repeatedly compared southern secession to Irish rebellion), neither group's members consisted largely of any particular class or belonged to any specific political persuasion. Nor did either group epitomize the views of any particular class or political persuasion as a whole. The number of each side's partisans shrinks even further when one excludes those who opposed the South because of slavery, or condemned the North because of apparent American aggression – expressed opposition to one side in the conflict rarely implied endorsement of the other. This distinction is important, because it goes to the heart of the question of how many in Britain actually supported either side.

For example, a recent retelling of the traditional account, dividing British opinion on the war on political grounds, largely ignores the diplomatic and political realm as well as society as a whole, and concentrates instead on the pro-southern and pro-northern lobbies' activities. The work fails to accurately note pro-northerners' and pro-southerners' political positions: John Arthur Roebuck's, William Schaw Lindsay's and William Scholefield's radical politics are not identified (apparently in the belief they were Tories) while other important radicals who sympathized with the South such as George Potter, J. T. Hibbert and Thomas Vize go unmentioned. Equally, very few conservatives are actually identified among the pro-southern ranks. The study also fails to recognize that British abolitionists were not necessarily radicals – the Halifax Ladies' Emancipation Society, for example, were actually the sort Dickens parodied by the character of Mrs Jellyby in *Bleak House*. Then there is the problem of numbers. The work provides estimates of the lobbies' membership numbers in 1863: the three pro-northern groups providing a combined total of 1,807 and the one pro-southern group providing 661 (and this last may well have shrunk to around 15 by the end of the year). Acknowledging there were other, smaller organizations which orbited these, but at the same time remembering that there was overlapping membership among the various groups, this nonetheless puts the combined number of dedicated southern and northern partisans in Britain and Ireland at 2,468 individuals. In 1863, the population of Britain and Ireland exceeded 29 million.[22]

Exclusive focus on a squabble between two diminutive lobby groups, the views of which were demonstrably unrepresentative of society as a whole, will certainly create the impression that British hearts were divided over the Civil War. Yet even an examination of their activities raises questions. For instance, the numbers at the three largest pro-northern gatherings were: 6,000 in Manchester, December 1862; 6,000 at Exeter Hall, London, January 1863; and 2,500–3,000 at St James's Hall, London, March 1863. By contrast, the numbers at the three largest pro-southern gatherings were: 6,000 at Ashton-under-Lyne, April 1862; 8,000 at Sheffield, May 1863; and 4,000 in Glasgow, November 1863. The numbers at these, by far the six largest meetings held in Britain on the subject of the conflict, are actually not that impressive. The April 1863 meeting held in support of the Polish rebellion in London, for example, exceeded 10,000 people. In that same month, Palmerston addressed a meeting in Glasgow containing 50,000 people. The Prime Minister could draw a crowd, but so could the radical George Potter. His meeting in favour of extending the electoral franchise in November 1866 drew 20,000–25,000 individuals. But nothing drew an audience like a hanging. The largest gathering that had anything to do with the United States was the crowd of over 50,000 which witnessed the execution of the murderer, Franz Muller, who had been extradited from America, outside Newgate Prison in November 1864. Indeed, the size and behaviour of that crowd so alarmed the authorities that executions were soon moved to behind prison walls. These were what constituted mass meetings (and gatherings) in nineteenth-century Britain.[23]

The numbers *at* the meetings not numbers *of* meetings are what matter. Some pro-Union meetings were nothing more than private soirées, such as one held by middle-class members of the Union and Emancipation Society in a tea room in Ashton-under-Lyne, in January 1864, which nonetheless sent an address to Lincoln. In comparison to the much larger pro-southern meeting at Ashton cited above, what did this private party signify? Indeed, it was a measure of how unpopular both the Union and the Confederacy made themselves that pro-northern and pro-southern meetings and lectures were regularly interrupted by outsiders. Pro-northerners especially had to restrict entry into their meetings and lectures by ticket because failure to do so often spelled trouble. Visiting Americans were especially targeted. For example, in 1863, Henry Ward Beecher was so barracked and heckled by audiences in Manchester and Glasgow that the proceedings were reduced to a shambles – despite there being arrangements in place to suppress disorder. These and other such actions were not the work of pro-southern activists or supporters of slavery, but rather public demonstrations of disapproval for propagandists from an apparently hostile government. The only consolation the pro-northerners could take was in the fact that their opponents were subjected to much the same abuse.[24]

What is most significant about the two sides' respective lobbies is how little they achieved. The pro-southerners, trying to obtain recognition of the Confederacy or intervention on its behalf, were pushing at a door nailed shut. The pro-northerners, meantime, had no effect on either Parliament's or the Palmerston ministry's views regarding the war. There is not even any convincing evidence to demonstrate that either lobby changed many minds regarding the moral worth or credibility of their respective causes. In the end, the tale of the pro-northern and pro-southern lobbies' activities was full of sound and fury, signifying nothing.

The myth that British views on the war were divided on a political basis, with progressives supporting the Union and conservatives supporting the Confederacy, constantly runs up against the fact that there is more evidence against this interpretation than supporting it. For example, beyond isolated individuals such as Robert Gascoyne-Cecil and A. J. Beresford Hope, few conservatives actually articulated any sympathy for the South while most others expressed distaste. Besides the anti-reform MPs Sir G. C. G. F. Berkeley, Charles Newdigate Newdegate and Edward Horsman, there was the view of Sir James Fitzjames Stephen, who fulsomely praised John Elliot Cairnes's anti-southern work *The Slave Power* (1862), agreeing with nearly all of its arguments and thus making it clear where his sympathies lay. Stephen was one of the leading conservative thinkers of his day, a staunch opponent of political reform, an apostle of strong (some might say, authoritarian) government, and the scourge of J. S. Mill's *On Liberty* (1859) in his *Liberty, Equality, Fraternity* (1872–73). Then there was William Rathbone Greg who strongly opposed enfranchising the working class because it would throw 'the supreme power of the State, into their hands'. During the Civil War he opined, 'We cannot be very zealous for the North ... but we still have much feeling of kinship and esteem. We cannot be at all zealous for the South; for though she is friendly and free-trading, she is fanatically SLAVE, and Slavery is the object of our rooted detestation.' It is probably superfluous to add that, like many opponents of the South, Greg also made repeated references to the 'Anglo-Saxon' heritage of the United States. There was, in fact, no correlation between opposing southern slavery and one's political outlook – at this time, denouncing slavery in Britain was akin to disparaging monarchy in America. Indeed, even Richard Cobden doubted the Tories were pro-South. In a letter to Bright he explicitly requested his friend cease making the accusation, going so far as to claim that the language of the leading Conservatives was 'far more reserved and conciliatory to the North' than that of the Liberals.[25]

This is unsurprising. If one actually examines the beliefs of nineteenth-century British conservatives, as opposed to creating them out of whole cloth, one can see a host of reasons why the Confederate cause carried so little appeal. With the obvious examples of Ireland and the Empire, conservatives opposed the doctrine of secession and revolutionary governments generally; they distrusted the new racial doctrines given apparent credence by Charles Darwin's *Origin of Species* (a work with which they were uncomfortable anyhow); they, in fact, distrusted Lincoln's and Davis's respective republics equally. Few, it is true, shed many tears at the dissolution of the Union, but they expressed as little sympathy for Russia's difficulties in Poland or France's in Mexico – imperial rivals' problems were not Britain's. To seriously claim that British conservatives thought differently in any meaningful way about the United States' difficulties than they did about any other imperial rivals' is to thoroughly misrepresent their beliefs. Americans – in both the North and the South – may have viewed themselves and their struggle as being somehow different; British conservatives did not.

The myth of widespread British radical support for the Union is even less tenable. Even leaving aside that it was the two radicals, Roebuck, one of the authors of the People's Charter, and Lindsay of the Manchester School, who made the most determined effort to persuade Parliament to recognize the South, there were other radical MPs who demonstrated obvious anti-Union sentiment such as William Scholefield, Acton Smee Ayrton and J. T. Hibbert. London's radical leaders also provided a large crop of anti-Union and, in some cases, pro-Confederate sympathizers, such as George Potter, T. J. Dunning, W. Newton, J. F. Bray, Thomas Vize, John Bedford Leno and George W. M. Reynolds. The last was the proprietor and editor of *Reynolds's Weekly Newspaper*, the largest selling radical (some would say republican) journal in Britain, whose campaign from 1861–62 demanding the government break the northern blockade for the sake of getting cotton into Lancashire and its hostility to Lincoln's government generally, went well beyond anything expressed by the mainstream or Tory press. Nor was Reynolds's journal the exception among the radical press – it was the rule. As two scholars working independently of each other demonstrated, very few radical journals supported the North, the predominant tendency, if anything, being decidedly the other way. The exceptions were the *Bee-Hive* which was not mass-circulated, the *Daily News*, the circulation of which plummeted during the war and the *Daily Star* which was Bright's organ. There was some radical support for the North; the trouble was it was representative of only a small minority of the movement.[26]

By the time of the Civil War, British radicals had already largely ceased looking at the United States as a useful political model. Further, the Union's apparent sympathetic alliance with Russia, to the extent of providing a rapturous reception to the visiting Russian fleets in 1863, the same year the Polish rebellion began, angered many radicals. The reason *Punch* published cartoons depicting Tsar Alexander II and Lincoln greeting each other as friends was that Russian naval officers were received at the White House (and that no government was as staunch a supporter of the Union as Russia's). In any event, given the state of Anglo-American relations during the conflict, radical anger at the North was predictable. As George Grote complained in late 1862, 'I never expected to have lived and think of them [Americans] as unfavourably as I do at present ... the worst of all is their appetite for throwing all of the blame of their misfortunes upon guiltless England.' Most nineteenth-century British radicals were patriots, if not outright nationalists. They saw their own nation, flaws and all, as being in the vanguard of human progress – it was, indeed, a crucial part of their national identity. There was never any question that they might be willing to take ideas from the United States, but as *Reynolds's Weekly* put it, 'the principles of civil and religious liberty which are embodied in their institutions, were elaborated in England in the course of some hundreds of years. All their noble thoughts and ideas are the product of British brains.' When the United States became belligerent, radicals responded to it in much the same way they did any other foreign power which behaved thus. The majority of British radicals certainly did rally around the Union flag during the Civil War – not the one with the stars and stripes, but the one with the three crosses.[27]

The notion that British radicals believed that the preservation of the

Union was crucial to political reform and that the upper classes and
conservatives supported the Confederacy in hopes of preventing political change at home, are owed essentially to Bright who repeated this
charge throughout the war. Bright was assisted in his endeavour, at least
in part, by his long-time ally Cobden as well as a few others, including
lawyer Edmund Beales, the professors Goldwin Smith and Edward
Beesly, as well as the businessman Thomas Bayley Potter who served as
chief financial supporter and president of the Union and Emancipation
Society. By this time, however, working-class radicals wanting economic
justice had increasingly turned against Bright's and his allies' *laissez-
faire* policies. Further, when it came to foreign affairs, Bright and British
radicalism often diverged. Bright's peace-at-any-price mentality, or
appeasement in plain English, found few backers. Aside from America,
British radicals disagreed with him regarding the Crimean War; they
had little time for his studied indifference to both the Italian and Polish
struggles for independence (two movements which they overwhelmingly supported); and they were especially contemptuous of his
apparent benevolence towards Louis Napoleon, whose dictatorship
impressed few.[28]

The nickname applied to Cobden and Bright, the 'Members for
America', was not a reference to their radicalism, but an imputation
that their loyalties lay with a foreign government, one which appeared
hostile to Britain. Indeed, Bright did serious damage to Anglo-American
relations. His constant refrain, both in public and in his private correspondence with the Massachusetts senator Charles Sumner, that the
British establishment supported the Confederacy, could well have had
serious consequences. Those historians wondering why Sumner was so
violently anti-British and why, after the war, he wildly accused Palmerston's ministry of conspiring with the South, should read the correspondence between this elected representative of the United States
and the self-appointed one in Britain. George Orwell is supposed to
have complained of political activity that amounted to 'playing with fire
by people who don't even know that fire is hot'. In many respects this
effectively sums up Bright's conduct during the conflict.

Even many of those predisposed to favour the Union demonstrated a
tendency to distance themselves from Bright and his allies. Thus, the
anti-Confederate *Spectator*, reporting on the pro-northern Liberal MP
W. E. Forster's speech on the war, noted, 'he does not belong to that
school which prefers America to England, and is disposed, like most
Englishmen to meet menace with a very clear defiance'. John Stuart Mill

and John Elliot Cairnes, who were arguably responsible for the two most effective publications in defence of the North, 'The Contest in America', in *Fraser's* 1862 and *The Slave Power*, in 1862, took a very different view of the war than Bright. Both opposed the South because of slavery, not because of any particular faith in American institutions, of which Mill was suspicious and Cairnes frankly dismissive. Nor did either man support re-union until very late in the war – Mill regarding it as a 'moot point', and Cairnes declaring that 'I do not expect, nor desire to see the Union restored.'[29]

It was Lincoln's assassination and later Anglo-American relations that allowed Bright, his supporters and then American nationalists to portray British attitudes towards the conflict as being divided by political persuasion and class. The pro-northern lobby's radical membership held a number of meetings which, attempting to make political capital out of Lincoln's murder, while concomitantly maligning their political opponents, accused both conservatives and the British establishment of supporting slavery. This was seized upon by others, such as the *Westminster Review*, which began the war supporting secession and refused to draw any comparisons between British politics and events in America during it, but then declared, three months after the close of hostilities, that the conflict was in fact a test of republicanism and that the upper classes feared the triumph of democracy more than that of slavery. Evidence, if any were needed, that history is always at its most vulnerable in the aftermath of the event.

Another motive for the pro-northern lobby's activities, however, was appeasement. In 1865 tensions between Britain and the United States appeared serious: there were calls in America to seek revenge for the *Alabama*, and Palmerston's hardly conciliatory language alarmed the pro-northern camp. The beginnings of this process could already be seen in Cobden's letter to Sumner, 11 January 1865, where, recognizing that his and Bright's alarmist misrepresentations of Palmerston's ministry's position might have serious consequences, he begged the senator to remember that 'the common folk of England were true to the cause of freedom' (something he had never hitherto believed) and unctuously agreed with the senator that 'you are fighting the battle of liberalism in Europe as well as the battle of freedom in America'. This was a cry of appeasement, not a *cri de coeur*.

When, instead of conflict, the basis of the rapprochement between the two countries was laid with the 1871 Treaty of Washington, these post-war fables assumed the trappings of fact. Thus, Mill would claim in his autobiography, published in 1873, that he had witnessed 'the rush of nearly the whole upper and middle classes of my country, even those who passed for liberals, into a furious pro-Southern partisanship'. What Mill said during the war – particularly in his private correspondence – differed greatly to what he said in his autobiography, but this was true for nearly all the memoirs written by the, usually at best, anti-Confederate Britons in later years. These views were given a fillip when, on the other side of the Atlantic, Americans celebrating the centennial of the Declaration of Independence in 1876, promoted the myth that the United States taught the world the meaning of democracy and claimed that Britain's 1867 Reform Act was a result of the Union victory. Again, as with the War of 1812, the Adams family muddied the waters through the writings of the American minister's two sons, Henry Adams's *The Education of Henry Adams* (1907) and Charles Francis Adams's assisting the research of E. D. Adams, whose *Great Britain and the American Civil War* (1925) essentially established the traditional interpretation and was, up until the 1960s, considered the standard work on the topic.[30]

As regards the Reform Act of 1867, Bright and some of his allies certainly tried to link the example of the preservation of the Union to political reform, declaring that the North's victory in the Civil War proved the worth of an extended franchise. The evidence demonstrates, however, that they convinced very few. In the 1866 parliamentary debates on Gladstone's and Russell's unsuccessful reform bill – preceded by the equally unsuccessful attempts in 1852, 1854, 1859 and 1860 – less than ten per cent of the speakers referred to America. By the time of the parliamentary debates on the this time successful 1867 reform bill, less than two per cent of the speeches contained references to the United States. The claim, then, that the Civil War seriously influenced the 1867 Reform Act is not borne out by any evidence. The truth is that the conflict was primarily a foreign policy problem and had about as much impact upon British political reform as the Crimean War had on the domestic policies of the United States.[31]

Fundamentally, the most important question regarding Britain and the American Civil War is why the British did not become involved, either through accident or design, in the manner of the Americans during the Napoleonic wars in 1812? The answer is diplomacy born of experience. The legacy of Anglo-American diplomatic relations accumulated from 1815–60, resulted in distrust, certainly, but also in discernment. British and American statesmen – whatever their public declarations – sought to reach peaceful accommodation. Despite all the cacophony during the war, after the *Trent* affair both Palmerston's and Lincoln's governments followed the path laid down by previous administrations – above all else, avoid open conflict. Neither administration needed a war. Palmerston, who unleashed the Royal Navy on slave traders (and was thus a great emancipator long before Lincoln), did not want the Confederacy as a friend or the Union as an enemy. Lincoln, recognizing that British intervention would mean the end of the Union, did not want Britain as an enemy either. As the war progressed, both Washington, increasingly involved in a protracted war against the Confederacy, and London, facing serious diplomatic problems in Europe, actually found themselves cooperating on increasingly reasonable terms, whether as regards to the slave trade or problems caused by Confederate agents on the Canadian-American border. Indeed, despite the Morrill Tariff, their continuing commercial dealings were of such importance that both administrations tried to save the Canadian-American reciprocity treaty in 1864 from congressional termination. In this respect, then, however unfashionable it may be nowadays to express such views, the approach taken by the political elites of both the liberal state and the democratic one proved to be more accommodating of each other than either the press or public on both sides of the Atlantic.[32]

Just as there was real anger in America towards Britain, the British public were equally incensed by both sides in the Civil War. This was based as much on relations before the conflict as during it. Not only had the American public never demonstrated much sympathy towards Britain during the Napoleonic wars, the Canadian rebellions of 1837–38 or the Crimean War, 1854–56; they had, in fact, from the British perspective, pretty well manifested the reverse sentiment in each and every case. Even those willing to overlook all of this, and the tangled legacy of antebellum Anglo-American diplomatic relations, still had to contend with the *Trent* affair and the apparent northern belligerence shown throughout the conflict. Slavery was simply too much of a barrier to widespread support for the South, but there were equally very few reasons to feel any affinity with the North. Palmerston's policy of non-intercourse with the Confederacy and armed neutrality towards the Union was irrefutably popular with the overwhelming majority of the British public – whatever their class or political affiliation.[33]

Comprehending British views of the American Civil War requires an understanding of their history, society, politics and culture. Britain remained the pre-eminent world power with global, as opposed to regional, interests. The British witnessed a civil war in America, a rebellion in Poland from 1863–65, a war between Prussia and Denmark in 1864, and all the while observed the machinations of Louis Napoleon in both North America and Europe. This was a lot to digest; the American war was only one of many topics that exercised the British mind. To some degree, the United States did impact upon British cultural and political thought, but in the mid-nineteenth century, the balance of influence was decidedly the other way: culturally, economically and politically. This is why the partitioning of British society by political persuasion or, in a new incarnation, on the basis of love or hatred of Americanization (a term that meant nothing to mid-nineteenth-century Britons) is both crudely reductive and simply wrong. If anything, by becoming urbanized, industrialized, more politically centralized, a nation rather than a union, and indeed, by abolishing slavery, the United States was, in fact, becoming Anglicized. It is a measure of Britain's cultural dominance that the play Lincoln attended that fateful Good Friday when he was assassinated, *Our American Cousin*, was a British farce. Global powers rarely stake their political development on the outcome of regional ones' internal affairs – even those with which they share a common language – unless they come into direct conflict. It is little wonder, therefore, that the *Trent* affair generated by far and away the greatest amount of British commentary on the Civil War.[34]

In any event, insofar as Anglo-American relations are concerned, there was one individual who described the situation better than most and this was Lincoln. He compared the two nations' relationship to an elaborate story concerning a man who, convinced that he was dying, made a most affecting peace with his worst enemy. When the latter turned to go, however, 'the sick man rose up on his elbow and said, "But see here, Brown, if I should happen to get well, mind, that old grudge stands".' By 1865 a whole host of grudges had been built up among the public on both sides of the Atlantic. How these were resolved and what were the lasting consequences is the topic of our next chapter.[35]

7

The Road to Rapprochement: Anglo-American Diplomatic Relations from 1865 to the First World War

On 17 January 1917 in the Old Building, next to Admiralty House, the duty officer, Royal Navy Intelligence, examined the first German wireless intercept to arrive that morning. Noting that it was in non-naval code, he forwarded it to the Political Section in Room 40. This, the Admiralty's cipher room, contained a mixture of linguists, classical scholars as well as crossword and other puzzle addicts; in short, people very good at cracking codes. Germany's problem was that the British had cut their transatlantic cables (an act committed at dawn on the first day of the war) and had also tapped cables owned by other countries, including Sweden and the United States. This meant that, aside from courier, all German communications could be intercepted by the British – hence this use of insecure radio and thus the use of their code. The Germans were not especially concerned; they believed their code was unbreakable. Unfortunately for them, it was not. In Room 40, two civilians, the Reverend William Montgomery and Nigel de Grey, a scholar and a publisher, respectively, identified the code as a form of encryption used only for high-level diplomacy and set to work with alacrity. It took them two weeks to completely finish the job, but they deciphered the message. Their accomplishment would have crucial repercussions.

The message was from the new German Foreign Minister, Arthur Zimmermann, to the Reich's ambassador in Washington to be forwarded to his colleague in Mexico. The first part read:

> We intend to begin on the first of February unrestricted submarine warfare. We shall endeavour in spite of this to keep the USA neutral. In the event of this not succeeding we make Mexico a proposal of alliance on the following basis: Make war together[.] Make peace together[.] Generous financial support and an understanding on our part that Mexico is to reconquer the lost territory in Texas, New Mexico + Arizona. The settlement in detail is left to you.

The implications of unrestricted submarine warfare were important for reasons we shall come to, but it was the second part of the message that really mattered. Leaving aside that this was an obvious violation of the spirit, if not the letter of the Monroe Doctrine, Germany was encouraging an attack on the United States which, if successful, would dismember it. If anything would provoke the Americans into abandoning their neutrality and enter the war as a British ally, their being made aware of this communication would be it. The deciphered communiqué was passed to the Director of Naval Intelligence, Sir William Hall. Events were about to move in a direction favourable to Britain – and not before time.[1]

The war against Germany and its allies was not progressing well. The British offensive at the Somme had been called off just two months previously and although not quite the futile bloodbath of popular imagination (it saved the French at Verdun), it had nonetheless failed to produce the anticipated breakthrough. Russia, one of Britain's key allies, meanwhile, was looking politically unstable after its offensives of the previous autumn had ended in a serious reversal and cost the lives of almost a million men. Indeed, within two months, the Tsar would abdicate the throne. Then there were the revenues of the Treasury – or what was left of them. With the war costing £150 million per month, Britain was facing insolvency. The only good news, if it could be called such, was that if Britain was suffering, so too was Germany. The latter was experiencing severe food shortages, thanks to the British blockade and this, among other things, made their position in many respects even more desperate. The Germans, however, had a plan.[2]

With tenacious ingenuity, they had hit upon a method to not only counter Britain's century-old domination of the high seas but at the same time deal the nation a mortal blow. The weapon was the *unterseeboot*, or U-boat as it became known. By using unrestricted submarine warfare – meaning the targeting of any ship within the war-zone declared by Germany surrounding British waters – the Germans had found the solution to the problem that eluded them at the Battle of Jutland in 1916. Instead of attempting to lift the blockade by a futile attempt to openly engage the Royal Navy, the Germans would simply circumvent the latter and, at the same time, give the British a taste of their own medicine. Fortress Britain would be placed under siege and starved into submission.[3]

Significantly, the German plan had already enjoyed a successful trial run. The U-boat campaign had started in 1915 and had proven its worth.

From October 1916 to January 1917 the U-boats had sunk over 1.4 million tons of shipping. Indeed, within months of initiating their unrestricted submarine warfare policy, Britain would be reduced to less than six weeks' supply of food. By January 1917, over two hundred U-boats had been constructed and it was now time for the Germans to tighten the noose. As Zimmermann's message had also said, on 1 February 1917, 'the ruthless employment of our submarines now offers the prospect of compelling England in a few months to make peace'. There remained, however, one minor snag.

Unrestricted submarine warfare was bound to provoke the anger of a powerful neutral, the United States of America. Indeed, the Germans had ended their first attempt at unrestricted submarine warfare in part because of American outrage at the accidental sinking of some US merchantmen, and particularly the torpedoing of the RMS *Lusitania* in May 1915, resulting in the deaths of over a hundred Americans. During the policy's suspension, however, the Germans had built a massive submarine fleet and were now ready for a fresh attempt. The question was what to do about the American anger that would inevitably follow? Not that Berlin much cared for the American attitude. The British were blockading them and war was war. In any event, the Germans reasoned, the Americans should keep their noses out of European affairs – just as, from their perspective, so should have the British (they had been shocked by Britain's declaration of war in 1914 – whatever happened to 'splendid isolation'?). Besides, Washington had offered to mediate and bring an end to the conflict – and it was London who repeatedly rebuffed them. Thus, from Berlin's viewpoint, it was hardly they who were the unreasonable party. Further, there was a not entirely unfounded suspicion in Berlin that the American President, Woodrow Wilson, favoured the British, and was thus not an honest broker. So, if the Americans would insist on poking their noses into Europe's business, perhaps they should be kept occupied on their own continent. Hence Zimmermann's remarkable offer to the Mexican government.

While possession of Zimmermann's message could prove to be the weapon that would counter the U-boat, the British still faced a dilemma. They did not want the Germans to know they had broken their code and they did not want to allow them to take advantage of what is now termed 'plausible deniability'. Hall solved the first problem by ensuring that the copy of Zimmermann's telegram sent to the German minister in Mexico from the German ambassador to the United States was stolen by a British agent (it was this unencrypted version that the Foreign

Secretary, Sir Arthur Balfour, handed to the American ambassador, Walter Paige). The second problem was solved by Zimmermann himself who, when the American press got hold of his communication's contents, or the 'Prussian invasion plot' as they called it, gave a news conference on 3 March, admitting authorship. Why the German Foreign Minister made such a confession remains a mystery. Most probably he believed that Wilson's administration already had an original copy of his communication and, therefore, because the situation was beyond remedy by an official denial, he had best explain his actions. Zimmermann's defence was that the plan had not been offensive, but defensive: only if the United States declared war as a result of unrestricted submarine warfare was the proposed alliance with Mexico to occur. This, however, did little to mitigate the effects of his fatal admission. The American public, already angered by the recent sinking of US merchantmen, was outraged beyond measure. From their perspective, Germany, not content with starting a war in Europe, now wanted to start one in North America, too. Further, not only had the Germans been plotting against the United States, they now openly admitted it.

This was the final straw for Wilson, who regarded Berlin's activities as a treacherous response to his attempts at brokering peace among the belligerents. Three months earlier, he had declared that it would be a 'crime against civilization' to lead the United States into the war. On 21 March, after a cabinet meeting, Wilson reconvened Congress for 2 April, two weeks ahead of schedule, to hear a message from the President. On that date, citing Germany's unrestricted submarine warfare policy and the Zimmermann telegram, he declared that 'the world must be made safe for democracy', and requested that Congress declare war on Germany. On 4 April, the Senate voted 82–6 in favour; the House of Representatives voted the same two days' later by a 373–50 margin. The British now had one ally, Russia, which wobbled and ultimately faltered, replaced by another, the United States, which would do neither. They had outmanoeuvred Germany and had influenced the course of the war in a direction more favourable to them. The British had acquired an ace to be sure, but they had also known how to play it. True, Anglo-American relations had improved a lot since the early years of the nineteenth century, but the British had learned a lot from that awkward and, at times, acrimonious, earlier relationship with the United States. Certainly, it gave them an understanding of the Americans that Berlin – as shown by Zimmermann's suicidal confession – lacked. And they had just used that knowledge very effectively indeed.[4]

Before we turn to the greatest war since the one against Napoleon we need to examine what happened after the end of the bloodiest conflict in the western world that occurred between those two struggles, the American Civil War. For it was in this period that the British and Americans – at the diplomatic level at least – settled their half-century of accumulated grievances and placed their relationship on the road to the 'great rapprochement' that would be cemented by the United States' entry into the First World War.

When the Civil War ended, the public rancour on both sides of the Atlantic was intense. From the American popular perspective, London had supported the Confederacy, without whose aid and sympathy the South could have never resisted for so long, as demonstrated by the unleashing of the *Alabama* and other cruisers upon northern shipping – this being proof of treachery of the deepest dye. Clearly, British hatred of the sacred Union greatly outweighed their alleged opposition to slavery. On the other hand, from the popular British viewpoint, both the American people and their government had demanded a degree of support and sympathy they had never demonstrated towards Britain in their entire history, had throughout the conflict repeatedly threatened an unprovoked attack upon their territory, had traduced the nation's policy of neutrality and whose (very) late conversion to the cause of abolitionism was merely a hypocritical cloaking of the Union's real motive – the self-seeking retention of territorial possession. The escape of the *Alabama*, while unfortunate, and certainly not in Britain's long-term interests irrespective of whoever won the war, was primarily the fault of southern agents, not the government. Palmerston, speaking for the overwhelming majority of the population, had already made his views clear in the House of Commons when he declared on 13 March 1865,

> No doubt during the contest there has been expressed, both in the North and the South, feelings of irritation against this country. The irritation was caused by the natural feeling of the two parties against a third who does not espouse their cause, and who therefore think he is doing them an injury. The North wished us to declare on their side and the South on theirs, and we wished to maintain a perfect neutrality.

Although Palmerston knew it was unlikely, his position was that if the United States wanted to attempt revenge for the *Alabama* by attempting the annexation of Britain's Canadian colonies, they were welcome to try – the United Kingdom was a far more powerful nation than the Confederate States had ever been. From his point of view, any concessions to the Americans would be tantamount to appeasement and, as such, would take place only over his dead body.[5]

In some respects, this was what happened. On 18 October of that year, Palmerston, whose career spanned from the age of Napoleon Bonaparte to that of Otto Von Bismarck, passed away. His death was not the only factor that contributed to the post-war settlement, but his departure meant the removal of a major barrier. There were, however, other problems that militated against a successful resolution of Anglo-American difficulties, including the termination of the 1854 Marcy-Elgin Treaty, which besides ending trade reciprocity also ended American fishing privileges in Canadian waters and soon resulted in clashes between fishermen on both sides of the border. More problematic, however, were the activities of the Fenian Brotherhood, an Irish-American organization consisting of Irish rebels and Union veterans who, under the proclaimed aim of securing Ireland's independence, launched a series of raids into Canada, either to secure it as a hostage in exchange for Irish independence, or in order to provoke an Anglo-American war which would somehow achieve the same goal. Unfortunately for the Fenians they were unwelcome in Canada. Despite winning some skirmishes, their incursions were all halted and they were frequently repulsed not by British regulars, but by Canadian militia. Although the Fenians' military accomplishments were, in the end, negligible, the political influence the Irish-American electorate enjoyed, combined with the already existing level of animosity between Britain and the United States, made them appear a much bigger threat than they were in actuality. On top of all of this, there remained the disputed territory in the Northwest, including San Juan Island. All of this, combined with America's demands for damages accruing from the *Alabama*'s activities, made for a genuine diplomatic headache – for both Washington and London.[6]

British suspicions were aggravated by the United States' purchase of the remaining Russian territory in North America, now present-day Alaska, in 1867, which like the Fenian activities fuelled annexationist concerns. Moscow, viewing the territory as a too-easily taken hostage by the British in any future conflict between them, and deciding against making an offer to a potential foe, concluded that selling it to their friends the Americans represented the better option. Secretary of state William H. Seward proved a very keen customer and the deal was done. The United States would purchase the roughly 600,000 square mile territory for $7.2 million. Even though the Russians had initiated the deal, Seward had obtained a real bargain on behalf of his nation.

To his chagrin, his countrymen disagreed, seeing no reason why their government should purchase what they regarded as little more than a frozen wilderness. The secretary of state's deal was soon derided as 'Seward's Folly' and 'Seward's Icebox'. Stung by this ingratitude, Seward played the annexationist card, claiming that the purchase would hasten the day when Canada and the United States would be joined. He found an ally in Massachusetts senator Charles Sumner, who defended the deal as being a strategic necessity for the United States. Contrasting Russia's friendship during the Civil War to Britain's alleged enmity, Sumner argued that it made sense to help Moscow while discomfiting London. Once put in these terms, the purchase found allies in the press. The *New York Herald*, long interested in the annexation of Canada, took up the notion, declaring that the acquisition was a 'hint' from the Tsar to the British that they had 'no business on this continent'. The *New York Tribune*, hardly any more pro-British, meantime described events as 'a flank movement' upon Canada, and warming to its theme declared that John Bull would soon recognize that selling Canada to Cousin Jonathan was his only option. Successfully advocating ratification of the purchase in the Senate, Sumner, besides citing the value of the territory, declared that its acquisition by the United States would 'dismiss one more monarch from this continent'. His rather obvious implication being that another, Queen Victoria, would soon likewise be dispatched. Although Sumner won the day regarding the Tsar, his forecast regarding Her Majesty was to prove rather less accurate.[7]

Opportunity had not only knocked on Washington's door, but on London's as well. While the United States added to their North American acquisitions, the British – thanks to their colonists – consolidated theirs. This was the confederation of several of the Canadian colonies into a self-governing dominion. This long-standing British policy had, thanks to disputes among the future provinces, taken a long time to reach fruition. Upper and Lower Canada had already been united in the 1840 Act of Union, creating the province of United Canada, but this excluded Nova Scotia, New Brunswick, Newfoundland and Prince Edward Island and territory in the west, including crucially, British Columbia. By the end of the 1850s, however, colonial politicians openly proposed union and advanced plans to bring it about. At a meeting in September 1864 to discuss a union among the maritime colonies in Charlottetown, Prince Edward Island, the Prime Minister of

United Canada, the Scottish-born John Alexander MacDonald, contrived to secure an invitation for a Canadian delegation, including himself. Once there he proposed a union of all British colonies in North America. Encountering interest, but also suspicions regarding United Canada's ambitions, the Canadians suggested a second conference in Quebec City that October. Thus in a manner similar to that of American federation – an initial conference in Annapolis leading to the one in Philadelphia – the delegates in Quebec (who like America's Founding Fathers kept the proceedings private) produced 72 resolutions laying the foundation for a federation of Britain's North American colonies. A necessary follow-up conference in London, chaired by MacDonald, essentially completed matters and Parliament passed the British North America Act with the minimum of debate. Queen Victoria signed the Act into law on 29 March 1867, to take effect on 1 July.

Although some of the colonies, such as Prince Edward Island (echoing Rhode Island's contumaciousness regarding American federation), initially declined to join, they eventually gave way, in part thanks to pressure from London. In a manner similar to Seward's purchase of Alaska, the new Canadian Prime Minister, now Sir John A. MacDonald, bought Rupert's Land and the North-Western Territory from the Hudson's Bay Company for £300,000 and persuaded British Columbia to enter confederation in 1871. Yet MacDonald's political genius was only part of the story. If the Canadian colonies confederated for internal reasons, such as the promise of better economic prospects and political representation, there were external causes besides British imperial policy. While the push for confederation began before the Civil War, the Union's victory in 1865 gave the movement further impetus. The fear of American annexation was a constant presence in the Canadian mind and the loose talk by some politicians south of the border demanding revenge for British policy in the Civil War, the Fenian raids, as well as the negotiations resulting in the purchase of Alaska, all served to concentrate minds. While it would be exaggerating to claim that the Union's victory in the Civil War was a key factor in Canadian confederation, it was important enough. As one delegate, D'Arcy McGee (ironically enough, a repentant Fenian who was later assassinated by one of his former comrades), put it in the debates, 'They [the Americans] coveted Florida, and seized it; they coveted Louisiana, and purchased it; and they picked a quarrel with Mexico, which ended by their getting California ... had we not the strong arm of England over us, we would not now have a separate existence.' The legacy of the American War of Independence, the War of 1812 and all the subsequent Anglo-American differences including during the Civil War made it obvious that the Canadians, in Benjamin Franklin's words, needed to join or die.

Yet the American example was not simply negative. True, the delegates at the confederation conferences specifically denied they were creating a union akin to America's. MacDonald noted they were avoiding the 'mistakes and weaknesses of the United States' system', while Sir George-Étienne Cartier declared that they were adopting British principles over American ones, 'In our Federation the monarchical principle would form the leading feature, while on the other side of the line, judging by past history and present conditions of the country, the ruling power was the will of the mob.' Further, the British North America Act specifically emphasized that all powers not allocated to the provinces belonged to the federal government, the complete opposite of the American Constitution that awarded any powers not delegated to the federal government to the states. Historians may dispute the importance of the states' rights ideology as a cause of the Civil War, but the Canadians were determined to nip the doctrine in the bud. On the other hand, as we have seen, the path towards confederation, not to mention the form of government chosen, resembled that of the United States. Further, Canadian judges, when ruling on issues dividing the provinces and the federal government, cited American precedents, these being the most accessible and convenient. In many respects, they did what American judges did in the Early National period, especially the Chief Justice John Marshall, who cited precedents from English Common Law when necessary. Whatever the British, Americans or Canadians thought about each other, they showed a tremendous propensity to learn from one other – and all the while indignantly denying that they were doing any such thing.[8]

Thus, later claims by American nationalists that the British essentially withdrew from North America in response to the Union's victory in the Civil War, recognizing that there was no place for them on the continent, are wrong. London had always intended, even before the 1839 Durham Report (which provided the blueprint), that their Canadian colonies would become self-reliant and self-governing. It was not London that delayed confederation, but rather the disagreements among the future Canadian provinces themselves on the form of unification. Newfoundland, meantime, did not join confederation until after the Second World War and only received dominion status in the twentieth century (this was appropriate, for Newfoundland, even before Virginia, was the site of Britain's first involvement with the North American continent). Equally, Halifax, in Nova Scotia, remained an important Royal Naval base until the Canadians began building their own fleet in the twentieth century. In any event, Canada did not become an independent nation in 1867, only a self-governing dominion. So, for example, when Britain declared war on Germany in 1914, the Dominion was also at war – its parliament had no say in the decision, not gaining control over foreign policy until 1931. Indeed, Canadians remained British subjects until 1947, Canadian citizenship not actually existing until then. Whatever later scribes might claim, the United States, both at the time and afterwards, more accurately recognized the true state of affairs – demands that Britain ought to cede Canada would be made long after confederation. The United States' contribution to Canadian confederation was much akin to Britain's role regarding the preservation of the American Union from 1861–65 – it stood aside from developments. In the end, when it came to the final act in North America, Britain and the United States to an extent swapped places. It had been the British, with their global concerns, who usually muddled through while the Americans, focusing closely on their continent, had the clearer goals and ambitions. Yet regarding what to do about Canada, the United States had finally proven uncertain; the British, by contrast, played for a stalemate. In 1867, that was exactly what they achieved.

The United States was, however, determined to deal with Louis Napoleon, who had taken advantage of the Civil War to install a puppet emperor in Mexico, Ferdinand Maximilian, in 1864. Maximilian's rule was upheld by the French military; the plebiscite making him Emperor being held under the watch of French troops. Thus, Mexican rebels, led by Benito Juárez, refused to recognize his reign and fought the French army upholding his rule. With the Civil War ended, the United States sought to reverse this violation of the Monroe Doctrine by sending an army of 50,000 men to the Mexican–American border and formally advising Napoleon to withdraw. Napoleon had no choice but to oblige and, in the absence of French soldiers, Maximilian's regime collapsed, the Emperor being shot by the victorious rebels in June 1867. The British, initially relieved by Napoleon's activities in North America on the grounds that he could cause far less trouble there than in Europe, now found that they were stuck with him again. London and Washington had, in effect played pass-the-parcel with Napoleon III, but in the end neither one was responsible for his final downfall. Nemesis came in the form of Otto Von Bismarck and the Franco-Prussian war (1870–71) where the Emperor was deposed.[9]

There was thus rather a lot going on in the background when the British and Americans began negotiations regarding the *Alabama*, and yet this is still not the whole accounting. The British, as we have discussed elsewhere, had concerns far beyond North America. On the imperial front, from 1867–68 they fought the Abyssinian War, successfully rescuing Europeans and diplomats held by King Theodore of Abyssinia in his capital Magdala. Closer to home, there were concerns about developments in Europe, particularly the actions of that new rising power, Prussia and the unification movement it directed, resulting in the North German Confederation in 1867, and its successor, the German Empire, in 1871. The British found they were rapidly becoming mere spectators to European events. They failed to intervene in either the Polish Rebellion from 1863–65 or the Prussian-Danish war in 1864. In the case of the first, much as the British sympathized with the Poles, by not intervening they gave the Russians a free hand to crush the rebellion. In the case of the second, despite strong language from London about the need for a just settlement, Prussia and Austria defeated Denmark militarily then seized and divided the duchies of Schleswig and Holstein between them. This was followed by the Austro-Prussian war in 1866 in which Britain also declined to become involved. Although Britain somewhat reasserted its influence at a May 1867 conference of the Powers, where the Foreign Secretary Lord Stanley (Derby) acted as President, which settled the dispute between France and Prussia over Luxembourg, events in Europe were being increasingly dictated by Bismarck and the Prussian army. This point was underlined by Britain's failure to prevent the outbreak of the Franco-Prussian war. All of this certainly encouraged settling matters peaceably with the United States.[10]

In the case of the Americans, they had enough internal problems to keep them equally busy. The period from 1865 to 1877 is generally referred to as 'Reconstruction', wherein the United States was faced with the dual task of politically (as opposed to militarily) reuniting the nation and, at the same time, providing at least a measure of justice for the newly liberated slaves. The Confederate States, whatever one thought of secession, had largely enjoyed the support of its citizenry. The United States, being a democratic republic, needed to regain the loyalty of these disaffected citizens. Few southerners, however, were prepared to accept African Americans as political or social equals. The latter, on the other hand, were understandably unprepared to accept anything less than full citizenship, with all the rights and privileges thereof. Lincoln's successor, President Andrew Johnson, pursued, in effect, a policy aimed at conciliating white southerners while ignoring the situation of African Americans. This angered the radicals of the Republican Party who wanted the southerners to be treated more harshly and the freedmen more justly, and who eventually impeached Johnson in the House of Representatives (the first presidential impeachment in American history), and missed removing him from office by only one vote in the Senate. Johnson's successor, the Union general Ulysses S. Grant, proved less hostile to the radical agenda, but at the same time managed to become embroiled in a series of serious financial scandals and these, plus the economic recession which began in 1873, marred his presidency. With the American domestic political scene ridden with upheaval, coming to some sort of accommodation with London was, in many respects, one of the last of Washington's priorities.[11]

While Johnson's domestic policies might have been dubious, diplomatically he picked up where Lincoln's and Palmerston's administrations had left off. Besides telling the British minister to Washington, Sir Frederick Bruce, that he regarded the two nations to be on friendly terms, he demobilized the US Army quickly, reducing it to 38,000 men by the end of 1866. Further, his administration was no friend to the Fenians – the army confiscated their weapons while the government provided rail tickets home to those who promised to behave themselves. Although this was done quietly, as few politicians wished to tangle with the Irish-American lobby or their supporters in Congress, it was nonetheless helpful from a British perspective (although it also allowed Canadian nationalists to portray the Fenians as an American plot). Thus, even if Seward, at least in public, persisted in making annexationist noises, actions spoke louder than words. In this sort of climate, the British could consider negotiations over the *Alabama* and, in 1866, Lord Derby's Conservative administration offered a limited arbitration. This proposal was rejected by Seward as too little, meaning the issue remained unsettled, but at least some sort of offer had been placed on the table. This allowed Seward to make a fresh attempt in 1868, after Gladstone became Prime Minister and Grant was elected, although not inaugurated, as President. The American minister to London, Reverdy Johnson and the British Foreign Secretary, Lord Clarendon, concluded the Johnson-Clarendon Commission in January 1869. It provided a framework for individual Americans to submit claims to a commission. The problem seemed on the way to a solution acceptable to both parties.

Unfortunately, however reasonable this all appeared, the Senate rejected the convention by 54 votes to one. The opposition was led by the Chairman of the Foreign Relations Committee, Charles Sumner (coincidentally, one of Andrew Johnson's fiercest critics and who had now fallen out with Seward). Sumner, who had been fed a series of alarmist and, at times, dishonest, accounts of the Palmerston ministry's beliefs and conduct in the Civil War by Richard Cobden and John Bright, wanted, if not retaliation against Britain, certainly retribution. On 13 April 1869, he made a speech that was as ill-tempered as it was ill-informed. Sumner, after declaring that the convention represented a 'capitulation' to Britain, then damned the Queen's Proclamation of Neutrality as both a premature act and a spur to rebel resistance. Further, the convention contained no apology from London and no recognition that the claims were not those of individuals, but of the nation. Citing the rise of insurance on American ships, the loss of vessels and the destruction of the mercantile marine's prospects, Sumner, by some strange fiscal alchemy, calculated the damages at $125 million. These were the direct claims, but the senator was not yet done. He then argued that because the Confederacy was fed by British supplies and blockade runners thus 'If through British intervention, the war was doubled in duration, or in any way extended, as cannot be doubted, then England is justly liable for the additional expenditure to which our country was doomed.' Besides ignoring the fact that the Union had been an even bigger purchaser of munitions than had the Confederacy, this charge appeared to be an open-ended claim for any amount of damages the United States saw fit to demand. According to Sumner's calculations the final sum, including these indirect claims, was over $2 billion; by British accounting this was naked extortion.

Sumner's speech received a rapturous reception in the United States and, in line with his previous declarations regarding Canada, it was assumed that he was proposing Britain cede the Dominion in lieu of the debt. In fairness to the intemperate senator, this was not what he was suggesting, but others took up the cry and annexationist chatter filled the American press. Having noted that, others, while approving of the speech, nonetheless decried war with Britain. In Britain, the reception was very different. In the first place, if the United States was resentful about Britain's conduct during the Civil War, the British returned the compliment. The Johnson-Clarendon Commission had not been at all popular and was regarded by many as an unacceptable concession to the Americans. Now the British concession had been hurled back at them by a notoriously Anglophobe senator who had simply exponentially increased his nation's demands. As for the suggestion that Canada be ceded, that, as the old pun had it, was simply the red rag to John Bull. Even Bright, usually willing to appease the United States on every issue, was outraged. As one American visitor put it, he denounced Sumner 'quite violently, for a Quaker'. Yet Bright, of course, was in part the architect of Sumner's views thanks to his misguided correspondence during the war. As the actions of both the Conservatives and the Liberals demonstrated, London recognized that because the *Alabama* had escaped from her ports, the United States was owed some restitution. Nonetheless, Britain was not going to apologize for its neutrality, pay a blackmailer's bill or cede Canada. Thus, all hopes of any deal or reconciliation between the two nations appeared to be as sunk as the *Alabama* itself.[12]

Unrelated events changed the situation. Later that year, the Red River Rebellion took place in what is now Manitoba, which the Canadian government suppressed with British troops and without American interference. In the United States meanwhile, Grant's administration locked horns with Congress as the President tried unsuccessfully to annex Santo Domingo (now the Dominican Republic). The Santo Domingo fiasco placed Grant and Sumner on a collision course when the senator led the opposition to the President's scheme. Hitherto, Grant had basically agreed with Sumner regarding Britain and the *Alabama* claims. Now they were political enemies. Grant, the conqueror of the Confederacy, was not a man to be trifled with. First he replaced Sumner's protégé John Motley as British minister to Britain (who succeeded Reverdy Johnson in 1869), then he successfully conspired to remove Sumner from the chairmanship of the Senate Committee on Foreign Affairs. A major obstacle to Anglo-American negotiations had just been neutered.[13]

Even with Sumner's departure, it took a year and some behind-the-scenes negotiations to get talks back on track, but resume they did. Canada's finance minister John Rose, meeting with Grant's secretary of state Hamilton Fish to discuss trade reciprocity, had his offer to take a message to Britain regarding the frozen *Alabama* negotiations accepted. This led to talks between the British minister to Washington, Sir Edward Thornton and the secretary of state. There were some hiccups, including a demand at the outset from Fish that Canada be ceded (he was responding to Sumner's insistence that British withdrawal from the western hemisphere was a precondition to talks). When this oft-made proposal met with the same brusque response accorded to all its previous incarnations, the secretary of state abandoned Sumner's precondition and the talks resumed. Although the British refused to accept liability up front for the *Alabama*, or to pologize either for its escape or the proclamation of neutrality, both nations finally agreed to discuss some method of arbitration. There remained, unfortunately, a hitch: it was never made clear if the indirect claims would also be up for discussion. Washington would not disavow them, while London would not recognize them – but had either nation insisted upon having its way at this point, no agreement would have been possible. Yet this oversight would almost prove fatal.

The Joint High Commission, the American delegation led by Fish, the British by Earl de Grey, first met in February 1871 and concluded the Treaty of Washington in two months. The commission referred the San Juan Island boundary dispute – the site of the 'Pig War' – to arbitration by the German Emperor (who decided in favour of the Americans) and agreed on a method of arbitration to settle the fishery disputes. Regarding the *Alabama*, they agreed that the issue of claims would be determined by five arbitrators, one each from Britain, the United States, Switzerland, Brazil and Italy, to meet in Geneva. London even threw in an 'expression of regret' that the Confederate cruisers had escaped British custody. Both nations ratified the treaty – even a chastened Sumner voted with the majority in the Senate. At that point, however, the deal unravelled.

When in December 1871, Washington presented its case to London, the indirect claims were included, which amounted to all the expenses since the Battle of Gettysburg plus seven per cent interest. To say this caused an explosion in Britain, both at the political and public level, would be an understatement. Throughout the negotiations resulting in the Treaty of Washington, the American delegation had never mentioned the indirect claims – only the direct ones. More importantly, the British had made it clear that they would not agree to submit any indirect claims to arbitration. To many in Britain, the United States was attempting to foist its massive war debt onto the shoulders of the British taxpayer. When Queen Victoria opened Parliament on 6 February 1872 with the declaration that the indirect claims were not 'within the province of the Arbitrators', the cheers were as loud as they were long. On the other side of the Atlantic, Grant, running for re-election, could not repudiate the United States' position, even if he had been so inclined. Further, all American suggestions to break the deadlock – which included, among other things, ceding Vancouver Island or rescinding any counter-claims for the Fenian raids – simply enraged the British even more.

Recognizing that the prospect of arbitration and, with it, any possibility of restitution, was rapidly receding, the American arbitrator, Charles Francis Adams, made it clear that he opposed the indirect claims. London, however, was unwilling to trust that Adams would vote against the indirect claims or that the other three arbitrators would do likewise, and refused to reverse its decision. When the Tribunal at Geneva met in June 1872, the British simply declared that they would not submit their case until the issue of the indirect claims was settled, forcing adjournment. In an effort to resolve the dispute, the British representative, Lord Tenterden, and his American colleague concocted an arrangement where the Tribunal would recognize that it had no authority on the matter of indirect claims, but would make a non-binding decision on whether there was any merit to them. As both the American and British negotiators now wanted the indirect claims dropped, the Tribunal's decision was virtually a foregone conclusion – but it went further: it refused to even consider the issue. The language used was certainly diplomatic, but the message was clear: the indirect claims could not be substantiated and were outside the terms of the Treaty. Washington could now drop the issue of indirect claims, arguing the Tribunal had rejected them; London could now allow the proceedings to take place.[14]

The verdict of the Tribunal was, on the whole, reasonable. Regarding the Confederate raiders' escapes and activities, Britain was variously found liable, not liable and only partially liable depending upon the individual case and required to pay the United States $15.5 million. A fair sum, to be sure, but far short of Sumner's $125 million to say nothing of the over $2 billion in indirect claims. This award was partially offset by the almost $2 million that the United States was required to pay Britain for claims against it during the war and, later, the almost $5.5 million it paid Canada in order to solve the fishing disputes. Put in imperial terms, the British really paid $8 million, but as Canada absorbed the lion's share of Washington's money, it was the British Treasury that really carried the costs.

Although later seen as a landmark in international law, there was a lot of opposition to the decision in both nations and this hostile public response ought to remind us of what British and American politicians often had to factor into their negotiations and the pitfalls they had to circumvent. In Britain, many regarded the award as both humiliating and unjustifiably large. Many reminisced about the good old days of Palmerston and if not a reason for Gladstone's ministry's fall in 1874, the outcome of the Treaty of Washington did nothing to help the Grand Old Man's administration. In the United States, meantime, there remained resentment that the indirect claims had been rejected and accusations were levelled that 'Unconditional Surrender' Grant had capitulated to the British. To claim that the Treaty of Washington was one of the reasons the Republicans nearly lost the presidency in 1876 would be to exaggerate, but it certainly did little to help the party's electoral prospects. On the other hand, despite the outcry, most individuals in both countries were happy to renounce the *Alabama* and all her works. From the American perspective, an expression of regret and $15.5 million was better than nothing; from the British perspective, that no *Alabama*s would be unleashed against them in any future war was a reasonable outcome. In truth, both nations had gained about as much as they had a right to expect. Further, while the Treaty of Washington did not turn them into good friends, it did at the very least make such an event possible – something that appeared virtually unthinkable in 1865.[15]

Acknowledging that, acrimonious diplomatic disputes were not yet a thing of the past, including those concerning issues that still required resolution under the Treaty of Washington. These involved, most significantly, compensation for British subjects which resulted from the fishing disputes in Nova Scotia and Newfoundland. Particularly problematic was the assertion by the American negotiator, Ensign Kellogg, only made after the British were awarded $5 million (they had asked for $15 million) that unanimity among the tribunal's three members (Britain, the United States and Belgium) was required. Kellogg found both public and political support within the United States, especially when American and Canadian fishermen became involved in a series of serious altercations (including a particularly ugly incident in Newfoundland). This led to a counter-suit for damages by the United States which nearly derailed the entire agreement. In the end, the United States paid up, after receiving some compensation for the Newfoundland incident, but the entire imbroglio caused resentment. Indeed, quarrels over fishing rights, as well as seal-hunting disputes on the Alaska–

Canadian border, would keep British, Canadian and American diplomats busy for the rest of the century. Arguments over territory had apparently given way to disputes over wildlife.[16]

Not that the last remaining territorial dispute, over the Alaska-Yukon boundary in 1903, was settled quietly. What made the stakes higher than they should have been was the discovery of gold in the area and some not especially clever talk both before and during the negotiations. To settle the dispute, a Joint Commission consisting of six officials, three Americans and three British subjects was established. The British appointed two Canadians and a senior British judge, Viscount Alverstone (Richard Webster), to negotiate. President Theodore Roosevelt, besides picking three men who he knew would take a hard line on the issue, dropped some far-from-subtle hints that he expected an outcome favourable to the United States. Alverstone, however, received contrary instructions from the Colonial Secretary Joseph Chamberlain, who being a staunch proponent of Imperial Federation (discussed in the following chapter), wanted the judge to vote with the Canadians. Although Alverstone made the right decision and voted with the Americans on the logical grounds that their claims most closely matched those of the original 1825 Russian-British Treaty, he received no credit for his integrity. The Canadians damned both him and London for betraying their interests in a quest for American friendship, while jubilant remarks about Roosevelt's tactics – including some silly comments from the President himself – in the United States apparently confirmed their verdict. The scramble for North America had finally come to an end and, in light of its long and tangled history, it somehow seemed appropriate that it was finally laid to rest to a chorus of dim-witted cacophony.[17]

Much the same must be said of the last potentially dangerous diplomatic dispute between Britain and the United States, the Venezuela Crisis of 1895–96. Although it is sometimes cited as the last time Britain and the United States nearly went to war, there is not much substance to the claim. The cause of the confrontation was another boundary dispute, this time between British Guiana and Venezuela, which had never been properly established. The British had tried to arrange its settlement in 1844, but upon receiving no encouragement from Venezuela, withdrew their offer. Doubtless the boundary would have been eventually settled without any crisis whatsoever but, as is so often the case, something turned up; in this case, gold. It was discovered in the disputed territory and both Britain and Venezuela claimed the land –

the latter going so far as to include hitherto undisputed areas of British Guiana as belonging to it, too. Wanting a favourable settlement and recognizing that in the case of a military show-down Venezuela would be the loser, the South Americans pressed Washington to intervene, citing the 'immortal Monroe', meaning the Monroe Doctrine, as a justification.

Washington was initially loath to interfere, especially as the Monroe Doctrine was hardly applicable. Indeed, in the same year as the Venezuela Crisis, 1895, America had stood by when Britain sent troops into Nicaragua to collect damages, temporarily occupying a number of ports. This action, however, had not passed unnoticed by some American politicians, particularly on the part of the new imperialists, men such as Theodore Roosevelt and the Republican senator Henry Cabot Lodge, who wanted the United States to take its place as a world power and international player. As the first rule of world powers is to extend hegemony over their self-proclaimed spheres of influence, these new imperialists turned on Britain, Lodge going so far as to accuse the British of trying to turn the Caribbean into a 'British lake'.[18]

Thus, although it is true that President Grover Cleveland was under pressure from the imperialists and experiencing domestic problems at home (his Democrats had lost both Houses of Congress in the 1894 elections), there was more to his actions than mere political expediency. His expressions of concern, sent through official diplomatic channels, received vague answers from London. The British, involved in a dispute with Russia and outraged about Turkish massacres of Armenians, simply did not regard the business with Venezuela as important. Suspicions aroused by these apparent evasions, Cleveland made a point of writing to the British Prime Minister on 20 July 1895. In his letter, he cited the Monroe Doctrine and insisted Latin America was not open to colonization.

A prompt and courteous reply from London would probably have ended the matter there and then. As it was, the response from the Prime Minister, Lord Salisbury, was neither. After an interlude of four and a half months, Salisbury's blunt reply arrived in Washington. After stating that Britain had no designs on Venezuelan sovereignty (which was true enough), the Prime Minister declared that although the Monroe Doctrine 'must always be mentioned with respect . . . no statesman, however eminent, and no nation, however powerful, are competent to insert into the code of international law a novel principle which was never recognized before, and which has not since been accepted by the

Government of any other country'. In short, Salisbury was stating not only that the Monroe Doctrine was inapplicable to the situation in Venezuela, but that it had no standing in international law. Salisbury was dismissive rather than deliberately offensive. As far as he could see it, the at best minor matter was between Britain and Venezuela and was none of the United States' business. Further, as the Monroe Doctrine had at least in part been instigated by British efforts to prevent the recolonization of the South American republics by Europeans and been entirely enforced by the Royal Navy, Salisbury had at least half a point.[19]

Although all available evidence suggests the tone of Cleveland's letter took Salisbury by surprise and that he had no intention of provoking anything, his response had that effect. Enraged by Salisbury's high-handed dismissal, of both himself and sacred American doctrine, Cleveland, on 17 December, sent a message to Congress which, in effect, declared that the United States would send a commission to establish the 'true divisional line' between British Guiana and Venezuela and 'resist by any means in its power' British claims to territory 'we have determined of right belongs to Venezuela'. In other words, the United States was declaring its intent to enforce arbitration – with or without British consent.

A wave of patriotic fervour swept the United States. Calls for the invasion of Canada were heard, while the *New York Sun* carried the headline 'War if Necessary'. It was almost as if the bad old days of the *New York Herald* and the Civil War had returned. Certainly, that was how the Canadians saw it. They prepared to raise volunteers to fight their traditional foe. The British response, by contrast, was one of surprise, if not shock, for this American response, from their perspective, came from out of the blue. The surprise then transformed into anger and outrage. Voices – not necessarily 'High Tory' as has been tiresomely claimed by some, forgetting that nineteenth-century nationalism was a bipartisan phenomenon – called for the defence of Canada and war with the United States if it interfered in the Venezuelan issue. As had been the case in the past, both countries were locked in a standoff, for, if the United States had the undeniable advantage on land, the British with fifty battleships, compared to America's three, held the best cards when it came to the sea.[20]

Ultimately, like every Anglo-American dispute since the War of 1812, the political elites both decided that 'jaw–jaw' was better than war. This time, however, the decision was not entirely theirs to make. Joseph Pulitzer, editor of the *New York World*, speaking for many Americans declared, 'There is no menace in the boundary line, it is not our frontier, it is none of our business', and published numerous letters from leading Americans and Britons decrying war. Many British newspapers followed his lead. Scores of memorials and petitions against war soon flooded each nation's capital from the public on both sides of the Atlantic, smothering what war fever existed. Personal, professional and political connections across the Atlantic were now just simply too powerful to be discounted. When Colonial Secretary Joseph Chamberlain declared that 'War between the two nations would be an absurdity as well as a crime', and that 'The two nations are allied and more closely allied in sentiment and interest than any other nations on the face of the earth', he was as much genuflecting towards public opinion as declaring his own.[21]

Despite the initial anger on both sides (and it lasted about three days in the United States), the sensible minority, when it came to Anglo-American relations, had grown into a majority and an entrenched one at that. The relieved politicians were thus able to bow to the inevitable and negotiate without losing face. Finally, after much diplomatic manoeuvring, on 12 November 1896 an Anglo-American commission, including a Russian expert on international law, was established to settle the boundary. It contained not a single Venezuelan. That was the insult. The injury occurred when the commission awarded most of the disputed territory to Britain. To the Venezuelans' chagrin, the United States instructed them to accept the settlement. Thus, the last serious war scare in Anglo-American relations came to an end accompanied by, appropriately enough, a great deal of commotion, followed by common sense. The postscript to the Venezuelan Crisis came in 1902, when Britain (along with Germany) blockaded Venezuela to force its dictator, Cipriano Castro, to pay debts outstanding. This time, the American response was that of President Roosevelt: 'If any South American State misbehaves towards any European country, let the European country spank it.' Clearly, the Monroe Doctrine was a flexible instrument.[22]

The truth is that by the end of the nineteenth century, the United States and Britain were moving in increasingly similar directions. Both were now fully fledged imperialists whose interests rarely conflicted and at times even became complementary as the Spanish-American War (1898), Boer War (1899–1902) and Boxer Rebellion (1900) demonstrate. The parallels had already been long apparent, and sometimes in the form of failures as well as successes. So, for example, where the Lakota-Cheyenne massacred Lieutenant-General George Armstrong Custer and

the 7th Cavalry at the Battle of Little Bighorn in June 1876, the Zulus
achieved much the same feat when they annihilated a battalion of the
2nd Warwickshire regiment at the Battle of Isandlwana in January 1879.
In the end, it was the Americans and British who prevailed in both
conflicts, but the Lakota-Cheyenne and Zulus were peoples with a
warrior culture who both demonstrated that they would not be meekly
pushed around.[23]

The origins of the Spanish-American War lie in the 1897 Cuban
rebellion against Spain. American public opinion, and that of the
President William McKinley, was generally sympathetic to the rebels.
Finding his offer to persuade Spain to withdraw gracefully rebuffed,
McKinley sent a warship, the USS Maine, to allegedly observe the
proceedings in January 1898. Spain warned that it would not tolerate
foreign intervention in its affairs and, shortly after this, on 9 February, a
letter written by the Spanish Minister to Washington, outlining
McKinley's personal defects, somehow made its way to the American
press, which published it. Six days after this, an explosion ripped
through the Maine, anchored in Havana, killing some 260 officers and
men. The American press, already incensed by the minister's letter,
accused the Spanish of planting a bomb (hence the battle-cry
'Remember the Maine!') and clamoured for war. Modern research has
subsequently exonerated Spain, but that meant nothing then. Finding
his efforts to mediate rebuffed, McKinley successfully requested Congress to give him permission to end the fighting in Cuba by force if
necessary. Spain responded to this intervention in its affairs by declaring
war. It was a decidedly one-sided affair. The United States was far
wealthier and far more powerful than Spain. On 1 May 1898 the Spanish
Navy was defeated in a battle in Manila Bay in the Philippines and
another American naval victory at the Harbour of Santiago de Cuba,
accompanied by an invasion of the island and decisive Spanish defeat at
the Battle of San Juan Hill, brought the lop-sided contest to an end.
Spain sued for peace in August 1878. As a result of the war, the United
States acquired the Philippines, Guam and Puerto Rico (it also annexed
Hawaii), while Cuba obtained independence. It was, in the words of
secretary of state John Hay, 'a splendid little war'.

As regards Spain, that was true enough; the occupation of the Philippines was decidedly less so. The Filipinos, who had been fighting for
independence from Spain since 1896; were not inclined to accept rule by
another foreign power. The rebellion, which lasted from 1899–1902, took
70,000 American troops to suppress. In desperation, the Filipinos

turned to guerrilla warfare. In retaliation, US forces burned whole villages to the ground and established concentration camps to intern
suspected guerrillas and supporters in which thousands died. By 1902,
with the last effective Filipino guerrillas dead or captured, the United
States was able to declare the insurgency over (although there was
sporadic fighting until 1913). The United States lost less than 5,000 men;
the Filipinos lost between 15,000–20,000 combatants and around ten
times that number of civilians.[24]

If the American activities in the Philippines were hardly an
impressive spectacle, the British accomplishments in the Boer War were
no better and no one ever mistook this conflict for a splendid little war,
even though it was called 'the last gentleman's war' by those who lived
to see the slaughter of 1914–18. Technically, the Boer War of 1899–1902
was the second of two. The first, 1880–81, was a more limited and
somewhat inconclusive affair although, on balance, the Boers had the
better of it, winning independence from Britain in all matters except
foreign affairs. The second was very different. With the discovery of
gold in the nominally independent Transvaal (the other Boer republic
being the Orange Free State), thousands of prospectors from Britain
and elsewhere flooded the territory. These foreigners, 'Uitlanders' was
the Boers' phrase, essentially settlers, found themselves denied the vote
and subject to discriminatory taxation. When they informed the President of the Transvaal, 'Oom' Paul Kruger, that they would protest, he
responded with the immortal reply: 'Protest all you like, I have the
guns.' The treatment of the Uitlanders, Boer attempts to undermine
British economic hegemony in Southern Africa and apparent flirtations
with Imperial Germany, led London to believe that the Boers needed to
be brought back under control. A clumsy attempt to orchestrate a *coup
d'état* in 1895, the Jameson Raid, sponsored by Cecil Rhodes, ended in
abject failure. Having proven unsuccessful through indirect means,
London chose a more direct method. Demanding that the Uitlanders be
given full civil rights, troops began to be sent to the Cape Province and
from there to the Transvaal border to force Boer cooperation. This
provoked, as was probably intended, an ultimatum from Kruger that
the British withdraw their troops from the Transvaal border or else the
Boer republics would declare war. This was rejected and, on 11 October,
war was declared.

The Boers had just declared war on the most powerful nation on the
globe and, like the Spanish declaration of war on the United States, it
proved an unwise decision. True, the Boers scored some spectacular

military successes early in the contest, especially during the so-called 'Black Week' in December 1899, advancing deep into the Natal and Cape Colonies and placing several British garrisons under siege – most importantly Mafeking, Kimberly and Ladysmith. Unfortunately for them, as with the American southern states' contest against the northern ones, they were a primarily agrarian society fighting an industrial power with a lot more men (including from the Dominions) and a lot more methods of prosecuting war at its disposal. In 1900, with increasingly large numbers of reinforcements, the British began to turn the tide of the contest. The besieged garrisons were relieved, the Orange Free States' capital, Bloemfontein, fell in March, Johannesburg surrendered in May and in June British troops marched into Pretoria, the capital of the Transvaal. Kruger fled to the Netherlands; the war appeared to be over.

The Boers, however, were not quite finished. Like the Filipinos, they turned to guerrilla warfare. The British response was to divide the country by means of blockhouses and barbed wire in order to corner the Boer commandos and, like the Americans in the Philippines, they began interning Boer civilians (as well as prisoners-of-war) in concentration camps. The conditions of the camps, including quality of food and medicine, resulted in the deaths of almost 30,000 inmates. These tactics, brutal as they were, worked: in May 1902 the last Boer commandos surrendered. The war had cost the lives of some 6,000 British soldiers, some 6,000 Boer combatants, some 28,000 Boer civilians and some 20,000 Africans.[25]

If Britain and the United States moved in parallel directions in the Boer War and the Spanish-American War, they collaborated outright, along with other powers, during the Boxer Rebellion in China. China had, during the course of the nineteenth century, been encroached upon by the much-stronger western Powers (and later, Japan) and been forced to sign various treaties, giving foreigners special rights and privileges. In 1900, an organization called the Righteous Harmonious Fists (named the Boxers by westerners) decided it was time for the foreign powers to vacate China and launched a revolt with the connivance of the Chinese government. Trapping the foreign nationals (including the Dutch, French, Belgians, Germans, Russians, Japanese, as well as the British and Americans) in the walled Legation Quarter in then Peking, the revolt initially went in the Boxers' direction. In response and fortified by reports of murder and torture of captured foreign nationals, an Eight-Nation Alliance (consisting of Italy, France, Austria-Hungary,

Japan, Germany, Russia as well as Britain and the United States) despatched an international force to bring China to heel. After a failed first attempt, the alliance forces, commanded by British Lieutenant-General Sir Alfred Gaselee, finally captured Peking in August. In September, the Chinese government was forced to sign a peace treaty with the Alliance which included almost $333 million in reparations. Although the forces which suppressed the Boxer Rebellion were not purely Anglo-American, one of the major battles, fought at Yangcun, witnessed British and American troops leading the assault. For the first time since the War of Independence, British and American soldiers had fought on the same side in a major engagement. The times were clearly changing.[26]

Yet Britain was already adjusting to the new realities, represented by the increasing importance not simply of the United States, but of other powers, too. Splendid Isolation came to an end when Britain signed the Anglo-Japanese Treaty in 1902 (which secured each nation's interests in Asia). Perhaps more significantly, in April 1904 Britain finally came to a formal accord with its ancient foe France, signing the Entente Cordiale. This was followed three years later by the Anglo-Russian Entente in August 1907. Britain had thus made accord with the leading powers on two of its three imperial frontiers. Further, if it had no formal entente with the United States, relations with that nation were friendly and likely to be increasingly so. In light of nineteenth-century history, progress must have appeared as inevitable as it was unstoppable. There remained, however, one rising power with which accord seemed impossible to achieve: Germany.

The subject of the causes of the First World War remains controversial and will not be definitively answered here. There were many factors, all of which have to be weighed in the balance. The alliances that had been built up, the Triple Alliance of Germany, Austro-Hungary and Italy and the Triple Entente of Britain, France and Russia were a factor, although these did not actually commit the participants to war. That Germany wanted to rule Europe, essentially attempting what the United Sates had already achieved, hegemony over their continent, tends to be overstated as a cause. Germany certainly had territorial ambitions but of a likely more limited kind and, in any event, so did other powers such as France (namely recovering territory lost in the Franco-Prussian War) and Russia. Britain's traditional maintenance of the balance of power in Europe was a factor but, despite its alliances, at the war's outset it remained concerned about France or Russia upsetting said balance.

True enough, Anglo-German relations before the war were problematic. The two nations were involved in a naval race that had led to the construction of the dreadnoughts, but France and Britain had competed in the building of ironclads in the nineteenth century without going to war. In any event, by the time hostilities broke out, Britain had won the naval race. Further, when Germany went to war, it assumed Britain would not become involved. Equally, the British cabinet only slowly realized that Britain would have to decide on whether or not to parti-cipate in the contest and experienced divisions among itself when the decision was made. When on 3 August 1914 the Foreign Secretary Sir Edward Grey outlined the reasons for declaring war, one member of the cabinet questioned why nothing was said about Britain's national or imperial interests, while two others resigned. Thus, when on 4 August 1914 Britain declared war on Germany after it violated Belgian neu-trality, it embarked upon an uncertain cause with unclear objectives. The long nineteenth century and, with it, the Pax Britannica had just come to an end.[27]

Initially, British military support was given in such a manner that neither France nor Russia would emerge as the single, overweening and dominant European power, but by 1915 this policy had collapsed in the face of German tenacity. Despite acquiring new (if unreliable) allies in the form of Italy and Japan, the Gallipoli/Dardanelles campaign against the Turks from 1915–16 proved a costly failure. Although Germany's African colonies proved soft targets, these were all sideshows to the war in Europe, and here precious little was gained. Britain retained her naval superiority by her strategic, as opposed to tactical, victory at Jutland in May 1916 when the Kaiser's fleet retreated to its ports. An important achievement certainly, but it was no Trafalgar. Further, despite the fact that ultimately at least one third of the forces Britain raised for the war came from the Empire (most notably, Canada, Australia, New Zealand, South Africa and India – the last of the quintet's numbers virtually equalling the combined amount of the first four) more men were needed and, in 1916, Britain had introduced conscription for the first time in its history.

With fresh troops and a recognition that it had to make a complete commitment to the war in Europe, Britain along with France launched the Somme offensive in July. Plans changed when the Germans laun-ched their offensive against Verdun, resulting in the diversion of French troops to that theatre. By the time the fighting ended, in November, less than eight miles had been gained at the cost of some 420,000 British casualties, 195,000 French and 500–650,000 German. Despite acquiring a new Prime Minister when David Lloyd George replaced Herbert Asquith in December, 1917 began as a bleak year for Britain, one that became even more so as Germany stepped up its U-boat campaign and Russia started to look distinctly unstable.[28]

Across the Atlantic, most Americans supported President Wilson's policy of neutrality. If there were few grounds for British entry into the war, there were even fewer for the United States. There certainly were Americans sympathetic to the Entente, but others, including those of German descent (roughly equal by now to those of British descent), tended to sympathize with the Triple Alliance while others such as the Irish-Americans openly supported it (and the latter's outright encouragement became even more vocal when Britain smashed the so-called Easter Uprising in Dublin and executed the ringleaders in 1916). Washington accepted the British blockade of Germany and its allies and the consequent loss of trade, and although it protested London's declaration that all neutral shipping headed for Europe had to undergo inspection, it ultimately accepted it. The precedent of the Union's blockade in the American Civil War meant that the United States had few grounds for complaint.

The neutrality of the United States, however, did little to endear it to Britain, any more than British neutrality had been appreciated by the Americans in their Civil War. From the British perspective, they were fighting, as usual, a war for liberty and the Americans should have understood that. Anti-American sentiment was actually quite common in Britain during the period of the United States' neutrality, especially when Wilson offered to mediate following a German offer to negotiate an end to hostilities in 1916. King George V was allegedly moved to tears by this act, staggered that Wilson could believe that the British cause was the moral equivalent of the German one. Well, Abraham Lincoln could have told him a thing about that; so, too, for that matter could have Lord Castlereagh. The British, however, unlike in 1812 (or the Union in 1861), from the war's beginning attempted to win neutral opinion over to their cause. An aggressive propaganda campaign was launched highlighting German atrocities, both real and imaginary, and London for the most part remained as cordial as possible towards the United States. Berlin, by contrast, instead established a clandestine network of German-American and Irish-American saboteurs that destroyed goods (including munitions) stockpiled in American ports destined for Europe. This, though, was tactical brilliance trumping strategic logic because such activities did little to help Germany's reputation in the eyes of the American public.

These last activities were essentially the result of German desperation. Thanks to the blockade, Britain and her allies had access to America's markets denied to Germany. Munitions, foodstuffs and other commodities were increasingly purchased in order to prosecute the war. Before long, Britain was borrowing money from American banks, J. P. Morgan becoming a valuable ally. These loans were an absolute necessity to Britain which, as we have seen, was expending vast sums of money on the war. This gradually resulted in New York displacing London as the world's financial centre, while the United States and Britain began to swap places as creditor and debtor. This situation where Britain could obtain both money and supplies denied to Germany was not likely to be appreciated by the latter. Increasingly, the Germans began to resent, as they saw it, the one-sided neutrality of the United States. This belief in the hollowness of American neutrality increased when Americans loudly denounced their U-boat campaign – the only method the Germans had at their disposal to strike back at Britain's international operations. Thus, by 1917, although not actually wanting a war with the United States, Berlin decided to risk one through its unrestricted U-boat war and made plans to counter any potential American involvement – plans that ended up being deciphered in Room 40 in the Old Building next to Admiralty House.[29]

The entry of the United States on the side of Britain and France was a catastrophic blow to German ambitions. Although they managed to halt the British assault at the third battle of Ypres (usually referred to as Passchendaele) from July to November in 1917 and with their divisions on the eastern front now free to move to the west thanks to the armistice signed with now Bolshevik Russia in December, the arrival of thousands and ultimately over a million American soldiers in France threatened to offset these victories. Equally, by moving to a convoy system, the British finally neutralized the worst effects of the U-boat campaign. In spring 1918, at the end of their material and manpower resources, the Germans launched a last desperate assault consisting of five major offensives, to force Britain and France to sue for peace before the number of American reinforcements could be put to use. Although they initially made headway, getting to within 75 miles of Paris, French, British and British Imperial forces' resistance stiffened and the German offensives petered out. In August 1918, with American reinforcements available, the Allied counter-offensives, including Amiens and, in

September, Meuse-Argonne, forced the Germans to retreat. By the end of the month, the defensive Hindenburg line had been breached and the German army was beginning to disintegrate. In May and June 1918, the British had taken fewer than 3,000 German prisoners; from July to September, the number was 90,000. Facing complete collapse, the German High Command on 29 September demanded an armistice, finally negotiated on 11 November.

To claim that America's intervention in the war prevented a German victory is inaccurate. What is true is that they broke the stalemate. Further, with end of the conflict and the negotiations at Versailles in 1919, the United States was now undeniably a world power, if not the world power. Britain remained a powerful player and, even in the 1930s, thanks in part to American isolationism, remained the only genuine international power on the globe. Yet the First World War had changed the situation – in more ways than one. Lytton Strachey's *Eminent Victorians* (1918) marked the opening shots, even if the term 'Victorian' had already acquired a pejorative edge. The new age increasingly defined itself against its predecessors.[30]

As for Anglo-American relations, that Britain and the United States had emerged as allies in what was then the greatest war in history, irrevocably changed relations. It was, indeed, the period of the great rapprochement. Yet despite this, tensions remained. The United States' refusal to join the League of Nations was seen by many in Britain as a dereliction of duty. Vicious tongues wagged that the Americans had only entered the war when all sides were exhausted in order to dictate the terms of peace; more slanderous was the accusation that the United States only joined when they knew which side was winning. Both the existence of War Plan Red by the US Army for conflict against the British Empire (which essentially involved the annexation of Canada) and the Royal Navy's plans for hostilities against the United States (by shelling American coastal cities) in the 1930s, demonstrates that there still existed those in each nation who remained essentially unconvinced about the other's benignity. In the 1930s, the British government did not regard the United States as an ally in any genuine sense of the term (although it was regarded as a friendly power). In some respects, it was the Second World War that really sealed the Anglo-American friendship. This time the two were allies in an undeniably just war. By that time, however, their positions were completely reversed: the twentieth century would be the American one.[31]

8

Arguing Affinities; Debating Differences: British Politics and the United States in the Later Nineteenth Century

Grover Cleveland was the only President to leave the White House and return for a second term four years later; he was the first Democrat to be elected President after the American Civil War and he was the first President to be elected by secret ballot (in 1892). The secret ballot – called the 'Australian ballot' in the United States for reasons we shall come to – had been a demand of the Populists (who later formed the People's Party), an amalgamation of working-class and agrarian interests who had suffered especially during the economic recession of the 1880s. They called the secret ballot the 'Australian ballot' because Britain's Australian colonies had pioneered its use, beginning with Tasmania in February 1856 and, in the following month, Victoria (which subsequently took the credit, meaning the term 'Victoria ballot' was also in use). Other Australian colonies (this was before federation) followed their examples, and by 1870 its use had spread to New Zealand and, finally, to the motherland, Britain, in 1872. The secret ballot reduced both fraud and intimidation at elections and, although first put into practice in Australia, began life as one of the six demands of the People's Charter, its adoption being yet another posthumous victory for Chartism. Indeed, it was the combination of Chartists being transported to Australia, plus the publication of the People's Charter in the colonial press, that alerted Britain's Australian colonists to the value of the idea. Thus, despite claims that the Chartist demand for the secret ballot was owed to the example of the United States, it is, in fact, rather more an example of British democracy influencing that of the United States (via the Empire) than the reverse.[1]

Yet this kind of free and open exchange of ideas on representative government, among other issues, could only take place once Britons and Americans ceased seeing the other as putative foes and viewed them instead as potential friends. This, in turn, could only begin to take place when the numerous outstanding grievances from the period up to and including the Civil War had been settled and the (at times) apparently incessant rancour in Anglo-American affairs finally began to subside. This did not happen all at once, nor was it a particularly smooth process, but rather one that occurred in fits and starts. For example, the decidedly pro-American Goldwin Smith, who moved to the United States to assume a position at Cornell University, New York, in 1868, became disillusioned by his experiences there, particularly the rampant anti-British sentiment stemming from the rancour raised by the Civil War in general and the *Alabama*'s activities in particular. The situation became such that in 1871 he retreated to the now Dominion of Canada and spent the rest of his days in Toronto, for a time levelling venomous attacks on the United States, even going so far as to express the heretical belief that John Bright's and Richard Cobden's views of it had been 'too ideal'.

Nonetheless, as the relationship between the two nations began moving in a direction of increased amity, Britons started to examine the United States, its society, politics and culture, with fresh eyes. At the same time, this sentiment was slowly reciprocated on the other side of the Atlantic and so the age of transatlantic cultural and political affinity gradually developed, influenced by, and influencing in turn, the manoeuvrings preceding, during and following the 1871 Treaty of Washington. This movement, like the treaty itself, helped both the Americans and the British look beyond the difficulties that had characterized their relationship from 1812 to 1871, and if many of those involved were responsible for both mythologizing certain incidents or overlooking many inconvenient truths of this earlier period, such were the requirements of reconciliation after almost sixty years of serious tensions.[2]

On the British side, some of the influential individuals leading this re-evaluation of the United States included, among others, William Gladstone; Archibald Primrose, Earl of Rosebery and future Prime Minister; the triumvirate of Liberal MPs John Morley, Joseph Chamberlain and Charles Wentworth Dilke, who would formulate the Radical Programme of 1885; the liberal politicians William Vernon Harcourt (who married the American John Lothrop Motley's daughter in 1877) and James Bryce; as well as Albert and Edward Dicey and Leslie Stephen. Some of them, Bryce, Stephen and E. Dicey, joined Goldwin Smith in contributing to *Essays on Reform* (1867), the rebuttal to Robert Lowe, Edward Horsman and the other denizens of the Cave of Adullam (Bright's derisive term for those Liberal MPs who opposed Russell's

1866 reform measures). A couple of the essays did cite the example of the United States as a model for political reform but equally closely examined was Australia, in large part because it was the latter that had turned Lowe against democratic reform when he visited it – rather than America (which had, in fact, comparatively little impact upon the leading Adullamite's ideas). In certain respects, these men continued and expanded upon the efforts of George J. D. Campbell, the Duke of Argyll; novelist Thomas Hughes; philosopher Herbert Spencer (founder of social Darwinism); as well as the Liberal MPs William E. Forster and Thomas Milner Gibson. Although many of these individuals were anti-Confederate during the Civil War (Gladstone is an obvious exception), none could be credibly accused of demonstrating either blind support for the North or tendencies towards appeasement. Harcourt, for example, one of the few pro-northern contributors to *The Times* as 'Historicus', made a point of reminding his critics that during the war, while he had declared in favour of the United States on some issues, he had found for Britain on others. More importantly, however, the atmosphere of improved Anglo-American relations meant that openly expressing pro-American sentiments were no longer akin to supporting a putatively hostile power. It no longer resulted in being associated with individuals such as James Polk, William Seward and Charles Sumner or with publications like the *New York Herald*.[3]

Most of these men, and their followers especially, were relatively young (Gladstone, again, is the exception). Morley, Stephen, Bryce, the Diceys and Chamberlain were all born in the 1830s while Rosebery and Dilke were born in the forties. This meant that their views of the United States were noticeably less shadowed by the numerous unpleasant incidents and quarrels that marred Anglo-American relations during the difficult years in the first half of the nineteenth century. Thus, their formative experiences took place in the improving climate of the 1850s and the Union victory in the Civil War, meantime, helped cement their pro-American views. That the older generation of Britons, whose memories and views of the United States were decidedly different, were dying out – Palmerston in 1865, trade unionist T. J. Dunning in 1873 and John Arthur Roebuck in 1879 – also served to assist them. Changing climates – political, social or cultural – are sometimes ultimately the result of whoever happens to be the last man standing (and this generational shift could be seen elsewhere – in 1868 when Gladstone and Disraeli became head of the Liberal and Conservative parties respectively, it marked the first time the leaders of the two parties were men born after 1800). As a result, for the sake of simplicity, these pro-American individuals shall be referred to herein as the young liberals.[4]

Before we discuss youth, however, precedence shall be given to age. At around the same time the young liberals, including a future Prime Minister, were building relations with the United States, one decidedly older liberal and current Prime Minister was concerned about his past conduct towards it. This was Gladstone, who was bitterly regretful about his 1862 'Jefferson Davis ... has made a nation' speech and his general pro-southern proclivities during the war itself. During the *Alabama* arbitration, the United States had cited Gladstone's Newcastle speech as 'conscious unfriendly purpose' towards the Union during the Civil War. Despite the fact that speech paled in comparison to the utterances of William Seward, Charles Sumner and Cassius Clay to name just three American politicians, this reference to his comments affected Gladstone deeply. Finally, in November 1872, over the objections of his cabinet colleagues, the Prime Minister sent a long explanatory letter to the American minister, Robert Schenck. Gladstone's cabinet colleagues may well have been wiser – it took the secretary of state Hamilton Fish four years to properly reply to the letter thanks to an alleged communication breakdown between the secretary of state and American minister. Further, Fish's response is best described as a grudging half-acceptance of Gladstone's apologies and explanations. Gladstone was understandably dissatisfied and decided to appeal to the American public directly. After obtaining permission from a reluctant Fish, Gladstone arranged for the American journal *Harper's New Monthly Magazine* to publish edited versions of their exchange in December 1876 (the centenary year of the Declaration of Independence). In 1878 he followed up these efforts with his article 'Kin Beyond Sea' in the *North American Review*.[5]

Gladstone's article was an important milestone in the changing Anglo-American relationship, one that reflected the transformation in one of its earliest sentences, 'I do not speak of the political controversies between them and us, which are happily, as I trust, at an end.' Noting that 'students of the future ... will have much to say in the way of comparison between American and British institutions. The relationship between these two is unique in history', Gladstone declared that while the 'prolific British mother' has 'sent forth her innumerable children all over the earth to be the founders of half a dozen empires ... among these children, there is one whose place in the world's eye and in history is superlative: it is the American Republic'. In short, this was a paean of praise for the United States. Noting America's rapid growth both in population and industry, Gladstone observed that,

> But while we have been advancing with this portentous rapidity, America is passing us by in a canter ... the England and the America of the present are probably the two strongest nations in the world. But there can hardly be a doubt, as between the America and England of the future, that the daughter, at some no very distant time, will, whether fairer or less fair, be unquestionably yet stronger than the mother.

Yet this was not a problem, in Gladstone's eyes, because the two nations essentially shared the same values. Both peoples preferred the practical to the abstract; they tolerated dissent; they 'set a high value on liberty for its own sake'; they deemed 'self-help to be immeasurably superior to help in any other form'; and they mistrusted 'the centralization of power'. Indeed, according to Gladstone, 'It would be difficult, in the case of any other pair of nations, to present an assemblage of traits at once so common and so distinctive.' In other words, Gladstone was identifying or, if one prefers, inventing, a common Anglo-American political tradition.

Gladstone was not claiming that Britain and the United States were mere reflections of each other – he noted that there were 'the strongest reasons why America could not grow into a reflection or repetition of England' – but he did trace (or create) a historical narrative accounting for the existence of this Anglo-American political tradition. Crediting 'not the Recusant in Maryland', nor 'the Cavalier of Virginia', Gladstone identified the Puritan of New England as 'the type and form of manhood for America'. These Puritans represented all 'that was democratic in the policy of England', and they carried it to America. The American War of Independence, which Gladstone called 'a conservative revolution', resulted in a constitution that could stand comparison to Britain's. 'But, as the British Constitution is the most subtle organism which has preceded from the womb and the long gestation of progressive history, the American constitution is, so far as I can see, the most wonderful work ever struck off at a given time by the brain and purpose of man.' Praising the United States for upholding its institutions during the Civil War, demilitarizing so quickly afterwards and starting to pay off its debts accrued so quickly, Gladstone explicitly compared and described both the American structure of government and the British, discussing republicanism and monarchy, congress and parliament, presidential and prime ministerial cabinets and the largely homogeneous, continental United States to the heterogeneous British Empire. The comparison was rather more favourable to the United States, as Gladstone even went so far as to declare that the 'English people are not believers in equality; they do not, with the famous Declaration of July 4, 1776, think it to be a self-evident truth that all men are born equal. They hold rather the reverse of that proposition. At any rate, in practice they are what I may call determined inequalitarians.' He concludes that the 'great acts, and the great forbearances' of the United States since the Civil War 'rendered a splendid service to the general cause of popular government throughout the world'.[6]

It was frankly inconceivable that any past British Prime Minister or statesman would have believed or even thought any of this, let alone published it in an American journal; certainly not Disraeli, then Prime Minister, nor Derby or Russell and absolutely not Palmerston. In the case of the last, he had remarked to Lord Shaftesbury shortly before his death: 'Gladstone will soon have it all his own way, and whenever he gets my place, we shall have strange doings.' Old 'Pam' had post-humously been proven prescient. While some Britons certainly agreed with Gladstone, a fair number were disturbed by this effusive praise of the United States, particularly *The Times*, but even the liberal *Pall Mall Gazette* and radical *Daily News* expressed serious reservations. Lord Hartington, former Chief Secretary for Ireland, meanwhile irritably asked the former Colonial Secretary, the Earl of Granville, 'What is the good of telling people that the Americans are going to beat us and that he [Gladstone] rather likes it?' All of which demonstrates that Gladstone was not simply following the current, but was in fact helping to direct it. Indeed, he has been credited, albeit somewhat controversially, with coining the term 'English-speaking peoples'.[7]

If Gladstone's own countrymen were not entirely delighted or necessarily convinced by his article's tone and arguments, the Americans proved more receptive. Although his reputation had been improving in the United States from its nadir during the Civil War even before the publication of 'Kin Beyond Sea' – he had been elected a 'foreign honorary member' of the American Academy of Arts and Sciences to replace the recently deceased John Stuart Mill in 1874 – its appearance cemented his reputation and largely exorcised the lingering miasma of his speech at Newcastle. Gladstone received countless invitations to visit the United States, including an offer to give a series of lectures at Harvard. In many respects, Gladstone had flattered the

Americans. For example, he declared that 'America whose attitude towards England has always been masculine and real, has no longer to anticipate at our hands the frivolous and offensive criticisms which were once in vogue among us', a statement whose first half would have come as a surprise to any British visitor to the United States in the past century or, indeed, casual reader of the American press, and the second half of which ignored the fact that not all criticism had been frivolous. Further, less commendable was his attempt to assist the *North American Review* in smearing Disraeli as having (in reality, non-existent) affiliations with the Confederacy – a clear example of Gladstone attempting to transfer his guilt onto another and so lessen his own. Nonetheless, whatever Gladstone's or the article's shortcomings, 'Kin Beyond Sea' marked a sea-change for the better in Anglo-American relations, and encouraged yet more communication between the two nations as British and Americans contributed more frequently and more sympathetically to each other's publications, discussing each other's, as well as their own, affairs.[8]

With the end of the Civil War, the volume of transatlantic travel greatly increased. Americans began to visit the United Kingdom (and indeed, Europe) in greater numbers and with greater frequency while Britons likewise increasingly journeyed to the United States. Just to give one example: in 1865, when the US minister to Paris, John Bigelow, sent out invitations for an Independence Day fête, it was possible for him to invite virtually every American citizen then living in Britain and Europe. Two years later, in 1867, there were over 4,000 American citizens living in Paris alone. Aware that British comprehension of the United States was as woeful as American knowledge of Britain, the young liberals both sought out potential American acquaintances and began travelling to the United States in order to improve their understanding. Thus, Hughes, Spencer and Morley formed the Anglo-American Association to increase British political knowledge of the United States in January 1871, while Dilke made his first trip there in 1866, Morley in 1867, Bryce in 1870 and Rosebery in 1873. The last of the three, Rosebery, was in part influenced by his friend, the former Liberal MP, Francis Lawley, who advised him to make his trip 'as prolonged as possible, as I think it [the United States] the most instructive country in the world for a politician; far more so than this buried past from which I am now writing [Italy]'. This phrase itself marked a changing outlook – the Italian struggle, and its leaders such as Giuseppe Garibaldi, had attracted enormous interest and sympathy from British liberals in the previous decades. Now Italy was old hat. Although these young liberals were not the only politicians to visit the United States – Conservative Randolph Churchill (father of Winston), whose wife was American, visited in 1876 while the future Tory MP Louis Jennings even edited the *New York Times*, from 1868 to 1876 (an unlikely occurrence at any time earlier in the century) – they were the ones who most treated it as a pilgrimage and were keen to bring back the fruits of their learning to Britain.[9]

Dilke's *Greater Britain: A Record of Travel in the English-Speaking Countries* (1868) was one of the first results of this young liberal phenomenon. Dilke, who 'followed England round the world', visiting 'English-speaking, or ... English-governed lands', including the United States, Canada, New Zealand and Australia, may to some extent be considered the first categorizer of what we now refer to as the Anglo-sphere or English-speaking world (although he would have doubtless preferred the term Anglo-Saxon world – an important distinction, as we shall see). 'If I remarked that climate, soil, manners of life, that mixture with other people had modified the blood', Dilke observed, 'I saw, too, that in essentials the race was always one.' This applied equally to that former colony the United States, where 'the peoples of the world are being fused together'; they were nonetheless so 'into an English mould'. The work demonstrated all the effusive enthusiasm of an author in his very early twenties (he was fresh out of Cambridge), but youthful energy carried its own advantages. Dilke was an indefatigable observer, describing Fenian conventions, Mormon polygamy, congressional debates and Harvard commencements. Among the many places he visited were Washington, New York, Boston, Denver, Salt Lake City and San Francisco – eating Chinese food in the last. He also met, among others, Ralph Waldo Emerson, Henry Wadsworth Longfellow and Oliver Wendell Holmes. Being pro-American, Dilke explicitly extolled what he regarded as the kinship between Britain, its empire, and the United States, thus equating the latter's success with British accomplishment. 'America offers the English race the moral directorship of the globe', he noted, 'by ruling mankind through Saxon institutions and the English tongue. Through America, England is speaking to the world.' Dilke's work praised American republicanism and democracy (in this he may even have exceeded Bright), including its party politics where he broadly endorsed the philosophy of the Republican Party. Dilke did have criticisms of the United States – he was, like most liberals, strenuously opposed to protectionism – but he actively promoted the notion of consanguinity between the nations. Indeed, he would refer to the example of the United States (and, for that matter, the Dominions, as they became) throughout his political career. To Dilke, the imperial rivalry that had characterized the Anglo-American relationship made no sense, because the British, their settler societies and the Americans were, in effect, one people, albeit with the last in the vanguard.[10]

This, however, leads us to the other aspect of Dilke's beliefs. His work, an instantaneous success going through several editions in various languages, was a pioneering effort in two respects, both of which were related: in the first, it helped pave the way for the new direction which British thought on imperialism would take; in the second, it was an important addition to the new corpus of works arguing in favour of congenital Anglo-Saxon superiority over other ethnic groups – notions given a fillip by the 1865 Jamaican rebellion – an idea with which Dilke would become increasingly enamoured as the century wore on (expressed clearly in his work's 1890 sequel, *Problems of Greater Britain*). In the case of the second notion, it is almost impossible to separate Dilke's admiration for American society and its political institutions from his belief in Anglo-Saxon racial superiority. So, if he supported African Americans receiving the franchise, he also believed the destruction of the Indians to be a positive good, '[t]he gradual extinction of the inferior races is not only a law of nature but a blessing to mankind', and noted with satisfaction that 'the Anglo-Saxon is the only extirpating race on earth'. Meantime, those non-Anglo-Saxons not exterminated would simply be absorbed:

> The first thing which strikes the Englishman just landed in New York is the apparent latinization of the English in America; but before he leaves the country, he comes to see that this is at most a local fact, and that the true moral of America is the vigour of the English race ... Excluding the Atlantic cities, the English in America are absorbing the Germans and the Celts, destroying the Red Indians, and checking the advance of the Chinese.

It is important to note that Dilke was not the first to argue for Anglo-Saxon racial superiority, but simply an assiduous promoter of the notion. Nonetheless, his promotion of Anglo-American amity was firmly anchored in this belief. True, Dilke's use of the term 'race' could sometimes be ambiguous and the distinction between culture and, for want of a better term, ethnicity, could sometimes be blurred. Yet it is instructive to note that John Stuart Mill, who greatly admired the work and became a friend and mentor, took very much the traditional British liberal view when he sharply criticized the young radical for placing too much emphasis on race in determining national character. In any event, notions of Anglo-Saxon superiority would prove to be a significant factor in the growing amity between Britain and the United States. In this respect, at least, Dilke was a pioneer.[11]

As regards the first point, the changing British views of empire, although Dilke was, in fact, anti-imperialist to the extent that he favoured the independence of the colonies on the grounds that they were too expensive to maintain, his notion that the expansion of the Anglo-Saxon race across the globe was what prevented Britain from becoming a provincial nation or, as he put it, 'Guernsey a little mag-nified', planted an important seed. Traditionally, John R. Seeley's *The Expansion of England* (1883), most famous for its quote 'We seem ... to have conquered and peopled half the world in a fit of absence of mind', is seen to mark the shift in British thought regarding the empire from the view that it was, at best, a necessary nuisance by liberals and con-servatives alike, to the notion that if Britain persisted in its absent-minded attitude it would lose out to its rivals and must therefore strengthen the links between the motherland and its Dominions. Yet Seeley drew heavily from Dilke, even using the term 'greater Britain', in reference to the Empire. There were differences, to be sure, particularly in that Seeley was less pro-American, taking the more traditional view that the United States was another imperial rival like Russia (although he cited America as a modern example of a political union of remote and diverse people) and he emphasized the potential contribution that modern technology could make to the project in a manner that Dilke did not, but the influence of the latter's ideas upon the former's central themes is undeniable.[12]

Furthermore, there was a direct link between the other young lib-erals' views of the United States and this later imperial outlook – Chamberlain, Rosebery and Bryce were, along with Dilke, all leading exponents of the Imperial Federation movement. Rosebery for a time was president of the Imperial Federation League and went so far as to declare that, 'I venture to say that the federation of the British Empire can be carried out with infinitely more ease, given goodwill on all sides, than the United States encountered in their formation.' In the end, of course, the notions of Imperial Federation faltered. Its moving lights could never decide whether it should be an Anglo-Saxon grouping (in which case the United States would presumably be involved) or a purely British one (in which case America would not be, but places such as India presumably would be). Although the Imperial Federation

movement initiated a series of regular conferences of the prime ministers of the colonies and Dominions – the first held in 1887 in connection with Victoria's Golden Jubilee; others at the Diamond Jubilee in
1897 and at the coronation in 1902, finally establishing regular meetings
at four-year intervals in 1907 – not a great deal was to result from them.
In many respects, the Dominions were acquiring greater political
autonomy, and this fact alone militated against notions of imperial
federalism. Indeed, although 'Empire Day' (24 May) was adopted by the
Dominions as a public holiday even before Britain, by 1879 some were
also starting to apply protective tariffs against British goods.[13]

Yet the question of tariffs and free trade were intimately linked to
that of the Imperial Federation movement and here the example of the
United States again proved germane. The most important individual in
the movement was Chamberlain who, in fact, was arguably the first self-
consciously imperial politician. Chamberlain, an admirer of Seeley's
work as well as James A. Froude's *Oceana or England and her Colonies*
(1886), which also derived lessons from America, publicly enunciated
his views in Toronto in 1887. Chamberlain, in Canada at the behest of
the Conservative Prime Minister Lord Salisbury, went to discourage a
commercial union between the former colony and the United States.
Noting that Canadians had achieved their own federation, Chamberlain
declared that they now ought to contemplate one involving the Empire
as a whole – and he would carry this faith in Imperial Federation to the
extent of turning down the posts of Home Secretary and Chancellor of
the Exchequer in favour of the Colonial Office so as to put his ideas into
practice. As for the plans for reciprocity between Canada and the United
States, they were torpedoed not by Chamberlain, but by local Canadian
politicians who led an anti-American campaign (although they were
assisted by some not very intelligent annexationist remarks made by US
politicians). This fear that the Americans were trying to annex Canada
economically, however, was not just a re-run of the old imperial rivalry,
but went to the heart of a new problem.[14]

As the nineteenth century wore on, certainly by the 1880s, Britain,
'the workshop of the world', began to face increased competition from
other industrializing and industrialized nations, particularly Germany
and the United States. As we have seen, the Americans had already
instituted tariffs against manufactured goods in the early years of the
century (followed, in 1879, by Germany, although these were not as
steep). While these tariffs had always aroused hostility in Britain, the
United States had not hitherto been a serious economic rival; now it

was, and this changed the tone of the debate. Free-traders had always claimed that protectionism harmed national economies; yet both protectionist Germany and the United States were now growing faster economically than Britain. Likewise, the economic slow-down, real or imagined, which took place from 1873 to the mid-1890s, not only helped increase the disillusionment with free trade, it also led to increases in both anti-German and anti-American rhetoric. By 1881, for example, a Yorkshireman, William Farrer Ecroyd, founded the National Fair Trade League, which demanded that Britain apply retaliatory tariffs on protectionist states. When America passed the 1890 McKinley Tariff (with an average duty of 48.4 per cent on imported goods), public anger grew. Demands, in the form of newspaper editorials and petitions, for retaliatory measures started to appear in ever greater numbers. Even the *Journal of the Board of Trade* now demanded action from the government. Besides the Fair Trade League, the Imperial Federation League and, more ominously, the Conservative Protectionist League, started to challenge the status quo. One MP even went so far as to demand that Britain form an Anglo-German free-trade area in retaliation against American tariffs – a potential forerunner of the European Economic Community.[15]

Anger was directed at a United States which barred British manufactures from its market, but there was also concern regarding the increasing volume of corn imported. In the view of many, Britain was dangerously reliant on a single foreign power for its food (the majority of American imports were foodstuffs and raw material until the First World War). It was therefore essential to secure an alternative source of supply – Canada was a logical alternative, provided a North American *zollverein* was prevented. The only way this could be achieved was to offer the Dominion an alternative – imperial preferences. Through such a system, Canada and, indeed, the other Dominions could provide the raw materials and especially food currently provided by the United States, except that, unlike America, they would do so in exchange for British manufactures. Further, according to this argument, as Germany and America had vast internal markets, Britain must turn her Dominions into the same in order to compete with these new rivals.

Although the British establishment (including especially the Foreign Office) defended its virtually sacrosanct doctrines of free trade, by the 1890s the opposition it faced was now serious. Calls for preferential treatments and imperial commercial reciprocity now increased in volume and intensity. Free-traders warned that counter-tariffs on

American corn and raw materials would merely make bread more expensive and increase the costs of British manufactures. They cited the examples of the British ship-building and shipping industry – two areas where Britain remained a world leader – which they attributed to lack of protectionism. Another area in which Britain was a world leader was international finance – huge amounts of trade between foreign nations were financed through London. The free-traders also argued that British manufactures tended to be of greater value and quality than those of the United States. Finally, they insisted that international trade could not be seen from a purely bilateral perspective – meaning merely between Britain and the United States – but from a multilateral one. The free-traders had a point: while Britain was running trade deficits with the United States and Germany, these were financed by surpluses with Turkey, Japan, British Africa, parts of Latin America and especially India. Nonetheless, the debate between the free-traders and the pro-tectionists – the latter containing both 'Little Englanders' and suppor-ters of Imperial Federation – continued and both relied on the example of the United States to support their arguments while denigrating those of their opponents.[16]

Despite the strength of their arguments, in the end the free-traders lost the debate. The beginning of the end came in May 1903, when Chamberlain gave a speech at Birmingham announcing his conversion from the doctrine of free trade to that of imperial tariffs – all foreign imports were to be taxed throughout the Empire while colonial pro-ducts, chiefly foodstuffs, would be admitted duty-free, creating an Empire-wide free-trade area – and resigned his cabinet position in order to press for this at the next election. Although Chamberlain had been moving in this direction for some time already, the speech was the logical culmination of his ideas on Imperial Federation (that the prime ministers of the Dominions had called for a common imperial tariff in order to guarantee access to one another's markets was an additional factor). Although Chamberlain's campaign failed spectacularly in the 1906 election – where he split the Tories in much the same manner as he had earlier the Liberals over Home Rule for Ireland – this would turn out to be the last great victory for free trade. With the First World War and its aftermath, featuring the erection of tariffs across the globe, Britain's free-trade policy would be replaced by imperial preferences. The first great age of free trade had come to an end; not with a whimper, but with a bang.[17]

If the question of protectionism versus free trade assisted notions of

Imperial Federation, the question of Ireland exposed its shortcomings and, once again, the United States proved to be an important reference point. As so often in British history, Ireland proved problematic. In many respects, the Irish Home Rule movement of the 1880s essentially demanded no more than what the Canadians, Australians and New Zealanders already enjoyed or were about to. Ireland, however, was seen to be different. It was an integral part of the United Kingdom (since 1801) in the way that the Dominions were not. There was also the Catholic–Protestant divide, which greatly complicated matters. Then, of course, there was good old-fashioned prejudice, greatly exacerbated by the activities of the Irish Republican Brotherhood, better known as the Fenians, which involved an uprising in 1867, some failed invasions of Canada from the United States and a bombing campaign in the 1880s.

All of these factors, which divided the Liberals, would contribute to the failure of Gladstone's Home Rule bills of 1885 and 1893. Although they did not often do so publicly, many of the young liberals used the example of American federalism in their debates and discussions over Ireland's future. Here, however, they split. A. Dicey, for example, cited Gladstone's 'Jeff Davis' speech at Newcastle, and accused him of holding the same views of Ireland as he had of the Confederacy. Likewise, Dicey accused Bryce and the other young liberals in favour of Home Rule of bad faith: they had supported the Union cause in the American Civil War, but were now ardent supporters of states' rights when it came to Britain. Much of this was rhetoric, of course, but Dicey was drawing on historical reality – Irish nationalists had, in fact, supported Confederate independence during the war. Further, older politicians who had supported the North made similar equations between Ireland and the Confederacy. In 1892, the Duke of Argyll, for example, told the readers of the *North American Review* that the British were fighting to save the union just as the North had done in the Civil War (he also cited Gladstone's speech at Newcastle – and as a former member of Palmerston's cabinet could have mentioned a lot more besides). Goldwin Smith, writing from Canada, also denied any applicability of American federalism to the question of Irish Home rule (and further claimed that American support for the measure was owed to inveterate hatred of Britain). Chamberlain, meanwhile, dismissed Bryce's arguments equating Home Rule with American federalism and formally broke with the Liberals over the 1886 debates, joining the Liberal Unionists and eventually the Tories. In the end, of course, Home Rule was derailed by a number of factors, including Charles Parnell's affair with Kitty O'Shea (and his being cited as co-respondent in the O'Shea's divorce) and the obstruction by the House of Lords. Thus, while it would be incorrect to claim that either the American federal system or Civil War was in any way a decisive factor in the outcome, there must be a lingering suspicion that the latter event might well have taught at least some Britons the wrong lessons regarding Ireland. In any event, the use or abuse of the American example in the Home Rule debates reveals how much the United States was selectively used, even in the late nineteenth century.[18]

When it came to late nineteenth-century thought regarding both imperialism and Anglo-Saxon notions, the Americans were hardly passive observers. There was certainly some resistance to the notion that the British and American experiences were the same. So, for example, Frederick Jackson Turner's 'The Significance of the Frontier in American History' (1893) was, in part, a response to Dilke's ideas of Greater Britain. Turner posited that the frontier had been the determining development in American culture, making it different to those of Europe generally and Britain specifically. In other words, if the American character had initially been British, the frontier had wrought upon it a profound transformation. Turner's ideas, although initially resisted by those who preferred to cite America's European and British antecedents, proved extremely influential in shaping Americans' national self-perception. Yet, as at least one scholar has observed, Turner's novelty has been exaggerated. He, too, remained at least partially in thrall to German cultural ideas and, in many ways, simply replaced the Teutonic by the Mississippi forests.[19]

Turner aside, just as the British were deriving ideas from the Americans, the latter were also taking ideas from the former. In 1885, the commander of the USS *Waschusett*, stationed in the South Pacific, found himself making frequent stops at Callao, Peru. From there he made regular nine-mile trips to Lima, where he availed himself of the facilities of the British Club's library. Hitherto, the American naval officer, a stickler for probity, had done his career no favours by his exposing corruption in the Boston Navy Yard. Nor did his outspoken criticism of senior officers and politicians, or his constant bemoaning the weakness of the United States Navy (which at this point had fewer armoured ships than landlocked Austria-Hungary), win him many friends. It was a book in the British Club's library that would change his life and ensure him a place in American history. The work was a translation of the German historian Theodor Mommsen's three-volume *History of Rome*. Reading the story of the Punic Wars, the naval officer noted Mommsen's argument that Rome had beaten Carthage through its command of the Mediterranean Sea. The commander was suddenly struck by the realization that control of the seas had never been systemically analysed as a historic factor. There had been no overall approach focusing on the influence of sea power on world history. It took some wangling, but he managed to obtain a position at the Naval War College at Newport where, after a good deal of research with a great deal of focus on the history of the Royal Navy, he produced a series of lectures that filled this gap in historical analysis. He soon made the acquaintance of a young Harvard graduate who had published a book on the naval dimension of the War of 1812 and who helped shape his ideas. The young graduate was Theodore, later, President Roosevelt. The US Navy commander was Alfred T. Mahan.

Mahan is famous for his *The Influence of Sea-Power in History, 1660–1783* (1890). What made this rather dry work of history influential was a first chapter, inserted at the publisher's insistence, which summarized Mahan's views in a somewhat polemical manner. One of his main points, influenced by his discussions with Roosevelt, was that Britain's rise to world power status was owed to her control of the seas. After first turning itself into an island fortress, thanks to the Royal Navy, Britain had established bases further afield that secured trade routes and became colonies. This enabled it to defeat potential rivals such as France (his sequel, *The Influence of Sea Power on the French Revolution and Empire, 1793–1812*, published in 1892, argued that Britain's control of the seas was what ensured its victory in the Napoleonic wars). That Britain had achieved world power status was thus owed to her command of the oceans. America must do the same, even if only to have the power to uphold the Monroe Doctrine and defend its hemisphere. America, Mahan demanded, must abandon its isolationist thinking and look outward. Although some in the United States still regarded Britain as a rival or, indeed, potential foe, Mahan was at least partially an Anglophile; and if he did not favour a formal alliance, he saw a 'cordial recognition of the similarity of character and ideas [giving] birth to sympathy'.[20]

Mahan's work was hugely influential (and a glowing review by Roosevelt in the *Atlantic Monthly* helped its reputation). Besides Roosevelt, Mahan's work influenced secretaries of state James G. Blaine and John Hay, the senator Henry Cabot Lodge and, eventually, even secretaries of the US Navy (and it influenced others besides; Kaiser Wilhelm II was an early admirer). By the time of the Spanish-American

War of 1898 and William McKinley's and Roosevelt's presidencies (1897–1909), Mahan's ideas had taken on orthodox status. So much so that one scholar has even compared his influence in the nineteenth century to that of George Kennan's in the twentieth. Contrary to what has sometimes been claimed, Mahan did not initiate America's late nineteenth-century imperialist thought – Roosevelt, among others, was already convinced of America's need to expand globally – but, in a very real sense, he provided the blueprint. Not a negligible result, then, of the time spent in the library of the British Club in Lima, Peru.[21]

Anglo-Saxonism and imperialism were not the only ideas that were shared on both sides of the Atlantic. There were plenty of other intellectual, cultural and political exchanges taking place. It was not long after Dilke visited the United States that John Morley followed suit. Morley who, like Dilke, intended to write a book about his trip, proved unlucky. He fell violently ill while in America, necessitating a premature return home. As a result, his influence on Anglo-American relations would be most felt by his editorship of the *Fortnightly Review*. This he turned into a regular platform for articles promoting both knowledge about the United States and Anglo-American amity. Among his American contributors were Moncure Conway, a minister; Horace White, former editor of the *Chicago Tribune*; and most importantly, Charles Elliot Norton. Norton, a Harvard professor, was a scholar and man of letters. Coming from a Massachusetts family of intellectuals, Norton was more cosmopolitan than most. From 1849–76, he visited India and Europe as well as Britain, forming friendships with Thomas Carlyle, John Ruskin and Leslie Stephen among others. He was an assiduous promoter of both Anglo-American relationships and his nation's interests – he persuaded the novelist Elizabeth Gaskell to support the Union during the American Civil War, for example. Editing the *North American Review* from 1864–68 along with poet James Russell Lowell, Norton, in collusion with Morely, helped encourage the now burgeoning transatlantic world of letters and exchange of political ideas. Their friendship, which included visits to Britain by Norton in 1868–69 and 1872–73, and a lengthy epistolary relationship, was a sustained one, highlighting the greater development of Anglo-American accord.[22]

Lord Rosebery, who was the first future Prime Minister ever to visit the United States – by contrast, future American Presidents had made visits to Britain since John Adams in 1783 – did so a little later than the other young liberals, making three trips there from 1873–76. Rosebery was taken with the United States – so much so, that one scholar has bemoaned the fact that his evaluations were so uncritical as to be dis-appointing. He demonstrated a fascination with the Civil War, visiting Jefferson Davis and former general Pierre T. Beauregard and speaking to former combatants about the campaigns. Making friends with, among others, the Democrat Samuel Ward, called 'the King of the Lobby' who introduced Rosebery to his vast array of political contacts including the future secretaries of state William Evarts and James Blaine, as well as the Republican senator and friend of President Ulysses S. Grant, Roscoe Conkling. Through Ward, this future Prime Minister also made the acquaintance of the future Presidents James Garfield and Chester Arthur. Indeed, Rosebery made so many such acquaintances in the United States that he became for many later British politicians and others an important source of letters of introduction into American political society. Equally significantly, Rosebery, who married Hannah Rothschild of the banking family, ensured that his estates became the foci of prominent Anglo-American literary, political and social gath-erings. Some of his more notable guests included Andrew Carnegie and Henry James.[23]

Another of the young liberals to strike up important American friendships was James Bryce, a student of Goldwin Smith's at Oxford, who first visited the United States in 1870 and, travelling with A. Dicey, was introduced to various leading American intellectuals and public men including Oliver Wendell Holmes, the future Supreme Court Justice; James Russell Lowell, future minister to Britain; and Charles Eliot, president of Harvard University among others. Upon his return to Britain, Bryce penned a series of articles on the United States, in *Macmillan's Magazine*, discussing in sympathetic depth issues such as poor relief, the legal profession, and the nation's politics and culture. Overall, Bryce insisted that both nations had a great deal in common, but that Britain had much to learn from the United States in numerous areas. In response to earlier accounts of the American political cor-ruption, about which Bryce had concerns, particularly as regards Tammany Hall, he nonetheless insisted that New York with its Irish population was rather more the exception than the rule. All of this would ultimately lay the groundwork for his 1888 magnum opus *The American Commonwealth*.[24]

This work, considered by some to be second only to Alexis de Tocqueville's *Democracy in America* as an analysis of the American political and constitutional system, represented a marked improvement in British intellectual understanding of the United States, far surpassing anything previously published. Despite this, it owed a lot to some earlier ideas regarding the United States as well as incorporating some of the nascent intellectual ideas now being promulgated. Bryce was unable to escape the influence of two scholars: his old Oxford tutor Goldwin Smith and the Regius Professor E. A. Freeman. In 1864, while the Civil War was raging, Smith had published a series of essays in Britain and the United States. Containing the Manchester School's standard praise of the United States, Smith also argued that the schism in the Anglo-Saxon world was not geographical and occurred not in the eighteenth century, but the seventeenth, when the Pilgrim Fathers, sailing to America, took with them the heritage of Puritan dissent. England was thus deprived of an important engine of radicalism. Deprived of England's balancing influence, the Americans, in turn, misread their revolution and incorrectly dated the origins of their political creed to 1776 instead of 1620. Concerned that Britain and America at loggerheads would 'give the world over to evil', Smith urged that the two might 'have a league of the heart. We are united by blood. We are united in common allegiance to the cause of freedom.' These powers of evil included, among others, the Papacy in general and Irish-Americans in particular through their party, the Democrats. E. A. Freeman, meanwhile, a pronounced Germanophile, enamoured with Teutonic myth, traced the so-called Aryan race's development in the Anglo-Saxon world, thus demonstrating that the New England town meeting developed from the English vestry meeting which, in turn, was owed to the Teutonic gemôt. Turning to the United States, Freeman argued that modernization, resulting in racial mixing and diversity, was less in evidence there. Indeed, according to the professor the Americans, inhabiting a pre-industrial wilderness, had reasserted their Teutonic nature. Both Freeman's and Smith's ideas enjoyed some popularity on both sides of the Atlantic – the latter could count American historian Herbert Baxter Adams as an admirer – but their impact on Bryce was twofold: a belief in Anglo-American racial supremacy and that the American was an Englishman on the frontier.[25]

Armed with such doctrines, Bryce posited that the American Revolution was entirely unlike the French version. Influenced by Smith and Freeman, but especially by his friend E. Dicey, Bryce argued that the American Revolution was a conservative one (he emphasized especially the importance of the Constitution over the Declaration of Independence), far more akin to the Glorious Revolution of 1688 than what occurred in France. The Gallic temperament, it seemed, was overcome by the ancient and specific rights of the Anglo-Saxon community and, obsessed with arcane theory, was driven to madness and bloodshed. On the subject of matters French, Bryce deliberately intended to critique, update and even surpass Tocqueville's analysis, believing it too much based on deductive theory and conjecture rather than empirical research. In particular, he wished to dismantle what he saw as Tocqueville's simplistic equation America = Democracy, and his concept of a 'democratic spirit' which allegedly imbued all American institutions. At the same time, he explicitly dismissed Tocqueville's belief that democracy necessarily led to either tyranny of the majority or the destruction of intellectual life. As Bryce noted,

> American democracy has certainly produced no age of Pericles. Neither has it dwarfed literature and led a wretched people, so dull as not even to realize their dulness [sic], into a barren plain of featureless mediocrity. To ascribe the deficiencies, such as they are, of art and culture in America, solely or even mainly to her form of government, is not less absurd than to ascribe, as many Americans of what I may call the trumpeting school do, her marvellous material progress to the same cause. It is not Democracy that has paid off a gigantic debt and raised Chicago out of a swamp. Neither is it Democracy that has hitherto denied the United States philosophers like Burke and poets like Wordsworth. Most writers who have dealt with these matters have not only laid more upon the shoulders of democratic government than it ought to bear, but have preferred abstract speculations to the humbler task of ascertaining and weighing the facts. They have spun ingenious theories about democracy as the source of this or that, or whatever pleased them to assume; they have not tried to determine by a wide induction what specific results appear in countries which, differing in other respects, agree in being democratically governed.

Further, rather than arguing that America represented the future, Bryce instead posited that democracy in the United States was specifically and uniquely American and that Britons and Europeans would need to apply its lessons selectively. 'So, although the character of democratic government in the United States is full of instructions for Europeans, it supplies few conclusions directly bearing on the present politics of any European country.'

Bryce's analysis was not altogether new and, as we have seen in an earlier chapter, numerous Britons had already made similar points, but it seems that every generation is compelled to rediscover its predecessor's knowledge. Bryce's work, however, was nothing if not thorough. In the first volume, he described the origins and workings of the national government, including the presidency, the cabinet, both houses of Congress and their committees, the Supreme Court and federal courts as well as constitutional developments and amendments. This was followed by an analysis and description of the state governments including their courts, legislatures, and governorships, one which extended all the way to American municipal government. There was even discussion of lobbyists:

> 'The Lobby' is the name given in America to persons, not being members of the legislature, who undertake to influence its members, and thereby to secure the passing of bills ... Efforts have been made to check the practice of lobbying, both in Congress and the State legislatures. Statutes have been passed severely punishing any person who offers any money or value to any member with a view to influence his vote.

His second volume, meantime, examined political parties, their campaigning, the primaries and conventions. Public opinion in the United States was also explored, noting the regional differences found among the North, South and West.

Bryce concluded with a discussion of the influence of Wall Street, the universities and the colleges, the churches and the clergy as well as religion in American life. Yet, if there was no prior examination of such depth made by any Briton previous to Bryce of the United States, there were also some familiar criticisms: 'Lynch law is not unknown in more civilized regions, such as Indiana and Illinois. A case occurred recently not far from New York City.' He also complained of corruption and 'bribery at popular elections'. Further, one can still detect a tone of British cultural superiority. Besides the chapters entitled 'Why Great Men are not Chosen Presidents' in volume one, and 'Why the Best Men do not go into Politics', Bryce's claim that the United States produced no political philosopher equal to Edmund Burke was rather a disservice to James Madison, Alexander Hamilton and even Thomas Jefferson. As for his note that the United States had failed to provide a poet of William Wordsworth's status, surely Walt Whitman provided at least some competition. His chapter entitled 'Creative Intellectual Power', meanwhile, effectively described America as a cultural and intellectual colony of Britain.[26]

Nonetheless, Bryce's work was immediately recognized as a classic – on both sides of the Atlantic – with new editions appearing from 1889 to 1920. That Tocqueville's work has regained its position as the seminal study of American democracy should not blind us to the *American Commonwealth*'s influence in the late nineteenth and early twentieth centuries. Theodore Roosevelt and Oliver Wendell Holmes admired it; so too did Woodrow Wilson, who declared that Bryce's 'conspicuous merit consists in seeing that our politics are no explanation of our character, but that our character is the explanation of our politics'. Yet even less intellectually inclined individuals such as Presidents Warren Harding and Calvin Coolidge made references to it. There is also evidence to support the contention that it influenced scholarship of the American historians Charles Francis Adams Jr, James Ford Rhodes and William Dunning, all of whom were friends of Bryce. In Britain, meantime, besides the young liberals, Bertrand Russell, Beatrice Webb and C. P. Trevelyan all regarded it as the last word on the United States. Bryce would maintain his links with the United States until the end of his life. He was active in bringing about Anglo-American agreement during the Venezuela Crisis 1895–96, even if he was contemptuous of the Monroe Doctrine, particularly through his friendship with Roosevelt. From 1914–17 he was deeply involved in British efforts to win America over to their side in the First World War. In many respects, Bryce personified the growing and increasing links between the United States and Britain's political classes.[27]

It remains, however, important to note that these changes took time, and tariffs and Turner aside, the old animosities could still re-surface. British and American views of one another remained, in some respects, ambiguous. On the British side, this still applied even to those who visited the United States. For example, when asked what his trip to America had taught him, Charles Kingsley replied many things, but 'especially to thank God I am an Englishman'. Yet, despite remarks such as these and lingering suspicions, the developing rapprochement continued apace. This can be seen in Matthew Arnold's 'A Word about America', published in the *Nineteenth Century* in May 1882. Arnold's work was a response to James Russell Lowell's 'interesting, but rather tart', article 'On a certain condescension in foreigners'. In it, Lowell (who was serving as American minister to Britain at the time) made the usual (and by now, threadbare) accusation, 'I never blamed England for not wishing well to democracy', and demanded that 'Let them [the British] give up trying to understand us, still more thinking that they do, and acting in various absurd ways as the necessary consequence; for they will never arrive at that devoutly to be wished consummation, till they learn to look at us as we are, not as they suppose us to be.' Arnold brushed aside this example of transference, merely to observe that 'from some quarters in America come reproaches to us for not speaking about America enough, for not making sufficient use of her in illustration of what we bring forward'. More problematic still was that whatever a Briton might say was unlikely to be accurately reported, as Arnold noted, 'A Boston newspaper supposes me to "speak of American manners as vulgar"', while another journal, 'commenting on this supposed utterance of mine, adopts it and carries it further'. Retorted Arnold, 'I do not remember to have anywhere, in my too numerous writings, to have spoken of American manners as vulgar, or to have expressed my dislike of them.' Arnold insisted that he adhered 'to my old persuasion, the Americans of the United States are English people on the other side of the Atlantic', yet 'from the time of their constitution as an independent power', there developed distinct differences between the two peoples.

Noting that he had never visited the United States ('with the best will in the world I have never yet been able to go to America') and accepting Lowell's complaint that 'Englishmen may easily fall into absurdities in criticizing America, most easily of all when they do not, and cannot see it with their own eyes, but have to speak of it from what they read', Arnold nonetheless noted,

> When one has confessed a belief that the social system of one's own country is far from being perfect, that it presents us with the spectacle of an upper class materialised, a middle class vulgarised, a lower class brutalised, one has earned the right, perhaps, to speak with candour of the social systems of other countries.

As for American democracy, Arnold noted that he had long stated 'that we suffer from a want of equality', and that 'Nothing would please me better than to find the difficulty solved in America, to find democracy a success there', adding, 'I have long been convinced that English society must transform itself, and long looking in vain for a model by which we might be guided and inspired in the bringing forth of our new civilisation'. Unfortunately, he observed, 'But I own that hitherto I have thought that, as we in England have to transform our civilisation, so America has still hers to make; and that, though her example and co-operation might, and probably would, be of the greatest value to us in the future, yet they were not of much use to our civilisation now.'[28]

The problem regarding both Britain and the United States, in

Arnold's view, was the existence of widespread middle-class materialist arrogance and intellectual complacency. Identifying these 'serious and effective forces of our middle class', and noting that 'it is easy to praise them, to flatter them, to express unbounded satisfaction in them, to speak as if they gave us all we needed', certainly, such was the view of 'the newspapers [and] our great orators take up the same strain. The middle-class doers of the English race, with their industry and religion are the salt of the earth.' Arnold identified this point of view with Bright in particular, and, somewhat uncharitably, claimed the latter's admiration for the United States was based on little more than a belief that it was simply a larger canvas upon which the middle class could work its designs. The problem was, according to Arnold,

> the English middle class presents us at this day, for our actual needs, and for the purposes of national civilisation, with a defective type of religion, a narrow range of intellect and knowledge, a stunted sense of beauty, a low standard of manners. For the building up of human life, as men are now beginning to see, there are needed not only the powers of industry and conduct, but the power also, of intellect and knowledge, the power of beauty, the power of social life and manners.

For Arnold, the bourgeois society was essentially provincial, philistine, narrowly utilitarian and materialist and that 'which we call the middle class is in America virtually the nation'. Thus, what many praised in Britain and delighted to see writ large in America, Arnold criticized and condemned.[29]

Although Arnold's harshest remarks were reserved for British society, he quoted extensively from the American press to demonstrate that what he bemoaned in Britain existed equally in the United States and was similarly condemned:

> The complaints one hears of the state of public life in America, of the increasing impossibility and intolerableness of it to self-respecting men, of the 'corruption and feebleness', of the blatant violence and exaggeration of language, the profligacy of clap-trap – the complaints we hear from America of all of this.

Indeed, as Arnold noted, Lowell himself had condemned 'the sad experience in America of "government by declamation"'. Furthermore, Arnold mischievously added, Lowell himself had been accused by his own people of doing exactly that for which he excoriated the British: '"This Lowell is a fraud and disgrace to the American nation; Minister

Lowell has scoffed at his own country, and disowned everything in its history and institutions that makes it free and great".'

Arnold's article was thus both riposte and appeal, and its message was simple enough. As both societies suffered from a surfeit of self-satisfied bourgeois provincialism, insular arrogance and pervasive philistinism, that minority represented by individuals of a more cos-mopolitan and cultural outlook on both sides of the Atlantic should, rather than attempt to score points regarding the merits of their respective nations, instead form a sympathetic alliance to bring about the transformation of genuinely civilized, sophisticated and intellectually elevated culture. Clearly, it was not just the political elites who were developing and sustaining relationships; the self-appointed guardians of cultural sophistication and cosmopolitanism were not far behind. Could the relationship between the two nations move from anarchy to culture (to paraphrase Arnold)? Possibly so, but any movement taking on such a responsibility would, from that day to this, be the preserve of a minority. But that would probably always be the case, no matter what society one was dealing with – liberal or democratic.[30]

It was but a relatively short step from Arnold's ideas to those found in American sociologist Thorstein Veblen's *The Theory of the Leisure Class* (1899). Veblen coined the term 'conspicuous consumption' to describe the habits of those at the top of society. According to Veblen, this group spent much more than they needed to on items both impractical and practical alike to demonstrate its status as members of the leisure class. Arnold's article appeared during the period in America that Mark Twain named 'the Gilded Age' in his novel of the same title published in 1873. Twain's work came to be used as a label for the entire period from 1877 to the start of the twentieth century, which he satirized as an age of corrupt politicians and fraudulent entrepreneurs, the age of the Robber Barons.[31]

Such a period was always going to be a richer and more complex age than the satirist would have one believe, of course, and Twain was the first to realize that. Yet how to respond to the changing societal com-plexities in the latter part of the nineteenth century was an issue that would bring Britons and Americans intellectually and socially, as much as politically, closer together than ever before. Then there is Twain himself, who was as much a literary phenomenon in Britain as he was in the United States, representing the increasing interconnectedness of cultural ties to the extent that it was becoming increasingly difficult to demarcate where American and British ideas and activities both began and left off. Thus, Arnold's desire for greater Anglo-American cultural and intellectual exchange would come true in so many ways except for perhaps in the fashion which he had hoped. He did, in the end, manage to visit the United States – the year after his essay above was published, in fact. There, his daughter would fall in love with, and marry, an American citizen. It was, indeed, increasingly becoming a transatlantic age. The young liberals proved merely to be a foretaste of what was to come.

9

Towards a Transatlantic Culture

The consulting detective was concerned. The mystery he faced had been brought to him by one Mr Hilton Cubitt, of Riding Thorpe Manor, Norfolk. Cubitt, the previous year, had married an American lady, Elsie Patrick, whom he had met at Queen Victoria's Diamond Jubilee in London. As with most marriages, there was a catch: Miss Patrick had, on the day before their wedding, told Cubitt that she had had 'some very disagreeable associations in her life', and that while she had 'nothing that she need be personally ashamed of', because she wished to forget all about them, her future husband must allow her 'to be silent as to all that passed up to the time' before she met him. Cubitt, 'as much in love as a man could be', had accepted these terms. In some respects, it was a mistake which he would not live to regret.

During their first year of marriage, his wife received a letter from the United States which she burned upon reading. Some time after this, a series of chalk pictograms, described as being like 'dancing men', looking as innocuous as a child's drawing, began appearing on the exterior walls and doors of the Norfolk squire's manor. These hieroglyphics, while puzzling Cubitt, drove his wife to distraction but she would not say why. Unable to directly confront his wife as to the nature of the drawings – 'a promise is a promise', Cubitt had replied to the detective when asked why he did not directly appeal to his spouse as to their secret – the squire required outside help. The detective had agreed to solve the mystery, and asking for and receiving copies of future drawings had set to uncover the riddle.

The detective recognized from the beginning that the pictograms represented a code somehow connected to Elsie Cubitt's American past and set to work deciphering it in order to solve the mystery of the dancing men. Upon finally breaking the code, and discovering the name of the individual sending the messages to Elsie Cubitt to be one Abe Slaney, the detective sent a telegram to his friend, Wilson Hargreave of the New York Police Bureau, asking if this individual was known to him. The response arrived at almost the same time as the detective solved the last set of hieroglyphics Cubitt would ever send him. The translated pictograms read: 'Elsie prepare to meet thy God'; Hargreave's telegram said of Abe Slaney: 'The most dangerous crook in Chicago'. Recognizing that he had let events go too far, the detective made ready to head to Norfolk, only to miss the last train. This delay would lead to tragedy including the death of Cubitt. If only the detective had been able to get from London to Norfolk as easily as he had been able to send and receive a telegram from New York.[1]

The events described above never happened, being one of the adventures of Sir Arthur Conan Doyle's creation, Sherlock Holmes, in 'The Adventure of the Dancing Men'. The work was first published in Britain in the *Strand Magazine* in December 1903 and simultaneously in America in *Collier's Weekly*. The choice of one of the stories from adventures of the most famous detective in literature has not been made for reasons of whimsy, but because it illustrates how popular culture closely reflected the degree to which the United States and Britain were becoming intertwined by the late nineteenth and early twentieth century. Take, for example, the use of the telegram, or the 'Victorian internet' as one scholar has labelled it. It took several attempts – in 1858, 1865 and 1866 – before a permanent connection was laid from Valentia Island, Ireland to Trinity Bay, Newfoundland. The first official telegram to pass between Britain and the United States was the message of congratulations from Queen Victoria to President James Buchanan. Although the cable carrying that message was broken, meaning that there was no instantaneous communication between the two nations during the Civil War (a fact usually considered fortuitous by most historians) with a permanent connection made afterwards and more and more cables being laid, the days of waiting for important information by ship had come to an end. It should be noted that this achievement was thanks to entrepreneurs, in the form of the Atlantic Telegraph Company, the Telegraph Construction and Maintenance Company and, finally, the Anglo-American Telegraph Company, rather than politicians; the last expressing both anti-American and Anglophobic sentiment initially proved extremely reluctant to help underwrite the venture, though both Congress and Parliament finally released funds in the form of grants and loans. In this instance, at least, transatlantic capitalism and entrepreneurship proved more foresighted and progressive than the political leadership.[2]

Equally, on another level, although Sherlock Holmes is an undeniably British fictional character, in many respects he is very much American, too. Or, if that is too much, there is an obvious American thread running through not only the stories, but also in the development of his publishing history. For example, Holmes himself is largely modelled on Edgar Allan Poe's French detective, C. Auguste Dupin, published in the 1840s. The second part of the very first Holmes story, *A Study in Scarlet* (1887), takes place among the Mormons in the American mid-west while in an early adventure, *The Five Orange Pips* (1891), the Ku Klux Klan are the villains.

More significantly, it was an American who brought the detective back to life (as it were) when his creator killed the character off in 1893. As is well known, Conan Doyle's feelings about Holmes were ambiguous at best, believing the stories overshadowed what he regarded as his more important works of historical fiction. Despite protests from readers, including an irritated Queen Victoria, Conan Doyle relented only to write *The Hound of the Baskervilles* (1901–02), which he insisted was an old case of the detective's. Apart from that, his readers would have to make do with his other stories and novels – or so the author hoped. Conan Doyle was forced to change his mind when the American P. F. Collier of *Collier's Weekly* wrote to him asking for more Sherlock Holmes stories at whatever price the author sought fit to ask. Conan Doyle, in an effort to get rid of him, named a sum he believed beyond the latter's means of paying. The American answer arrived by cable: Conan Doyle had himself a deal. Thus, in a very real sense, Holmes was pulled out of the Reichenbach Falls, where his creator had hoped to permanently deposit him, by a rope made of American dollars.[3]

Understandably, in the subsequent tales there were rather more references to the United States (Dr Watson has a picture of Henry Ward Beecher, for example) and there were more frequent appearances of American characters (including 'The Adventure of the Dancing Men', above). Yet there was always a strong degree of pro-American sentiment in the Holmes stories, as the detective himself declares in 'The Adventure of the Noble Bachelor' (1892):

> It is always a joy to meet an American ... for I am one of those who believe that the folly of a monarch and the blundering of a minister in far-gone years will not prevent our children from being some day citizens of the same world-wide country under a flag which shall be a quartering of the Union Jack with the Stars and Stripes.

Indeed, the American aspects of the detective's stories were so pronounced that one of his more famous aficionados, President Franklin

Roosevelt, wrote an article 'Sherlock Holmes was an American', insisting that his character was such that he could only be a citizen of the United States. It was 'Elementary, my dear Watson', as Holmes never actually said.[4]

The detective was not, and is not, to everybody's tastes. Many have agreed with George Bernard Shaw's verdict that 'Holmes was a drug addict without a single amiable trait', referring to the latter's rather enthusiastic use of cocaine (then legal on both sides of the Atlantic) as well as to the fact that he was as conceited as he was clever. Yet the stories remain an illustrative example of how much popular culture was increasingly becoming transatlantic as opposed to merely national. In the case of Conan Doyle's creation, plays and then films would be made featuring his exploits on both sides of the Atlantic.[5]

Conan Doyle's works were hardly the first transatlantic literary phenomenon. As discussed in a previous chapter, Charles Dickens, Harriet Beecher Stowe and others preceded him. Yet he and the other later British and American nineteenth-century writers had an advantage: copyright. It took until the 1870s for British writers to start winning support from the United States in favour of it. In 1876, a Royal Commission was appointed on copyright and, after hearing testimony from, among others, Matthew Arnold, Edward Dicey, Thomas Huxley, Herbert Spencer, and the American publisher George Putnam, proposed ideas for an Anglo-American arrangement. As the Commission noted, pirated editions in the United States were the biggest concern of British authors. American agreement was initially slow to materialize and so the problem remained. By the 1880s, however, the American Copyright League (ACL) was formed and began agitating for a bilateral agreement. On 12 January 1884, the League passed a resolution which called upon the State Department to 'complete an International Treaty with Great Britain, securing to the authors of each country the full recognition of property rights in both countries'. British and American authors soon began a transatlantic campaign, the leader of the ACL, Robert Underwood Johnson, becoming a correspondent of William Gladstone, who promoted a plan of his own and wrote articles in support of an agreement. Thanks to these efforts, led largely by Johnson in America and James Bryce in Britain, success was finally secured on 4 March 1891 when President Benjamin Harrison signed a copyright bill and the House of Commons reciprocated. On 1 July 1891, the agreement took effect and a long-standing problem besetting Anglo-American literary relations was finally solved. British and American authors could breathe a sigh of relief – their property rights would be respected in each other's largest foreign market.[6]

Britons and Americans were not simply entertaining each other by the printed word, of course; the stage had always been an avenue and, in 1887, during the occasion of Queen Victoria's Golden Jubilee, a major American show made its British debut: Buffalo Bill's Wild West Exhibition. It has been suggested that the United States in effect gate-crashed, as the expression has it, the very British occasion when, without receiving any invitation, it announced it was sending a large delegation, but this belief demonstrates a misunderstanding of the Jubilee's nature. Unlike the Great Exhibition of 1851, the Golden Jubilee was not a world fair, but the celebration of the fiftieth anniversary of the monarch's coronation. The invited delegations included the various European royal houses which were related to the Queen as well as those from the colonies and dominions of which she was head of state. The United States, falling into neither category, and being both determinedly and loudly republican, was thus not an obvious potential guest. Further, while the American announcement certainly came as a surprise it was nonetheless warmly welcomed as a friendly overture, the *Illustrated London News* declaring that, 'we take it kindly of the great kindred people of the United States, that they now send such a magnificent representation to the Fatherland, determined to take some part in celebrating the Jubilee of her Majesty the Queen.'[7]

The American delegation was expected to put on a good show; the United States had, after all, managed a very impressive – and much remarked upon – display in the Great Exhibition of 1851. Not only that, but one member of that delegation, Buffalo Bill (and his show), was already known to many Britons. Colonel William Frederick Cody – to provide his real name – and his exploits had already been the subject of numerous American 'dime novels', the equivalent of Britain's 'penny dreadfuls' which had made their way across the Atlantic. Buffalo Bill was thus already something of a celebrity in Britain before he set foot on British soil. Thus, his arrival (and that of the rest of the American delegation) was awaited with some excitement. He did not disappoint.

Although Buffalo Bill's reputation was as much mythology as hard fact, he was a genuine frontiersman. Born in 1846 and growing up in the then unsettled territories of Kansas and Utah, Cody experienced his first encounter with hostile Indians at the age of 12. By the age of 14 he was a rider with the Pony Express – a band of horsemen who delivered the mail between Missouri and California in ten days. He served with the

Union armies in the American Civil War, and took on a variety of jobs from cattle driving, to stage-coach driver, to unsuccessful hotel manager, to hunting buffalo to provide fresh meat for the workers of the Kansas Pacific railroad, all of which were followed by another stint in the army fighting Indians. It was following the last of these activities, an engagement with a Cheyenne Chief, Tall Bull, and his warriors, that Cody was interviewed by a popular novelist, Edward Judson, who went under the *nom de plume* of Ned Buntline, and shortly afterwards read of his own exploits (in somewhat exaggerated form) in the popular press. Although he never received a penny from Buntline, Cody soon found himself in demand to lead hunting parties of, first, wealthy Americans from the east and then foreigners, including the Grand Duke Alexei of Russia, keen to hunt with the legendary Buffalo Bill. Invited to New York and enjoying the fruits of celebrity there while on a furlough from the army, Cody was urged to return to star in plays written by Buntline. Recognizing an opportunity to make money when he saw it, Cody obliged and although the first play, *The Scouts of the Prairie*, was savaged by the critics, it was a huge success. It was also, arguably, the first western. It did not take long for Cody, with the help of one Nate Salsbury, to establish his own show: an outdoor extravaganza featuring real cowboys, Indians and buffalo, based loosely on his exploits. According to Salsbury, the two men intended to take their show to Britain from the start, recognizing it would be a bigger novelty there than anywhere else.

The specially built circular arena in which the show would take place was a third of a mile in diameter, surrounded by an amphitheatre which had boxes for 20,000 spectators, standing room for another 10,000 and open-air standing for a further 10,000 people. To whet public appetite still more, associates of Buffalo Bill acted as public relations men, and planted stories about the show and its performers in the British press. Likewise, the performers themselves, upon arrival in Britain, gave interviews, as well as riding through the streets in full regalia, while the arena was being prepared. The Indian delegation, speaking through interpreters, attracted by far the most curiosity (they themselves were most taken with Westminster Abbey where they attended a service, as well as the Tower of London, which attracted multiple visits). With all of this publicity, the only concern was that the troupe would not deliver; that fear was assuaged with the very first performance.

Given the modern-day familiarity with the western as a genre, particularly in films, it is probably impossible to capture the sheer sense of novelty the spectacle presented to that original British audience. The souvenir programme – over seventy pages in length – featured, among other things, bands playing 'The Star Spangled Banner' and 'Dixie', as well as other popular American tunes; horse races between Mexicans and Indians riding bareback in purported national costume; sharp-shooter Annie Oakley's skills; a recreation of the Pony Express ride, featuring Indians and bandits; a large wagon train which circled to defend itself against an Indian attack, and was saved by the arrival of the cavalry; a genuine former sheriff arresting various desperados; various battles on horseback by Indians and cowboys; a series of riding and rope tricks, including bucking broncos and lassoing objects held up by members of the audience; stagecoach adventures; braves doing war and other dances in a recreation of an Indian village with tepees; the expert herding of 18 American bison; and the activities of a pioneer family in a log cabin who defended themselves against Indian attacks (as regards to this last, *Punch* complained that the Indians should be allowed to win now and again). It was, quite literally, sensational; and like most such things, a resounding commercial and popular success. To claim that Buffalo Bill stole the show when it came to the Golden Jubilee would be to exaggerate, but it was one of the most talked-about events sur-rounding it.[8]

Not that her Majesty appeared to mind – Queen Victoria herself enjoyed a royal command performance. She also insisted on meeting members of the troupe, shaking hands with many, including the Indian performers, whom she called 'the best-looking people' she knew. While the members of Buffalo Bill's troupe were delighted to meet and be praised by the Queen, there was some disgruntled commentary in the realm itself. Several newspapers criticized the Queen because she had 'insisted on having the Wild West all to herself', meaning that 'thousands who came to see the American exhibition to pay their money and see the show were told to go away and come back another day'. But such are the prerogatives of the sovereign. Victoria was hardly the only major figure to make acquaintance with the troupe. Sir Henry Irving; Ellen Terry; Randolph Churchill; Oscar Wilde; Edward, Prince of Wales; and Gladstone were some of the many who did so. In the case of the last, he made a point of meeting the head of the Indian delegation, Red Shirt (inaccurately billed as 'the Chief of the Sioux Nation'), in the latter's tepee. By all accounts, the two men thought highly of each other, so much so that cartoons appeared depicting Gladstone in Indian dress, smoking a peace pipe with Red Shirt.

Buffalo Bill's Wild West show toured the British Isles and went on from there to Europe. Despite the usual problems all travelling shows encounter, such as accidents, loss of property or persons and the occasional brush with the law, the troupe, which was a study of professionalism, pretty well met with success wherever it went. The show, with changes, returned to tour both Britain and Europe throughout the end of the nineteenth and early twentieth century, by 1902 travelling to over a hundred different locations by means of railway trains pulling 150 carriages, the final farewell tour taking place in 1912. By the time Buffalo Bill died in 1917, some of his exploits had been captured on crude movies; that most American of genres, the western, was now a permanent fixture in the British imagination.[9]

Sherlock Holmes and Buffalo Bill are or were reflections of popular culture, and the realm of entertainment. Yet the relationship between Britain and the United States was also developing in other realms as well, particularly in the field of industrial relations and other social areas. In the case of industrial production, the Americans had a lot to teach the British – they pioneered the use of interchangeable parts, for example, which became known as the American method of manufacturing. The United States, suffering labour shortages that Britain did not, had more incentive to develop new technology. Yet despite this eventual American lead in industrial output and production, many observers from the United States still believed they had much to learn when it came to industrial relations. In 1903, for example, A. Maurice Low, a US Bureau of Labor investigator, reported on British employers' and union leaders' opinions:

[I]n the United States, the unions are at the present time passing through the same stage which is part of the history of unionism in the United Kingdom a quarter of a century ago. Questions which have been settled in Great Britain are yet to be settled in the United States ... [I]n the United States trade unionism has not yet advanced to the high level it now occupies in Great Britain. This is one reason why ... the relations between capital and labor in America are not so cordial as in England; and it also explains why strikes in America are more common than in England and are carried on with greater bitterness on both sides.

Furthermore, the issues at heart often extended beyond only industrial relations. Edith Abbott, a lecturer in sociology, went so far as to declare that,

England [is] proceeding much more rapidly to embody our democratic ideals into social legislation than [are] most of the American states ... England led the civilized nations of the world and is still in advance of most of them, including our own, in the establishment of social control over industry through the establishment of a minimum wage, the prohibition of long hours and night work for working-women, and the prohibition of child labor.

These opinions on how the British managed labour relations and other social issues would endure for a surprisingly long time. As late as the 1940s, American Mary B. Gilson recalled her visits to Britain in the late 1920s to report on the crisis in labour relations for Industrial Relations Counselors: 'Great Britain has long furnished a happy hunting ground for American students of political, social, and economic questions. There are various reasons for this, among them the primary one that England was the first country in the world to proceed along the now commonly travelled route of industrialization.' What was the cause of this American interest in British labour relations and social legislation?[10]

The origins and reason for these investigations lay in the widespread labour unrest which occurred in the United States from 1873 onwards. In 1873, existing unprecedented high levels of unemployment led to mass meetings and demonstrations within the United States, as well as violence. Among coal miners in Pennsylvania, members of a secret Irish organization (initially formed to protect Irish workers from discrimination), the so-called 'Molly Maguires', engaged in acts, including murder, for which several were executed. In 1877 a railway strike, which began in West Virginia, spread to Maryland and Pennsylvania. By the time it was broken by state militias and the army, over a hundred people were dead and thousands more imprisoned. Then there was the Haymarket Riot in Chicago 1886, where a bomb was thrown at the police who fired upon the crowd in retaliation. This sort of unrest caused a fair degree of uneasiness and, as a result, ideas were sought to mitigate it. Britain, it must be noted, was hardly free of either industrial unrest or, indeed, social problems – far from it, as American observers were perfectly aware. One need only cite events such as the 'Jubilee Riots' or the Trafalgar Square demonstrations in 1887 and the great London dock strike of 1889, or publications such as Andrew Mearn's *The Bitter Cry of Outcast London: An Inquiry into the Abject Poor* (1883) or Charles Booth's *Life and Labour of the People of London* (1902) to demonstrate this. Further, as one scholar has shown, nineteenth-century London –

whether of conservative, liberal or radical persuasion – believed itself to be almost permanently threatened by the casual labouring classes. Despite this, many American reformers believed that how the British dealt with the problems of labour unrest, and other social issues, seemed to be worth examining, if not necessarily entirely emulating.[11]

As we have already seen, the improving relationship between Britain and the United States during the latter part of the nineteenth century, not to mention improved methods of transport and communication, meant that individuals from both were looking to the other for ideas, including solutions to social problems. In the 1870s, the Liberal MPs Thomas Hughes and A. J. Mundella embarked upon an American lecture tour which, among other topics, covered trade unionism and boards of arbitration in Britain. With the labour unrest in the United States, the two men appeared to have something to offer, especially their descriptions of the findings of the Royal Commissions on Trade Unions, 1867–69, that unions often contributed to social peace. In response at least in part to this, American journalists, politicians and others were travelling to the world's first industrial nation to examine the British model first-hand and report on their discoveries. Thus, by 1893, Josephine Shaw Lowell's *Industrial Arbitration and Conciliation* devoted a third of her pioneering study's twelve chapters to the British experience which, she assumed, was the most ready guide as to how the United States should settle its industrial disputes.[12]

As one scholar has noted, the period from the 1870s until after the First World War marked a distinct period of American willingness to learn from British methods of handling labour relations and other social issues. It was only after the Second World War that ideas of American exceptionalism again came into vogue, including the belief that there was a distinctive American way of dealing with such issues, and that other nations had little to offer except in a negative sense. To be sure, part of this belief that the two nations were on a similar path was, in many respects, owed to late nineteenth-century beliefs of Anglo-Saxon racial superiority, as the words of the president of the American Society of Mechanical Engineers, Henry R. Towne, spoken in 1889 demonstrate: '[T]ogether we constitute the two branches of the great Anglo-Saxon, English-speaking race, which, in accomplishment, especially in the industrial world, is at present easily the leader among the nations in the march of civilization.' Yet there was more to it than this. As one scholar has pointed out, we are perhaps too used to thinking of Britain unappreciatively, in terms of its long relative decline and certainly by the early years of the twentieth century some evidence of a declinist mentality can be identified in the British public discourse. Yet in the last years of the nineteenth century and early ones of the twentieth, Britain actually only faced two serious industrial rivals: the United States and Germany. At this time, there were neither differences of scale nor qualitative ones great enough to convince America that Britain's experience was not relative to them. As late as 1907, the ratio of British to American wage earners in 26 different trades was roughly four to five and the standard of living for common labour was arguably more closely comparable. We are talking here of the era before the First World War, a conflict which did catastrophic damage to the British economy and society as a whole. Further, as late as 1914, British overseas investment dwarfed that of Germany and the United States (indeed, more British capital was invested in the Americas from 1865 to 1914 than in Britain itself). Only 6 per cent of this stock of capital in overseas investment was in western Europe while around 45 per cent was in the United States and the Dominions with some 20 per cent invested in Latin America. Britain was, prior to the First World War, the world's banker. Thus, prior to the conflict and, indeed, for a time afterwards, Britain was simply not viewed as a declining – let alone foundering – state, even if the United States, in terms of industrial output and economic growth, had already begun to overtake it.[13]

Further, it is important to note that, in both political and social terms, Britain was not simply an island off the continent of Europe, but the headquarters of a world empire or, as the phrase then had it, a 'greater Britain'. Thus, we are talking of an organization consisting of a series of British Dominions – Australia, Canada, New Zealand, and later, South Africa, among others – which, although following one another in achieving degrees of autonomy, nonetheless had a political and economic relationship with Britain in certain respects akin to those of American states within the United States. These Dominions were further connected to the rest of the Empire, including places like India, parts of Africa and the West Indies. The Dominions themselves were places of social experimentation which affected, and were affected by, developments in Britain. So, for example, New Zealand's Liberal–Labour alliance lasting from 1891 to 1906, which introduced a programme of progressive land taxes, comprehensive factory regulation and old-age pensions in effect acted as pioneer for other autonomous members of the Empire as well as Britain itself. New Zealand's enfranchising of women in 1893 (followed by Australia in 1902) spurred the achievement of woman's suffrage in Britain in 1918 (by contrast, American women gained the vote in 1920). Not only that, but these connections were being maintained, and in some cases strengthened, by travel and trade among British subjects. Indeed, in the last quarter of the nineteenth century, British emigration to the Dominions now exceeded that to the United States.[14]

By the 1880s and certainly by the end of the nineteenth century, 'the annihilation of distance', as one historian has termed it, by improved technology, not to mention promotion and propaganda, meant that the British Empire held a prominent place in both the imagination and political life of Britain and its subjects at both home and abroad. So, for example, in 1895, the *Castle Line Atlas of South Africa* contained a map of 'The British Empire Coloured Red'. Canada, at the same time, issued postage stamps illustrating the same, declaring 'We hold a greater empire than has ever been.' This was the era of Rudyard Kipling, the poet of Empire, and the financier, Cecil Rhodes (who would seriously talk of 'the ultimate recovery of the United States of America as an integral part of the British Empire'). All of this meant that Britain still remained a focal point of both American and world attention.[15]

This imperial aspect brings us to another point about the Anglo-American relationship. In a previous chapter we discussed the parallels between the Spanish-American War, and the exploits in the Philippines and the second Anglo-Boer War. One parallel not discussed was the anti-imperial reaction that took place in response to the conflicts in both the United States and Britain. In the case of the former, the American Anti-Imperial League was established and circulated more than a million pieces of literature against the annexation of the Phi-lippines. The League, which contained notable Americans such as Democratic presidential candidate, William Jennings Bryan, Mark Twain, Andrew Carnegie, Charles Francis Adams Jr, novelist Ambrose Bierce, former president Grover Cleveland, philosophers John Dewey and William James, social reformer Jane Addams, and labour leader Samuel Gompers were only some of the well-known names within the organization. The League's supporters were an eclectic bunch: they included racists who wanted to avoid the likely immigration of non-whites into the United States, as well as African Americans who saw the war as a racist one. Despite these contradictions, it proved an influential and powerful lobby: when the Senate ratified the treaty annexing the Philippines, it did so by only one vote.[16]

In Britain, meantime, editor and journalist William Thomas Stead founded the Stop the War committee in an effort to stave off hostilities with the Boer Republics. The committee included, among others, future British Prime Minister, David Lloyd George and the labour leader and founder of the Labour Party, Keir Hardie. Other opponents included the Liberal MP Phillip Stanmore, the Labour MP John Burns and the writers G. K. Chesterton and Hilaire Belloc. At the same time, the owner and editor of the *Manchester Guardian* and MP, C. P. Scott, used his newspaper as a forum for anti-war activity and continued to do so even though the journal's circulation declined by 15 per cent. In 1900, meanwhile, the Trades Union Congress passed a resolution condemning the war 'to secure the goldfields of South Africa'. The 'Pro-Boers', as they were known, were initially at odds with the public – a fact underlined when the Conservatives, prematurely declaring victory upon the fall of Pretoria, won another majority government in the 'khaki election' in October 1900. Then came the guerrilla war and, perhaps worse from the Conservatives' point of view, Emily Hobhouse. Hobhouse, a social reformer, visited South Africa and exposed the appalling conditions of the concentration camps in which the Boer (both civilian and military) population was held. Her reports galvanized the Liberal opposition, their leader Henry Campbell-Bannerman declaring, 'When is a war not a war? When it is carried on by methods of barbarism in South Africa.' Lord Salisbury's Conservative administration was forced to establish the Boer War Concentration Camp Commission, a committee of women chaired by the feminist Millicent Fawcett. Although the government had dismissed Hobhouse as a 'hysterical female', the Fawcett Commission inconveniently vindicated most of her claims. Women had just exposed the façade of the gentleman's war. This was bad news for the Conservatives, because this and the guerrilla war, among other things, resulted in the Liberal landslide of 1906.[17]

Although, like the American activities in the Philippines, the opponents of the Boer War included a wide array of opinion – cries that the war was fought for the benefit of Jewish financiers were common – these two movements represented the first serious domestic challenge to the United States' and Britain's expansionist activities. Some scholars have even claimed that modern pacifist movements owe their origins to the opponents of the Boer War, but if this is true, surely the American Anti-Imperial League must also share the credit. Not that either the British or American publics' views of each other were necessarily improved by the war. Most in Britain had sympathized with the United States in the Spanish-American War (in contrast with Europe), and were outraged when the American public largely sided with the Boers (Irish-Americans especially, but Irish nationalists in Britain demonstrated similar sentiments).

At the level of government, however, things were different. Remembering Britain's pro-American neutrality in the first conflict, both William McKinley's and Theodore Roosevelt's administrations returned the compliment in the latter. In September 1899, Secretary of State John Hay had written to the First Secretary at the London Embassy, Henry White, 'The one indispensable feature of our foreign policy should be a friendly understanding with Britain.' The next year he was writing, 'The fight of England is the fight of civilization and progress and all our interests are bound up in her success.' Not for the first time, governments went against the public grain. Yet the more intelligent of the American opponents of the British in the Boer War criticized it because they recognized the parallels between it and what was occurring in the Philippines. William Jennings Bryan and Andrew Carnegie both saw the similarities, while Mark Twain remarked, 'I think that England sinned when she got herself into a war in South Africa which she could have avoided, just as we have sinned in getting into a similar war in the Philippines.' Governments were now usually in agreement on both sides of the Atlantic but so too, increasingly, were the opponents and critics of their actions. Lord Salisbury might complain that 'England is the only country in which, during a great war, eminent men write and speak as if they belonged to the enemy', but this was true of the United States as well.[18]

Yet, at least at this stage, it was the supporters of Anglo-American imperialism who had their way. That popular propagandist for Empire, G. A. Henty, the children's novelist, or 'boys' Dumas' as he was known, author of *With Clive in India* (1884) and *With Buller in Natal* (1901), also wrote *With Lee in Virginia* (1880). Rudyard Kipling, meantime, would publish his famous 'White Man's Burden' in 1899 in response to the United States' activities in the Philippines. Opening with the ringing exhortation, 'Take up the White Man's burden/ Send forth the best ye breed/ Go bind your sons to exile/ To serve your captives' need;/ To wait in heavy harness/ On fluttered folk and wild/ Your new-caught, sullen peoples/ Half-devil and half-child', and speaking of, 'The blame of those ye better/ The hate of those ye guard', this poem was a great favourite with the American imperialists, particularly with its recipient, Theodore Roosevelt. It was little wonder that the President struck up a friendship with the poet, even if he liked to tease Kipling on the subject of Anglo-Saxon heritage by repeatedly noting that he had not a drop of English blood in his veins.[19]

That the late nineteenth and early twentieth century was the high point in educated Americans' familiarity with and belief in a shared Anglo-American culture was another contributing factor to this trans-atlantic cross-fertilization of ideas. After 1889, for example, the influence of the American Historical Society (one of whose presidents, lest we forget, was Briton Goldwin Smith in 1904) on the American high school curricula meant that more US citizens than ever before (and probably since) studied British history in depth as the precursor to their own. This, combined with the rapidly converging economic development of Britain and the United States (and, indeed, Europe), meant that the accompanying material forces became important centralizers of experience. With this process underway, it was almost inevitable that social-political networks would develop alongside. The process was essentially symbiotic.[20]

Thus, Britain's Liberal administrations of 1906–14 embarked upon a process of social reform that influenced Franklin Roosevelt's New Deal. Toynbee Hall, the British settlement house established in London's East End in 1884, attracted visitors such as American social reformers Jane Addams, Margaret Dreier and Robert Woods. The American radical economist Henry George made five very popular tours of the United Kingdom from the 1880s onwards. Even British higher education began to attract American students (although Germany was always the more common destination). American historian Charles Beard made his way to Oxford in the 1890s while the London School of Economics took on American recruits. Britain's lead in urbanization meant that its sanitary movements, including the provision of fresh water and sewerage, came under American scrutiny. Joseph Chamberlain's Birmingham (he was mayor from 1873–75), where slums were cleared, public libraries built, and the water, gas and sewerage systems placed under municipal con-trol, served as a magnet for American urban reformers. American Richard Ely in the 1880s urged the adoption of a programme of British (and German) municipal services. Woodrow Wilson declared in 1912 on the campaign trail that 'one of the best governed cities in the world is the great Scotch city of Glasgow'. The first British charity organization to provide poor relief was established in London 1869, to be followed by an American offshoot in Buffalo, New York, 1877, by a former volunteer in England.[21]

This movement of people and ideas was reciprocated, of course, by

British social reformers, some of which we have noted in the previous chapter. The American system of public parks in urban areas was noted and adopted by British municipal reformers. Charles Booth admired Manhattan's skyscrapers, believing they represented the nation's magnificent energy. Beatrice and Sidney Webb visited the United States in 1898 (this was not the first trip for either – Beatrice, as an adolescent, had visited with her father in 1873, while Sidney had crossed the Atlantic in 1888). Beatrice made a point of noting in her diary, 'Who would recognize as distinctly American the essentially eccentric and ugly individuals portrayed by [Charles] Dickens, [Frances] Trollope and [Harriet] Martineau?' She was also impressed by the United States' ability to integrate its immigrant population, declaring that 'one of the surprises' was how 'the heterogeneous population' settled down 'to the orderly ways and clean habits typical of American civilization'. She was not entirely uncritical, especially of the government, noting 'who can deny the truth of Professor Bryce's remark that for the last twenty years the Federal Congress had shirked every problem and evaded every issue'. If, however, the Webbs were not entirely struck with the United States, other Fabians were and the organization maintained strong transatlantic connections. William Clarke, for example, became a regular contributor to the *New England Magazine*, while American feminist Charlotte Gilman Perkins, among others of her fellow countrymen, became a member of the British society.[22]

Another social reformer who visited the United States was the novelist H. G. Wells, author of *The Time Machine* (1895), *The Island of Doctor Moreau* (1896) and *The War of the Worlds* (1898) among numerous others, who published an account, *The Future in America*, in 1906. Wells was less interested in the United States as it was, but rather, as befitted a writer of science fiction, what it would come to do. Inclined towards favouring the United States, his verdict was ultimately mixed. Although long an admirer of American writers such as James Fenimore Cooper, Washington Irving and friends with both Henry James and Stephen Crane, before he crossed the Atlantic, Wells had been very much influenced by the American Henry George's criticisms of his nation's social problems and substantially upheld the latter's views. Being a socialist, he regarded the pervasiveness of private property and commercialism to be more extensive (and therefore problematic) than in Britain. In a chapter, 'The tragedy of colour', he commented upon the issue of American race relations and the efforts of black reformers such as

Booker T. Washington and W. E. B. Du Bois, both of whom he met on his trip.

He was especially sceptical of the claim that America was a new country, remarking that it was 'an older country than any European one, for she has not rejuvenesced for a hundred and thirty years. In endless ways America fails to be contemporary.' Yet for all that, he identified the United States as an experiment – something few nineteenth-century Britons did – asking, 'Is America a giant childhood or gigantic futility, a mere latest phase of that long secession of experiments which has been and may be for interminable years – may, indeed, altogether until the end – man's social history?' He had no particular answer to that question, but he did make some predictions, including that Boston, 'America's Athens', represented the nation's past, not future: 'My main thesis is that culture, as it is conceived in Boston, is no contribution to the future of America'; that honour belonged to New York which was more interesting, more significant, more stimulating and better represented the 'crude splendour of the possibilities of America now'. Wells was amazed, appalled and intrigued by the potential of the United States and for at least one very good reason: 'It seems to me that in America, by sheer virtue of its size, its free traditions, and the habit of initiative in its people, the leadership of progress must ultimately rest.' Yet that, for Wells, was always the problem, the question of where humanity was ultimately headed was a subject about which he would become increasingly pessimistic.[23]

Wells's American friendships and love of American fiction, his multiple travels to the United States, in 1921, 1934, 1935, 1937 and 1940, and his involvement in transatlantic reform, represent just how much British and American travel and trade in products, ideas and culture was beginning to make it difficult to tell where each nation's influence began and left off. They had, of course, never been hermetically sealed off from one another, but the boundaries were being increasingly blurred and difficult to demarcate. An example of this phenomenon is the writer Henry James, born an American citizen in 1843; dying a British subject in 1916 (he adopted the latter nationality partly in protest at his native land's refusal to enter the First World War).

Sensibly classified as an American novelist, James to an extent bought into and elaborated upon the by now mouldy American views of Britain and Europe for, as is frequently noted, his works often juxtapose characters from the New World and Old World. The former tend towards brashness, openness and assertiveness, the latter to corruption, reserve and retirement. This is not to say James was simply trading in stereotypes – that would be absurd – and his admirers are correct to claim that he analysed the English character with extreme subtlety. Yet in some ways, he was partially a throwback to an earlier age, because the growing transatlantic links were rendering the peoples on both sides more similar rather than more distinct. His earlier novels, such as *Roderick Hudson* (1876) and *Portrait of a Lady* (1881), explored the impact of Europe on American life; after this he tended to focus on the British and more specifically, English character, in works such as *The Tragic Muse* (1890) and *The Awkward Age* (1899), returning to a transatlantic theme in his last great novels *The Ambassadors* (1903) and *The Golden Bowl* (1904). Although his novels were not widely popular during his lifetime, he was well known as a critic, and struck up friendships with Robert Louis Stevenson, fellow American Edith Wharton (who explored some of the same themes as James) and Polish-Briton Joseph Conrad. Literature was now almost determinedly transatlantic in character.

Yet, as with American novelists earlier in the century, James faced accusations that he had, figuratively speaking, de-nationalized himself (long before he did literally). Although several British authors at the receiving end of his criticism remarked that he was effeminate – Thomas Hardy, for example, dismissed him as a virtuous female – several Americans pitched in on that score. Theodore Roosevelt, whom James dismissed as 'Theodore Rex', complained of his supposed lack of American masculinity. Meanwhile, after his death, American critics such as Van Wyck Brooks condemned his self-imposed expatriation and break with the United States. The snide observations about James's manhood aside, this was a repetition of the same accusations that had been previously levelled against Washington Irving, James Fenimore Cooper and Nathanial Hawthorne. In the words of the French critic Alphonse Karr: '*Plus ça change, plus c'est la meme chose.*' (The more things change, the more they stay the same).[24]

All the same, the literary exchanges kept growing. Oscar Wilde travelled to the United States in 1882 to embark upon a lecture tour, the story of his telling the New York customs official that he had nothing to declare but his genius being probably apocryphal. His tour was lucrative; Wilde claimed that he was a bigger hit than even Dickens had been. The trip was a success, even if not a few commentators disapproved of his flamboyant dress and dandy mannerisms. He may or may not have coined the phrase 'America is the only country that went from barbarism to decadence without civilisation in between' – the quote has also been ascribed to Georges Clemenceau – but Wilde found much to marvel at in the United States. He also made the acquaintance of Walt Whitman, the two men by all accounts getting on famously. Indeed, Wilde boasted to a friend, 'I have the kiss of Walt Whitman still on my lips.' Ultimately, this sort of thing would land Wilde in serious trouble. The late nineteenth century was not a good time to be homosexual or, if one prefers, to practise homosexual acts. Unlike in the early part of the century, when it was often ignored rather than tolerated, by the late 1800s the increasing categorization of human sexual activity and accompanying laws passed against certain acts, on both sides of the Atlantic, criminalized such behaviour and made legal prosecution more common.[25]

Another great literary celebrity on both sides of the Atlantic was Samuel Langhone Clemens or, to use his pen-name, Mark Twain. Best known for his novels *The Adventures of Tom Sawyer* (1876) and *The Adventures of Huckleberry Finn* (1885) and called 'the father of American literature' by William Faulkner, Twain first visited Britain in 1872. Twain's works were already popular in Britain, appearing in pirated copies. This was part of the reason he was visiting – to strike a deal with the publishers Routledge (who were themselves guilty of literary piracy) to produce an 'official' version of his works. With this arranged, he stayed on, making the acquaintance of Charles Reade, Charles Kingsley, Charles Dilke, Robert Browning, Alexander Kinglake and Charles Villiers, among others. It was a measure of his works' popularity that Twain found himself dining with the Lord High Chancellor and the Lord Mayor of London, both of whom were readers. Indeed, Twain remarked that he received a better reception from the gentlemen of old England than 'the literary gods of New England'.

If Twain was not an Anglophile before this trip, he was afterwards and made plans to return again, doing so the following year and embarking upon a successful lecture tour. He flattered British audiences, by telling them, and repeating his sentiments in the British edition of the *Gilded Age* (1873), that their government, which he had been taught to regard as corrupt, tyrannical and oppressive towards the masses, seemed in fact to allow the best persons to assume positions of authority rather than the worst, as was often the case in America. He also promoted certain British ideas and institutions while in the United States. He even, albeit privately, after readings of Thomas Carlyle, began to heretically wonder if Britain's (still) limited suffrage might in fact have a point.

Twain's relationship and views of Britain would fluctuate throughout his life. He never became an Anglophobe, but he did not much care for the threadbare British charge that American manners were crude, nor did he much appreciate the occasional adverse (and at times distinctly snooty) criticism his works received (particularly from Matthew Arnold). He patriotically sided with his own nation over the Venezuela crisis (although like most sensible people hoped for a peaceful resolution) and quietly condemned the Boer War. Yet he nonetheless struck up a friendship with Kipling and the latter's American wife, Caroline Balestier (whom Henry James gave away at the wedding), particularly when the couple resided in the United States for four years (it was while in the United States that Kipling would write both *Jungle Books* as well as *Captain Courageous*). Further, a number of Twain's best-known tales, including *The Prince and the Pauper* (1882) and *A Connecticut Yankee in King Arthur's Court* (1889), not to mention non-fiction works of travel and on Queen Victoria's Jubilees, were either based in Britain or had themes relating to the nation. The most interesting work as regards Anglo-American connections is *A Connecticut Yankee in King Arthur's Court*, because although broadly a satire of its age, Twain, to some degree, parodied British and American views of each other and differences between them. This was to be expected, because in the age of Henry James, Rudyard Kipling, H. G. Wells and Mark Twain, among others, the transatlantic current was now a flood. That said, the current was now beginning to change direction: even the legendary King Arthur now had to engage with American visitors and their influence.[26]

The work which first identified this development was W. T. Stead's *The Americanisation of the World or the Trend of the Twentieth Century* (1902). Stead, an enterprising and activist newspaper editor, was arguably the creator of the modern tabloid. An outspoken pacifist and social crusader, Stead came to national attention in 1876 by exposing the massacre of some 12,000 Christians in Bulgaria when the Turks suppressed rebellion there. Castigating Disraeli and his 'whole tribe of moral eunuchs' for doing nothing, Stead provided a platform for Gladstone to re-establish his political ascendancy. He later attracted even more attention when he exposed the trade in child prostitution, in his series of articles 'Maiden Tribute of Modern Babylon', in 1885. The public outcry forced the government to raise the age of consent to 16 from 13 (and for purchasing a girl aged 13 to prove his point, Stead ended up serving three months in gaol). Several times nominated for the Nobel Peace Prize, Stead ended his days in a manner that, in some ways perhaps, befit his tumultuous career – he was among those who drowned in the sinking of the *Titanic* in April 1912. He was en route to a peace congress at Carnegie Hall, New York, at the invitation of President William Howard Taft.[27]

It was thus hardly unusual that someone like Stead would note the rise and growing power of the United States and comment upon it. True, his work repeated the ideas found in Charles Dilke's *Greater Britain* (although Stead and Dilke were political enemies), namely those of Anglo-Saxon commonalities, but he took these notions further and in certain respects, a different direction. Stead did not place Britain and the United States on an equal footing: he believed that the Anglicization of the world had already been surpassed by its Americanization. Further, rather than seeing American society and culture as merely a derivative of Britain's (immigration and integration meant that 'the American, it is evident, is no mere Englishman transplanted to another continent'), Stead instead viewed Americanization as something new and different to Anglicization, going so far as to compare the two respectively to Christianity and Judaism. What Stead wanted was full-fledged Anglo-American political unity under this new phenomenon Americanization. Or, as he forthrightly expressed it, the United States and Britain should 'merge the British Empire in the English-speaking United States of the World', substituting 'the insular patriotism of our nation' into 'the broader patriotism of the race', and 'realise the great idea of Race Union', in order to enter 'a new era of power and prosperity'. Pointing to the fact that German unity must have appeared as idle a dream in 1801 as Anglo-American unity seemed in 1901, Stead noted, 'The tendency of the last half century has been all in favour of the unification of peoples who speak the same language' and argued that this was 'not likely to slacken in the new century'.[28]

All this was pretty heady stuff, as was his proposed blueprint for political unification between the United States and the British Empire. Arguing that the constituent parts of the United Kingdom, including Scotland and Wales, to say nothing of Ireland would probably prefer to be part of the American Union than the British one, Stead stated that Britain's Dominions, Australia and Canada, were already federations with written constitutions and that their culture was closer to that of the United States' than that of the motherland. He observed, for example, that none of them had adopted British notions of aristocracy and that 'the English segment of Great Britain may be true to the distinctive British institutions, but Greater Britain repudiates them with absolute unanimity'. Thus, although when Britons referred to 'the possible pull' of American 'gravitation upon their Empire', they usually referred to Canada, all the colonies and indeed, Britain itself, were already falling under American influence. Not everyone agreed with Stead on this point; Sidney Webb, who visited both the United States and Australia, insisted the latter 'is utterly and completely unlike America in every respect'. That noted, although Stead danced around the topic in a decidedly nimble fashion (largely by craftily quoting others), he did, in effect, imply that the United Kingdom and British Empire should be broken up and become individual states of a greater American Union. Failing this, he made it clear that he would be satisfied with some sort of Anglosphere league – but an alliance would be a poor substitute. Considering that at this stage the two nations did not even enjoy a formal alliance, these proposals, taken as a whole, were frankly astounding.[29]

Remarkable as all of this was, what made Stead's analysis most interesting was his definition of the term 'Americanization' (which he spelt with an 's' as most Britons then did) because he was the individual who gave the expression its modern meaning. Before Stead, the term Americanization, if used at all, simply referred to methods of manufacture, individual practices or actions that originated (or were believed to have) in the United States, things such as slang terms, modes of address, or for some, behaviour in the style of Sam Slick (whose enduring influence Stead noted). Stead, however, identified the phenomenon as a process, less dependent on either the economic or military might of the United States or its political ideas (although he did acknowledge the political aspects) and rather more on the spread of the nation's culture, including art, music, journalism, theatre, popular entertainment, as well as notions regarding religion and gender relations. More importantly, this Americanization – or 'American invasion' as Stead also called it – came about because people wanted it to. They wanted American products, liked American cultural ideas and manners because they found them attractive, and by adopting them, found their societies transformed by them (sometimes, as in the case of Britons, without really noticing). Thus, although Stead did not express it so, the process of Americanization succeeded because it was seduction, not rape. As regards to this process, he could be as literal as figurative, pointing to, for example, the 'remarkable fact that four English statesmen of Cabinet rank have married American wives' (Joseph Chamberlain, Sir William Harcourt, James Bryce and Lord Randolph

Churchill). According to Stead, this process, which he believed had been occurring for the past two decades in Britain, would prove to be the moving force – or trend – of the twentieth century.[30]

Stead, who referred to the United States by the friendly sobriquet 'Uncle Sam' rather than the less affable 'Cousin Jonathan', also recognized (and it pained him to do so, for he thought Americanization was, on the whole, a good thing) an awareness of and opposition to the process. Believing that most Britons, thanks to the common language, accepted it without too many problems (and here he was possibly too sanguine), he identified the forces of anti-Americanization as being located in Europe, particularly among societal elites. So, despite the fact there were 'no more Americanised cities in Europe than Hamburg and Berlin' and that there was 'a constant movement of men and ideas between the Social Democrats and the German electorate in the United States', Berlin was the 'centre of resistance to American principles in Europe', particularly in the person of the Kaiser. Indeed, according to Stead, French journalists had reported that:

> the Kaiser foresees the necessity of forming a European Customs Union against the United States on similar lines to the Continental blockade devised by Napoleon against England in order to safeguard the interests and assure the freedom of Continental commerce at the expense of America's development. And he declared to us without circumlocution that, in such an eventuality, England would be forced to choose the alternative of two absolutely opposite policies: either to adhere to the blockade and place herself on the European side against the United States, or else join the latter against the Powers of the Continent.

Although Stead acknowledged that the German Foreign Ministry had categorically denied that the Kaiser had said any such thing, like the good sensationalist journalist he was, he insisted it was nonetheless probable the German Monarch had in fact said it, especially as the French stood by their story. Further, Stead noted, the Kaiser was hardly alone. Apparently the German Industrial Union's Secretary, one Dr Wilhelm Vendlandt, had declared that 'We propose to work for an all European Union. The commercial interests of the hour are paramount, and a discriminatory alliance of all European Powers, including England, will be the inevitable result of the American invasion.'

Nor, apparently, were such ideas confined to Germany, for in Austria there were cries of 'America for the Americans, Europe for the Europeans'. Thus, noted Stead, there 'seems to be no doubt that the

American invasion has somewhat scared Europeans, nor is the scare confined to Germany or Austria', going on to cite Prince Albert of Belgium's lament that 'Alas! You Americans will eat us all up!' Not to mention a statement by Italian politicians declaring the need for 'European nations to consider the possibility and the necessity of uniting against America, as the future of civilization would require them to do'. Stead dismissed these concerns, which he believed were both misguided and overwrought, observing that to 'defend themselves against the United States of America these thinkers advocate the creation of what ... would be the United States of Europe'. Nonetheless, he recommended a course of action for America to allay or at least vitiate these fears: that it should abandon its tariff policies. This, Stead believed, was the only real grievance people had against the United States and its removal would undercut the more spurious complaints.[31]

In any event, Stead believed Americanization was unstoppable, whatever the hopes or plans of politicians or intellectuals. The process was simply too attractive to too many people (even the Canadians, whose long-standing anti-American attitude he saw as the biggest barrier to an Anglo-American union, were apparently succumbing). He provided a fairly comprehensive list of how Britain had been Americanized in the past two decades, including in the areas of religion, journalism, the stage, literature, art, music, science, sport, industry and social mores. Yet all of this was despite the fact,

> The fathers of the American Constitution, the statesmen and political thinkers and judges who moulded its early development, are practically unknown to the ordinary European. Educated Englishmen, and some politicians interested in the working of the federal principle, have read books which form the political Scriptures of the American politicians; but, speaking broadly, we get their influence second-hand through Tocqueville and Mr. Bryce.

Indeed, according to Stead, Charles Dickens and Frances Trollope were still regarded as among the leading authorities on the subject of the United States, even if their influence was waning. Thus, according to Stead, where Americanization had made the least headway in Britain was in the political realm. This was thus the final barrier to a complete embrace of Americanization by the United Kingdom; hence, his somewhat extravagant blueprint.[32]

A cynic might say that Stead's proposals amounted to little more than a 'if you can't beat them, join them' argument, but this would be to misread his sincerity. Fair enough, Stead certainly got a lot wrong; Britain, Canada, Australia and the West Indies, no matter how much or how little Americanized they may be, still retain at least nominal political independence. Yet his definition of the term Americanization and his prediction that the Americanization of the world would be the trend of the twentieth century did, despite the best efforts of Nazi Germany, Imperial Japan and the Soviet Union (as well as other rather more humane individuals and movements) prove to be correct. So, too, did his recognition that the phenomenon would meet resistance, including where it had proven most successful, even if popular opposition to it would perhaps turn out to be more widespread than he anticipated. His outlook was thus that of a visionary who, if not proven entirely correct, was nonetheless largely vindicated. As for the trend of the twenty-first century, although it is early days yet, it will be interesting to see if Stead's modern equivalents prove to be as prescient.

Certainly Stead's essay demonstrates that even before the First World War, recognition existed that the Pax Britannica was giving way to the Pax Americana. This, in a sense, helps explain Sherlock Holmes's prediction of Anglo-American unity and how this most British of detectives could be so Americanized that a president of the United States would claim that he was a citizen of the republic rather than a subject of the Queen. As for the detective and the dancing men, this was one of Holmes's American cases that ended largely in failure. Upon arrival in Norfolk, Holmes learned that Cubitt had been murdered and the chief suspect was his wife, Elsie, who had shot herself in the head and although not dead, seemed unlikely to recover. To the local police, in the possession of a single revolver with two shots fired, it was an obvious case of murder-suicide (Americans were renowned for their obsession with firearms) and should the doctors save Elsiey's life it would be for the gallows.

Holmes solved the case as he nearly always did. Knowing what the police did not, he demonstrated that Cubitt's killer was Abe Slaney and that Elsie had shot herself in despair after witnessing her husband's murder. The detective then lured Slaney into the arms of the law by sending a message – ostensibly from Elsie – in the dancing men code: 'Come here at once'. In custody, Slaney confessed. Elsie was the daughter of a Chicago crime lord who had promised her hand in marriage to his lieutenant, Slaney. Elsie had fled to Britain and had ended up marrying Cubitt. Slaney had tried to communicate with her in the gang's code and then took a different approach, resulting in an exchange of gunfire with Cubitt. Cubitt missed; Slaney did not. Although this tragic and somewhat tawdry case, which exposed Holmes's limitations as much as his strengths, could never have a happy ending, at least it concluded with only one death. Elsie survived and with Slaney's confession retained her freedom. As for Slaney, although found guilty of a capital charge, there were extenuating circumstances: Cubitt had fired the first shot, meaning that there was an element of self-defence involved. The sentence of death was thus commuted.

While it is impossible to imagine 'The Adventure of the Dancing Men' as any kind of metaphor for nineteenth-century Anglo-American relations, the story contains many of the same ingredients: failure and success, hostility and friendship, misapprehension and understanding, mystification and revelation, ignorance and knowledge, deception and disclosure, ambiguity and clarity, prejudice and impartiality, opportunities missed and taken, scribes honest and dishonest, and yes, even a supposedly unbreakable code. Finally, whatever blood was shed in the often rancorous Anglo-American relationship, both parties managed to avoid, often by luck as much as judgement, spilling far more and arriving at a point of friendship where, at least between the two of them, war would be virtually unthinkable. It was progress, of a sort. We end with Mark Twain, who said that truth the was always stranger than fiction because the latter had to make sense. Yet in the end, the story of Anglo-American relations in the long nineteenth century made a strange kind of sense. Indeed, it did so to such an extent that one can almost imagine the shades of George Cockburn and Andrew Jackson permitting themselves a smile.

Conclusion: Closer Cousins?

In the United States and in England there seems to be more liberty in the customs than in the laws of the people.

Alexis de Tocqueville[1]

It goes without saying that we inhabit a very different world to that of the nineteenth century. Equally, we have also moved beyond the stale imagery of that era caricatured by Lytton Strachey and countless others to a greater appreciation of the achievements as well as the failings of nineteenth-century society – whether in Britain or the United States. In some respects, having left behind a decidedly bloody short twentieth century, the period from 1914 to 1991 and the collapse of the Soviet Union, this re-evaluation was probably overdue. As we look more sympathetically, not to say more honestly, at the nineteenth century, we can at least gain an idea of how the inhabitants of that era grappled with many similar problems and questions we face today. The list is endless, but certainly includes the movement of peoples and trade liberalization; the question of when is military action justifiable; how to democraticize without becoming demotic; guaranteeing that representative government is genuinely such; determining the rights and duties of both the individual and the state; and how nations should interact with each other in a just manner. Many of the people discussed herein grappled with these and other issues and, while we would adopt few of their conclusions, we can at least acknowledge that many of them asked the right questions.

In Chapter 6 we discussed Richard Cobden's belief that free trade would draw 'men together, thrusting aside the antagonism of race, and creed, and language, and uniting us in the bonds of eternal peace'. Unmentioned was Lord Palmerston's reply:

It would be very delightful if your Utopia could be realised, and if the nations of the world would think of nothing but peace and commerce, and would give up quarrelling and fighting altogether. But unfortunately, man is a fighting animal, and that this is human nature is proved by the fact that republics, where the masses govern, are far more quarrelsome, and more addicted to fighting than monarchies, which are governed by comparatively few persons.

Unfortunately, the history of both the nineteenth and twentieth centuries demonstrated that we needed Palmerstons as much as we did Cobdens, even if in the end one hopes that Cobden's views will ultimately prevail. Certainly, by looking at much of the world today, we see the spread of political liberalization – or democracy – and nations that were formerly antagonistic towards each other now enjoy relationships that have rendered war among them virtually unthinkable. At the same time, elsewhere in the world we see the exact opposite and the question remains, how do we ensure that the first situation becomes the norm and not the second? Or, how do we avoid in the twenty-first century the horrors of the twentieth, while maintaining and building upon the undeniable achievements also accrued?[2]

It would be remiss to conclude a book on the nineteenth-century Anglo-American relationship without recording Her Majesty's views on the United States. As it happened, Queen Victoria adopted a generally more friendly view earlier than did most of her subjects. Her father, the Duke of Kent, paved the way, offering a toast to American minister, and future President, John Quincy Adams, less than two years after the War of 1812: 'The United States of America, and to the perpetuity of the friendship between Great Britain and them'. Adams responded with a toast of his own, expressing the hope that 'the harmony between Great Britain and the United States may be as lasting as the language and principles common to both'. Queen Victoria herself corresponded with none other than Andrew Jackson, who referred to her as his 'little good friend'. American ministers to Britain mostly enjoyed their audiences with the Queen whether Edward Everett or James Buchanan. As for her royal speeches, these impressed even Anglophobes like Charles Sumner and George Bancroft. American ministers commented on her strong dislike of tobacco use (in any form) and in the days before trade liberalization her support for the duties levelled on the imported product. They also noted her staunch opposition to slavery and her complete lack of sympathy for American demands for reimbursement for slaves who escaped to British territory. After yet another Anglo-American dispute over the international slave trade, Everett, no Anglophile, was forced to concede, 'whatever else might or might not be true of England, she [Victoria] was honestly and actively trying to suppress a most shameful practice'.[3]

The Queen also, with President James Buchanan's assistance, ensured that her son, Edward, the Prince of Wales, visited the United States following his trip to Canada, in 1860. If that trip was not quite the success that legend has it, it was nonetheless the first time a member of the Royal Family toured the United States. During the American Civil War, the Queen demonstrated more sympathy towards the Union than did much of Palmerston's cabinet, not to say the Prime Minister himself. She also, recently widowed herself, sent a personal letter of condolence to Mary Todd Lincoln, after the President's assassination. She later had to send a telegram of condolence to Mrs Garfield after that President's assassination in 1881. Throughout her reign, while Victoria could prove militant in upholding British honour regarding the French and the Russians, she remained surprisingly temperate about the United States – except when it came to the Fenians. That said, she regarded the American people as a rather wild and unreserved lot. In 1877 she complained that British couples were no longer behaving modestly, 'they go about driving, walking and visiting, everywhere alone ... In short, young people are getting very American, I fear in views and ways.' She was sounding like W. T. Stead before even he was.[4]

A number of African Americans visited the Queen, too, including in 1877, Jonah Henson, the model for Uncle Tom in Harriet Beecher Stowe's eponymous novel. She also sent books to the United States to help establish a public library in Chicago after the great fire of 1871, and cabled her condolences to the people of Charleston, South Carolina after an earthquake struck that city in 1886. This low-level diplomacy began to pay dividends. By the time of her Golden Jubilee of 1887, President Grover Cleveland sent a personal letter of congratulations and, on the occasion of her Diamond Jubilee in 1897, President William McKinley sent a special American Jubilee emissary, Whitelaw Reid, who proudly rode in the great procession. When she passed away on 22 January 1901, the House of Representatives adjourned in her honour and McKinley immediately ordered that the flag be flown at half mast above the White House. This had never been done before for any monarch. On the day of her funeral, the New York Stock Exchange remained closed, while McKinley and his entire cabinet attended the memorial service at St John's Episcopal Church.[5]

Victoria's relationship with the United States certainly fluctuated; she did not see the point of the Spanish-American war (nor did many Americans) and her relationship improved as the state of affairs between the two nations did. That said, her early, friendly, attitude towards the United States, even when the two nations were barely on civil terms, suggests that she was in many respects ahead of most on both sides of the Atlantic. Indeed, her contribution to nineteenth-century Anglo-American accord may be one of the great untold stories of the period. It is ironic that a queen should take the lead in seeking rapprochement with a republic, but then in light of the nations' peculiar relationship, perhaps it was appropriate after all.

We have come a long way from the age of Victoria and the Pax Britannica, and now inhabit the American era. Two individuals who identified this transition early on were the satirists W. C. Sellar and R. J. Yeatman whose comic study of British history, *1066 and All That* (1930), finished with the First World War, and facetiously concluded:

> Chapter LXII: A Bad Thing
> America was thus clearly top nation, and History came to a .

Ah yes, the end of history. Well the end of this one at any rate.[6]

Notes

Notes to Introduction: Very Distant Cousins

1. Philip Schreiner Klein, *President James Buchanan: A Biography* (University Park, PA, 1962), p. 320.
2. *Quarterly Review* (September 1836), p. 135.
3. On the widespread view that the loss of the American colonies marked the end of Britain as a world power, see John Clarke, *British Diplomacy and Foreign Policy* (London, 1989), p. 57.
4. Winston Churchill, *A History of the English-Speaking Peoples*, 4 vols. (London, 1956–58). Volumes three and four are most germane to this study. H. C. Allen, *Great Britain and the United States: A History of Anglo-American Relations, 1783–1952* (Watford, 1954). See also Allen's *The Anglo-American Relationship since 1783* (Watford, 1959); W. A. Dunning, *The British Empire and the United States; A Review of their Relations during the Century of Peace Following the Treaty of Ghent* (New York, 1914); George Payne, *England: Her Treatment of America* (New York, 1931); Crane Brinton, *The United States and Britain* (Cambridge, MA, 1945); and John Bartlet Brebner, *North Atlantic Triangle: The Interplay of Canada, the United States and Great Britain* (New Haven, CN, 1945).
5. See, for example, Howard Temperley, *Britain and America since Independence* (Houndmills, 2002), a survey that adds to our understanding of Anglo-American relations but which still follows the grand parameters of Allen's work. See also Kevin Phillips, *The Cousins' Wars: Religion, Politics and the Triumph of Anglo-America* (New York, 1999) which, taking an ethno-cultural-historical-regional approach, also adheres to this interpretation.
6. These works, and their impact, are discussed in Chapter 8.
7. 'Sirrah, your tongue betrays your guilt. You are an Irishman, and that is always sufficient evidence with me.' Henry Fielding, *Amelia* (London, 1995 [1751]), p. 5.
8. For example, of Allen's work, one scholar notes its habit of 'exaggerating the friendliness of the [Anglo-American] relationship'. Charles S. Campbell, *From Revolution to Rapprochement: The United States and Great Britain, 1783–1900* (New York, 1974), p. 205.

9. Jean Baudrillard, *America*, trans. Chris Turner (London, 1988), p. 76. Bourne quoted in Benjamin Schwartz, 'The diversity myth: America's greatest export', *Atlantic Monthly* (May 1995), pp. 57–67 (62). Q. J. D. Whelpley, *British-American Relations* (London, 1924), p. 204. Allen declared this was true. Allen, *The Anglo-American Relationship*, p. 97.

10. A good introduction to the notion of American exceptionalism is Seymour Martin Lipset, *American Exceptionalism: A Double-edged Sword* (New York, 1997). For a counter-view, see Ian Tyrrell, 'American exceptionalism in an age of international history', *American Historical Review* 96 (4) (1991), pp. 1031–55.

11. Mark Neeley, Jr, *The Union Divided: Party Conflict in the Civil War North* (Cambridge, MA, 2002), Introduction.

Notes to Chapter 1: The War Both Sides Won

1. Anthony S. Pitch, *The Burning of Washington: The British Invasion of 1814* (Annapolis, MD, 1998), p. 118.

2. See Donald R. Hickey, *The War of 1812: A Forgotten Conflict* (Urbana, 1989). This is a good treatment of the conflict, but see also Glenn Tucker, *Poltroons and Patriots: A Popular Account of the War of 1812* (Indianapolis, 1954); Reginald Horsman, *The Causes of the War of 1812* (Philadelphia, 1962); *The War of 1812* (New York, 1969); J. Mackay Hitsman, *The Incredible War of 1812: A Military History* (Toronto, 1999); John K. Mahon, *The War of 1812* (Gainseville, 1972); Wesley B. Turner, *The War of 1812: The War Both Sides Won* (Toronto, 1990); Mary Alice Burke Robinson (ed.), *The War of 1812* (Carlisle, 1998); Walter R. Borneman, *1812: The War that Forged a Nation* (New York, 2004); and A. J. Langguth, *Union 1812: The Americans Who Fought the Second War of Independence* (New York, 2006). The author is especially indebted to Jon Latimer, *1812: War with America* (Cambridge, MA, forthcoming), who kindly allowed him to read and quote from his manuscript.

3. Bradford Perkins, *The First Rapprochement: England and the United States, 1795–1805* (Philadelphia, 1955) and Jerald A. Combs, *The Jay Treaty: Political Battleground of the Founding Fathers* (Berkeley, 1970).

4. See Joseph Charles, *The Origins of the American Party System: Three Essays* (Williamsburg, VA, 1956); John F. Hoadley, *Origins of American Political Parties* (Lexington, KY, 1986), and Stanley Elkins and Eric McKitrick, *The Age of Federalism* (New York, 1993).

5. Jefferson quoted in Perkins, *The First Rapprochement*, p. 27. Jefferson's infatuation with the French Revolution took a long time to dissipate – he

even went so far as to act as an apologist for the Terror – condemning it only after the fact. See Conor Cruise O'Brien, *The Long Affair: Thomas Jefferson and the French Revolution, 1785–1800* (London, 1996).

6. Alexander DeConde, *The Quasi-war: The Politics and Diplomacy of the Undeclared War with France, 1797–1801* (New York, 1966) and Stephen G. Kurtz, *The Presidency of John Adams: The Collapse of Federalism, 1795–1800* (Philadelphia, 1957).

7. Quoted in Paul Leicester Ford (ed.), *The Writings of Thomas Jefferson*, 10 vols. (New York, 1892–99), p. ix. 365. On the Louisiana Purchase and the impact of the British and French blockades on the United States, see Robert W. Tucker and David C. Hendrickson, *Empire for Liberty: The Statecraft of Thomas Jefferson* (Oxford, 1990). See also Frank Lawrence Owsley, Jr and Gene A. Smith, *Filibusters and Expansionists: Jeffersonian Manifest Destiny, 1800–1821* (Tuscaloosa, 1997). As one's views on the rights and wrongs of the Napoleonic wars are inevitably shaped by one's opinion of Bonaparte himself, it is best to state one's position. This author holds the traditional British view that the Emperor was decidedly a foe, and not friend, of political liberty. Opinion on Napoleon in Europe, however, is decidedly more mixed. For an introduction to this debate, see Pieter Geyl, *Napoleon: For and Against* (London, 1957). See also R. S. Alexander, *Napoleon* (Oxford, 2001) and Stuart Semmel, *Napoleon and the British* (New Haven, 2004).

8. A discussion of the history of the blockades and embargoes may be found in Horsman, *The Causes of the War of 1812*, pp. 96–97; Hickey, *The War of 1812*, pp. 17–26, 44–47; and Latimer, *1812: War with America*, pp. 26–40.

9. See James Zimmerman, *Impressment of American Seamen* (New York, 1925); Bradford Perkins, *Prologue to War: England and the United States, 1805–1812* (Berkeley, 1961), pp. 84–94; Hickey, *The War of 1812*, pp. 9–13, 26; Latimer, *1812: War with America*, pp. 23–26 and Borneman, *1812*, pp. 24–25.

10. *Niles' Weekly Register*, 7 March 1812, p. 5, quoted in Borneman, *1812*, p. 28. See also Perkins, *Prologue to War*, pp. 95–96 and J. Leitch Wright, Jr, *Britain and the American Frontier, 1783–1814* (Athens, GA, 1975).

11. On the war hawks, see Hickey, *The War of 1812*, pp. 30–39, 43–48; Latimer, *1812: War with America*, pp. 38–41 and Harry W. Fritz, 'The war hawks of 1812', *Capitol Studies* 5 (1977), pp. 25–42; Hickey, *The War of 1812*, p. 38.

12. James M. Banner, *To the Hartford Convention: The Federalists and the Origins of Party Politics in Massachusetts, 1789–1815* (New York, 1970). See also Perkins, *Prologue to War*, pp. 369–72. New England farmers would go so far as to provide the British with the beef necessary to feed their armies

in Spain. Thus while some Americans effectively allied with Napoleon, others did so with his enemies.

13. Just how much damage Napoleon's continental system caused Britain is disputed. The classic account, by E. F. Heckscher, argues its effects were relatively mild and undercut by smuggling. F. Crouzet's more recent account, however, claims the system did considerable damage to the British economy. E. F. Hecksher, *The Continental System: An Economic Interpretation* (Oxford, 1922) and F. Crouzet, 'Wars, blockades, and economic change in Europe: 1792–1815', *Journal of Economic History* 24 (1964), pp. 567–88. For Britain's war against Napoleon, see Ian Fletcher, *Napoleonic Wars: Wellington's Army* (London, 1996). See also Elizabeth Longford, *Wellington: Years of the Sword* (London, 1969) and Lawrence James, *The Iron Duke: A Military Biography of Wellington* (London, 1992).

14. Madison quoted in Gaillard Hunt (ed.), *The Writings of James Madison*, 9 vols. (New York, 1900–1910), VIII, pp. 191–201. That Madison consciously linked Britain's difficulties in Europe to the assumption that it would not be able to reinforce its North American colonies, see Lawrence S. Kaplan, 'France and the War of 1812', *Journal of American History* 57 (1971), pp. 36–47 (37); Latimer, *1812: War with America*, p. 43.

15. On the declaration of war, see Hickey, *The War of 1812*, ch. 2 and on the British reaction, Latimer, *1812: War with America*, ch. 2.

16. Mahon, *The War of 1812*, pp. 43–54; Borneman, *1812*, p. 68. See also Latimer, *1812: War with America*, ch. 3 and Pierre Berton, *The Invasion of Canada, 1812–13* (Toronto, 1980).

17. Albert Ellery Bergh (ed.), *The Writings of Thomas Jefferson*, 20 vols. (Washington, 1907), XIII, pp. 180–81. While it was Napoleon who coined the phrase 'General Winter', it was Tsar Nicholas I who, in 1854, spoke of Russia's generals January and February looking after the French and British during the Crimean War.

18. See C. S. Forester, *The Age of Fighting Sail: The Story of the Naval War of 1812* (New York, 1956).

19. Borneman, *1812*, pp. 77–95; Latimer, *1812: War with America*, chs 4–5, 7 and 11; Hickey, *The War of 1812*, pp. 90–99, 151–58, and ch 7; Mahon, *The War of 1812*, pp. 57–63, 86–95, 109–37, 247–66, 313–28.

20. Pierre Berton, *Flames across the Border, 1813–1814* (Toronto, 1981).

21. David Curtis Skaggs and Gerard T. Altoff, *A Signal Victory: The Lake Eire Campaign, 1812–1813* (Annapolis, MD, 1997). On Perry, see Richard Dillon, *We Have Met the Enemy: Oliver Hazard Perry: Wilderness Commodore* (New York, 1978).

22. Latimer, *1812: War with America*, ch. 8; Hickey, *The War of 1812*, pp. 135–39.

23. Quoted in Borneman, *1812*, p. 169. Donald E. Graves, *Field of Glory: The Battle of Crysler's Farm, 1813* (Toronto, 1999).

24. See Latimer, *1812: War with America*, chs 6, 8–10; and Hickey, *The War of 1812*, ch. 6.

25. Katherine Cave (ed.), *Diary of Joseph Faringdon*, 16 vols. (New Haven, 1978–84), vol. 13, p. 4492.

26. Donald E. Graves, *Where Right and Glory Lead! The Battle of Lundy's Lane, 1814* (Toronto, 1997); Latimer, *1812: War with America*, ch. 13 and Borneman, *1812*, pp. 183–99.

27. David Fitz-Enz, *The Final Invasion: Plattsbugh, the War of 1812's Most Decisive Battle* (New York, 2001); Borneman, *1812*, p. 215. See also Latimer, *1812: War with America*, ch. 16.

28. Tucker, *Poltroons and Patriots*, p. 550; Pitch, *Burning of Washington*, chs 1–7.

29. Pitch, *Burning of Washington*, chs 8–13.

30. Antoine Jomini, *The Art of War*, trans. G. H. Mendell and W. P. Craighill (Westport, Conn, 1971), p. 349.

31. Fred L. Engleman, *The Peace of Christmas Eve* (New York, 1962). See also Hickey, *The War of 1812*, ch. 11.

32. Pitch, *Burning of Washington*, p. 221. See also Latimer, *1812: War with America*, ch. 15.

33. See Robert Remini, *The Battle of New Orleans: Andrew Jackson and America's First Military Victory* (New York, 1999).

34. For a further discussion of this topic, see Andrew Lambert, 'Winning without fighting: British grand strategy and its application to the United States, 1815–1865', in B. A. Lee and K. F. Walling (eds), *Strategic Logic and Political Rationality: Essays in Honour of Michael I. Handel* (London, 2003), pp. 164–93. See also William James, *The Naval History of Great Britain during the French Revolutionary and Napoleonic Wars*, 6 vols., introduced by Andrew Lambert (Mechanicsburg, PA, 2002–2003), vol. 6. Future American President Theodore Roosevelt wrote his *The Naval War in 1812* (New York, 1882) in response to James's account. Neither study can be described as impartial.

35. Latimer provides a good discussion of the influence of the war on the Canadian national identity. Latimer, *1812: War with America*, introduction. See also J. L. Granatstein, *Yankee Go Home? Canadians and Anti-Americanism* (Toronto, 1996), ch. 1.

36. Allan Nevins (ed.), *The Diary of John Quincy Adams, 1794–1845* (New York, 1951), p. 151. Another negotiator was Henry Clay, the war hawk, who could justly claim to be one of the few individuals who both helped cause, and end, the war; a truly consummate politician, then.

Notes to Chapter 2: Who Reads an American Book?

1. Thomas C. Haliburton, *The Clockmaker; or the Sayings and Doings of Sam Slick of Slickville*, 3 vols. (London, 1837–40), I, pp. 10–17 and x.

2. Quoted in William B. Cairns, *British Criticisms of American Writings, 1783–1815* (Madison, 1918), p. 11. See also Benjamin Lease, *Anglo-American Encounters: England and the Rise of American Literature* (Cambridge, 1981), p. 4. The author is particularly indebted to this invaluable study of early Anglo-American literary relations.

3. *Edinburgh Review* (January 1820), pp. 79–80. Smith concluded by asking 'under what of the old tyrannical governments of Europe is every sixth man a slave, whom his fellow creatures may buy and sell and torture?' This last point would be a standard complaint. What is unusual here is that slavery had not yet been abolished in the British Empire, even if it had in Britain.

4. *Edinburgh Review* (July 1824), pp. 432–33. See also Lease, *Anglo-American Encounters*, pp. 10–11. Oddly enough, of all the scholarship on the nineteenth century that this author has read, American historians are far more likely to quote the wit and wisdom of Sydney Smith than their British counterparts, thus suggesting that his fame is more entrenched on the other side of the Atlantic. If this is so, the last laugh must surely be on the witty Whig himself.

5. Washington Irving, *The Sketch Book of Geoffrey Crayon, Gent*, 2 vols. (London, 1821), I, p. v, and Pierre M. Irving, *The Life and Letters of Washington Irving*, 4 vols. (London, 1862), I, p. 257. See also William Hedges, *Washington Irving: An American Study, 1802–1832* (Baltimore, 1965).

6. *John Bull* (7 July 1822), p. 653. See also Ben Harris McClary (ed.), *Washington Irving and the House of Murray: Geoffrey Crayon Charms the British, 1817–1856* (Knoxvillee, TN, 1965). Italics in the original.

7. Irving, *The Sketch Book*, pp. i, 3. See also M. I. Thomis and P. Holt, *Threats of Revolution in Britain, 1789–1848* (London, 1977), ch 2. See also Joyce Marlow, *The Peterloo Massacre* (London, 1969).

8. *North American Review* (November 1833), p. 66.

9. Dickens to Irving, 21 April 1841, Madeline House and Graham Storey (eds), *The Letters of Charles Dickens*, 12 vols. (Oxford, 1969–2002), II, p. 267.

10. Peter Ackroyd, *Introduction to Dickens* (London, 1991), p. 79.

11. Dickens to Forster, 29 January 1842; Dickens to Macready, 22 March 1842, *The Letters of Charles Dickens*, III, pp. 34 and 156.

12. Charles Dickens, *American Notes for General Circulation*, 2 vols. (London, 2000 [1842]), pp. 277 and 176. See also P. M. Ard, 'Charles Dickens's

stormy crossing: the rhetorical voyage from letters to *American Notes*', *Nineteenth-century Prose*, 23 (1996), pp. 30–45; J. Meckier, 'Dickens discovers America: the unflattering glass', *Dickens Studies Annual*, 15 (1986), pp. 61–72 and S. P. Moss, 'South Carolina contemplates banning Dickens's *American Notes*', *Dickens Studies Newsletter*, 10 (1979), pp. 1–20.

13. Charles Dickens, *The Life and Adventures of Martin Chuzzlewit* (Oxford, 1998 [London, 1843–44]), ch. 16.

14. Cooper to Carey and Lea, 20 April–3 May 1833, *The Letters and Journals of James Fenimore Cooper*, 6 vols., ed. J. F. Beard (Cambridge, MA, 1960–64), VI, p. 320; George E. Hastings, 'How Cooper became a novelist', *American Literature*, 12 (1940), pp. 20–51; Lease, *Anglo-American Encounters*, pp. 38–46. Although the idea of Hawkeye hitting William Elliot over the head with a tomahawk carries a certain appeal, there is, alas, no such scene in *Precaution*.

15. Cooper to Samuel Hall, 21 May 1831, *The Letters and Journals*, II, p. 84. See also Nicholas Mills, *American and English Fiction in the Nineteenth Century* (Bloomington, 1973).

16. James Fenimore Cooper, *England with Sketches of Society in the Metropolis* (London, 1837); *Gleanings from Europe: England* (Albany, NY, 1982), pp. 234, 240 and 304.

17. James Fenimore Cooper, *The American Democrat* (New York, 1956 [Cooperstown, 1838], pp. 157 and 182). See also John P. McWilliams, *Political Justice in a Republic: James Fenimore Cooper's America* (Berkeley, 1972).

18. Mark Twain, 'Fenimore Cooper's Literary Offenses', in Lawrence Teacher (ed.), *The Unabridged Mark Twain* (Philadelphia, 1976), pp. 1239–50.

19. Lease, *Anglo-American Encounters*, ch. 4. See also *That Wild Fellow John Neal and the American Literary Revolution* (Chicago, 1972), by the same author.

20. *Broadway Journal*, 4 October 1845, pp. 199–200. See also Michael Allen, *Poe and the British Magazine Tradition* (New York, 1969).

21. Jeffrey Meyers, *Edgar Allan Poe: His Life and Legacy* (New York, 2000).

22. *The Athenaeum*, 10 July 1852, p. 741.

23. *The English Notebooks by Nathanial Hawthorne*, ed., Randall Stewart (New York, 1941), p. 92.

24. Randall Stewart, introduction, in ibid., p. xxii. See also Terence Martin, *Nathaniel Hawthorne* (Boston, 1983).

25. Anthony Trollope, 'The genius of Nathaniel Hawthorne', *North American Review*, 129 (1879), p. 207, quoted in Lease, *Anglo-American Encounters*, p. 115.

26. On Carlyle's and Emerson's friendship, see Lease, *Anglo-American Encounters*, ch. 9. For Carlyle's influence on John Brown and George Fitzhugh, see David Reynolds, *John Brown, Abolitionist, the Man who Killed Slavery, Sparked the Civil War and Seeded Civil Rights* (New York, 2004) and C. Van Woodward, introduction, *Cannibals All! Or Slaves without Masters*, by George Fitzhugh (Cambridge, MA, 1960 [Richmond 1857]).

27. See Lease, *Anglo-American Encounters*, pp. 190–94; John Slater (ed.), *The Correspondence of Emerson and Carlyle* (New York, 1964) and J. Sowder, *Emerson's Impact on the British Isles and Canada* (Charlottesville, VA, 1966).

28. E. Wagenknecht, *Ralph Waldo Emerson: Portrait of a Balanced Soul* (New York, 1974), pp. 158–201; Kenneth Marc Harris, *Carlyle and Emerson, their Long Debate* (Cambridge, MA, 1978); Thomas Carlyle, 'Occasional discourse on the negro question', *Fraser's magazine*, January 1850; *Latter-day Pamphlets* (London, 1850); Slater, *The Correspondence of Emerson and Carlyle*, pp. 57–58; Donaldson Jordan and Edwin J. Pratt, *Europe and the American Civil War* (London, 1931), p. 73.

29. See William Ellery Channing, *Thoreau the Poet-Naturalist* (Boston, 1902), p. 50; Henry David Thoreau, *Walden, or Life in the Woods* (Oxford, 1999 [1854]); Lease, *Anglo-American Encounters*, pp. 208–28.

30. Harold Blodgett, *Walt Whitman in England* (Ithaca, 1934); Lease, *Anglo-American Encounters*, ch. 11. Lease provides an interesting critical comparison between Carlyle's and Whitman's works.

31. *Blackwood's Magazine*, November 1849, pp. 574–76 and William H. Gilman, *Melville's Early Life and Redburn* (New York, 1951), pp. 136–37.

32. Lease, *Anglo-American Encounters*, pp. 145–48. See also Lewis Mumford, *Herman Melville: A Study of his Life and Vision* (New York, 1962) and David Kirby, *Herman Melville* (New York, 1993).

33. William Thackeray, *The Virginians*, 2 vols. (London, 1859).

34. John Sutherland, *Thackeray at Work* (London, 1974) and D. J. Taylor, *Thackeray* (London, 1999).

35. Frank Thistlewaite, *America and the Atlantic Community: Anglo-American Aspects, 1790–1850* (New York, 1959), p. 119.

36. Lease, *Anglo-American Encounters*, p. 160. Lord Carlisle quoted in Catherine Gilbertson, *Harriet Beecher Stowe* (New York, 1937), p. 160. See also Forrest Wilson, *Crusader in Crinoline: The Life of Harriet Beecher Stowe* (Philadelphia, 1941) and John R. Adams, *Harriet Beecher Stowe* (Boston, 1989). Just how great a work of literature is *Uncle Tom's Cabin* remains in dispute. Its sentiments are certainly sincere but, as Oscar Wilde noted, so are those of all bad art.

Notes to Chapter 3: Trade, Immigration and the Transfer of Capital and Technology

1. As Marquis James points out, this quote was attributed to Jackson by the Whig congressman, Horace Greeley, in his *The American Conflict*, published in 1864 – almost twenty years after the President's death. Nonetheless, as James notes, 'Jackson may well have said it'. Marquis James, *Andrew Jackson: Portrait of a President* (New York, 1937), p. 304.

2. An excellent work on Smithson and his bequest is Nina Burleigh's *The Stranger and the Statesman: James Smithson, John Quincy Adams and the Making of America's Greatest Museum: the Smithsonian* (New York, 2003). Much of the information above has been gleaned form this source. For the debate in Congress regarding Smithson's bequest, see William J. Rhees, *The Smithsonian Institution: Documents Relative to its Origin and History, 1835–1899*, 2 vols. (Washington, 1901).

3. Frank Thistlewaite, *America and the Atlantic Community: Anglo-American Aspects, 1790–1850* (New York, 1959), p. 3. See also Brinley Thomas, *Migration and Economic Growth: A Study of Great Britain and the Atlantic Economy* (Cambridge, 1954). For a wider perspective, examining the intricate web of connections between politics and economics of the nineteenth century, Karl Polyani's *The Great Transformation: The Political and Economic Origins of our Time* (Boston, MA, 1985 [1944]), remains the classic account.

4. See Arthur Herman, *To Rule the Waves: How the British Navy Shaped the Modern World* (New York, 2004), ch. 17. See also W. W. Rostow, *British Economy of the Nineteenth Century* (Oxford, 1948); A. D. Gayer, W. W. Rostow and Anna J. Schwartz, *The Growth and Fluctuation of the British Economy, 1790–1850*, 2 vols. (Oxford, 1953); R. Tames, *Economy and Society in Nineteenth-century Britain* (London, 1972); A. J. Taylor, *Laissez-faire and State Intervention in Nineteenth-century Britain* (London, 1972).

5. Thistlewaite, *America and the Atlantic Community*, pp. 5–8.

6. See Cheryl Schonhardt-Bailey, *From the Corn Laws to Free Trade: Interests, Ideas and Institutions in Historical Perspective* (Cambridge, MA, 2006); A. Howe, *Free Trade and Liberal England, 1846–1946* (Oxford, 1997); T. A. Jenkins, *Sir Robert Peel* (London, 1998); Boyd Hilton, *Corn, Cash and Commerce: The Economic Policies of the Tory Governments, 1815–1830* (Oxford 1977); and Norman McCord, *The Anti-corn Law League* (London, 1958). See, in addition, Polyani, *The Great Transformation*, chs 12–13.

7. Harold Underwood Faulkner, *American Economic History*, 8th edn (New

York, 1954), pp. 163–68. See also Merrill D. Peterson, *The Great Trium-verate: Webster, Clay and Calhoun* (Oxford, 1987).

8. See William W. Freehling, *Prelude to Civil War: The Nullification Controversy in South Carolina, 1816–1830* (New York, 1965). See also Richard Ellis, *The Union at Risk: Jacksonian Democracy, States Rights and the Nullification Crisis* (New York, 1987).

9. See Anthony Howe, 'Free Trade and the International Order: The Anglo-American Tradition, 1846–1946', in Fred Leventhal and Roland Quinault (eds), *Anglo-American Attitudes: From Revolution to Partnership* (Aldershot, 2000), pp. 142–67.

10. Beckles Willson, *America's Ambassadors to England 1785–1928* (London, 1928), p. 368, original emphasis. See also Polyani, *The Great Transformation*, pp. 137–50 and David Green, 'The Friendly Societies and Adam-Smith Liberalism', in David Gladstone (ed.), *Before Beveridge: Welfare Before the Welfare State* (London, 1999), pp. 18–25.

11. Norman Sydney Buck, *The Development and Organization of Anglo-American Trade, 1800–1850* (New Haven, 1969 [1925]), pp. 32–33.

12. Thomas Nichols, *Forty Years of American Life* (London, 1864), vol. 2, p. 79, quoted in Thistlewaite, *America and the Atlantic Community*, p. 18.

13. On the Bank Wars, see Robert Remini, *Andrew Jackson and the Bank War: A Study in the Growth of Presidential Power* (New York, 1967). On the Bank of England, see Charles Goodhart and Norbert Schnadt, 'The Development of Central Banking', in Forrest Capie, Charles Goodhart, et al. (eds), *The Future of Central Banking: The Tercentury Symposium of the Bank of England* (Cambridge, 1994), pp. 1–97. For a discussion on the establishment of the Federal Reserve and the problems surrounding the lack of a central bank, see William Silber, *When Washington Shut Down Wall Street* (Princeton, 2007).

14. Faulkner, *American Economic History*, pp. 157–63. See also Hammond Bray, *Banks and Politics in America from the Revolution to the Civil War* (Princeton, NJ, 1957).

15. A. A. Iliasu, 'The Cobden-Chevalier Treaty of 1860', *The Historical Journal* 14 (1) (1971), pp. 67–98. On France and Britain's naval race, see C. I. Hamilton, *Anglo-French Naval Rivalry, 1840–1870* (Oxford, 1993). For an interesting discussion on the relationship between politics and economics, war and peace, see Niall Ferguson, *The Cash Nexus: Money and Power in the Modern World, 1700–2000* (New York, 2001).

16. See Brooke Hindle and Steven Lubar, *Engines of Change: The American Industrial Revolution, 1790–1860* (Washington, 1986).

17. David Jeremy, *Transatlantic Industrial Revolution: The Diffusion of Textile Technologies between Britain and America, 1790–1830* (Oxford, 1981).

18. William L. Burn, *The Age of Equipoise: A Study of the mid-Victorian Generation* (London, 1964), remains the classic account of this period, but see also Roy A. Church, *The Great Victorian Boom, 1850–1873* (London, 1975) and Geoffrey Best, *Mid-Victorian Britain, 1851–1875* (London, 1971).

19. See William E. Van Vugt, *Britain to America: Mid-nineteenth-century Immigrants to the United States* (Urbana, 1999), p. 10.

20. Van Vugt, *Britain to America*, p. 77.

21. Van Vugt, *Britain to America*, pp. 13–16.

22. See Theodore Blegen (ed.), *Land of their Choice: The Immigrants Write Home* (Minneapolis, 1955) and Alan Conway (ed.), *The Welsh in America: Letters from the Immigrants* (Cardiff, 1961). Another point of view is that of E. R. R. Green, who argues that such letters are often either forgeries or drastically edited to suit the individual journal's views on emigration. Green, 'Ulster emigrants' letters', in Charlotte Erickson (ed.), *Essays in Scotch-Irish History* (London, 1969), pp. 87–103 (89).

23. William Jones, '"Going into print": published immigrant letters, webs of personal relations, and the emergence of a Welsh public sphere', in Bruce S. Elliot, David A. Gerber and Suzanne M. Sinke (eds), *Letters across Borders: The Epistolary Practises of International Migrants* (Basingstoke, forthcoming). The author would like to thank Professor Jones for allowing him to read and quote from his manuscript.

24. Quoted in Howard Zinn, *A People's History of the United States* (New York, 2003), pp. 227–28.

25. Michael Chevalier, *Society, Manners and Politics in the United States* (Boston, 1839), pp. 143–44, quoted in H. J. Habakkuk, *American and British Technology in the Nineteenth Century* (Cambridge, 1962), p. 4.

26. See Geoffrey Tweedale, *Sheffield Steel and America: A Century of Commercial and Technological Interdependence, 1830–1930* (New York, 1987).

27. See Wray Vamplew, 'The protection of English cereal producers: the corn laws reassessed', *Economic History Review* 33 (August 1980), pp. 382–95.

28. William Brown, *America: Four Years' Residence in the United States and Canada* (Leeds, 1849), p. 32. See also Jonathan Chambers and G. E. Mingay, *The Agricultural Revolution, 1750–1880* (London, 1966).

29. Wilbur S. Shepperson, *British Migration to North America: Projects and Opinions in the Early Victorian Period* (New York, 1957). See also J. F. C. Harrison, *Robert Owen and the Owenites in Britain and America: The Quest for the New Moral World* (London, 1969).

30. Charlotte J. Erickson, *Invisible Immigrants: The Adaptation of English and*

Scottish Immigrants in Nineteenth-century America (Coral Gables, Florida, 1972). See, in addition, *Leaving England: Essays on British Immigration in the Nineteenth Century* (Ithaca, NY, 1994), by the same author.

31. John Wood to Wheatley Wood, 30 January 1853. Wood letter, Z109, West Yorkshire archive service, Wakefield, quoted in Van Vugt, *Britain to America*, p. 141. Van Vugt cites several such letters.

32. Ella Lonn, *Foreigners in the Union Army and Navy*, 2nd edn (New York, 1969), pp. 577–79. Seward quoted in Frank L. Owsley, *King Cotton Diplomacy: Foreign Relations of the Confederate States of America*, 2nd edn, rev. Harriet Owsley (Chicago, 1959), p. 498.

33. Marion Elizabeth Rodgers, *Mencken: American Iconoclast* (Oxford, 2006). On 25 September 2001, however, the United States Congress officially recognized Antonio Meucci as the inventor of the telephone, denying Bell's claim to its invention. See *The Guardian*, 17 June 2002.

34. See Burleigh, *The Stranger and the Statesman*, ch. 1.

Notes to Chapter 4: Taking Liberties and Beacons of Freedom

1. William Cobbett, '*The Scare-crow*: being an infamous letter sent to Mr John Olden, threatening destruction to his house, and violence to the person of his tenant, William Cobbett; with remarks on the same', by Peter Porcupine. Published as a pamphlet by Cobbett in Philadelphia, 1796, and reprinted in *Porcupine's Works*. J. E. Morpurgo (ed.), *Cobbett's America: A Selection from the Writings of William Cobbett* (London, 1985), pp. 100–12.

2. The definitive account of this phenomenon, especially as it applies to Britain, remains Elie Kedourie's *Nationalism*, rev. edn (New York, 1961) especially as pertains to his distinction between the 'civic' and 'ethnic' varieties, but see also Anthony D. Smith, *Nationalism: Theory, Ideology and History* (London, 2001) and Benedict Anderson, *Imagined Communities: Reflections on the Origin and Spread of Nationalism* (London, 1983).

3. See Harold Hyman (ed.), *Heard around the World: The Impact Abroad of the Civil War* (New York, 1969), p. viii. G. D. Lillibridge's *Beacon of Freedom: The Impact of American Democracy upon Great Britain 1830–1870* (Philadelphia, 1954), remains the standard version of this account, being repeated in Henry Pelling's *America and the British Left: From Bright to Bevan* (London, 1956), Frank Thistlewaite's *America and the Atlantic Community: Anglo-American Aspects, 1790–1850* (New York, 1959), as well as other more recent works. Lillibridge's analysis, however, was seriously undermined by David Paul Crook's *American Democracy in English Politics, 1815–50* (Oxford, 1965), which demonstrated factual and interpretative

errors in *Beacon of Freedom*, concluding that 'this analysis has outlived much of its usefulness', p. 8. Crook's study was followed by Jon Roper's *Democracy and its Critics: Anglo-American Democratic Thought in the Nineteenth Century* (London, 1989), which further demonstrates the complexity of the nineteenth-century Anglo-American political discourse. These last two works remain the most scholarly accounts of British views of the American political system and remain the starting point for any historian interested in the subject. But see also Andrew Robertson, *The Language of Democracy: Political Rhetoric in the United States and Britain 1790–1900* (Ithaca, NY, 1995) and Jamie Bronstein, *Land Reform and Working-class Experience in Britain and the United States, 1800–1862* (Stanford, CA, 1999).

4. Dicey quoted in Hugh Tulloch, *James Bryce's American Commonwealth: The Anglo-American Background* (Woodbridge, Suffolk, 1988), p. 48; Bright quoted in Asa Briggs, *Victorian People: A Reassessment of Persons and Themes, 1851–1867* (London, 1996 [1954]), p. 168; Cobden quoted in W. T. Stead, *The Americanization of the World, or the Trend of the Twentieth Century* (New York, 1902), pp. 412–13; *Quarterly Review* (April 1835), p. 551.

5. Woodrow Wilson in Charles Beard, *The Republic* (New York, 1943), pp. 29–33. See also Robert A. Dahl, *How Democratic is the American Constitution?* (New Haven, 2001). Dahl provides a good discussion of the uses of the term democracy in the United States' early years, especially in appendix A. For an interesting, if at times determinedly contrarian, view of British and American political development, see J. D. C. Clark, *The Language of Liberty, 1660–1832: Political Discourse and Social Dynamics in the Anglo-American World* (Cambridge, 1994). But see also Roy Porter, *Enlightenment: Britain and the Creation of the Modern World* (London, 2000).

6. The issue of the extent and speed of American democratization is noted by Roland Quinault, 'Anglo-American attitudes to democracy from Lincoln to Churchill', in Fred Leventhal and Roland Quinault (eds), *Anglo-American Attitudes: From Revolution to Partnership* (Aldershot, 2000), pp. 124–41 (127). On Jacksonian America, see Arthur Schlesinger, Jr, *The Age of Jackson* (New York, 1945). See also Marvin Gettleman, *The Dorr Rebellion* (New York, 1973) and Howard Zinn, *A People's History of the United States*, 2nd edn (New York, 2003), ch. 10.

7. See Linda Colley, *Britons: Forging the Nation, 1770–1837* (New Haven, 1992), pp. 30–42. This is also a recurring theme of Rebecca Fraser's *A People's History of Britain* (London, 2003). See also Peter Mandler (ed.), *Liberty and Authority in Victorian Britain* (Oxford, 2006). For

Schopenhauer, see David Berman, Introduction, in Arthur Schopenhauer, *The World as Will and Idea*, trans. Jill Berman (London, 1995), p. xvii. For Engels, see Friedrich Engels, Preface, in Karl Marx, *Das Kapital* (London, 1938), p. xiv. For Conrad, see Robert Conquest, *The Dragons of Expectation: Reality and Delusion in the Course of History* (New York, 2005), p. 63. For Freud, see Ernest Jones, *Sigmund Freud: Life and Work* (London, 1953), p. xiv. For Weil, see A. N. Wilson, *After the Victorians, 1901–1953* (London, 2005), p. 154.

8. Quoted in Rosemary Ashton, *Little Germany: Exile and Asylum in Victorian Britain* (Oxford, 1986), p. 166. A good introduction to the subject is Robert Winder's *Bloody Foreigners: The Story of Immigration to Britain* (London, 2004). Unlike the United States, Britain does not have a tradition of acknowledging, far less celebrating, its immigrant past; the evidence in Winder's book suggests that its significance to British history still needs to be properly acknowledged. See also Bernard Porter, *The Refugee Question in Mid-Victorian Politics* (Cambridge, 1979).

9. See W. D. Rubinstein, *A History of the Jews in the English-speaking World: Great Britain* (New York, 1996) and David Feldman, *Englishmen and Jews: Social Relations and Political Culture, 1840–1914* (New Haven, CN, 1994).

10. *Chamber's* quoted in Lucio Sponza, *Italian Immigrants in London: Realities and Images* (Leicester, 1988), p. 153.

11. Alexis de Tocqueville, *Journeys to England and to Ireland*, ed. J. P. Mayer, trans. George Lawrence and K. P. Mayer, 2nd edn (New Brunswick, NJ, 2003), Introduction, p. 13.

12. Analysis of nineteenth-century British reaction to Tocqueville's work really requires either Reeve's translation or the editions in the original French. The best version available for those who do not read French is *Democracy in America*, ed. and trans. Harvey C. Mansfield and Delba Winthrop (Chicago, 2000), hereafter cited as '*DA*'. For 'tyranny of the majority', see *DA* I: 2.4, 2.7 and 2.8; 'despotism of the majority', *DA* I: 1.8, 2.7 and 2.9; *Edinburgh Review* (April 1861), p. 430; Crook, *American Democracy in English Politics*, p. 191. This was surely in part owed to Reeve's translation.

13. *Blackwood's* (October 1840), pp. 467 and 470, original emphasis.

14. Crook, *American Democracy in English Politics*, p. 177; *Edinburgh Review* (October 1840), pp. 13–14.

15. See Crook, *American Democracy in English Politics*, pp. 180–81. For more on J. S. Mill and Tocqueville, see Roper, *Democracy and its Critics*, pp. 145–52.

16. Crook, *American Democracy in English Politics*, pp. 186–91.

17. For more discussion on the origins of the differing political views, developments and traditions of these three countries, see Gertrude Himmelfarb's *The Roads to Modernity: The British, French and American Enlightenments* (New York, 2004).

18. Hazlitt declared he was 'anti-American', and continually condemned the United States. For Hazlitt, see Crook, *American Democracy in English Politics*, pp. 79–80; Jeremy Bentham, *The Works of Jeremy Bentham, published under the superintendence of his executor John Bowring*, 12 vols. (London, 1838–43), X: 63, IX: 122–23. See also Roper, *Democracy and its Critics*, pp. 130–36.

19. An astute analysis of British radicalism's malleable views of the United States may be found in Gregory Claeys, 'The example of America as a warning to England? The transformation of America in British radicalism and socialism, 1790–1850', in Malcolm Chase and Ian Dyck (eds), *Living and Learning: Essays in Honour of J.F.C. Harrison* (Aldershot, 1996), pp. 66–80. See also Ira Katznelson, 'Working Class Formation and the State: Nineteenth-century England in American Perspective', in David Englander (ed.), *Britain and America: Studies in Comparative History, 1760–1970* (Bath, 1997), pp. 171–95.

20. For a discussion of this shift in emphasis in British working-class radical thought, see Margot C. Finn, *After Chartism: Class and Nation in English Radical Politics, 1848–1874* (Cambridge, 1993). For Jones, see *Notes to the People* (1851), p. 2, quoted in Ray Boston, *British Chartists in America, 1839–1900* (Manchester, 1971), p. 7.

21. Lillibridge cited examples of Chartist references to the United States in several publications, but as Francis H. Herrick points out, 'Few critical readers are likely to accept this thesis entire', for if the former had studied nineteenth-century documents generally not to mention examined diaries and letters, 'he would have seen how little the reforms achieved in the 'thirties were determined by American democracy, how secondary American influence was on the Chartists'. *American Historical Review*, 61 (1955), pp. 174–75. Alexander to O'Brien, *The Reformer*, 26 May 1849, p. 35, quoted in Boston, *British Chartists in America*, pp. 42 and 20. See especially ch 4: 'Political disillusionment', pp. 36–44.

22. *Blackwood's* (April 1846), pp. 440–41. In the case of the last, this was written during the Anglo-American dispute over the Oregon territory, which probably had a bearing on British opinion – conservative and radical alike.

23. Winder, *Bloody Foreigners*, p. 113 and Crook, *American Democracy in English Politics*, ch. iv, *passim*.

24. Hansard, 26 May 1820, 2nd series, I, p. 575, italics in original; Crook, *American Democracy in English Politics*, pp. 94–124.

25. *Edinburgh Review* (January 1846), p. 194; Crook, *American Democracy in English Politics*, ch. 3, *passim*; Roper, *Democracy and its Critics*, ch. 6, *passim*.

26. Max Berger, *The British Traveller in America, 1836–1860* (New York, 1943), p. 190. This and Allan Nevins's *America through British Eyes* (New York, 1948) remain the two best studies of nineteenth-century British travellers' observations. Some thoughtful observations on British and American views of each other's character may be found in Paul Langford, 'Manners and character in Anglo-American perceptions, 1750–1850', in Leventhal and Quinault, *Anglo-American Attitudes*, pp. 76–90. See also James Epstein, '"America" in the Victorian cultural imagination', in the same collection, pp. 107–123.

27. Frances Trollope, *Domestic Manners of the Americans*, 2 vols. (London, 1832). As the preface to Trollope's book noted, 'she leaves to abler pens the more ambitious task of commenting on the democratic form of the American government', I, p. vi. Shakespeare as obscene, I, p. 125; religious camp meeting, I, pp. 229–50; War of 1812, II, pp. 163–64; and ant's nest, II, pp. 136–37. An interesting analysis of Trollope's account may be found in Marcus Cunliffe, 'Frances Trollope, 1780–1863', in Marc Pachter and Frances Wein (eds), *Abroad in America: Visitors to the New Nation, 1776–1914* (Reading, MA, 1976), pp. 33–42.

28. Frederick Marryat, *A Diary in America*, first series, 3 vols., second series, 3 vols. (London, 1839), Introduction, second series, II, 103–104, original emphasis. See also Frederick Marryat, *Diary in America*, edited with a foreword by Jules Zanger (London, 1960). The introduction provides much useful background information about the Captain's trip.

29. Harriet Martineau, *Society in America*, 2 vols. (New York and London, 1837). There are a number of substantive works on Martineau, but a good discussion of her American observations is Marghanita Laski, 'Harriet Martineau, 1802–1877', in Pachter and Wein, *Abroad in America*, pp. 63–71. Alexander MacKay, *The Western World*, 3 vols. (London, 1849). A good introduction to the story of the infamous Tammany Hall is Oliver E. Allen's *The Tiger: The Rise and Fall of Tammany Hall* (Reading, MA, 1993).

30. J. S. Buckingham, *America*, 3 vols. (London, 1841), I, p. 288; Charles MacKay, *Life and Liberty in America*, 2 vols. (London, 1859), I, p. 128.

31. Berger, *The British Traveller in America*, p. 58; Martineau, *Society in America*, II, pp. 169–70 and James Logan, *Notes of a Journey through*

Canada, the United States of America and the West Indies (Edinburgh, 1838), p. 188.

32. Martineau, *Society in America*, I, pp. 120–34; William Thomson, *A Tradesman's Travels in the United States and Canada* (Edinburgh, 1842), pp. 163–68; J. S. Buckingham, *Eastern and Western States*, 3 vols. (London, 1842), III, p. 38 and I, pp. 153–59; C. R. Weld, *A Vacation Tour in the United States and Canada* (London, 1855), pp. 358–60; W. E. Baxter, *America and the Americans* (London, 1855), p. 100; and Logan, *Notes of a Journey*, pp. 189–90.

33. Although Cartwright established the rules of the modern game, 'baseball' is specifically referred to in Jane Austen's *Northanger Abbey*. Tocqueville, quoted in H. C. Allen, *The Anglo-American Relationship since 1783* (Watford, 1959), p. 198. Basil Hall, *Travels in North America in the Years 1827 and 1828*, 3 vols. (Edinburgh, 1829), III, p. 60 and *Quarterly Review* (September 1836), pp. 134–35.

34. Berger is somewhat in error when he claims that despite their opposition to slavery, 'English travellers were overwhelmingly opposed to abolitionism, also'. Examining the works he cites to support this claim, what numerous British writers criticized was the form of abolitionism espoused by William Lloyd Garrison, which opposed both gradual manumission and compensation. British writers predicted that slave owners would never accept the end of their institution without both. They were, therefore, recommending that the United States follow the approach used in the Empire. The exceptions to this were individuals such as Alfred Bunn who, largely untroubled by the institution and wanting better relations with the United States, told the British to get off their 'high horse' regarding slavery. See Berger, *The British Traveller in America*, p. 118 and Alfred Bunn, *New England and Old England*, 2 vols. (London, 1853), I, ch. x and II, ch. viii. Also, William Chambers, *Things as they are in America* (London, 1854), pp. 353–63; J. R. Godley, *Letters from America*, 2 vols. (London, 1844), II, pp. 67–75; Thomas Colley Grattan, *Civilised America*, 2 vols. (London, 1859), II, ch. xvi; Charles Lyell, *Travels in North America*, 2 vols. (London, 1845), I, ch. ix; and Charles Mackay, *Life and Liberty in America*, 2 vols. (London, 1859), II, pp. 25 and 43. The last even took time to sneer at George Fitzhugh's infamous pro-slavery work, *Cannibals All* (1857), noting 'Mr. Fitzhugh is a slave already – a slave to his theory', II, p. 72. The term abolitionist being almost as bad as murderer, Buckingham, *A Journey through the Slave States of America*, 2 vols. (London, 1842), I, p. 131; The Earl of Carlisle quoted in Berger, *The British Traveller in America*, p. 43; Martineau, *Society in America*, I, p. 373.

35. Frederick Douglass, *My Bondage, my Freedom*, ed. Philip S. Foner (New York, 1969 [1855]), p. 365; Alan J. Rice and Martin Crawford, 'Triumphant exile: Frederick Douglass in Britain, 1845–1847', in Alan J. Rice and Martin Crawford, *Liberating Sojourn: Frederick Douglass and Transatlantic Reform* (Athens, Georgia, 1999), p. 4. See also Richard Bradbury's 'Frederick Douglass and the Chartists', and David Turley, 'British Unitarian abolitionists, Frederick Douglass and racial equality', in the same edition.

36. Douglass in Rice and Crawford, 'Triumphant exile', p. 5; Melville in Winder, *Bloody Foreigners*, p. 169.

37. See Thistlewaite, *America and the Atlantic Community*, pp. 94 and 98 and ch. 3, *passim*. See also Richard Carwardine, *Translatlantic Revivalism: Popular Evangelicalism in Britain and America, 1790–1865* (Westport, Connecticut, 1978).

38. On Albert, see Winder, *Bloody Foreigners*, p. 121. For Anglo-American abolitionist efforts, see Betty Fladeland, *Men and Brothers: Anglo-American Anti-slavery Co-operation* (Urbana, 1972); Douglas Charles Strange, *British Unitarians against American Slavery, 1833–1865* (Toronto, 1984), and Clare Taylor (ed.), *British and American Abolitionists: An Episode in Anglo-American Understanding* (Edinburgh, 1974).

39. As Sarah Wilks points out, 'this patriotic pride is not easily distinguishable from the more selfish ambition to further your own interests', a point historians of both nations would do well to remember. See Sarah Wilks, 'An independent in politics: John Arthur Roebuck, 1802–1879', unpublished DPhil dissertation (Oxford, 1979), pp. 306–307. This invaluable work should have been published. John Stuart Mill, 'A few words on non-intervention', *Fraser's Magazine* (December 1859), pp. 766–76. Mill was responding in part to Richard Cobden and John Bright and their tendency towards appeasement of Britain's imperial rivals. See, in addition, Eileen P. Sullivan, 'Liberalism and imperialism: J. S. Mill's defense of the British Empire', *Journal of the History of Ideas*, 44(4) (1983), pp. 599–617.

Notes to Chapter 5: Squabbles and Squalls: The Scramble for North America and the Diplomatic Relationship from 1815 to 1860

1. Jasper Ridley, *Lord Palmerston* (London, 1970), p. 273; Jackson to F. P. Blair, 11 May 1844, and Jackson to Sam Houston, 15 March 1844, quoted in Marquis James, *Andrew Jackson* (New York, 1937), pp. 479 and 482.

2. See Ronald Hyam, *Britain's Imperial Century, 1815–1914: A Study in Empire and Expansion* (Basingstoke, 2002). See also Muriel Chamberlain, '*Pax*

Britannica? British Foreign Policy, 1789–1914 (New York, 1988); and Robert Kagan, *Dangerous Nation* (New York, 2006).

3. As Charles Campbell notes, 'But if Britain's policy toward the United States was low on the former's scale of priorities, it was very high on the American scale. In its foreign policy calculations Washington almost always had to consider, before anything else, the probable British reaction. The State Department kept its attention riveted on London to a much greater extent than any other capital'. Charles Campbell, *From Revolution to Rapprochement: The United States and Great Britain, 1783–1900* (New York, 1974), p. 34.

4. Phillip E. Myers argues that the British maintained a 'mask of indifference' towards the United States, believing that the latter's sensitivities and perceived political immaturity could only be guided to a more mature diplomatic accord by means of an ostensible 'hands-off' approach. Although this author places slightly more emphasis on luck than on skill when it came to Anglo-American diplomatic relations, because Dr Myers is one of a handful of scholars who demonstrates the same depth of understanding of British politics and foreign policy, as they have of American, this author is in debt to his interpretation. Phillip Myers, 'Mask of indifference: Great Britain's North American policy and the path to the treaty of Washington, 1815–1871', unpublished PhD dissertation (University of Iowa, 1978). Another overall survey is Reginald C. Stuart, *United States' Expansionism and British North America, 1775–1871* (Chapel Hill, NC, 1988).

5. Campbell, *From Revolution to Rapprochement*, pp. 29–32; Myers, 'Mask of indifference', ch. 1; Kenneth Bourne, *Britain and the Balance of Power in North America, 1815–1908* (London, 1967), pp. 3–53; Francis M. Carroll, *A Good and Wise Measure: The Search for the Canadian-American Boundary, 1783–1842* (Toronto, 2001), chs 2–6; Howard Jones, *To the Webster-Ashburton Treaty: A Study in Anglo-American Relations, 1783–1843* (Chapel Hill, 1977), ch. 1.

6. Bourne, *Balance of Power in North America*, ch. 3; J. W. Derry, *Castlereagh* (London, 1976), ch. 4 and William Kaufman, *British Policy and the Independence of Latin America, 1804–1828* (New Haven, 1951).

7. Castlereagh quoted in Paul W. Schroeder, *The Transformation of European Politics, 1763–1848* (Oxford, 1994), p. 52; Napoleon quoted in Harold Nicholson, *The Congress of Vienna: A Study in Allied Unity, 1812–1822* (London, 1946), p. 237. These are the two best studies of the Congress of Vienna, although Henry Kissinger's *A World Restored: Metternich,*

Castlereagh and the Problems of Peace 1812–1822 (Boston, 1957), is another intriguing analysis.

8. This argument is developed in some depth in Arthur Herman, *To Rule the Waves: How the British Navy Shaped the Modern World* (New York, 2004), pp. 416–18 and ch. 17.

9. See Schroeder, *The Transformation of European Politics*. See, in addition, Derry, *Castlereagh*, ch. 4; W. Hinde, *Castlereagh* (London, 1981), ch. 14 and John Clarke, *British Diplomacy and Foreign Policy, 1782–1865: The National Interest* (London, 1989), chs 1 and 4. See also Deepak Lal, *In Praise of Empires: Globalization and Order* (London, 2004).

10. Kaufman, *British Policy and the Independence of Latin America*, chs 5–6; Nicholson, *The Congress of Vienna*, chs 15–16.

11. See Bradford Perkins, *Castlereagh and Adams: England and the United States, 1812–1823* (Berkeley, 1964); P. Dixon, *Canning* (London, 1976), ch. 9 and Clarke, *British Diplomacy*, ch. 6.

12. Adams quoted in Dexter Perkins, *The Monroe Doctrine, 1823–1826* (Cambridge, 1927), p. 74.

13. On the Monroe Doctrine, see Ernest May, *The Making of the Monroe Doctrine* (Cambridge, 1975), and Gretchen Murphy, *Hemispheric Imaginings: The Monroe Doctrine and Narratives of U.S. Empire* (Durham, 2005).

14. Castlereagh quoted in Nicholson, *The Congress of Vienna*, p. 258. See also Clarke, *British Diplomacy*, chs 1 and 5–6.

15. One study highlighting some of these connections is D. M. Pletcher, *The Diplomacy of Annexation: Texas, Oregon and the Mexican War* (New York, 1973).

16. Carroll, *A Good and Wise Measure*, chs 7–10.

17. On the Texan war of independence, see Albert Nofi, *The Alamo and the Texas War of Independence, September 30, 1835 to April 21, 1836: Heroes, Myths and History* (New York, 1992).

18. Aberdeen to Sir Richard Pakenham (Minister to Washington), 26 December 1843, quoted in Campbell, *From Revolution to Rapprochement*, p. 63. See also M. K. Wisehart, *Sam Houston* (New York, 1962).

19. Aberdeen quoted in S. F. Bemis, *A Diplomatic History of the United States* (New York, 1942), pp. 228–29. For the impact of Anglophobia on the annexation of Texas, see Sam Haynes, 'Anglophobia and the annexation of Texas: the quest for national security', in Sam Haynes and Christopher Morris (eds), *Manifest Destiny and Empire: American Antebellum Expansionism* (College Station, TX, 1997), pp. 115–45.

20. On the rebellions, see Phillip A. Buckner, *The Transition to Responsible Government: British Policy in British North America, 1815–1850* (Westport,

1986), chs 5–7; Helen Taft Manning, *The Revolt of French Canada, 1800–1835* (London, 1962); Gerald M. Craig, *Upper Canada: The Formative Years, 1784–1841* (Toronto, 1963), chs 10–13; Donald Creighton, *Towards the Discovery of Canada: Selected Essays* (Toronto, 1972), pp. 103–21; and Elinor Kyte Senior, *Redcoats and Patriotes: The Rebellions in Lower Canada 1837–38* (Toronto, 1985). The British government, in response to the rebellions, would send John Lambton, Earl of Durham, to act as governor-in-chief of the colonies. Durham's 'Report on the Affairs of British North America' (1839) recommended both the union of Britain's Canadian colonies followed by local self-government. Hence, the blueprint for Canadian confederation, and thus the event itself, was the eventual result.

21. Bourne, *Balance of Power in North America*, pp. 84 and 96; Carroll, *A Good and Wise Measure*, ch. 9; Jones, *To the Webster-Ashburton Treaty*, chs 2–3.

22. It has been argued that Seward would have pardoned McLeod had he been found guilty, but this ignores the widespread rage expressed by the American public – McLeod was not only nearly lynched while in custody, but had to be smuggled out of the United States after his acquittal. An analysis of the affair, demonstrating the amount of pressure Palmerston came under both in Parliament and from the public, may be found in Ridley, *Palmerston*, pp. 269–72. The *Caroline* incident was later deemed to have established a precedent in international law – namely, the principle of 'anticipatory self-defense'. See also Bourne, *Balance of Power in North America*, pp. 75–79 and Wilbur Devereux Jones, *The American Problem in British Diplomacy, 1841–1861* (London, 1974), ch. 1.

23. Jones, *To the Webster-Ashburton Treaty*, chs 6–8; Carroll, *A Good and Wise Measure*, chs 11–13; Jones, *The American Problem in British Diplomacy*, ch. 2. On the Webster-Ashburton banking connection, see E. L. Woodward, *The Age of Reform: 1815–1870* (Oxford, 1949), p. 295 and R. W. Hidy, *The House of Baring in American Trade and Finance: English Merchant Bankers at Work, 1783–1861* (Cambridge, MA, 1949).

24. Many of these imperial incidents are covered in Saul David's *Victoria's Wars: The Rise of Empire* (London, 2006). On the Irish famine, see Colm Toibin, *The Irish Famine* (London, 1999) and Cecil Woodham-Smith, *The Great Hunger, Ireland, 1845–9* (London, 1962).

25. On the Oregon Territory and American expansionism, see Pletcher, *The Diplomacy of Annexation*; Jones, *The American Problem in British Diplomacy*, chs 3–4; Robert Leckie, *From Sea to Shining Sea: From the War of 1812 to the Mexican War, the Saga of American Expansionism* (New York, 1995); William Earl Weeks, *Building the Continental Empire: American Expansionism from the Revolution to the Civil War* (Chicago, 1996) and

Sam Haynes, *James Polk and the Expansionist Impulse* (Arlington, VA, 1997).

26. On the war, see John Eisenhower, *So Far from God: The U.S. War with Mexico, 1846–48* (New York, 1989). On sectionalism and Manifest Destiny, see Michael Morrison, *Slavery and the American West: The Eclipse of Manifest Destiny and the Coming of the Civil War* (Chapel Hill, NC, 1997).

27. See Myers, 'Mask of Indifference', ch. 3 and Donald Masters, *The Reciprocity Treaty of 1854: Its History, its Relations to British Colonial and Foreign Policy and to the Development of Canadian Fiscal Autonomy* (Toronto, 1963). See also David Brown, *Palmerston and the Politics of Foreign Policy, 1846–55* (Manchester, 2002).

28. See Campbell, *From Revolution to Rapprochement*, ch. 6; Ridley, *Palmerston*, pp. 455–58 and Jones, *The American Problem in British Diplomacy*, chs 5–6.

29. On filibustering, see Charles Brown, *Agents of Manifest Destiny: The Lives and Times of the Filibusters* (Chapel Hill, NC, 1980); Robert E. May, *The Southern Dream of a Caribbean Empire, 1854–1861* (Baton Rouge, LA, 1973); idem, *Manifest Destiny's Underworld: Filibustering in Antebellum America* (Chapel Hill, NC, 2002); and Haynes and Morris, *Manifest Destiny and Empire*.

30. Bourne, *Balance of Power in North America*, pp. 181–90 and Jones, *The American Problem in British Diplomacy*, chs 7–9.

31. A very good study of Anglo-American tensions during the Crimean War, including in relation to Central America, may be found in Alan Dowty, *The Limits of American Isolation: The United States and the Crimean War* (New York, 1971), especially chs 3–7. See also Frank A. Golder, 'Russian-American relations during the Crimean War', *American Historical Review*, 31(3) (1926), pp. 462–76. Golder is the scholar referred to in the paragraph. On the conflict itself, see Andrew Lambert and Stephen Badsey, *The Crimean War* (Dover, NH, 1994), and J. B. Conacher, *Britain and the Crimea, 1855–56: Problems of War and Peace* (New York, 1987).

32. For a discussion of the *Creole* affair, see Howard Jones, 'The peculiar institution and national honor: the case of the Creole slave revolt', *Civil War History* 12(1) (1975), pp. 28–50. See, additionally, his *To the Webster-Ashburton Treaty*, ch. 5.

33. For a discussion of this crisis see Richard D. Fulton, 'The London *Times* and the Anglo-American boarding dispute of 1858', *Nineteenth Century Contexts* 17 (1993), pp. 133–44. For a discussion of Anglo-American disputes over the slave trade generally, see Bernard Semmel, *Liberalism and*

Naval Strategy: Ideology, Interest and Sea Power during the Pax Britannica (Boston, 1986).

34. See Myers, 'Mask of indifference', ch. 4; Michael Vouri, *The Pig War: Standoff at Griffin Bay* (Friday Harbor, Washington State, 1999); and Scott Kaufman, *The Pig War: The United States, Britain and the Balance of Power in the Pacific Northwest, 1846–1872* (Lanham, MD, 2003). The last demonstrates an awareness of how difficult and, at times, hazardous, Anglo-American relations could be.

35. See Warren I. Cohen, *America's Response to China: An Interpretive History of Sino-American Relations* (New York, 1971), pp. 25–26. On the Indian Mutiny, see Saul David, *Indian Mutiny: 1857* (London, 2002) and William Dalrymple, *The Last Mughal: The Fall of a Dynasty, Dehli, 1857* (London, 2006).

Notes to Chapter 6: John Bull, Cousin Jonathan and Johnny Reb: Great Britain and the American Civil War, 1861–65

1. Letter to Legation in Sarah A. Wallace and Frances E. Gillespie (eds), *The Journal of Benjamin Moran 1857–1865*, 2 vols. (Chicago, 1948–49), II, p. 1220; promises of future hatred by *New York Times*, reproduced in *Saturday Review*, 6 December 1862, p. 669.

2. For a discussion of origins of the foundation of the traditional interpretation, see my *English Public Opinion and the American Civil War* (Woodbridge, Suffolk, 2003). See also Frank J. Merli, *The Alabama, British Neutrality and the American Civil War*, ed. David M. Fahey (Bloomington, 2004), ch. 1. The best overall study of Anglo-American relations during the conflict remains D. P. Crook's *The North, the South and the Powers* (New York, 1974), which retains the advantage of historical accuracy that too many recent works lack. Other useful broad studies include Brian Jenkins, *Britain and the War for the Union*, 2 vols. (Montreal, 1974 and 1980); David F. Krein, *The Last Palmerston Government: Foreign Policy, Domestic Policy and the Genesis of 'Splendid Isolation'* (Ames, IA, 1978); Howard Jones, *Union in Peril: The Crisis over British Intervention in the Civil War* (Chapel Hill, NC, 1992), *Abraham Lincoln and a New Birth of Freedom: The Union and Slavery in the Diplomacy of the American Civil War* (Lincoln, NE, 1999); Eugene Berwanger, *The British Foreign Service and the American Civil War* (Lexington, KY, 1994); and Charles M. Hubbard, *The Burden of Confederate Diplomacy* (Knoxville, TX, 1998). An outstanding work is that of Philip Myers, *Caution and Co-operation: The American Civil War in British-American Relations* (Kent, OH, forthcoming). The author would

like to thank Dr Myers for allowing him to read and quote from the manuscript. The older, traditional works on the subject include Brougham Villiers and W. H. Chesson, *Anglo-American Relations, 1861–1865* (London, 1919); E. D. Adams, *Great Britain and the American Civil War*, 2 vols. (London 1925), Donaldson Jordan and Edwin J. Pratt, *Europe and the American Civil War* (London, 1931) and Frank Lawrence Owsley, *King Cotton Diplomacy: Foreign Relations of the Confederate States of America*, 2nd edn (Chicago, 1959 [1931]).

3. John Quincy Adams, 'Jubilee of the constitution: a discourse', 30 April 1839; President Lincoln, Second inaugural address, 4 March 1865.

4. For an interesting discussion of the American Civil War within this international context including an intriguing comparison of Lincoln to Bismarck, see Carl Degler, *Lincoln: The War President* (Oxford, 1992). For studies of the conflict generally, see Shelby Foote, *The Civil War, a Narrative*, 3 vols. (New York, 1958–74); Peter Parish, *The American Civil War* (New York, 1975); and James McPherson, *Battle Cry of Freedom: The Civil War Era* (New York, 1989).

5. *Fraser's Magazine* (April 1861), p. 414; William L. Yancey and Ambrose D. Mann to Robert Toombs, 15 July 1861, in James D. Richardson (ed.), *The Messages and Papers of Jefferson Davis and the Confederacy, Including the Diplomatic Correspondence, 1861–1865*, 2 vols. (New York, 1966), II, p. 37.

6. William Howard Russell, *My Diary North and South* (Philadelphia, 1988 [London 1863]), p. 51. For a discussion of the South's King Cotton policy, see Hubbard, *The Burden of Confederate Diplomacy*, ch. 3 and Owsley, *King Cotton Diplomacy*, ch. 1; Mason to Confederate secretary of state Robert Hunter, 11 March 1862, in Virginia Mason (ed.), *The Public Life and Diplomatic Correspondence of James M. Mason with some Personal History by his Daughter* (Roanoke, VI, 1903), p. 260.

7. *Spectator*, 30 March 1861, pp. 333–34; Palmerston to Russell, 24 September 1861, quoted in Duncan A. Campbell, 'Palmerston and the American civil war', in Miles Taylor and David Brown (eds), *Palmerston Studies*, 2 vols. (Southampton, forthcoming). All correspondence among Palmerston's cabinet in this chapter are quoted from this essay unless otherwise noted.

8. John Bright and James Thorold Rogers (eds), *Speeches on Questions of Public Policy by Richard J. Cobden, M.P.*, 2 vols. (London 1870), II, pp. 362–63; *The Economist* (14 September 1861), p. 1012; Stephen in *Macmillan's Magazine* (December 1861), p. 128 and Martineau quoted in Betty Fladeland, *Abolitionists and Working-class Problems in the Age of Industrialisation* (Baton Rouge, LA, 1984), p. 87.

9. On Seward, see Crook, *The North, the South and the Powers*, pp. 35, 63–68;

Jones, *Union in Peril*, pp. 11–15; Gordon H. Warren, *Fountain of Discontent: The Trent Affair and Freedom of the Seas* (Boston, MA, 1981), pp. 50–60, and Norman Ferris, *Desperate Diplomacy: William H. Seward's Foreign Policy, 1861* (Knoxville, TX, 1976). 'Seward's man', quoted in David H. Donald, *Lincoln* (London, 1995), p. 321. This, and Richard Carwardine's, *Lincoln* (Harlow, Essex, 2003), are two outstanding biographies on the sixteenth President, but for those who prefer a bit more iconoclasm, see Thomas DiLorenzo, *The Real Lincoln* (New York, 2002), and *Lincoln Unmasked* (New York, 2006), by the same author.

10. For a discussion of the breakdown in relations, see Campbell, *English Public Opinion and the American Civil War*, ch. 1 and D. P. Crook, 'Portents of war: English opinion on secession', *Journal of American Studies*, 33 (1967), pp. 163–79. The *Spectator* (15 June 1861), p. 635; Palmerston to Russell, 9 September 1861.

11. Andrew and Palmerston quoted in Warren, *Fountain of Discontent*, pp. 27 and 109. On the Trent, see also Norman Ferris's *The Trent Affair: A Diplomatic Crisis* (Knoxville, TX, 1977); *British Quarterly Review* (January 1862), p. 236; Horsman quoted in *Reynolds's Weekly Newspaper*, 15 December 1861, p. 4; *Eclectic Review* (January 1862), pp. 55–56; Palmerston to Russell, 6 December 1861. Palmerston's response to Bright: Hansard, CLXV, 390 (7 February 1862).

12. Palmerston to Russell (paraphrasing John Gray), 11 December 1860; 13 June 1862; and 2 October 1862. For more details on the public reaction to Gladstone's speech, see Campbell, *English Public Opinion and the American Civil War*, pp. 177–79; Palmerston to Russell, 22 October 1862. E. D. Steele argues that Gladstone complained of finding himself alone in defending the French proposal of armistice, having been let down by *both* Palmerston and Russell. E. D. Steele, *Palmerston and Liberalism, 1855–1865* (Cambridge, 1991), p. 300. See also Jones, *Union in Peril*, pp. 217–19; Palmerston to Russell, 3 November 1862. On the Crimean war, see Miles Taylor, *The Decline of British Radicalism, 1847–1860* (Oxford, 1995), p. 258.

13. Gladstone's budget in Roy Jenkins, *Gladstone* (London, 1995), p. 241; Derby and Disraeli quoted in Krein, *Last Palmerston Government*, p. 62; for MPs' commentary on the war, see Campbell, *English Public Opinion and the American Civil War*, ch. 4. The most scholarly study of Lancashire during this period remains Mary Ellison's *Support for Secession: Lancashire and the American Civil War* (Chicago, 1972). The speeches of Massey, Hibbert and Peel may be found in *Reynolds's Weekly Newspaper*, 26 January 1862 and 8 February 1863. While there remains the need for a scholarly study on the impact of trade and economics on Anglo-American

relations during this period, Jay Sexton's *Debtor Diplomacy: Finance and American Foreign Relations in the Civil War Era 1837–1873* (Oxford, 1995) is not it. Demonstrating a conspicuous lack of familiarity with both nineteenth-century British politics and foreign policy, the assertions made in this work do not inspire much confidence on the part of the reader. For more scholarly studies on this topic, see Richard Lester, *Confederate Finance and Purchasing in Great Britain* (Charlottesville, VA, 1975) and Owsley, *King Cotton Diplomacy*.

14. *Spectator*, 15 June 1861, p. 635; Russell to Lindsay, 21 April 1862, Lindsay papers quoted in Campbell, *English Public Opinion and the American Civil War*, p. 167; Wallace and Gillespie, *The Journal of Benjamin Moran*, II, pp. 1040–42; *Illustrated London News*, 4 July 1863, pp. 732–33. Lindsay made a last attempt in July 1864, asking Palmerston if he would offer to mediate in the war. Palmerston's curt refusal ended the matter.

15. The definitive account of the *Alabama* saga is Frank J. Merli's *The Alabama, British Neutrality and the American Civil War*, chs 2–6, but see also *Great Britain and the Confederate Navy, 1861–1865* (Bloomington, IN, 1970), by the same author. Adams and Palmerston quoted in Crook, *The North, the South and the Powers*, p. 151.

16. *Spectator*, 18 August 1862, p. 901; Benjamin to Mason, 30 December 1864, in *Correspondence of James M. Mason*, p. 544. Given the national differences within the United Kingdom, two useful studies include: Joseph Hernon, *Celts, Catholics and Copperheads: Ireland Views the American Civil War* (Columbus, OH, 1968) and Lorraine Peters, 'Scotland and the American civil war: a local perspective', unpublished PhD dissertation, University of Edinburgh, 1999.

17. On British views on the suppression of civil liberties in the North, see Campbell, *English Public Opinion and the American Civil War*, pp. 102–20. See also Mark Neely, *The Fate of Liberty: Abraham Lincoln and Civil Liberties* (New York, 1991). On Sherman, see Mark Grimsley, *The Hard Hand of War: Union Military Policy toward Southern Civilians, 1861–1865* (Cambridge, 1995) and John B. Walters, *Merchant of Terror: General Sherman and Total War* (New York, 1973).

18. *Illustrated London News*, 17 January 1863, p. 63.

19. The work arguing that this shift can be traced back to the 1850s is Reginald Horsman's *Race and Manifest Destiny: The Origins of American Racial Anglo-Saxonism* (Cambridge, 1981). While this work's arguments may be correct regarding the United States, their applicability to Britain is questionable. Only one chapter deals with Britain and its evidence consists simply of the well-known examples of Carlyle, Knox and Hunt while

ignoring the opposition they engendered. A more convincing study, at least insofar as Britain is concerned, is Peter Mandler's 'Race and nation in mid-Victorian thought', in S. Collini, R. Whatmore and B. Young (eds), *History, Religion and Culture: Essays in British Intellectual History, 1750–1950* (Cambridge, 2000), pp. 224–44. The best general work on British views on race remains Douglas A. Lorimer, *Colour, Class and the Victorians* (Leicester, 1978), but see also 'Race, science and culture: historical continuities and discontinuities, 1850–1914', in Shearer West (ed.), *The Victorians and Race* (Aldershot, 1996), pp. 13–30 by the same author. Pope quoted in David Nichols, *Lincoln and the Indians: Civil War Policy and Politics* (Columbia, MO, 1978), p. 87.

20. Mason to Benjamin, 25 January 1864, in *Correspondence of James M. Mason*, p. 461; *Saturday Review*, 6 September 1862, p. 594; Maury quoted in Warren F. Spencer, *The Confederate Navy in Europe* (Tuscaloosa, Alabama, 1983), p. 136.

21. Benjamin to Slidell, 17 August 1863, *The Messages and Papers of Jefferson Davis*, II, p. 544; *Illustrated London News*, 26 December 1863, p. 532.

22. R. J. M. Blackett, *Divided Hearts: Britain and the American Civil War* (Baton Rouge, LA, 2001), p. 99. On the Southern Independence Association's membership shrinking to fifteen members, see A. J. Beresford Hope to Lindsay, 19 December 1863, quoted in Campbell, *English Public Opinion and the American Civil War*, p. 183. Going through Blackett's list of names, correcting his misidentifications of individuals' politics and adding pro-southern radicals and pro-northern conservatives he has omitted, this historian finds, proportionally speaking, similar numbers of radicals and conservatives on each side. Equally, when it comes to the number of northern and southern partisans, even if we claim that for every member of the lobby groups there were a hundred additional supporters, this is still less than one per cent of the British population actively supporting either side. Even if we raise that figure to a thousand additional supporters per member, and here we are inventing numbers, we are still talking less than ten per cent of the population. Less than ten per cent does not a divided society make.

23. Ellison, *Support for Secession*, pp. 80–82; Blackett, *Divided Hearts*, pp. 196–98; Campbell, *English Public Opinion and the American Civil War*, pp. 203 and 215–26; Royden Harrison, *Before the Socialists: Studies in Labour and Politics, 1861–1881*, 2nd edn (Ipswich, 1994), pp. 70–71.

24. Ellison originally noted that the pro-northern meetings were convened by ticket; see *Support for Secession*, pp. 67–71; Blackett concedes this was so; see *Divided Hearts*, pp. 191–211. On the Ashton meeting and Beecher, see

Campbell, *English Public Opinion and the American Civil War*, pp. 98–99 and 216–17.

25. Stephen, *Fraser's Magazine*, October 1863, pp. 420–37; Greg on reform and Anglo-Saxons, *Edinburgh Review*, October 1852, pp. 469 and 463–64; on the Civil War, *National Review*, July 1861, p. 162. See, in addition, Wilbur Devereux Jones, 'British conservatives and the American civil war', *American Historical Review*, 58 (1953), pp. 527–43. Cobden to Bright, 29 December 1862, Cobden papers, MS 43652, British Library.

26. See Harrison, *Before the Socialists*, p. 53; Thomas J. Keiser, 'The English press and the American civil war' (unpublished PhD dissertation, University of Reading, 1971), pp. 285–92; Lucy Brown, *Victorian News and Newspapers* (Oxford, 1985), p. 51, and Jordan and Pratt, *Europe and the American Civil War*, p. 85.

27. Grote to George Cornewall Lewis, 27 December 1862, Copy, Russell papers; National Archives, *Reynolds's Weekly*, 1 December 1861, p. 1.

28. See Margot Finn, *After Chartism: Class and Nation in English Radical Politics, 1848–1874* (Cambridge, 1993), ch. 5. Finn demonstrates that European events were far more important to British radicals than American.

29. Forster's Speech: *Spectator*, 26 September 1863, p. 2538; J. S. Mill, 'The contest in America', *Fraser's Magazine*, February 1862; J. E. Cairnes, *The Slave Power: Its Character, Career and Possible Designs* (London, 1862); *The Economist*, 1 March 1862, p. 232. On Cairnes's work, see Adelaide Weinberg, *John Elliot Cairnes and the American Civil War: A Study in Anglo-American Relations* (London, 1970).

30. Cobden to Sumner, 11 January 1865, Cobden papers, MSS 43676; J. S. Mill, *Autobiography* (London, 1873), p. 287.

31. These numbers are derived from H. C. Allen's 'Civil war, reconstruction and Great Britain', in Harold Hyman (ed.), *Heard around the World: The Impact Abroad of the Civil War* (New York, 1969), p. 84. An examination of Hansard, however, reveals that Allen inflated these numbers, counting any reference to the United States, including ones along the lines of an MP who merely noted that Bright was always infatuated by America. If one counts the number of speeches which actually referred to the United States as an example – for good or ill – the numbers are below five per cent and one per cent respectively. The debate on the reform bills may be found in Hansard, vols. CLXXXII–CLXXXIX (1866–67). A good discussion of the Reform Act of 1867 is Gertrude Himmelfarb's 'The politics of democracy: the English reform act of 1867', *Journal of British Studies*, 6(1) (1966), pp. 97–138.

32. See Myers, *Caution and Co-operation*, for a detailed analysis of the

increasing collaboration that took place between Palmerston's and Lincoln's administrations.

33. On the importance of antebellum relations, see Martin Crawford, *The Anglo-American Crisis of the Mid-nineteenth Century, The Times and America, 1850–1862* (Athens, GA, 1987).

34. Hugh Dubrulle, 'Fear of Americanization and the emergence of an Anglo-Saxon confederacy in England during the American civil war', *Albion*, 33(4) (2002), pp. 583–613; idem, 'War of wonders: the battle in Britain over Americanization and the American civil war' (unpublished PhD dissertation, University of California Santa Barbara, 1999). This academic who claims Britons divided between those who favoured Americanization (which he simplistically equates with democratization), and those who did not, is simply providing old wine in new bottles. Drawing sweeping conclusions from the opinions of selected extreme partisans for either side, combined with a conspiracy theory that anti-Americans controlled the British press creating radical hostility towards the Union, renders these works wholly unpersuasive. Nor does the obvious lack of familiarity with nineteenth-century British politics and Anglo-American diplomatic relations do much to help. Other recent works bearing a closer relationship to American nationalist mythology than to British history include Alfred Grant, *The American Civil War and the British Press* (Jefferson, NC, 2000) and Dean Mahin, *One War at a Time: The International Dimensions of the American Civil War* (Dulles, VI, 1999).

35. Quoted in H. C. Allen, *Great Britain and the United States: A History of Anglo-American Relations, 1783-1952* (Watford, 1954), p. 452.

Notes to Chapter 7: The Road to Rapprochement: Anglo-American Diplomatic Relations from 1865 to the First World War

1. See Patrick Beesly, *Room 40: British Naval Intelligence, 1914–1918* (New York, 1982) and Barbara Tuchman, *The Zimmermann Telegram* (London, 2004 [1958]). The telegram's decoded contents may be found on p. 27 in the 2004 edn.

2. A work challenging the popular perception that the Somme was nothing but a futile bloodbath is Christopher Duffy's *Through German Eyes: The British and the Somme 1916* (London, 2006). For the First World War generally, see John Keegan, *The First World War* (London, 1999); David Stevenson, *1914–1918: The History of the First World War* (London, 2005); Hew Strachan, *The First World War: A New History* (London, 2003) and

Gary Sheffield, *Forgotten Victory: The First World War: Myths and Realities* (London, 2001).

3. For an interesting account of the war at sea, see Paul G. Halpern, *A Naval History of World War I* (London, 2005).

4. Tuchman, *The Zimmermann Telegram*, pp. 167–71.

5. Hansard, CLXXVII, 13 March 1865, p. 1620.

6. See Brian Jenkins, *Fenians and Anglo-American Relations during Reconstruction* (Ithaca, NY, 1969) and Hereward Senior, *The Last Invasion of Canada* (Toronto, 1991). See also Kenneth Bourne, *Britain and the Balance of Power in North America, 1815–1908* (London, 1967), ch. 8.

7. On the Alaska Purchase, see Ronald J. Jensen, *The Alaska Purchase and Russian-American Relations* (Seattle, 1975). See also Glyn Barrett, *Russian Shadows on the Northwest Coast of North America, 1810–1890: A Study in the Rejection of Defence Responsibilities* (Vancouver, 1983).

8. On Canadian confederation see Ged Martin, *Britain and the Origins of Canadian Confederation, 1837–1867* (Basingstoke, 1995); Donald Creighton, *The Road to Confederation: The Emergence of Canada, 1863–1867* (Boston, MA, 1965). An interesting analysis of the various interpretations of confederation is Paul Romney, *Getting it Wrong: How Canadians Forgot their Past and Imperilled Confederation* (Toronto, 1999). D'Arcy McGee quoted in H. H. Herstein, L. J. Hughes and R. C. Kirbyson, *Challenge and Survival: A History of Canada* (Scarborough, Ontario, 1970), p. 223. McDonald quoted in Joseph Pope, *Memoirs of the Right Honourable Sir John Alexander MacDonald, G.C.B.*, 2 vols. (Ottawa, 1894), I, pp. 269–70; Cartier in Herstein et al., *Challenge and Survival*, p. 227.

9. See Jasper Ridley, *Maximilian and Juarez* (New York, 1992). For the Franco-Prussian War, see Stephen Badsey, *The Franco-Prussian War, 1870–1871* (London, 2003) and Michael Howard, *The Franco-Prussian War: The German Invasion of France, 1870–1871* (London, 2001 [1961]).

10. See P. Hayes, 'British foreign policy, 1867–1900: continuity and conflict', in T. R. Gourvish and A. O'Day (eds), *Later Victorian Britain, 1867–1900* (London, 1988). On Britain and Germany, the standard work remains Paul Kennedy's *The Rise of Anglo-German Antagonism, 1860–1914* (London, 1980), although it relies too heavily on the hindsight of the First World War. An interesting study which, among other things, reminds us that Anglo-German relations were not necessarily destined to end the way they did, is Karina Urbach, *Bismarck's Favourite Englishman: Lord Odo Russell's Mission to Berlin* (London, 2000).

11. On Reconstruction see A. O. Craven, *Reconstruction: Ending of the Civil War* (New York, 1969) and Eric Foner, *Reconstruction: America's*

Unfinished Revolution, 1863–1877 (New York, 1988). Hayes was awarded the presidency by a congressional committee with a Republican majority; aggrieved Democrats referred to him as 'Rutherfraud' after this.

12. Sumner's speech is discussed in Campbell, *From Revolution to Rapprochement: The United States and Great Britain, 1783–1900* (New York, 1974), pp. 114–15 and Adrian Cook, *The Alabama Claims: American Politics and Anglo-American Relations, 1865–1872* (Ithaca, NY, 1975), ch. 4. 'For a Quaker', from the latter, p. 85.

13. On the Red River Rebellion, see George Stanley, *Toil and Trouble: Military Expeditions to Red River* (Toronto, 1996). For Grant, Santo Domingo and Sumner, see David Herbert Donald, *Charles Sumner and the Rights of Man* (New York, 1970), pp. 434–52.

14. See Campbell, *From Revolution to Rapprochement*, ch. 9, and Cook, *The Alabama Claims*, chs 10–12.

15. See Bourne, *The Balance of Power in North America*, pp. 302–10; Cook, *The Alabama Claims*, conclusion and Campbell, *From Revolution to Rapprochement*, pp. 134–35.

16. See Campbell, *From Revolution to Rapprochement*, chs 10–12.

17. Norman Penlington, *The Alaska Boundary Dispute: A Critical Reappraisal* (Toronto, 1972). See also Edward P. Kohn, *This Kindred People: Canadian-American Relations and the Anglo-Saxon Idea, 1895–1903* (Montreal, 2005).

18. Warren Zimmerman, *First Great Triumph: How Five Americans Made their Country a World Power* (New York, 2002), p. 153.

19. For a critique of Salisbury, see Paul Gibb, 'Unmasterly Activity? Sir Julian Pauncefote, Lord Salisbury, and the Venezuela Boundary Dispute', *Diplomacy and Statescraft*, 16.1 (2005), 23–55.

20. On the Canadian connection, see Norman Penlington, *Canada and Imperialism, 1896–1899* (Toronto, 1965), esp. pp. 201–17.

21. Campbell, *From Revolution to Rapprochement*, pp. 183–84 and Bradford Perkins, *The Great Rapprochement: England and the United States, 1895–1911* (New York, 1968) ch. 1.

22. Zimmerman, *First Great Triumph*, pp. 438–39.

23. One scholar who makes a direct comparison between the experience of the American Indians and Africans is James O. Gump, *Dust Rose like Smoke: The Subjugation of the Zulus and the Sioux* (Nebraska, 1996). On parallels between American and British imperialism, see Robin Winks, 'American imperialism in comparative perspective', in C. Vann Woodward (ed.), *The Comparative Approach to American History* (New York, 1968). On the Zulu War, see Saul David, *Zulu: The Heroism and Tragedy of the Zulu War of 1879* (London, 2005).

24. On the Spanish-American War, see David Healy, *US Expansionism: The Imperialist Urge in the 1890s* (Madison, WI, 1970); John Offner, *An Unwanted War: The Diplomacy of the United States and Spain over Cuba, 1895–1898* (Chapel Hill, NC, 1992); John Tebbel, *America's Great Patriotic War with Spain: Mixed Motives, Lies and Racism in Cuba and the Philippines* (Manchester Center, 1996) and H. Wayne Morgan, *America's Road to Empire: The War with Spain and Overseas Expansion* (New York, 1965).

25. The best single-volume work on the Boer war is Thomas Pakenham's *The Boer War* (New York, 1979), although Rayne Kruger's *Good-Bye Dolly Gray: The Story of the Boer War* (London, 1959) remains a classic account. See also Thomas Pakenham, *The Scramble for Africa, 1876–1912* (New York, 1991) and Denis Judd and Keith Surridge, *The Boer War* (London, 2003).

26. On the rebellion, see Diana Preston, *The Boxer Rebellion* (New York, 2000). See also Sterling Seagrove, *Dragon Lady: The Life and Legend of the Last Empress of China* (New York, 1992). For an examination of Anglo-American diplomacy in this era see, Lestyn Adams, *Brothers Across the Ocean: British Foreign Policy and the Origins of the Anglo-American 'Special Relationship' 1900–1905* (London, 2005).

27. Several works that deal with this controversy include: Annika Mombauer, *The Origins of the First World War: Controversies and Consensus* (London, 2002); James Joll and Gordon Martel, *The Origins of the First World War*, 3rd rev. edn (London, 2006); Zara Steiner, *Britain and the Origins of the First World War, Making of the Twentieth Century* (London, 2003). See also Fritz Fischer, *Germany's Aims in the First World War*, trans. James Joll (London, 1967) and Niall Feguson, *The Pity of War* (New York, 1999).

28. In addition to the works named above, two good studies concentrating on British involvement in the First World War are J. M. Bourne, *Britain and the Great War, 1914–1918* (London, 1989) and T. Wilson, *The Myriad Faces of War: Britain and the Great War 1914–1918* (Oxford, 1986). The exact casualty totals for the Somme remain in dispute. These are the most common ones cited.

29. On America's role in the First World War, see Ross Gregory, *The Origins of American Intervention in the First World War* (New York, 1971); Robert Ferrell, *Woodrow Wilson and World War I, 1917–1921* (New York, 1985); Daniel Smith, *The Great Departure: The United States and World War 1914–1920* (New York, 1965); and Ernest May, *The World War and American Isolation, 1914–1917* (Cambridge, MA, 1959). On financing the First World War, see Theo Balderston, 'War Finance and Inflation in Britain and Germany, 1914–1918', *Economic History Review*, 2nd series 42

(1989), pp. 207–21. On the subject of New York replacing London as the world's financial centre, see William Silber, *When Washington Shut Down Wall Street* (Princeton, NJ, 2007).

30. On Versailles, see Margaret Macmillan, *Paris 1919: Six Months that Changed the World* (London, 2003). On the declining reputation of the Victorians, see Matthew Sweet, *Inventing the Victorians* (London, 2001), introduction.

31. The expert on 'War Plan Red' is Floyd Rudmin; see his 'Secret War Plans and the Malady of American Militarism', *CounterPunch*, 13 (1–15 January 2006), p. 1. For a more humorous account, see Peter Carlson, 'Raiding the Icebox', *The Washington Post*, 30 December 2005. The author should like to thank Jon Latimer for reminding him of this issue. For an introduction to twentieth-century Anglo-American relations, see Andrew Roberts, *A History of the English Speaking Peoples since 1900* (London, 2006).

Notes to Chapter 8: Arguing Affinities; Debating Differences: British Politics and the United States in the Later Nineteenth Century

1. Terry Newman, 'Tasmania and the secret ballot', *Australian Journal of Politics and History*, 49(1) (2003), pp. 93–101 and L. E. Fredman, *Australian Ballot: The Story of an American Reform* (East Lansing, MI, 1968), ch. 1, *passim*. As the author notes, 'By the middle of the nineteenth century it was obvious to many Americans that manipulation of the ballot box had made voting a meaningless procedure' (p. ix). Portions of some American states had made some use of ballots earlier, but so too had some English counties. Our modern version is nonetheless owed to the Australians.

2. On Goldwin Smith, see Hugh Tulloch, *James Bryce's American Commonwealth: The Anglo-American Background* (Woodbridge, Suffolk, 1988), p. 36.

3. Leslie Stephen (ed.), *Essays on Reform* (London, 1867). In the case of the Adullamites, Bright was referring to 1 Samuel 22 (King James Version): 'David therefore departed thence, and escaped to the cave of Adullam: and when his brethren and all his father's house heard it, they went thither to him.'

4. For much of the information in this chapter the author is greatly indebted to Murney Gerlach's *British Liberalism and the United States: Political and Social Thought in the Late Victorian Age* (Houndmills, Hampshire, 2001). Daniel T. Rodgers's *Atlantic Crossings: Social Politics in a Progressive Age* (Cambridge, MA, 1998), and Robert Kelley's *The Transatlantic Persuasion:*

The Liberal-Democratic Mind in the Age of Gladstone (New York, 1969), also contain much useful information.

5. On Gladstone's attempts at rapprochement with the United States, see H. C. G. Matthew, *Gladstone, 1809–1874* (Oxford, 1986), pp. 186–88 and Gerlach, *British Liberalism and the United States*, pp. 48–57.

6. William Gladstone, 'Kin beyond sea', *North American Review* (Sept–Oct 1878), pp. 179–212; 181–83, 183–85, 202 and 212. Despite often being referred to as 'Kin beyond the sea', there is no definite article in the original title.

7. 'Strange doings', quoted in E. Hodder, *Life and Work of Lord Shaftesbury*, 3 vols. (London, 1886), III, p. 187, from E. L. Woodward, *The Age of Reform 1815–1870* (Oxford, 1949), p. 175; *Pall Mall Gazette*, 20 September 1878, *Daily News*, 18 September 1878, and *The Times*, 19 September 1878; cited in Gerlach, *British Liberalism and the United States*, p. 56. On the 'English-speaking peoples', see Francis H. Herrick, 'Gladstone and the concept of "English-speaking Peoples"', *Journal of British Studies*, 12 (1972), pp. 150–56, but see also Peter Parish, 'Gladstone and America', in Peter J. Jagger (ed.), *Gladstone* (London, 1998), pp. 85–103 (101).

8. Gladstone, 'Kin beyond sea', p. 186.

9. On the phenomenon of the massive increase of American tourists to Britain and Europe after the Civil War, see James Buzzard, *The Beaten Track: European Tourism, Literature, and the Ways of Culture, 1800–1918* (Oxford, 1993). Lawley quoted in Gerlach, *British Liberalism and the United States*, p. 15.

10. Charles Dilke, *Greater Britain: A Record of Travel in the English-Speaking Countries during 1866 and 1867*, 2 vols. (London, 1868), I, pp. xvii, vii, 217–18, 230. On Dilke's radicalism see Miles Taylor, 'Republics versus empires: Charles Dilke's republicanism reconsidered', in David Nash and Antony Taylor (eds), *Republicanism in Victorian Society* (Stroud, Gloucestershire, 2000), pp. 25–34.

11. Dilke, *Greater Britain*, I, pp. 128 and 233. Two good biographies of Dilke are: Roy Jenkins, *Sir Charles Dilke: A Victorian Tragedy* (London, 1958; rev. edn, 1965) and David Nicholls, *The Lost Prime Minister: A Life of Sir Charles Dilke* (London, 1995). The second chapter in both works analyses *Greater Britain*. See also Paul Kramer, 'Empires, exceptions and Anglo-Saxons: race and rule between the British and the United States empires, 1880–1910', *Journal of American History*, 88 (2002), pp. 1315–53.

12. For a discussion of Dilke's influence upon Seeley, see James Epstein, 'Under America's sign: two nineteenth-century British readings', *European Journal of American Culture*, 24(3) (2005), pp. 205–19. Dilke, *Greater Britain*, II, p. 155; J. R. Seeley, *The Expansion of England* (London, 1883).

See, in addition, Andrew Porter (ed.), *The Oxford History of the British Empire: The Nineteenth Century* (Oxford, 1999), introduction, pp. 1–28; Niall Ferguson, *Empire: How Britain Made the Modern World* (London, 2003), pp. 240–64; and Lance E. Davis and R. A. Huttenback, *Mammon and the Pursuit of Empire: The Political Economy of British Imperialism, 1860–1912* (Cambridge, 1986).

13. Rosebery quoted in Gerlach, *British Liberalism and the United States*, p. 131.

14. See Donald Warner, *The Idea of Continental Union: Agitation for the Annexation of Canada to the United States, 1849–1893* (Lexington, KY, 1960), pp. 225–26 and D. C. Masters, *Reciprocity, 1846–1911* (Ottawa, 1961).

15. S. Pollard, *Britain's Prime and Britain's Decline: The British Economy 1870–1914* (London, 1989).

16. A very good discussion of this is Edmund Rogers, 'The United States and the fiscal debate in Britain, 1873–1913' (MPhil dissertation, Cambridge University, 2005). See also S. N. Broadbury, *The Productivity Race: British Manufacturing in International Perspective, 1850–1990* (Cambridge, 1997); E. H. H. Green, *The Crisis of Conservatism: The Politics, Economics and Ideology of the British Conservative Party, 1880–1914* (London, 1995); Anthony Howe, 'Free trade and the international order: the Anglo-American tradition, 1846–1946', in Fred M. Leventhal and Roland Quinault (eds), *Anglo-American Attitudes: From Revolution to Partnership* (Aldershot, 2000), pp. 142–67; and S. B. Saul, *Studies in British Overseas Trade, 1870–1914* (Liverpool, 1960).

17. See Peter Marsh, *Joseph Chamberlain: Entrepreneur in Politics* (London, 1994); Edward Kaplan and Thomas Ryley, *Prelude to Trade Wars: American Tariff Policy, 1890–1922* (Westport, CT, 1994); Frank Trentman, 'The strange death of free trade; the erosion of the "liberal consensus" in Great Britain', in Eugenio Biagini (ed.), *Citizenship and Community: Liberals, Radicals and Collective Identities in the British Isles, 1865–1931* (Cambridge, 1996); and Green, *The Crisis of Conservatism*.

18. For a good discussion of the American example in the Home Rule debates, see Gerlach, *British Liberalism and the United States*, pp. 101–10, 124–33 and 170–76 and Tulloch, *James Bryce's American Commonwealth*, pp. 128–36. On Home Rule generally, see Alan O'Day, *Irish Home Rule, 1867–1921* (Manchester, 1998) and Grenfell Morton, *Home Rule and the Irish Question* (London, 1980).

19. See Paul Kramer and John Plotz, 'Pairing empires: Britain and the United States, 1857–1947', *Journal of Colonialism and Colonial History* 2(1) (2001). On Teutonic and Mississippi forests, see Tulloch, *James Bryce's American Commonwealth*, p. 47.

20. Mahan quoted in Warren Zimmerman, *First Great Triumph: How Five Americans Made their Country a World Power* (New York, 2002), p. 113. Many Britons were, of course, aware of the importance of the Royal Navy's role in underpinning Britain's rise to world power status, whether we are talking of William James (see Chapter 1) or Lord Palmerston (who took care to keep the navy properly funded). Nonetheless, Mahan's work provided an intellectual and scholarly analysis that they at best understood instinctively.

21. Comparison to Kennan made by Zimmerman, *First Great Triumph*, p. 122. See, in addition, Robert Seager, *Alfred Thayer Mahan: The Man and his Letters* (Annapolis, MD, 1977); William E. Livezey, *Mahan on Sea Power* (Norman, OK, 1981); and Philip A. Crowl, 'Alfred Thayer Mahan: the naval historian', in Peter Paret (ed.), *Makers of Modern Strategy from Machiavelli to the Nuclear Age* (Oxford, 1981). The standard biography remains W. D. Puleston, *Mahan: The Life and Work of Captain Alfred Thayer Mahan* (New Haven, CT, 1939).

22. See James Turner, *The Liberal Education of Charles Eliot Norton* (Baltimore, MD, 1999).

23. See Gerlach, *British Liberalism and the United States*, p. 43.

24. Bryce's articles in *Macmillan's*: November 1871, pp. 54–65; January 1872, pp. 206–17; March 1872, pp. 422–32; December 1872, pp. 704–16. On his trip to America, see Tulloch, *James Bryce's American Commonwealth*, pp. 54–61.

25. See Tulloch, *James Bryce's American Commonwealth*, ch. 2. See also Goldwin Smith, *The Foundation of the American Colonies* (Oxford, 1861); *The Civil War in America* (London, 1866); E. A. Freeman, *Some Impressions of the United States* (London, 1883); and *Lectures to American Audiences* (London, 1882).

26. James Bryce, *The American Commonwealth*, 2 vols. (London, 1888, New York, 1910), II, pp. 824 and 656; I, pp. 691–95; II, p. 617; and I, p. 629. See also Tulloch, *James Bryce's American Commonwealth*, chs 3–5.

27. See Tulloch, *James Bryce's American Commonwealth*, p. 46 and ch. 6.

28. Matthew Arnold, 'A word about America', *The Nineteenth Century* (May 1882), pp. 680–96; 680–81; 682–84.

29. Ibid., pp. 684–87.

30. Ibid., pp. 690–96.

31. On this era in the United States generally, see John Sproat, *'The Best Men': Liberal Reformers in the Gilded Age* (New York, 1968); Mark W. Summers, *The Era of Good Stealings* (New York, 1993) and Charles W. Calhoun (ed.),

The Gilded Age: Essays on the Origins of Modern America (Wilmington, DE, 1996).

Notes to Chapter 9: Towards a Transatlantic Culture

1. Arthur Conan Doyle, 'The adventure of the dancing men', originally published in *Strand Magazine*, December 1903. *The Sherlock Holmes Mysteries*, introduction by Anne Perry (London, 2005), pp. 338–62.
2. See Tom Standage, *The Victorian Internet: The Remarkable Story of the Telegraph and the Nineteenth Century's On-line Pioneers* (New York, 1998); John S. Gordon, *A Thread across the Ocean: The Heroic Story of the Transatlantic Cable* (New York, 2002) and Bern Dibner, *The Atlantic Cable* (Norwalk, CN, 1959).
3. On this American connection, see Dean Dickensheet, 'The American profile of Sherlock Holmes', foreword in Bill Blackbeard, *Sherlock Holmes in America* (New York, 1981). See also Arthur Conan Doyle, *Memories and Adventures* (Oxford, 1989 [London, 1924]), ch. 9.
4. See Macdonald Hastings, 'Conan Doyle hated Sherlock Holmes' and Franklin Delano Roosevelt, 'Sherlock Holmes was a American', in Peter Haining (ed.), A *Sherlock Holmes Compendium* (London, 1980).
5. Much has been made, in some recent scholarship, of Conan Doyle's imperialist outlook, leading to accusations that his works are racist fantasies. This conveniently ignores the fact that Conan Doyle was known in his day for his opposition to the so-called 'colour bar' (a point his widow proudly reiterated in her memoriam), and the anti-racist message in some of his stories such as 'The Yellow Face', which is an obvious defence of interracial marriage. To claim that he held the same views on race as we do would be incorrect, but he was far more sympathetic to the idea of racial equality than the vast majority of his white contemporaries – on both sides of the Atlantic.
6. See Murney Gerlach, *British Liberalism and the United States: Political and Social Thought in the Late Victorian Age* (Houndmills, Hampshire, 2001), pp. 142–45 and A. J. Clark, *Movement for International Copyright in Nineteenth Century America* (New York, 1960).
7. See Alan Gallop, *Buffalo Bill's British Wild West* (Thrupp, Oxfordshire, 2001), p. x.
8. On the Jubilee itself, see John Fabb, *Victoria's Golden Jubilee* (London, 1987). See also Gallop, *Buffalo Bill's British Wild West*, pp. 40–130.
9. Gallop, *Buffalo Bill's British Wild West*, pp. 154–270.
10. Regarding this topic, I am indebted to Professor Howell Harris's article

'Between convergence and exceptionalism: Americans and the "British model" of Labor relations, c. 1867–1920', *Labor History*, 48(2) (2007), pp. 141–73. A. Maurice Low, 'Labor unions and British industry', *Bulletin of the Bureau of Labor*, 50 (January 1904), p. 4; Mary B. Gilson, *What's Past is Prologue: Reflections on my Industrial Experience* (New York, 1940), p. 250; both quoted in Harris. See also S. B. Saul, 'The American impact on British industry, 1895–1914', *Business History*, 3 (1967), pp. 19–38.

11. See Robert V. Bruce, *1877: Year of Violence* (Chicago, 1989); James Green, *Death in the Haymarket: A Story of Chicago, the First Labor Movement, and the Bombing that Divided Gilded Age America* (New York, 2006); and Gareth Stedman Jones, *Outcast London: A Study in Relationship between Classes in Victorian Society* (London, 1984). See also Clive Emsley, 'Police and industrial disputes in Britain and the United States', in David Englander (ed.), *Britain and America: Studies in Comparative History, 1760–1970* (Bath, 1997), pp. 112–31.

12. On the Hughes-Mundella visit and 'arbitration', see David Montgomery, *Beyond Equality: Labor and the Radical Republicans, 1862–1872* (New York, 1967), pp. 154–55; Josephine Shaw Lowell, *Industrial Arbitration and Conciliation: Some Chapters from the Industrial History of the Past Thirty Years* (New York, 1893), chs 2–5.

13. The scholar referred to in both cases is Harris. Harris, 'Between convergence and exceptionalism'; Henry R. Towne, 'President's address, 1889', *Transactions of the American Society of Mechanical Engineers*, 11 (1889–90), pp. 50–71 (57–58). Daniel Rodgers argues that ideas of American exceptionalism re-emerged after the Second World War. Rodgers, *Atlantic Crossings: Political Politics in a Progressive Age* (Cambridge, MA, 1998), p. 3. For British economic statistics, see Niall Ferguson, *Empire: How Britain Made the Modern World* (London, 2003), pp. 241–42. See also Michael Edelstein, *Overseas Investment in the Age of High Imperialism: The United Kingdom, 1850-1914* (New York, 1982).

14. For an interesting discussion on the broader issues of the Empire, see Paul Kennedy and P. K. O'Brien, 'The Costs and Benefits of British Imperialism, 1846–1914', *Past and Present*, 120 (1988), pp. 163–200 and Paul Kennedy, 'Debate: The Costs and Benefits of British Imperialism, 1846–1914', *Past and Present*, 125 (1989), pp. 186–99. See also Avner Offer, 'The British Empire, 1870–1914: A Waste of Money?', *Economic History Review*, 46(2) (1993), pp. 215–38.

15. See Lawrence James, *The Rise and Fall of the British Empire* (London, 2005), pp. 209–348; Ferguson, *Empire*, ch. 5, pp. 164 and 243. Ferguson is the scholar quoted above. Rodgers, *Atlantic Crossings*, pp. 55–56. Rodgers

does not give due consideration to the political and cultural ties linking the Dominions and Britain, referring to Australia and New Zealand as merely 'outposts' of the 'North Atlantic economy'; in other words, assuming these had the same relationship with, say, Germany or France or the United States as they did to Britain. This would be akin to referring to California merely as an outpost of the Pacific economy.

16. See Robert Beisner, *Twelve Against Empire: The Anti-imperialists, 1898–1902* (New York, 1968) and Daniel Schirmer, *Republic or Empire: American Resistance to the Philippine War* (Cambridge, MA, 1972).

17. See Stephen Koss, *The Pro-Boers* (Chicago, 1973) and Arthur Davey, *The British Pro-Boers, 1877–1902* (Cape Town, 1978).

18. Andrew Roberts, *A History of the English-speaking Peoples since 1900* (New York, 2006), pp. 6, 31–34; Richard Mulnaux, *The Boer War and American Politics and Diplomacy* (Lanham, MD, 1994) and Bryon Farwell, 'Taking sides in the Boer war', *American Heritage* (April 1976), pp. 18–30 (25). It was, of course, in response to the Boer War that J. A. Hobson wrote his seminal *Imperialism: A Study* in 1902. In some respects he was the progenitor of all anti-imperial texts.

19. For a thoughtful essay on Kipling's imperialism and late nineteenth-century European imperialism in general, see Geoffrey Wheatcroft, 'Send forth the best ye breed', *The New Statesman*, 5 July 1999.

20. See Anna Maria Martellone, 'In the name of Anglo-Saxondom, for empire and for democracy: the Anglo-American discourse, 1880–1920', in David K. Adams and Cornelis A. van Minnen (eds), *Reflections on American Exceptionalism* (Keele, Staffordshire, 1994), pp. 83–96. See also Cushing Strout, *The American Image of the Old World* (New York, 1963), ch. 8.

21. Rodgers, *Atlantic Crossings*, chs 2–6. See also Leon S. Marshall, 'The English and American industrial city of the nineteenth century', in Englander, *Britain and America: Studies in Comparative History*, pp. 103–11.

22. David A. Shannon (ed.), *Beatrice Webb's American Diary* (Madison, WI, 1963), pp. 42–43 and 151.

23. H. G. Wells, *The Future of America: A Search after Realities* (London, 1906); George Shepperson, 'H. G. Wells, 1866–1946', in Marc Pachter and Frances Wein (eds), *Abroad in America: Visitors to the New Nation, 1776–1914* (Reading, MA, 1976), pp. 293–301.

24. On James, see Leon Edel, *Henry James, the Conquest of London* (Philadelphia, 1962), and *Henry James: A Life* (New York, 1985). See also Adeline Tintner, *The Cosmopolitan World of Henry James: An Intertextual Study* (Baton Rouge, 1991) and Van Wyck Brooks, *A Pilgrimage of Henry James* (New York, 1925).

25. On this subject and Wilde, see Neil McKenna, *The Secret Life of Oscar Wilde* (London, 2003). See also Richard Ellman, *Oscar Wilde* (New York, 1987). On nineteenth-century changing views of sexuality and classification, see Mathew Sweet, *Inventing the Victorians* (London, 2001), ch. 12.

26. Two excellent works on Mark Twain's personal and literary British connections are Howard G. Baetzhold, *Mark Twain and John Bull, the British Connection* (Bloomington, IN, 1970) and Denis Welland, *Mark Twain in England* (London, 1978).

27. On Stead, see Victor Pierce Jones, *Saint or Sensationalist? The Story of W. T. Stead, 1849–1912* (Chichester, 1988).

28. W. T. Stead, *The Americanisation of the World; Or, The Trend of the Twentieth Century* (London, 1902), pp. 1–16.

29. Sidney Webb on Australia quoted in Shannon (ed.), *Beatrice Webb's American Diary*, p. 152, n. 9. Stead, *The Americanisation of the World*, pp. 16–60 and 147–64.

30. Stead, *The Americanisation of the World*, pp. 99–150.

31. Ibid., pp. 65–73.

32. Ibid, pp. 96–157 and 106.

Notes to Conclusion: Closer Cousins?

1. Quoted in Hugh Tulloch, *James Bryce's American Commonwealth: The Anglo-American Background* (Woodbridge, Suffolk, 1988), p. 125. For some considerations on the short twentieth century, see Paul Johnson, *Modern Times: A History of the World From the 1920s to the 1980s* (London, 1984); Robert Conquest, *Reflections on a Ravaged Century* (New York, 2001); and Niall Ferguson, *War of the World: History's Age of Hatred* (London, 2006).

2. Palmerston quoted in E. L. Woodward, *The Age of Reform, 1815–1870* (Oxford, 1949), p. 214.

3. See Walter Arnstein, 'Queen Victoria and the United States', in Fred M. Leventhal and Roland Quinault (eds), *Anglo-American Attitudes: From Revolution to Partnership* (Aldershot, 2000), pp. 91–106, pp. 92–95.

4. Ibid., pp. 96–99.

5. Ibid., pp. 96–99.

6. W. C. Sellar and R. J. Yeatman, *1066 and All That* (London, 1960), p. 113.

Index